EVENT TOURISM AND SUSTAINABLE COMMUNITY DEVELOPMENT

Advances, Effects, and Implications

EVENT TOURISM AND SUSTAINABLE COMMUNITY DEVELOPMENT

Advances, Effects, and Implications

Edited by
Ekta Dhariwal
Shruti Arora
Anukrati Sharma
Azizul Hassan

First edition published 2024

Apple Academic Press Inc.
1265 Goldenrod Circle, NE,
Palm Bay, FL 32905 USA

760 Laurentian Drive, Unit 19,
Burlington, ON L7N 0A4, CANADA

CRC Press
2385 NW Executive Center Drive,
Suite 320, Boca Raton FL 33431

4 Park Square, Milton Park,
Abingdon, Oxon, OX14 4RN UK

© 2024 by Apple Academic Press, Inc.

Apple Academic Press exclusively co-publishes with CRC Press, an imprint of Taylor & Francis Group, LLC

Reasonable efforts have been made to publish reliable data and information, but the authors, editors, and publisher cannot assume responsibility for the validity of all materials or the consequences of their use. The authors are solely responsible for all the chapter content, figures, tables, data etc. provided by them. The authors, editors, and publishers have attempted to trace the copyright holders of all material reproduced in this publication and apologize to copyright holders if permission to publish in this form has not been obtained. If any copyright material has not been acknowledged, please write and let us know so we may rectify in any future reprint.

Except as permitted under U.S. Copyright Law, no part of this book may be reprinted, reproduced, transmitted, or utilized in any form by any electronic, mechanical, or other means, now known or hereafter invented, including photocopying, microfilming, and recording, or in any information storage or retrieval system, without written permission from the publishers.

For permission to photocopy or use material electronically from this work, access www.copyright.com or contact the Copyright Clearance Center, Inc. (CCC), 222 Rosewood Drive, Danvers, MA 01923, 978-750-8400. For works that are not available on CCC please contact mpkbookspermissions@tandf.co.uk

Trademark notice: Product or corporate names may be trademarks or registered trademarks and are used only for identification and explanation without intent to infringe.

Library and Archives Canada Cataloguing in Publication

Title: Event tourism and sustainable community development : advances, effects, and implications / edited by Ekta Dhariwal, Shruti Arora, Anukrati Sharma, Azizul Hassan.
Names: Dhariwal, Ekta, editor. | Arora, Shruti, editor. | Sharma, Anukrati, 1981- editor. | Hassan, Azizul, editor.
Description: First edition. | Includes bibliographical references and index.
Identifiers: Canadiana (print) 20230442722 | Canadiana (ebook) 20230442773 | ISBN 9781774912416 (hardcover) | ISBN 9781774912423 (softcover) | ISBN 9781003332213 (ebook)
Subjects: LCSH: Tourism—Planning. | LCSH: Tourism—Marketing. | LCSH: Culture and tourism. | LCSH: Community development. | LCSH: Special events.
Classification: LCC G155.A1 E94 2023 | DDC 338.4/791—dc23

Library of Congress Cataloging-in-Publication Data

....

CIP data on file with US Library of Congress

....

ISBN: 978-1-77491-241-6 (hbk)
ISBN: 978-1-77491-242-3 (pbk)
ISBN: 978-1-00333-221-3 (ebk)

About the Editors

Ekta Dhariwal, PhD

Ekta Dhariwal, PhD, post graduated in history from University of Kota and in continual way obtained her Doctorate Degree in the subject "Women in Rajasthan: Awakening, Empowerment and Social Changes (1915-2016 AD); she is also doing her D. Litt. in, 'Infinite Aura of Jainism in Rajasthan'. As the author opened her eyes in the marvellous city of marble monument Taj Mahal, she is grasped with historical sensation. She realised that kept under the protection and keen eyes of the male counterparts a women is pronounced to be safer, yet to safe guard in itself is proved as the bottleneck of her talent and creativity. Opting to be a social activist she has served various organisations, societies, and associations in different walks. She is an honorary consultant to many women's organisations and NGOs in Rajasthan. She has participated in many national and international conferences and presented books like: Lineage Light (L2): Reminiscences of Rajput History, An Indian Blueprint: Stone Age Art, etc. Her research papers include: Because we are Women, Is Girl Child Curse for Parents, Temple-No Bars Whether Men or Women, Modern Women Self-Guard Herself, Female: The Change Agent, Is Women's Voice Remains Faint in Politics, Elders- Are a Boon, Covid-19: Ushering the Hope among Horror, Ancient Banking and Currency, From War Zones to People Home, Food Freedom and Health in Jainism, Yoga and Dhyana in Jainism, Kalpvraksha: The Theory, The Female: Silver Lining in Jainism, Mask : The Pandemic Control in Jainism and Influence of Jainism in Rajasthan. She is the recipient of "SUMITRA Women Entrepreneur Award." She has directed Documentary Film of Late Industrial Minister of Rajasthan on the "Biography of Rikhab Chand Dhariwal."

She has an NGO named, "Aksham Kalyan Sansthan," where she has been nourishing the social aspirations in various fields. It is evident that she stepped into a revolutionary path by providing thousands of girls with the sanitary napkins every month. In 2021, by virtue of her academics she has been nominated a member of the Board of Management in the University of Kota by the government of Rajasthan. she is also the only woman chairperson of sports of the Kota University, which includes 200 affiliated colleges. She is also a member of Rajasthan Medical Relief Society (RMRS), nominated by the government of Rajasthan. Her philosophical depth moved into being nominated as a member of Kota Jain Association. As a President of her second NGO, "Dhariwal Sports Society," she has been actively organising various tournaments to picked out new talents in Kota (Rajasthan). Apart from this, her ultimate passion is to strive ahead to help the female section of the society to become self-dependent, especially in Rajasthan, India.

Shruti Arora, PhD

Shruti Arora, PhD, is currently working as a guest faculty in the Department of Commerce and Management, University of Kota, Kota, Rajasthan, India. She has 13 years of experience in the education industry. Her core subjects are marketing, general management, international business management, and customer relationship management. She has attended various international conferences. Her publications include various chapters in edited books published by Routledge, Emerald, and Springer. Her research papers have been published in in national and international UGC-approved and peer-reviewed journals. She has authored the book *Event Management and Marketing: Theory, Practical Approaches and Planning* (2018), co-edited the book Event Tourism in Asian Countries: Challenges and Prospects (Apple Academic Press/CRC Press, as well as a book with NOVA Science Publishers, USA. She described the term "Food Walk Tourism" in *the Encyclopedia of Tourism Management and Marketing*, edited by Dimitrios Buhalis, published by Edward Elgar Publishing Limited.

Anukrati Sharma, PhD

Anukrati Sharma, PhD, is the Head and Associate Professor of the Department of Commerce and Management at the University of Kota (A State Govt. University) in Kota, Rajasthan, India. She is also the Director of the Skill Development Centre at the same university and Dean (Honorary) of two faculties: Tourism and Hospitality and Aviation and Aerospace, at Rajasthan Skill University (A Govt.

About the Editors

State University) in Jaipur, India. In 2015, she received a research award from the University Grants Commission (UGC), New Delhi, for her project "Analysis of the Status of Tourism in Hadoti and Shekhawati Region/Circuit (Rajasthan): Opportunities, Challenges, and Future Prospects." Her special interest areas are tourism, tourism marketing, strategic management, and international business management. She has been appointed as an Official Partner of a BRICS-funded project for the years 2022–2024. Dr. Sharma is a Routledge featured author. She is the Book Series Editor for *Building the Future of Tourism*, published by Emerald Publishing, UK; *Routledge Insights in Tourism Series*, Routledge, UK; *Perspectives and Anthropology in Tourism and Hospitality* (PATH), Apple Academic Press (CRC Press, a Taylor and Francis Group). She has edited several books: *Tourism—Opportunities and Ventures; Maximizing Business Performance and Efficiency through Intelligent Systems* (IGI Global) (Scopus indexed); *Sustainable Tourism Development: Futuristic Approaches* (Apple Academic Press), under the series *Advances in Hospitality and Tourism; Tourism Events in Asia Marketing and Development* (Routledge); *Sustainable Destination Branding and Marketing: Strategies for Tourism Development* (CABI, UK); *Future of Tourism: An Asian Perspective* (Springer); *Overtourism as Destination Risk: Impacts and Solutions* (Emerald Publishing); *Overtourism, Technology Solutions and Decimated Destinations* (Springer); *Event Tourism in Asian Countries: Challenges and Prospects* (Apple Academic Press); and *The Emerald Handbook of ICT in Tourism and Hospitality* (Emerald). She also authored a book titled *Event Management and Marketing Theory, Practical Approaches, and Planning.* Another book she wrote is *International Best Practice in Event Management*, published by the United Kingdom Event Industry Academy Ltd. and Prasetiya Mulya Publishing, Indonesia. Her current projects include editing the book *COVID-19 and Tourism Sustainability: Ethics, Responsibilities, Challenges and New Directions* for Routledge, USA; *Festivals and Event Tourism: Building Resilience and Promoting Sustainability* for CABI, UK; *The Emerald Handbook of Destination Recovery in Tourism and Hospitality* (Emerald); *COVID-19 and the Tourism Industry: Sustainability, Resilience and New Directions* (Routledge); *Event Tourism and Sustainable Community Development: Advances, Effects, and Implications* (Apple Academic Press); *Crisis, Resilience and Recovery in Tourism and Hospitality* (Springer Nature); *Strategic Tourism Planning for Communities: Restructuring and Rebranding* (Nova Science Publishers); *Dynamics of Tourism Industry Post-Pandemic and Disasters* (Apple Academic Press); and *Resilient and Sustainable Destinations after*

Disaster: Challenges and Strategies (Emerald). She is also working on a major research project under the Mahatma Gandhi National Council of Rural Education, Ministry of Human Resource Development, Government of India. A member of seven professional bodies, she has attended a number of national and international conferences and presented over 44 papers. She has been invited as a keynote speaker and panel member by different countries, such as Sri Lanka, Uzbekistan, Nepal, and Turkey. She has also been invited as Visiting Professor in Kazakhstan and Uzbekistan. Her doctorate from the University of Rajasthan is in Tourism Marketing with dissertation research on Tourism in Rajasthan—Progress and Prospects. She has two postgraduate degree specialties: one in International Business (Master of International Business) and the other in Business Administration (Master of Commerce).

Azizul Hassan, PhD

Azizul Hassan, PhD, is a member of the Tourism Consultants Network of the UK Tourism Society. His areas of research interest are technology-supported marketing for tourism and hospitality, immersive technology applications in the tourism and hospitality industry, technology-influenced marketing suggestions for sustainable tourism, and hospitality industry in developing countries. He authored over 100 articles and book chapters in leading tourism outlets. He is also part of the editorial team of 15 book projects from Routledge, Springer, CAB International, and Emerald Group Publishing Limited. He is a regular reviewer *for Tourism Management, Journal of Hospitality and Tourism Management, Tourism Analysis,* the *International Journal of Human Resource Management, Journal of Ecotourism, Journal of Business Research, eReview of Tourism Research* (eRTR), *International Interdisciplinary Business-Economics Advancement Journal, International Journal of Tourism Cities, Heliyon,* and *Technology in Society.*

Contents

Contributors .... *xi*

About the Contributors .... *xiii*

Abbreviations .... *xxiii*

Preface .... *xxv*

1. **Tracing the Journey of Event Tourism: Coevolution to Synergic Merger** 1
   Samik Ray

2. **Pull Factors That Influence Millennials to Visit Citrawarna Cultural Festival** 19
   Ahmad R. Albattat, Nur Amirah Binti Mazme, Trisha Anne Joseph, Wan Ahmad Azfaruddin Azif, and Ainul Husna Abdullah

3. **Effects and Implications of Event Tourism on Sustainable Community Development: A Review** 31
   Parag Sunil Shukla and Sofia Devi Shamurailatpam

4. **Rural Event Tourism and Community Development** 51
   Karabi Kabir and Md. Ashikur Rahman Avi

5. **Growth and Development of Catamaran: A New Luxury Tourism Demand** 65
   Anukrati Sharma and Shruti Arora

6. **Role and Importance of Event Tourism in Economic and Social Development** 75
   Jeetesh Kumar and Farhad Nazir

7. **The Terror, the Spectacle, and the Worker: The Role of Security Guards in the Organization of Mega Events and Festivals** 87
   Maximiliano E. Korstanje

8. **Advancing Women's Roles and Empowerment in Event Tourism in Rajasthan** 103
   Ekta Dhariwal

x   Contents

9. **Collaborative Involvement of Major and Minor Stakeholders for Organizing Community Events** 113
Monika Barnwal and Vijay Kumar

10. **Promoting Events and Festivals Through Digital Marketing Tools: A Conceptual Framework** 129
Betül Kodaş

11. **Events Create a Successful Destination Imaging: Case of Kirkpinar Oil Wrestling Festival** 141
Kaplan Uğurlu and Aydemir Ay

12. **A Feasibility Study of Resurrecting Elephant Marriage Ceremonies in Mondulkiri, as a Tourism Event: Case Studies of Pu Trom and Pu Tang Villages** 157
Orn Kimtek

13. **Antecedents and Challenges of Sustainable Event Management Practices in Sri Lanka** 187
A. M. D. B. Nawarathna and R. S. S. W. Arachchi

14. **Event Organizations Issues and Challenges of Disabled Youths** 201
Sharala Subramaniam, Thilagavathi Shanmuganathan, Ang Pei Soo, and Jeetesh Kumar

15. **Case Study of Tripura as a Destination Brand with Post-Pandemic Perspectives** 211
Manishankar Chakraborty

16. **Impact of Pandemic, Crises, and Challenges on Event Tourism** 231
Santus Kumar Deb and Shohel Md. Nafi

17. **Opportunities and Challenges in Event Tourism Education** 247
Abdullah USLU and Erkan GÜNEŞ

18. **Enhancing Entrepreneurship in the Event Tourism Industry** 263
Anurodh Godha

19. **Rural Event Tourism: Developing Sustainable Rural Event Tourism for the Development of the Community** 279
Anila Thomas

Index *301*

Contributors

Ainul Husna Abdullah
School of Hospitality and Creative Arts, Management and Science University, University Drive, Off Persiaran Olahraga, Section 13, Selangor, Malaysia

Ahmad Rasmi Albattat
Post Graduate Centre, Management and Science University, University Drive, Off Persiaran Olahraga, Section 13, Selangor, Malaysia

R. S. S. W. Arachchi
Faculty of Management Studies, Sabaragamuwa University of Sri Lanka, Belihuloya, Sri Lanka

Shruti Arora
Department of Commerce and Management, University of Kota, Kota, Rajasthan, India

Md. Ashikur Rahman Avi
Department of Tourism and Hospitality Management, Pabna University of Science and Technology, Pabna, Bangladesh

Aydemir Ay
Municipality of Edirne, Edirne, Turkey

Wan Ahmad Azfaruddin Azif
School of Hospitality and Creative Arts, Management and Science University, University Drive, Off Persiaran Olahraga, Section 13, Selangor, Malaysia

Monika Barnwal
Jamia Millia Islamia (Central University), New Delhi, India

Manishankar Chakraborty
Higher Colleges of Technology, United Arab Emirates

Santus Kumar Deb
Service Management and Marketing, Department of Tourism and Hospitality Management, University of Dhaka, Dhaka, Bangladesh

Ekta Dhariwal
Honorary consultant to many women's organizations and NGO's, Rajasthan, India

Anurodh Godha
Vardhman Mahaveer Open University, Kota, Rajasthan, India

Erkan GÜNEŞ
Vocational School of Tourism and Hotel Management at Erzincan Binali Yıldırım University, Turkey

Trisha Anne Joseph
School of Hospitality and Creative Arts, Management and Science University, University Drive, Off Persiaran Olahraga, Section 13, Selangor, Malaysia

Karabi Kabir
Tourism and Hospitality Management at University of Dhaka, Dhaka, Bangladesh

Orn Kimtek
Royal University of Phnom Penh, Major Tourism Management, Cambodia

Betül Kodaş
Department of Tourism Management in Faculty of Tourism, Mardin Artuklu University, Turkey

Maximiliano E. Korstanje
Department of Economics, University of Palermo, Buenos Aires, Argentina

Jeetesh Kumar
School of Hospitality, Tourism and Events, Taylor's University, Malaysia

Vijay Kumar
Department of Tourism and Hospitality, Jamia Millia Islamia Central University, New Delhi, India

Nur Amirah Binti Mazme
School of Hospitality and Creative Arts, Management and Science University, University Drive, Off Persiaran Olahraga, Section 13, Selangor, Malaysia

Shohel Md. Nafi
Department of Tourism and Hospitality Management, Noakhali Science and Technology University, Noakhali, Bangladesh

A. M. D. B. Nawarathna
Department of Tourism Studies, Faculty of Management, Uva Wellassa University of Sri Lanka, Badulla, Sri Lanka

Farhad Nazir
Institute of Cultural Heritage, Tourism, and Hospitality Management ICHTHM, University of Swat, Pakistan

Samik Ray
IITG, Department of Tourism, Government of India, Kolkata, West Bengal, India

Sofia Devi Shamurailatpam
Department of Banking and Insurance, Faculty of Commerce, Maharaja Sayajirao University of Baroda, Vadodara, Gujarat, India

Thilagavathi Shanmuganathan
Faculty of Languages and Linguistics, Universiti Malaya, Kuala Lumpur, Malaysia

Anukrati Sharma
Department of Commerce and Management, University of Kota, Kota, Rajasthan, India

Parag Sunil Shukla
Department of Commerce & Business Management, Faculty of Commerce, The M.S University of Baroda, Vadodara, Gujarat, India

Ang Pei Soo
Faculty of Languages & Linguistics, University of Malaya, Kuala Lumpur, Malaysia

Sharala Subramaniam
Faculty of Social Science & Leisure Management, Taylor's University Lakeside Campus, Malaysia

Anila Thomas
Department of Tourism and Travel Management, Jyoti Nivas College Autonomous, Bangalore, Karnataka, India

Kaplan Uğurlu
Kırklareli University, Faculty of Tourism in Kırklareli, Turkey

Abdullah USLU
Faculty of Manavgat Tourism, Akdeniz University, Manavgat, Antalya-Turkey

About the Contributors

Samik Ray is an ex-faculty of Department of Folklore, University of Kalyani; Travel and Tourism Management in MPTI (Kolkata); and WTCC School of Trade and Commerce (Kolkata); ex-trainer and Faculty of Regional Level Guide (RLG) Training (Govt. of India, Department of Tourism), presently working as IITG (Incredible India Tourist Guide) (Govt. of India, Department of Tourism); Visiting faculty in the Department of Tourism Management, Rãmãkrishna Mission Vidyãmandira autonomous college with potentials with Swami Vivekananda Institute of Modern Science (Maulana Azad University of Technology) and for excellence, UGC; Editor of *Tourism Theory and Practice*, the Author of several essays on tourism studies and management, social science, and literary criticism, and received National Tourism Award in the category of "The Best Tourist Guide."

Ahmad R. Albattat, is a senior lecturer in Postgraduate Centre, Management and Science University, Shah Alam, Selangor, Malaysia. He is also a visiting professor and external examiner in Medan Academy of Tourism (Akpar Medan). He holds a doctoral degree in Hospitality Management from University Sains Malaysia (USM). He was working for the Jordanian hospitality industry for 17 years. He is an active member of scientific and editorial review board on hospitality management, hotel, tourism, events, emergency planning, disaster management, human resource management.

Nur Amirah Binti Mazme is a program manager in Event Management, School of Hospitality and Creative Arts, Management and Science University, Malaysia. She holds a master's degree in mass communication from University of Technology Mara (UiTM). She is an active member of Asia Pacific International Events Management (APIEM).

Trisha Anne Joseph is an undergraduate student in Event Management, School of Hospitality & Creative Arts, Management & Science University, Malaysia.

Wan Ahmad Azfaruddin Azif is an undergraduate student in Event Management, School of Hospitality & Creative Arts, Management & Science University, Malaysia.

Ainul Husna Abdullah is an undergraduate student in Event Management, School of Hospitality & Creative Arts, Management & Science University, Malaysia.

Parag Sunil Shukla holds a PhD degree in Commerce and Business Management with focus on Strategic Marketing in the area of "retailing." He has been working as an Assistant Professor in The Maharaja Sayajirao University of Baroda since 2009. He has presented and published many research papers in contemporary areas of Marketing in National and International Journals. He is also an author in a book entitled *Retail Shoppers' Behaviour in Brick and Mortar Stores—A Strategic Marketing Approach* which is published by a reputed publisher. His major research area of interests include retailing, services marketing, and consumer behavior to name a few.

Sofia Devi Shamurailatpam holds a PhD in Economics with specialization in the area of Banking and Financial Economics. Currently, she is serving as an Assistant Professor in the Department of Banking and Insurance, Faculty of Commerce, The Maharaja Sayajirao University of Baroda. She has published several research papers and authored a book entitled *Banking Reforms in India: Consolidation, Restructuring and Performance*, published by Palgrave Macmillan, UK (2017). Her major research areas of interest include economics of banking, financial economics, economics of gender, agricultural economics, and development economics, particularly, contemporary issues on sustainability.

Karabi Kabir is an assistant professor in Tourism and Hospitality Management department at the University of Dhaka, Bangladesh (on study leave). She is currently doing her Ph.D. in Hospitality and Tourism Management at the University of Surrey, UK. She obtained her Bachelor and Master's degrees in tourism and hospitality management from the University of Dhaka. Her research interests include sustainable tourism development, tourism entrepreneurs, and gender in tourism.

Md. Ashikur Rahman Avi is an academician and researcher in the tourism and hospitality industry. He has been teaching at the university level since 2017. Presently, Avi is working as Assistant Professor in the Tourism and Hospitality Management department at the Pabna University of Science and Technology, Bangladesh. Previously, he had an appointment as a lecturer in the Department of International Tourism and Hospitality Management at Primeasia University for almost three years. Avi did both Bachelor

About the Contributors

and Master's Degrees in Tourism and Hospitality Management from the University of Dhaka. He received the "Dean's Honor Award 2015" for his outstanding results at Master level. He also received the "Research Honor Award-2022" from Pabna University of Science and Technology for his significant contribution to tourism and hospitality research. Avi has conducted 10 research papers that are published in reputed national and international journals, and he has also contributed 10 chapters in 3 books published by Springer, Singapore and Germany. As the keynote speaker, Avi conducted a session on 'Technology Applications in Tourism and Hospitality Industry in Asia: Present Status and Future Trends' at 1st International Conference on Business and Tourism Management (ICBT-2022) organized by Primeasia University, Dhaka, Bangladesh. His research interests include destination development, sustainable tourism management, tourism and technology, rural tourism, marine and coastal tourism, medical tourism, tourism planning, and tourism marketing.

Anukrati Sharma is currently an associate professor in the Department of Commerce and Management, University of Kota, Kota, Rajasthan, India. She has edited and authored several books and has attended a number of national and international conferences, presenting over 45 papers. She has been invited to talks, lectures, and panel discussions by different universities. Her special interest areas are tourism, tourism marketing, strategic management, and international business management.

Shruti Arora is currently working as a guest faculty in the Department of Commerce and Management, University of Kota, Kota, Rajasthan, India. She had an experience of 13 years in education industry. Her core subjects are marketing, general management, international business management, and customer relationship management. She has authored a book on *Event Management and Marketing: Theory, Practical Approaches and Planning* in 2018 and edited a book *Event Tourism in Asian Countries: Challenges and Prospects* under Apple Academic Press (Taylor and Francis Group), USA. She has attended various international conferences and her publications include various chapters in edited books and research papers in national and international peer-reviewed journals.

Jeetesh Kumar is a senior lecturer in the School of Hospitality, Tourism and Events, Taylor's University, Malaysia. His doctorate is from the Taylor's University in Hospitality and Tourism with research on Economic Impacts of Business Events in Malaysia. He has two postgraduate degrees; professional master's in Hospitality Management and International Tourism from University of Toulouse, France and the other in Business Administration (MBA—Marketing) from Hamdard University, Pakistan. His research areas include economic impacts, economic modeling, MICE, medical tourism, and behavioral studies. He has worked on consultancy and research projects at the national level and authored 35+ publications including research articles and book chapters.

Farhad Nazir is Lecturer at Institute of Cultural Heritage, Tourism, and Hospitality Management ICHTHM, University of Swat, Pakistan. Before joining University of Swat, he served as Coordinator at Marriott Hotel International. Presently, he is pursuing doctorate in tourism, heritage, and territory from University of Coimbra, Portugal. He has MPhil degree in Development Studies from Pakistan Institute of Development Economics PIDE, Islamabad. He obtained master's degree in Tourism and Hospitality from Hazara University, Pakistan and was awarded Gold Medal as well. His research lines are Cultural Tourism Sites and Cultural Identity, Islamic Legislation and Tourism Laws, and Hospitality Laws in the Islamic Preview. He has attended a number of national and international conferences and presented conference papers.

Maximiliano E Korstanje is a Senior Lecturer at Department of Economics, University of Palermo, Argentina. He is book series editor of Advances in Hospitality, and the Services Industries (IGI Global, US) and Tourism Security Safety and Post Conflict destinations (Emerald Group Publishing, UK). In 2015, he was awarded as Visiting Research Fellow at School of Sociology and Social Policy, University of Leeds, UK and the University of La Habana, Cuba. In 2017, he was elected as Foreign Faculty Member of AMIT, Mexican Academy in the Study of Tourism, which is the most prominent institution dedicated to tourism research in Mexico. He has also recently been selected to take part in the 2018 Albert Nelson Marquis Lifetime Achievement Award, a great distinction given by Marquis Who's Who in the world.

Ekta Dhariwal is a postgraduate from the University of Kota. Later, she obtained her doctorate degree from Career Point University in the year 2018. She is honorary consultant to many women's organizations and NGO's in Rajasthan. She has participated in many national and international conferences and presented papers as well. She is the recipient of *Sumitra Women Entrepreneur Award.* She is a famous panel discussant and raises her voice

About the Contributors xvii

for women empowerment. Hosting the flag of her NGO, Aksham Kalyan Sansthan, she has been nourishing social aspirations in various fields.

Monika Barnwal completed her graduation from SRM University in Computer Science and MBA from Indian Institute of Tourism and Travel Management, Gwalior. Currently, she is pursuing her PhD from Jamia Millia Islamia, Central University, New Delhi along with a JRF. Her topic is related to Branding of Smart Tourism Destination. She has published research papers in UGC Care journals and in Scopus listed journals. Her tourism interests are in sustainability, destination branding, and smart tourism destination. She has authored Ready Reckoner Tourism Guidebook for UGC Net Aspirants. She has four years of working experience in tourism corporate field and one year of teaching experience.

Vijay Kumar has done his MBA and PhD from Jamia Millia Islamia. His teaching interests are in the fields of Sustainability in Tourism and Domestic Tourism. He successfully completed his PhD with JRF. He currently teaches in the Department of Tourism and Hospitality, Jamia Millia Islamia Central University, New Delhi as Assistant Professor. He has teaching experience of more than 15 years and has a very significant teaching record among his students. He has more than 20 research papers and chapters published under his name. The research articles are published widely in UGC care listed journals and Scopus listed journals. He has also authored books related to tourism and has been supervising PhD candidates.

Betül Kodaş is an Assistant Professor in the Department of Tourism Management in Faculty of Tourism, Mardin Artuklu University, Turkey. She holds a bachelor's degree from School of Tourism and Hotel Management in Adnan Menderes University (Turkey), master's degree from Dokuz Eylül University and PhD from Eskişehir Osmangazi University (2018) in Turkey. Her research interests are tourism management, destination marketing and management, and information communication technologies.

Kaplan Uğurlu is an Associate Professor at Kırklareli University, Faculty of Tourism in Kırklareli, Turkey. He has been working in Turkey for 13 years as an Academician. He has worked as a Senior Manager for 28 years in the tourism sector. He is specialized in marketing, finance, accounting, cost controlling, and hotel openings. After his bachelor's degree at Uludağ University, Turkey (BSc in Tourism and Hotel Management), he completed his master's degree at the University of Surrey, England (MSc in International

Hotel Management). He received his PhD at Marmara University, Turkey (PhD in Production Management and Marketing). He has more than 65 papers presented and published in national and international congresses, journals, and books. His academic research interests include tourism and hotel management, tourism and hotel marketing, accounting, and finance.

Aydemir Ay is a PhD student and is also working as Tourism Consultant at the Municipality of Edirne, Turkey. Ay studied Tourism and Hospitality Management at Eastern Mediterranean University of the Turkish Republic of Northern Cyprus, and completed his master's degree at the University of Beykent, Istanbul. His working area is in tourism marketing, tourist behavior, cross-border tourism, and local gastronomy. Also, Ay studies specifically the Jewish Population and Culture of Edirne. With over 15 years in both public and private sectors, Ay has experience in tourism, management, and the successful completion of more than 20 festival projects and five books.

Orn Kimtek is a former graduate student from Royal University of Phnom Penh, Cambodia. He completed his bachelor's degree in Tourism Management in 2018. He has strong interest in exploratory and descriptive research concerning natural, community-based, and cultural tourism. Additionally, he was involved in a few community-based tourism and service-learning projects while he was studying at university. After graduating, Kimtek directly started his career as a monitoring and results measurement officer for a skills development project partly related to tourism in a non-governmental organization where he is working nowadays. His hobbies include reading, surfing the internet, and listening to music.

A.M.D.B. Nawarathna graduated in Hospitality, Tourism and Events Management (BBM) from Uva Wellassa University of Sri Lanka and currently reading for MBA in Tourism from Sabaragamuwa University of Sri Lanka. He is a full-time faculty lecturer at the Department of Tourism Studies, Faculty of Management, Uva Wellassa University, Sri Lanka. He is also a member of different committees and projects in the university and has coordinated a number of events organized in the university. His research interests are in event management, MICE tourism, travel agency and tour operations management, tourism planning and management, destination management and marketing, etc.

R. S. S. W. Arachchi graduated from Sabaragamuwa University, Sri Lanka, before receiving his master's degree from Colombo University, Sri Lanka and PhD degree from Management and Science University in Malaysia. He is the former Head, Department of Tourism Management. He is senior lecturer of Faculty of Management Studies, Sabaragamuwa University of Sri Lanka, Belihuloya. His major teaching and research areas are ecotourism, community-based tourism, sustainable tourism development, responsible tourism, environment and tourism resources, and homestay tourism in Asian Countries. He has published nearly 20 articles in well-recognized journals, both in Sri Lanka and overseas. Dr. Arachchi is an editorial board member of *Journal of Tourism and Hospitality Management, International Journal of Education Humanities and Social Science, International Journal of Studies in Social Science Research* (SSSR), and a member of Global Association for Humanities and Social Science Research.

Sharala Subramaniam is Lecturer in the Faculty of Social Science & Leisure Management at the Taylor's University where she has been a faculty member since 2015. Sharala completed her PhD at the National University of Malaysia and her undergraduate studies are also from the same University. Her research interests lie in the area of education. She has collaborated actively with researchers in several other disciplines of hospitality, particularly tourism and events management. Sharala has served on roughly four conference and workshop program committees. Sharala also organized MoU signing ceremony with Dewan Bahasa dan Pustaka (government industry) and considers it an accomplishment to have created a collaboration between Taylor's University and government industry.

Thilagavathi Shanmuganathan is Associate Professor in linguistics at the Faculty of Languages and Linguistics, Universiti Malaya, Malaysia. Since October 2016, she has jointly worked on an EU-funded, 3-year Erasmus+ Marco Polo project in cooperation with the University of Seville, Spain, and Heriot-Watt University, Scotland. Her recent roles include being coeditor for the book *Internationalization of Higher Education in Southeast Asia: A Perspective from the Marco Polo Project* (2020, with Rupert Beinhaeur), reviewer for the *International Journal of Language and Culture*, and Principal Investigator for a government-funded project "Hear Me! Empowering Disadvantaged Youth." Her current research focuses on language, conceptualization, and culture within the framework of cultural linguistics and discourse analysis. The main fields of her present linguistic investigation include cultural schemas in marriage, naming practices, and death among Malaysian Indians.

Pei Soo ANG is a Senior Lecturer at the Faculty of Languages, Linguistics, University of Malaya, Kuala Lumpur. Her areas of research interest include discourses of disability, critical disability studies, critical discourse analysis, social semiotics, and multimodality. Her current research work centers on characterizing the discourses of disability as represented in the Malaysian news media, employing a critical semiotic theoretical approach and a multi-perspectival methodology.

Manishankar Chakraborty is employed with the Higher Colleges of Technology, United Arab Emirates. His core teaching and applied research areas entail entrepreneurship, human resource management, marketing management, soft skills, tourism management, teaching and learning. He has published more than 20 research papers in several peer-reviewed journals globally, contributed more than 10 chapters in edited books, more than 45 publications in conferences across the Gulf Cooperation Council (GCC) region, Middle-East and North Africa (MENA) region, Europe, Americas and South Asia, and has also written more than 500 articles with leading dailies and periodicals across, Middle-East and North Africa (MENA) region and South Asia. After his doctoral studies, he has also been certified by MCIPD, UK as an academic fellow, and has also completed his Fellowship of the Higher Education Academy, UK (FHEA).

Santus Kumar Deb is Professor and currently serving as a chairman of the department of Tourism and Hospitality Management, University of Dhaka, Bangladesh. Santus Kumar Deb is Professor and currently serving as a chairman of the department of Tourism and Hospitality Management, University of Dhaka, Bangladesh. He earned his PhD in Service Management and Erasmus Mundus Scholar. He has completed an Executive Program in Strategic Digital Marketing (EPSDM), PGD in Supply Chain Management, and MBA in Marketing. His core subjects are marketing, e-tourism, service management, sustainable tourism, digital marketing, and logistics. Deb is a regular reviewer of ABDC ranked journals. He has conducted classes in Vincent Pol University, Lublin, Poland, as a visiting professor. He has many international publications on the era of business and tourism in renowned journals.

Shohel Md. Nafi is currently Chairperson and Assistant Professor in the Department of Tourism and Hospitality Management, Noakhali Science and Technology University, Bangladesh. He has an MBA in Tourism and Hospitality Management. His core subjects are sustainable tourism,

About the Contributors

digital tourism, event management, and community-based tourism. He has conducted classes in many renowned private universities in Bangladesh. He has many international and national publications on the era of tourism in ABDC-ranked journals.

Abdullah USLU is an Associate Professor in the Faculty of Manavgat Tourism at Akdeniz University. His main research areas are tourism marketing, tourist behaviour, destination image and management, service quality, residents' perceptions of the impacts of tourism in the local communities, residents' attitudes toward tourism and tourism development, and sustainable tourism.

Erkan GÜNEŞ is an Associate Professor in Vocational School of Tourism and Hotel Management at Erzincan Binali Yıldırım University. His research interests are destination marketing and management, destination quality, tourism education, cultural heritage tourism and sustainable tourism.

Anurodh Godha is working as Assistant Professor at Vardhman Mahaveer Open University, Kota, Rajasthan, India since August 2009. He is also looking after the Affairs of Centre for Entrepreneurship and Skill Development (CESD) as Dy. Director at VM Open University, Kota. His field of specialization is finance, tourism, and entrepreneurship. As editor, he has many books to his credit. He has also contributed in various edited books at national level. He has published many research papers in various journals. In administrative capacity, he is working as Dy. Director, School of Commerce & Management at VM Open University, Kota.

Anila Thomas is working as Associate Professor and Head in the Department of Tourism and Travel Management, Jyoti Nivas College Autonomous, Bangalore, Karnataka. A highly dedicated organizer, an enthusiastic researcher and an academician of soft nature, Dr. Thomas has a long teaching experience of 22 years. She has been an invited resource person and session chair for many international and national conferences and has been extensively published in both research journals and books. She completed her PhD thesis in Tourism Management in 2012 from Mother Teresa Women's University, Kodaikanal, Tamil Nadu. Her research areas include tourism resources, tourism geography, destination marketing, destination planning and policy-making, women's contributions in the field of ayurvedic medical tourism, and community involvement for sustaining tourism resources.

Abbreviations

AHC	Australian Heritage Commission
CBA	cost benefit analysis
CC	carrying capacity
CP	community participation
CRM	Collective Responsibilities Model
ELIE	Elephant Livelihood Initiative Environment Organization
FTAs	foreign tourist arrivals
GO	government official
GTI	global tourism industry
HRMP	human resource management policy
IATO	Indian Association of Tour Operators
ITY	integrated tourism yield
LAC	limits of acceptable change
LAO	Lalon Academy Official
LC	local community
LEAF	Local Environmental Awareness Foundation
LTC	leave travel concession
MICE	meeting, incentives, conferences and exhibitions
MoT	Ministry of Tourism
NGOs	nongovernmental organizations
NTOs	national tourism offices
PPP	public–private partnerships
PWD	person with disabilities
ROI	return on investment
SDS	Swadesh Darshan Scheme
SLA	sustainable livelihoods approach
STBT	sustainable tourism benchmarking tool
T	tourist
TEP	Tourism Empowerment Programme
TBL	triple bottom line
TO	tour operator
USP	unique selling propositions
VFR	visit friend and relative
WGDP	world's gross domestic product

Preface

The need to develop event tourism sustainably has become a significant concern as the event tourism business is becoming increasingly essential to community development around the world. It is critical to the development of a more successful and appealing destination. As tourists not only travel for leisure, but also for entertainment and business purposes like meetings or conferences, or attending an event etc, these people have contributed to the enlargement of the destinations they have visited and at large, developed the event tourism industry as a whole.

Event tourism can generate huge economic benefits for the entire economy of the destinations. At the same time, it also impacts the local economies. For a destination, event tourism can act as tourist attractions, catalysts, animators, image-makers, and place marketers. Local festivals, fairs, events, and tourism are the livelihood of society. They are inextricably linked and essential to the development and maintenance of a community's quality of life since they strengthen communities, provide exclusive events, raise knowledge of diverse cultures and identities, and serve as a basis for community smugness.

Traditional cultural celebrations, such as music, dancing, gastronomy, arts, and sports, are covered by events tourism. These events can occur around the same time each year and last anywhere from one to many days. Community events, festivals, and fairs provide jobs, support local businesses such as vendors, craftsmen, and crafters, and draw tourists from all over the world. In fact, governments of many countries provide a variety of products and services to support the promotion of event tourism. Organizing events has become an important aspect of healhty community development all over the world.

Our edited book brings together a wide range of festivals, events, and event tourism from around the world that focuses on many world events rather than on a single event. The book exclusively covers event tourism, community festivals, sustainable, community development, culture, and local communities. It highlights rural as well as urban event tourism, impact of event tourism on communities, managing event tourism during and after COVID-19, women empowerment in event tourism, promoting event tourism and community development, opportunities and challenges in event tourism education, and much more. The book is a meticulous effort of many minds from various countries like India, Sri Lanka, Turkey, Malaysia, United Arab Emirates, Bangladesh, Cambodia, Portugal, Argentina, and Zimbabwe and we are thankful to all the contributors.

Dr. Ekta Dhariwal
Dr. Shruti Arora
Dr. Anukrati Sharma
Dr. Azizul Hassan

CHAPTER 1

Tracing the Journey of Event Tourism: Coevolution to Synergic Merger

SAMIK RAY

IITG, Department of Tourism, Government of India, Kolkata, West Bengal India

ABSTRACT

Both events and tourism, disjunctively or conjunctively, are crucial in the new emerging world economy. While tourism is a few centuries-old phenomenon, participation in events is age-old culture. Although traveling is imperative to event participation, the interaction between tourism and event begins only with the event's emergence as a tourism motivator. Increasing demand for specialized and skilled services made events and tourism more interdependent and interactive to grow together. The growth of event tourism becomes the economic development indicator within the world's new emerging economy. The present chapter will trace the journey of coevolution and then the synergic merger of event and tourism that led event tourism to emerge as a distinct field of the service sector. It will also study the rationale and conceptual swings that shape event tourism.

1.1 INTRODUCTION

An event refers to social/cultural/economic/political/scientific happenings of personal/local/regional/national/global significance (Ray, 2019). It is either planned or unplanned, chance-directed or purpose-directed, organized or unorganized, regional or local, national or international, traditional; geosocial; ethnic identity or market-value-driven and as big as the Olympics or as small as a get-together or celebration of achievements. Tourism refers to

Please note that few chapters were submitted during the peak of the pandemic. The long period of time to publish (due to supply chain and other issues) may have changed the perspectives presented in the chapter altogether.

Event Tourism and Sustainable Community Development: Advances, Effects, and Implications.
Ekta Dhariwal, Shruti Arora, Anukrati Sharma, Azizul Hassan (Eds.)
© 2024 Apple Academic Press, Inc. Co-published with CRC Press (Taylor & Francis)

travel and stays away from home for motives such as exploring cultural and natural novelties or marvels, leisure, recreation, business, gatherings, events, health, education, and religion. Interaction between events and tourism was evident from ancient days as both share comparable and analogous hospitality conditions and homologous logistics environments. Moreover, travel motivators are somewhat analogous to event drivers. Thus, events and travel became naturally and logically selected allies. Their relationship is defined to be more complementary, causally interdependent, and reciprocal than competitive. An event always motivates people to travel and stay away from home, while travel-stay logistics make the event happen. Functional reciprocity, selective causal factors, complementary function, and shared logistics environment primarily made the event and the travel-stay logistics grow simultaneously and lately coevolve. In the process of coevolution, each sector adopts potential changes within its system and functions in conformity with the experience gathered by the other. Thus, bidirectional causation and changes take place in tandem. The relationship turned out to be mutually bidirectional dependency and connectivity. Moreover, temperance campaign events or the Great Exhibition, London, organized by Prince Albert and Henry Cole, caused the earliest appearances of organized package tourism by the middle of the 19th century. There were shreds of evidence of tourists visiting music or theatres though those events were not the sole motivation for the tours.

The mobility of capital for the market tearing down every spatial barrier (Marx, 1973) across the earth in the post-1950 world contributes to the intensification of trade-business-commerce globally. It escalates the demand for trade fairs and exhibitions, business-meet, incentive programs, trade summits and other events. The growth of various economic and geopolitical or strategic regional and international blocs also escalates the demand for interstate and intrastate economic, political, trade, and cultural events. Similarly, tourism in the post-1950 era experienced a rapid increment in tourist footfalls. Thus, unprecedented growth and spread of tourism become evident. Conversion of space, place, landscape, ethnocultural contents and events into a commodity appeared as a logical extension of the mass-scale mobility of tourists involving people from cross-sections. Thus, the event becomes an increasingly significant driver of tourism growth and an important motivator of travel since event-centric tour packages contribute to the escalation of tourist footfall. By the end of the last century, tourism advocating counter-goals like controlled and sustainable interaction between tourist and host and tourism growth and resources champions the niche alternatives to mass tourism. Concern for tourist choices and demands, authentic tourist experiences, better host life, preservation of hosts' ethnocultural identity, ill impacts, and other social responsibility agendas (Ray, 2017) become crucial. The tourism and event industry begins to be multifaceted, complex, and specialized. Thus, dependency and connectivity between two increases at a large scale logically. While tourism uses the event as growth and diversification drivers, utilization of tourism logistics and management mechanisms for effective marketing, promotion, development, and operation of growing multifaceted and exclusive event products becomes the need of the hour. As interconnection and interdependence increase rapidly, a shift in the relationship paradigm from the coevolved functional partnership of mutual interaction to the synergistic collaboration is overtly apparent. By the late 20th and early 21st century, the synergistic collaboration led the event industry to operate with the support of specialized tourism logistics and mechanisms, making both the tourism and event industry stakeholders experienced vertical and horizontal growth. The growth opportunity, a rapid increase of market-oriented economic systems and intensified international trade, differentiation in market segments, the necessity of place promotion, branding, imaging, and the ascendency of authentic experience paradigm in tourism eventually led the event industry to merge with tourism and then makes a way of the emergence of event tourism.

1.2 TRENDS IN EVENT TOURISM STUDIES: A SKETCH

While travel, hospitality logistics, and event have a long-established partnership, the development of tourism and event research is only a post-World War phenomenon. Researchers hardly combined two fields except for Goldblatt (1995) and Getz (2005). The emergence of event tourism as a crucial business field in the last few decades made scholars and researchers of various disciplines study this emerging field. The volume of research done on event tourism of late indicates the growth of academic interest in it though practices spread faster than research. General discussion, impact studies, and typology have received much attention. Management, marketing, planning, designing, evaluation, and concept-building aspects received much importance in this context. Borostin (1961) possibly made the earliest reference to the planned event, whereas Greenwood (1972) and Gunn (1979) noted the significance of festivals and conventions in tourism without perceiving an event as an attraction. Syme et al. (1989), Getz (1998, 2002, 2007), Rittichainuwat et al.

(2001), Weed (2005), Mackellar (2006), Bowdin et al. (2011), and Krajnović et al. (2016) endeavored to conceptualize event tourism. Getz (2000, 2000a, 2000b, 2005) studied event management by systematically broadening its research scope. Simultaneously, works on the evaluation of management effectiveness (Getz, 1989), risk management (Berlonghi, 1990; Tarlow, 2002), and event management education (Hawkins and Goldblatt, 1995) widened the area of the event study.

The most notable contribution to planning and marketing research is convention strategies in destination planning (Getz et al., 1998, 2001; Getz, 2004; Hoyle, 2002; Berridge, 2006; Masterman and Wood, 2006). Studies on the role of information and communication technology in tourism events (Arora and Sharma, 2019, 2020) and social media in traditional cultural tourism event promotion (Djumrianti, 2019), sports events' media management (Getz and Fairley, 2004), and the effectiveness of social media sharing on tourism event choice (Dedeoğlu and Küçükergin, 2019) are also crucial. A good number of scholars contributed significantly to the field of impact studies. Among those, the criticals are mega events' role in generating tourism (Bos, 1994) and its impact on tourism (Getz, 1999; Mossberg, 2000), resident perceptions about event impacts (Fredline and Faulkner, 2002), hallmark events to contest tourism seasonality (Ritchie and Beliveau, 1974) and social media's impact on tourism events (Ahmad et al., 2019). Economic impact enquiries include bearings on festival visitors (Scotinform Ltd., 1991), effects of expositions on tourism (Ritchie, 1984), and event tourism impact analysis (Della Bitta et al., 1978; Vaughan, 1979; Crompton and McKay, 1994; Bond, 2008). Indeed sociocultural and economic impact studies on the festival and sports events received much attention (Greenwood, 1972; Janiskee, 1980; Getz, 2000, 2000a; Small and Edwards, 2003; Xie, 2003; Matheson, 2005; Fredline, 2006; Chang, 2006; Quinn, 2009; Phipps and Slater, 2010; Ljudevit et al., 2012; Sharma, 2019). Type-specific studies largely delved into business, MICE, festival, and sports event tourism. Getz (2000), Allen et al. (2011), Getz et al. (2007) and Quinn (2009) focus on festival event's contributions to tourism, while Sharma (2019) discusses tourism festival marketing aspect. Hassan (2019) and Shabnam et al. (2019) deal with the role of cultural events in destination image and identity building. Lee and Back (2005) explored varied aspects of MICE tourism events. Research works of Getz (2003), Supovitz and Goldblatt (2004), and Ljudevit et al. (2012) on the aspects of sports event and tourism and the works of Getz (1989, 1991, 2000b, 2002), Hall (1992), Formica (1998), and Goldblatt (2007) on special interest tourism are notably significant. The present chapter endeavors to trace the journey of events and tourism and the rationale that shapes and leads to the emergence of event tourism, which is still a missing research area.

1.3   DIACHRONY OF TOURISM AND EVENT COEVOLUTION

The primitive hunger impulse-driven group hunting was possibly the earliest evidence of the event and travel linkage. A naturally and logically selected partnership between event and travel developed within the primitive group hunting frame since a shared homologous travel-hospitality logistics environment was the integral part or prerequisite to both. There was evidence of sociocultural and trade events in ancient Egypt, Greece, Rome (Kotsori, 2019), India, and China. Sonepur cattle fair and Prayag's pilgrimage bathing (India); Tekh Festival (Egypt); Dionysia Festival (Greece); Nottingham Goose Fair, and European Mop fairs; Chinese Miaohui festival were few examples of ancient events. Crowds, merchants, farmers, and artisans of far and near distances used to travel and participate in fairs, festivals, and trade events. They usually gather along the known trade routes of ancient and medieval Eurasian territory to buy and sell.

Between the eighth century BCE and the fourth century CE, more or less 40,000 spectators, pilgrims, and sportspersons from the Greek city-states and kingdoms usually traveled to Olympia to attend a 5-day-long Olympic. Merchants, fortune tellers, and jugglers also traveled there to do business. Intellectuals like Herodotus traveled to Olympia to meet people and politicians or make political propaganda. There were rented houses and tents for accommodation and temporary stalls for food. Usually, conflicting kingdoms went on a mutual and temporary truce to allow the people traveling to Olympia unmolested. Athenian Panathenaic Games, Greek equestrian sports and Roman jumping, wrestling, boxing, racing, and gladiatorial combats were the other examples of ancient events. The descriptions of contemporary Indian chariot racing, hunting and wrestling, swimming, and archery competitions were present in the Ramayana and Mahabharata. While the civilians entertain themselves gazing at those events, the warrior caste participates to enjoy and display military abilities and supremacy.

The modern conference concept originated from a series of events, such as the 7-month-long first Buddhist council of 500 spiritually enlightened at Rājgir in 400 BCE, the Second Buddhist Council of 700 monks at Vaishali in 383 BCE, the Third Buddhist council of 1000 monk participants across Asia at Pataliputra in 240 BCE and Ecumenical Council of 1800 bishops from churches across Roman and Sassanid empires at Nicaea in 325 CE. Occurrences of religious events, such as the commemoration of the birth and death anniversary of Lord Buddha at Lumbini and Kushinagar, were common in ancient times. Rigveda supplement (pariśiṣṭa) and Buddhist cannons such as Majjhima Nikāya referred to the event of pilgrimage bathing and occurrences of the fair at Prayag, the ancient form of Kumbha melā. By the late pre-Christian time, socioeconomic and cultural activities or various entertainments, such as folk music and dance performances; magic shows; races; jugglery; fire-eating; sword-swallowing; stilt-walking; gambling; wrestling; and animal fights became part of the events besides the primary goals, such as trading, sports or religious performances.

Besides migration and military achievement, people travel to attend various sociocultural and socioeconomic events in ancient days. The event drivers were closely analogous to the travel motivations. Fairs, festivals, trading, meeting people, religious conferences, pilgrimages, and sports were the event drivers, while event participation and those event drivers motivated people to travel. Indeed traveling and events were individual or community-managed, and socioeconomic need driven as the concept of professionally managed travel and event was utterly absent. Instances of traveling without event and event participation without travel were not abundant. Event locations emerged as the center of creative spending and social gatherings by the 13th century. It prompted people across different social strata to travel to and stay at event locations and consume, enjoy, and experience cultural performances and services required during their stay there. Then the rationale or motivation for traveling and event participation extended beyond the early impulses.

Efforts of imperial and merchant – guilds to develop better event infrastructure, accessibility, and accommodations for attendees gradually turned fairs, festivals, sports, and conferences internationally significant by the 12th century (Ray, 2019). Sociocultural, religious, and entertainment value appeared to be equally crucial to trading value in livestock fairs though its significance at the outset is located only in its trade value. Similarly, the rationale of religious fairs like the Kumbha Mela of India extended to various sociocultural values. Bhutan's Tsechu, a religious event instituted by Guru Padmasambhava in the eighth and ninth centuries, gradually gathered social and trading value.

The better infrastructure, facilities, and amenities contributed to the cross-national mobility growth at events. An immense and overt economic impact on Baku, Bukhara, Kashgar, Khurasan, Merv, Samarkand, Xinjiang,

Pushkar, Sonepur, and many other destinations became apparent. Events usually rotated periodically in association with a lifestream and took place at a permanent venue set aside for the event, thus get social sanctions. Changes in the event venue were uncommon except for a few cases. It happened to accommodate better infrastructure and socioeconomic or political compulsions. The shift of Harihar Kshetra fair from Hajipur to Sonepur by Mughal emperor Aurangzeb or changes of lantern festival venue at the Chinese emperors' wish were notable examples. With venue change initiatives, new infrastructure developments, such as well digging; security picket posting; building of structures for trading, selling, and storing of produces or for religious rites; construction of new styled accommodation with food, fun, and security provisions (inns, serāī, Traven, pānthasālā, dharamsālā) were evident. Hence, market-cum-fair and festivals became internationally significant institutions within medieval urban fabrics as commoners, pilgrims, inquisitives, merchants, and producers across boundaries attended those events regularly. Medieval Indian livestock fairs of Pushkar and Sonepur were participated by the military, state, cattle breeders, and traders across Asia for the finest livestock. Then, those fairs rose to prominence by scale and significance with immense cross-national socioeconomic consequences. With the patronization of princely states in the post-Great Mughal era and the introduction of better road-rail transportation and infrastructure during the colonial period, millions of pilgrims, merchants, missionaries, and curious Europeans began to attend those fairs. Pushkar, Sonepur, *Kumbha,* and *Gangasagar* fairs, thus, continued to be significant by the scale and nature of gatherings. A shift from unorganized local control to organized state support was evident as the state gradually began to provide better infrastructure and look after public health, security, and logistics management. Further, event hosting and travel to the event became commercial pursuits by the medieval period as state and event authorities earned large amounts as logistics management tax.

Participation in events primarily involves traveling, staying away from home, food–beverage, and hospitality service consumption, and experiencing various activities. Event participation since ancient days could be one of many impulses of early traveling phenomena. Though the modern concept of tourism was missing, travel and staying away from home to participate or gaze at an event for a while and consumption practice of various services while participating in the event established a significant link between event and tourism. The grand tour in the 17th and 18th centuries often encouraged tourists to visit the musical events and theatre performances. The story of organized tourism's emergence in the mid-19th century is also inextricably intertwined with a Victorian event since Thomas Cook, the father of modern tourism, arranged a train trip from Leicester to Loughborough and back along with band entertainment, food, and tea for one shilling per attendee to a temperance meeting.

1.4 COEVOLUTION: RATIONALE OF PROGRESS

The term coevolution is borrowed from biology (Hjalager, 2020) to describe the development of travel and event in reciprocal responding and mutually interdependent circumstances. Traveling for primitive group hunting, migration, military exercise, trading, pilgrimage, reunion, fair, festival, sports, conference, and any other sociocultural or socioeconomic causes is a common phenomenon in the civilization. Thus, traveling was overtly event-centric till the emergence of leisure-centric modern tourism. Similarly, participation in events without travel is impossible except for a few specific local ones. Since traveling was event-centric, a close interaction between the two led to the growth of an interdependency, thus natural and logical. Events and phenomena of travel evolve together in association with each other due to close interaction, mutual interdependence, and collaborative operational involvement. So, traveling and events are apparently detached but causally attached or interdependent sectors/phenomena/systems, began to coevolve while sharing similar growth drivers or motivations, interacting within comparable analogous hospitality conditions, homologous logistics environment, and exerting mutual pressure. Coevolution occurs in specificity, reciprocity, and simultaneity (Janzen, 1980). Sequential actions such as reciprocal influence or stimulation, causal pressure, bilateral change, and adaptation involve in the coevolution process. With the shift in the perception of events from primitive impulsions to the opportunity of socialization and economic growth, mobility from cross-section and cross-boundary toward events' participation had increased substantially. Increased mobility at the outset stimulates the condition to create causal pressure for improved travel logistics to facilitate a cost-effective, safe, less time-consuming, and less hazardous traveling experience. This pressure led to a change in travel logistics and on-road hospitality from the 10th century, thus making the event destination accessible better than before. More people began to travel, attend, and participate in events. A reciprocal influence and subsequent pressure grew for better event logistics. An overt shift in event perception and practice from locally managed to state or event logistic provider-controlled activity typically led event destinations equipped with orderly logistic support, such as transportation, accommodation, venue management, warehousing, storing and other amenities, and facilities for the attendees, visitors, and participants. Initiatives of digging well, posting security pickets, and making accommodations with food, fun, and security provisions at the event destinations were customary. Those initiatives were analogous to on-travel hospitality logistics. In parallel, the construction of make-shifts to create trading, storing, and selling space and arrangements for religious rites (Ray, 2019) made the destinations logistically ordered to host events successfully. As a result, market-cum-fair and festivals turned out to be cross-nationally accepted institutions within medieval and colonial urban fabrics as were attended by the people of diverse backgrounds across boundaries (Ray, 2019). Each entity (event and traveling) stimulates and pressurizes other reciprocally linked and closely interacting entities (Kallis, 2007) substantially to evolve and grow in parallel and tandem with changes in the prevailing system. Change in one is caused by the other or under the other's pressure, thus occuring in specificity and reciprocity. When both evolve together, evolutionary change and adaptation will be reciprocal. Thereby increased demand for event participation causes changes in on-road hospitality and on-travel logistics, and adaptation of change further causes changes in on-site event logistics. It is indeed an ongoing process. Sometimes changes and then adoption may not occur in tandem or simultaneity as the nature of causal pressure, intensities of reciprocal influence or stimulation, and the scale of mutual interactions were not symmetrical always. Thus, the present perception of simultaneity varies from the biological coevolution theory.

1.5 TRANSITION FROM COEVOLUTION TO SYNERGY

The use of 19th century technological innovation to invent railways, advanced technology-supported vehicles, new cruise lines, and advanced roadways ushered in a new travel logistic era. Thomas Cook and Reiseburo Rominger were among a few who had foreseen the pragmatic future of technological innovation-supported emerging logistic mechanisms. Cook successfully experimented with this new mechanism initiating an organized package tour for 570 people to attend a temperance event at Leicester (1841). Tourism stakeholders marked this incident as the beginning of modern tourism.

The meaning of logistics had been redefined when Cook, Rominger, and American Express put effort into making the flow of all kinds of tangible and intangible tourism services and experiences from tourist origin to the tourist destination a better way. The organized package tour logistics then introduce a series of new services and facilities to make the flow of the tourist experience better than before. Reservation on the ship and railway passages, advance accommodation booking, hotel coupon, money order, circular note, credit note, travelers' cheque, assistance to the cross-border travel formalities, and transport arrangements from a collection point to the point of disembarkation were a few of many innovations introduced in the service paradigm. Foreign exchange, interpreter–translator–tutor–guide service, on-travel security, various meal plans, on-board entertainment were instances of facility innovations.

Those innovations and the opportunities to visit attractions and participate in or attend the events, such as temperance meetings, the great exhibition of London, and the international exhibition at Paris and London, and merry-making functions, made several changes in the perception of organized tour packages logistics. A shift from medieval travel logistic concepts and practices to modern tourism logistics was overtly visible by then. Evolution from mere travel to organized package tourism contributed to increasing mobility from cross-section and cross-boundary to events, as was found in the initiatives of Thomas Cook to organize tours to different contemporary events. Indeed, it ascertained constant tourist or visitor flow to events. The pressure of visitor flow coupled with national pride and rivalry among event-hosting nations to boost their standing as the world leader stimulate the condition to create causal pressure for improved event logistics to facilitate a better event experience. A shift in event hosting from man-managed or human labor-dependent logistics to modern technology-driven logistics became evident. Thus, event destinations became equipped with technology-supported logistics. It includes the construction of the technology-supported venue, the provision of lodging near it, and the arrangement of security pickets and a rapid transit system for the to and fro movement of participants, organizers, attendees, and visitors from the respective overnight stay place. The construction of display, warehousing, storing sites, orderly management of exhibits, personnel, information, knowledge, energy,waste, fund, capital flow, and arrangement of other amenities and facilities for the attendees, visitors, and participants, such as banquet, rotunda for the concert, and conference venue gradually became crucial for an orderly event logistic arrangement by 1900. The story of tourism and event coevolution amid reciprocal influence or

Tracing the Journey of Event Tourism

stimulation and mutual causal pressure continued even in the late 19th and early 20th centuries as event and tourism were in comparable changes and common adaptation, that is, technology-driven logistics.

The beginning of modern tourism in the organized package tour format is also inextricably intertwined with several Victorian events since Thomas Cook arranged a series of package trips to temperance meetings, the great exhibition of London, the international exhibition in Paris, and other places. Moreover, requests come to increase the visitor flow to the events by organizing package trips. For example, Sir Joseph Paxton, an organizer of the Great Exhibition of London, once persuaded Thomas Cook to bring visitors to the exhibition. The dependence of event organizers on organized package tours for visitor flow grew highly with the repeated success of event-centric package trips in bringing visitors to the site. Indeed, event-centric package tours are usually all-inclusive type. Thus, event and tourism logistic functions frequently overlap in arranging accommodation, transportation, visit the attraction and entertainment for visitors. Additionally, both share the five most crucial elements, that is, tourists/visitors, destination, tourist attraction, hospitality, and motivations and play the role of a prime driver of destination identities, attractiveness, and competitiveness either together or separately. All these happenings and phenomena indicate that synergistic collaboration between events and tourism is necessary for improved efficiency in operations, greater exploitation of opportunities, and better utilization of resources and operational logistics.

1.6 JOURNEY TO SYNERGIC MERGER

The journey takes place in two steps. Primarily, it is synergistic collaboration and then a synergic merger. The synergistic collaboration between events and tourism was initiated in the late 19th century when event organizers set out to persuade organized package tour operators for regular visitor flow to the events. Event organizers use tourism logistics frequently to achieve the best possible outcome. In the post-1950 era event sector and tourism, separately or together, caused a makeover in the destination economy. As the era is of demand escalation for leisure or recreation-related travel and tours, tourism turns out to be the year-round driver of destinations' economic improvement. In fact, in the unknown or lesser-known destinations, where tourism is yet to flourish, events may become crucial for place imaging, promotion, attractiveness, positioning, and competitiveness. It then contributes to portraying a place as a potential tourist destination. In known tourism circuits, events appear as the crucial attraction of package offers, thus, increasing competitiveness and demand for organized package tours. Since both share comparable and analogous hospitality conditions and homologous logistics environments, the frequent a mutual operational or functional overlap is quite logical. By the end of the 20th century, event hosting and tourism operations became specialized services. The relationship between the two turned out to be more interconnected and interdependent since connectivity and dependency among those sectors mark by different complementary specialized-skill cooperation. It leads the two to continue interaction for business and leisure travel promotion. While sports and festivals encourages the leisure travel and cultural tourism, MICE promotes business tourism. All those phenomena together create a perspective for synergistic collaboration between the two. Indeed, the collaboration process is effectively evident in the mutual and reciprocal use of logistic supports and promotional systems. Utilization of existing tourism logistic support to make Durga festival (Kolkata), Hornbill festival (Nagaland), Bhutan's Tsechu, and carnivals of Italy, Notting Hill, and Tobago successful is customary. Sometimes historic event sites turn out to be tourist attractions, for example, Barcelona Olympic sites. The use of logistic support, developed for a particular event at a destination, is often incorporated into tourism logistic mechanisms such as Delhi in the post-Asian games.

Synergic collaboration gradually pushes the event and tourism industry to set off cross-promotion and cross-sell to increase revenue and build a better image. Bhutan's Tsechu-centric tourism promotion is a notable example in this regard. During the Durga festival, the festive organizers collaborate with tourism stakeholders and the government to increase innovation, efficiency, and effectiveness. They also do it to make the festival a success. Similarly, Tsechu and Hornbill festival organizers work with tourism stakeholders jointly for better logistic support and increased visitor flow. Event and tourism, then, begin to share management mechanisms and logistics that are both separately devised. The development of cross-sector or cross-industry activity legitimized the need for a synergic merger between events and tourism. The event industry then merges with the tourism industry to evolve as event tourism, thus creating a separate entity becomes crucial driver of 21st-century destinations' identities, attractiveness, and competitiveness. Further, it portrays a destination as an emerging place for events and tourism. Thus, the objective of the merger is to increase the synergistic effectiveness by sharing perceptions and experiences, insights, and knowledge, maximize resource utilization, and minimize operational overlaps.

1.7 CONCLUSIONS

Traveling is imperative to event participation. The coevolution of the two thus becomes an age-old phenomenon. But tourism and event interaction began overtly only with the event's emergence as a motivator of organized package tours in the mid-19th century. Emergence as a tourism motivator contributed to a crucial change in the event's value. Therefore, a conceptual swing from traditional social value to market value makes the event a specialized area of creative exchanges and experiences within the periphery of tourism art and creativity. Increasing demand for skilled services made events and tourism more interdependent and interactive to coevolve. Examples from around the world illustrate the formats of coevolution, which benefits tourism and event sectors alike. The coevolution of events and tourism opens possibilities for diversification and economic opportunities. As soon as the market value of collaborative, cooperative, and mutual interaction rises to a greater extent than the sum of its parts, the world of tourism and event understood the necessity of synergistic collaboration. Conditions such as the rapid increase of market-oriented economic systems and intensified international trade, differentiation in market segments, the need for place promotion, branding and imaging, and the ascendency of authentic experience paradigm have led event and tourism to set off cross-promotion and cross-sell. It contributed to generating more revenue and building a better image than the outcome of the event and tourism industries. Growing demand for specialized services toward managing events and tourism together leads to the emergence of event tourism. Neither of them perceived this fact before New Zealand's Tourist and Publicity Department's acceptance of the term "Event Tourism" in 1987 or the construction of a structured frame toward event tourism planning by Getz (1989). Event tourism plays a crucial role in attracting visitors at an increased scale (Lee et al., 2005). It increases tourist spending and length of stay, provides a unique experience, draws increased investment, improves infrastructure, and creates a destination image identifying the soul and tradition of the host destination and community. Altogether, it contributes decisively to the better positioning and competitive advantage for the place and its economy.

KEYWORDS

- **change**
- **coevolution**
- **event tourism**
- **interdependence**
- **reciprocal causal pressure**
- **synergic merger**

REFERENCES

Ahmad, A.; Tadros, S.; Fernandez, K. Social Media Impact on Tourism Events: A Case Study in Jordan. In *Tourism Events in Asia*; Hassan, A., Sharma, A., Eds.; Routledge: London, 2019; pp.82–97.

Allen, J. et al. *Festival & Special Event Manage.*, 5th ed.; John Wiley & Sons: Brisbane, 2011.

Arora, S.; Sharma, A. Digital Marketing for Religious Event of India for Tourism Sustainability and Promotion. In *The Emerald Handbook of ICT in Tourism and Hospitality*; Hassan, A., Sharma, A., Eds.; Emerald Publishing Limited: Bingley, 2020; pp 453–465. https://doi.org/10.1108/978-1-83982-688-720201029

Arora, S.; Sharma, A. Role of Information and Communication Technology in Marketing and Promoting Tourism Events of Rajasthan. In *Tourism Events in Asia*; Hassan, A., Sharma, A., Eds.; Routledge: London, 2019; pp.71–81.

Berlonghi, A. *The Special Event Risk Management Manual*; Self-Published. A. Berlonghi, P.O. Box 3454 Dana Point, CA, 1990.

Berridge, G. *Event Design*; Butterworth-Heinemann; Oxford, 2006.

Bond, H. *Estimating the Economic Benefits of Event Tourism*; Impacts 08 – Bond; University of Liverpool, 2008.

Boorstin, D. *The Image: A Guide to Pseudo-Events in America*; Harper & Row: New York, 1961.

Bos, H. The Importance of Mega-Events in the Development of Tourism Demand. *Fest. Manage. Event Tour.* **1994,** *2* (1), 55–58.

Bowdin, G.; Allen, J.; O'Toole, W.; Harris, R.; McDonnell, I. *Events Management*, 3rd ed.; Butterworth-Heinemann: Oxford, 2011.

Chang, J. Segmenting Tourists to Aboriginal Cultural Festivals: An Example in the Rukai Tribal Area, Taiwan. *Tour. Manage.* **2006,** *27*, 1224–1234.

Crompton, J.; McKay, S. Measuring the Economic Impact of Festivals and Events: Some Myths, Misapplications and Ethical Dilemmas. *Fest. Manage. Event Tour.* **1994,** *2* (1), 33–43.

Dedeoğlu, B.B.; Küçükergin, K.G. Effectiveness of Social Media Sharing on Tourism Event Choice. In *Tourism Events in Asia*; Hassan, A., Sharma, A., Eds.; Routledge: London, 2019; pp 98–113.

Della Bitta, A.; Loudon, D.; Booth, G.; Weeks, R. Estimating the Economic Impact of a Short-Term Tourist Event. *J. Travel Res.* **1978,** *16,* 10–15.

Desloehal Djumrianti, D. The Roles of Social Media in the Promotion of Traditional Cultural Tourism Events in Indonesia. In *Tourism Events in Asia*; Hassan, A., Sharma, A., Eds.; Routledge: London, 2019; pp 114–122.

Formica, S. The Development of Festivals and Special Events Studies. *Fest. Manage. Event Tour.* **1998,** *5* (3), 131–137.

Fredline, E. Host and Guest Relations and Sport Tourism. In *Sport Tourism: Concepts and Theories*; Gibson, H., Ed.; Routledge: London, 2006; pp 131–147.

Fredline, E.; Faulkner, B. Variations in Residents' Reactions to Major Motorsport Events: Why Residents Perceive the Impacts of Events Differently. *Event Manage.* **2002,** *7* (2), 115–125.

Getz, D. Bidding on Events: Critical Success Factors. *J. Conv. Exhib. Manage.* **2004,** *5* (2), 1–24.

Getz, D. Developing a Research Agenda for the Event Management Field. In *Events Beyond 2000: Setting the Agenda, Proceedings of Conference on Event Evaluation, Research and Education*; Allen, J. et al., Eds.; Australian Centre for Event Management, University of Technology: Sydney, 2000b; pp 10–21.

Getz, D. *Event Management and Event Tourism*, 2nd ed.; Cognizant: New York, 2005.

Getz, D. Event Studies and Event Management: On Becoming an Academic Discipline. *J. Hospital. Tour. Manage.* **2002,** *9* (1), 12–23.

Getz, D. *Event Studies: Theory, Research and Policy for Planned Events*; Elsevier: Oxford, 2007.

Getz, D. Event Tourism and the Authenticity Dilemma. In *Global Tourism*; Theobald, W., Ed., 2nd ed.; Butterworth-Heinemann: Oxford, 1998; pp 409–427.

Getz, D. Festivals and Special Events: Life Cycle and Saturation Issues. In *Trends in Outdoor Recreation, Leisure and Tourism*; Garter, W., Lime, D., Eds.; CABI: Wallingford, 2000a; pp 175–185.

Getz, D. *Festivals, Special Events, and Tourism*; Van Nostrand Rheinhold: New York, 1991.

Getz, D. Special Events: Defining the Product. *Tour. Manage.* **1989,** *10* (2), 135–137.

Getz, D. Sport Event Tourism: Planning, Development, and Marketing. In *Sport and Adventure Tourism*; Hudson, S., Ed.; Haworth, New York, 2003; pp 49–88.

Getz, D. The Impacts of Mega Events on Tourism: Strategies for Destinations. In *The Impact of Mega Events*; Andersson, T., Persson, C., Sahlberg, B., Strom, L., Eds.; European Tourism Research Institute: Ostersund, Sweden, 1999; pp 5–32.

Getz, D.; Anderson, D.; Sheehan, L. Roles, Issues and Strategies for Convention and Visitors Bureaux in Destination Planning and Product Development: A Survey of Canadian Bureaux. *Tour. Manage.* **1998,** *19* (4), 331–340.

Getz, D.; Fairley, S. Media Management at Sport Events for Destination Promotion. *Event Manage.* **2004,** *8* (3), 127–139.

Getz, D.; O'Neill, M.; Carlsen, J. Service Quality Evaluation at Events Through Service Mapping. *J. Travel Res.* **2001,** *39* (4), 380–390.

Goldblatt, J. *Special Events: The Roots and Wings of Celebration*, 5th ed.; Wiley: New York, 2007.

Greenwood, D. Tourism as an Agent of Change: A Spanish Basque Case Study. *Ethnology* **1972,** *11,* 80–91.

Gunn, C. *Tourism Planning*; Crane Russak: New York, 1979.

Hall, C. M. *Hallmark Tourist Events: Impacts, Management and Planning*; Belhaven: London, 1992.

Hassan, A. National Identity and Dark Tourism: Symbolising the 'Omor Ekushey February'. In *Tourism Events in Asia*; Hassan, A., Sharma, A., Eds.; Routledge: London, 2019; pp.132–139.

Hawkins, D.; Goldblatt, J. Event Management Implications for Tourism Education. *Tour. Recreat. Res.* **1995,** *20* (2), 42–45.

Hjalager, A. M. The Coevolution of Tourism and Agriculture **Source.** *J. Gastron. Tour* **2020,** *4* **(4),** 175–191. https://doi.org/10.3727/216929720X15846938924058

Hoyle, L. *Event Marketing: How to Successfully Promote Events, Festivals, Conventions, and Expositions*; Wiley: New York, 2002.

Janiskee, R. South Carolina's Harvest Festivals: Rural Delights for Day Tripping Urbanites. *J. Cult. Geogr.* **1980,** *1* (Fall/Winter), 96–104.

Janzen, D. H. When Is It Coevolution? *Evolution* **1980,** *34* (3), 611–612. https://doi.org/10.1111/j.1558–5646.1980.tb04849.x

Kallis, G. When Is It Coevolution? *Ecol. Econ.* **2007,** *62* (1), 1–6. https://doi.org/10.1016/j.ecolecon.2006.12.016

Kotsori, I-S. Ancient Festivals and Their Cultural Contribution to Society. *Open J. Stud. Hist.* **2019,** *2* (1), 19–26. https://doi.org/10.32591/coas.ojsh.0201.02019k

Krajnović, A.; Buškulić, A.; Bosna, J. The Role of the Tourist Boards in the Development of Event Tourism of Zadar County, Tourism & Hospitality Industry Congress Proceedings; 2016; pp 174–187.

Lee, J.; Back, K. A Review of Convention and Meeting Management Research. *J. Conv. Event Tour.* **2005,** *7* (2), 1–19.

Ljudevit, P.; Lidija, P.; Liljana, C. Host Population Perceptions of the Social Impacts of Sport Tourism Events in Transition Countries: Evidence from Croatia. *Int. J. Event Fest. Manage.* **2012,** *3* (3), 236–256.

Mackellar, J. Conventions, Festivals, and Tourism: Exploring the Network That Binds. *J. Conv. Event Tour.* **2006,** *8* (2), 45–56.

Marx, K. *Grundrisse: Foundations of the Critique of Political Economy (Rough Draft)*; Penguin: Hamondsworth, 1973.

Masterman, G.; Wood, E. *Innovative Marketing Communications: Strategies for the Events Industry*; Butterworth-Heinemann: Oxford, 2006.

Matheson, C. M. Festivity and Sociability: A Study of a Celtic Music Festival. *Tour. Cult. Commun.* **2005,** *5*, 149–163.

Mossberg, L., Ed. *Evaluation of Events: Scandinavian Experiences*; Cognizant Communication Corp: New York, 2000.

Phipps, P.; Slater, L. *Indigenous Cultural Festivals: Evaluating Impact on Community Health and Wellbeing*; Globalism Research Centre, Royal Melbourne Institute of Technology: Melbourne, Australia, 2010.

Quinn, B., Eds. *Festivals, Events and Tourism*; Sage: London, 2009.

Ray, S. Approaches Towards Ethno-Cultural Contents of the Hosts and Socially Responsible Tourism. *Tour.: Theor. Prac.* **2017,** *15* (1 and 2), 28–58.

Ray, S. Event Tourism in Asian Context. In *Tourism Events in Asia*; Hassan, A., Sharma, A., Eds.; Routledge: London, 2019; pp 4–19.

Ritchie, J. R. B. Assessing the Impacts of Hallmark Events: Conceptual and Research Issues. *J. Travel Res.* **1984,** *23* (1), 2–11.

Ritchie, J. R. B.; Beliveau, D. Hallmark Events: An Evaluation of a Strategic Response to Seasonality in the Travel Market. *J. Travel Res.* **1974,** *14*, 14–20.

Rittichainuwat, B.; Beck, J.; LaLopa, J. Understanding Motivations, Inhibitors, and Facilitators of Association Members in Attending International Conferences. *J. Conv. Exhib. Manage.* **2001,** *3* (3), 45–62.

Scotinform Ltd.*Edinburgh Festivals Study 1990/91: Visitor Survey and Economic Impact Assessment. Final Report*; Scottish Tourist Board: Edinburgh, 1991.

Shabnam, S.; Ramkissoon, H.; Choudhury, A. Role of Ethnic Cultural Events to Build an Authentic Destination Image: A Case of 'Pohela Boishakh' in Bangladesh. In *Tourism Events in Asia*; Hassan, A., Sharma, A., Eds.; Routledge: London, 2019; pp 47–63.

Sharma, A. (2019) Creating New Event Opportunities and Re-Creating Old Events in an Innovative Way: Case Study of Hadoti Region. In *Tourism Events in Asia*; Hassan, A., Sharma, A., Eds.; Routledge: London, 2019; pp 36–46.

Sharma, S. Malana Heritage Village: The Gateway for Great Tourism Events. In *Tourism Events in Asia*; Hassan, A., Sharma, A., Eds.; Routledge: London, 2019; pp 64–70.

Small, K.; Edwards, D. Evaluating the Socio-Cultural Impacts of a Festival on a Host Community: A Case Study of the Australian Festival of the Book. In *Proceedings of the 9th Annual Conference of the Asia Pacific Tourism Association*; Griffin, T.; Harris, R., Eds.; School of Leisure, Sport and Tourism, University of Technology: Sydney, 2003; pp 580–593.

Supovitz, F.; Goldblatt, J. *The Sports Event Management and Marketing Handbook*; Wiley: New York, 2004.

Syme, G.; Shaw, B.; Fenton, D.; Mueller, W., Eds. *The Planning and Evaluation of Hallmark Events*; Gower: Aldershot, 1989.

Tarlow, P. *Event Risk Management and Safety*; Wiley: New York, 2002.

Vaughan, R. Does a Festival Pay? A Case Study of the Edinburgh Festival in 1976. *Tourism Recreation Research Unit*, Working Paper 5, University of Edinburgh, 1979.

Weed, M. Sports Tourism Theory and Method: Concepts, Issues and Epistemologies. *Eur. Sport Manage. Quart.* **2005,** *5* (3), 229–242.

Xie, P.F. The Bamboo-Beating Dance in Hainan, China: Authenticity and Commodification. *J. Sustain. Tour.* **2003,** *11* (1), 5–16.

CHAPTER 2

Pull Factors That Influence Millennials to Visit, Citrawarna Cultural Festival

AHMAD R. ALBATTAT[1], NUR AMIRAH BINTI MAZME[2],
TRISHA ANNE JOSEPH[2], WAN AHMAD AZFARUDDIN AZIF[2], and
AINUL HUSNA ABDULLAH[2]

[1]*Post Graduate Centre, Management and Science University,
University Drive, Off Persiaran Olahraga, Section 13, Selangor, Malaysia*

[2]*School of Hospitality and Creative Arts, Management and Science University,
University Drive, Off Persiaran Olahraga, Section 13, Selangor, Malaysia*

ABSTRACT

There is a paucity of information regarding the real behaviour of millennials who visit cultural venues. This information is lacking in cultural destinations. Because they came of age at a period of widespread economic growth, the next generation's expectations for their participation in cultural celebrations are very different from those of the generation before them. This study's primary purpose is to determine the pull factors of programmes, services, and entertainment that inspired millennials to attend a cultural festival. The researcher relied on non-probability sampling, also known as convenience sampling, in order to obtain the necessary data. The researcher's quantitative method was based on the distribution of a questionnaire to 370 millennials who had visited the site. The Statistical Package for the Social Science (SPSS) version 25 was utilised in order to do the analysis on the data. According to the findings, there is a considerable association between pull factors and the likelihood of millennials attending cultural festivals. The most significant contribution to this research study came from the entertainment industry.

Please note that few chapters were submitted during the peak of the pandemic. The long period of time to publish (due to supply chain and other issues) may have changed the perspectives presented in the chapter altogether.

Event Tourism and Sustainable Community Development: Advances, Effects, and Implications.
Ekta Dhariwal, Shruti Arora, Anukrati Sharma, Azizul Hassan (Eds.)
© 2024 Apple Academic Press, Inc. Co-published with CRC Press (Taylor & Francis)

This is due to the fact that entertainment captures people's attention and keeps them occupied, as seen by people listening to live entertainment performances at the festival. The findings also indicated that there are certain recommendations that may be used to increase intention-setting among millennials and to improve the efficiency of the design of future festivals.

2.1 INTRODUCTION

Citrawarna, also known as Malaysia's Colors, was first held in 1999 to promote and celebrate the country's arts, heritage, nature, and culture via a spectacular night of music, fireworks, and performance. Citrawarna is a Malaysian yearly event that includes street performances, dance routines, and cultural demonstrations. It is organized by the Ministry of Tourism, Arts, and Culture. According to Window Malaysia (2019), over 7000 people, including millennials, public and private higher education institutions, local cultural organizations, and non-governmental organizations, participated in the festival, showcasing everything Malaysia has to offer. Around 100,000 people attend the festival.

Young people, on the other hand, are essential cultural consumers in cultural destinations, and more research is needed to understand the youth culture consumption tendencies (Scottish Executive, 2001). Although culture is usually associated with elderly people, it also affects youthful tourists (Fraser, 2001). According to the United Nations (2003), the words "youth" and "young people" are used for statistical purposes and comparisons for those aged 15–24. Furthermore, another term for "youth" is "millennials," which refers to people born between 1981 and 1997, or those who are currently 18–34 years old (Canada, 2015). This age group is sometimes referred to as the "digital generation," because technology has had a significant impact on their lives. Tech-savvy millennials account for 75% of the population (Coletto, 2012).

There have been numerous definitions of festivals in the literature. Festivals, according to Jackson (2014), are social events that convey societal norms and values. Festivals are events that provide entertainment to tourists, draw visitors to certain sites, and generate demand for lodging in the region where the festival is conducted (Litvin, 2006). The literature highlights the cultural, the three components (economic, sociocultural, and environmental), and a synthetic function to attract the younger. The importance of participants' incentive to attend a cultural festival and their perceptions of the effects on the surrounding community. Rural places have effectively grabbed tourists' interest and intention to visit due to their distinctiveness in terms of environmental, cultural, and ethnical components (Hernandez, 2016).

2.2 LITERATURE REVIEW

2.2.1 CULTURAL FESTIVAL

According to Kinnunen (2018), a cultural festival is a special event that features a cultural program created or performed by multiple artists. It is open to the public and held once a year or less frequently. A cultural festival is a short-term event that consists of a number of events held in the same location or region. Furthermore, cultural festival festivals are defined as an event that reflects a specific cultural genre, includes a program of performing or visual arts, occurs once a year or every 2 years in the same location or region, and is open to the public for a fee or without any charge.

2.2.2 CULTURAL FESTIVAL ATTRIBUTE

The features of festivals are the most important factors for attendees to consider while judging them (Akhoondnejad, 2016). Attributes that highlight the different aspects that contribute to their financial performance include program quality, services supplied, physical surroundings, and sponsorship (Lee, 2019). Huang et al. (2010) defined attributes in the context of festivals as items that are linked to the festival's distinctive qualities, such as facilities, activities, and entertainment opportunities.

Baker and Crompton (2000) discovered that the quality of the performance was a significant driver of audience satisfaction and behavioral intentions. Variety of food, well-organized, calm, natural atmosphere, exhilarating experience, great beaches, and vast shopping opportunities were all highlighted by Anrwar and Sohail (2004) as festival attributes. Festival qualities and programming have been connected to the consumption of festival products and services, as well as satisfaction, according to research.

2.2.3 FACTOR TO VISIT CULTURAL FESTIVAL

Cultural festivals increase residents' perceptions of a local community as a good place to live and enhance community interconnection and residents' pride in being individuals of a host community by providing opportunities for entertainment and recreation for all generations of visitors' festivals. (Kim and Uysal, 2003). People benefit from the festivals because they improve citizens' learning, awareness of community pride, ethnic identity, tolerance of others, and the opening of small and medium-sized family businesses (Sdnali and Chazapi, 2007). To put it in another way, one of the motivations to attend a festival is because of its distinctiveness and symbolic significance

(Gursoy, 2006). The inference is that these shared events or experiences during formative years have an impact on factors like worldview, values, and behavior in a certain age cohort throughout their life (Li and Hudson, 2013).

2.2.4 MILLENNIAL PULL FACTORS TO VISIT CULTURAL FESTIVAL

Pull-motivating elements vary for every tourist, but they include amenities and qualities like nightlife, natural and cultural attractions, and social and physical facilities that influence destination selection (Prayag and Ryan, 2010). These elements are usually destination-specific, which means that the place has traits that attract visitors, such as features, attractions, or attributes (Mohammad and Som, 2010).

2.2.5 ATTRACTIONS

According to Duran and Hamarat (2014), festivals are critical for the social and cultural evolution of local communities as well as the creation of tourist attractions. In industrialized countries, leisure and culture account for a significant portion of household spending. They represent a net rise in aggregate demand, which has a negative impact on the rest of the economy. In an increasingly globalized world, economic and cultural imperatives are two of the most powerful factors shaping human behavior (Throsby, 2001). The festival's main attraction should be greater inventiveness in order to generate a festive atmosphere. Because of their differences from the past generations, millennials pose a problem for marketers, according to Fromm and Garton (2013). However, considering the largely hedonic nature of tourism, this should not come as a surprise.

2.2.6 PROGRAMS

Festival plans, according to Yan (2012), outline scheduled events and offer festival products and services as a creative process in a way that is appealing to festival attendees. The festival organizers are in charge of the programs, which include on-site signs, commercial, and organization booths, printed materials, and free gifts (Cole and Chancellor, 2009). As a result, festival organizers can modify the quality of the programming to improve the overall experience of attendance. Within the good experience categories, the study found that programs and atmosphere are the most important success factors, while site, participants, services, and arrangements could be differentiators that give festivals a competitive edge.

2.2.7 AMENITIES

Festival facilities, according to Cole and Chancellor (2009), include the provision of restrooms, accessibility for persons with special needs, cleanliness, seating and eating areas, and food and drinks. Amenities are also defined by Merriam-Webster (2019) as something that helps to bring comfort, convenience, or ease. A variety of sorts of amenities are one of the pull elements that drive millennials to attend cultural festivals, according to the pull factors that influence millennials to attend cultural festivals. According to Rodrigue (2016), each mode of transportation has its own unique performance and space requirements. The automobile is the most relevant example. It needs road space to go around, yet it also spends at least 98% of its time motionless in a parking space. As a result, a large amount of urban space should be set aside to accommodate the needs of the automobile, particularly when it is parked.

2.2.8 ENTERTAINMENT

Entertainment and experience brand communities, according to Armstrong (2011), create shared rituals through activities including parties, gatherings, and shared consumption. Friendship groups or cultural institution members participate in similar amusing activities. This motive is strongly linked to the awareness self-actualization motive, as well as the millennials' consumption motives of balance in work–life or education–entertainment. This motivation can also assist cultural organizations in addressing one of the most pressing issues: how to strike a balance between education and entertainment, as well as the necessity to incorporate entertainment into marketing activities.

2.3 METHODOLOGY

This study took a quantitative approach, with the target demographic being millennial youth, both male and female, between the ages of 18 and 29. The survey's respondents are millennials who are attending the festival. The sample size was determined through convenience sampling, which involved the distribution of 350 questionnaires. The questionnaires are made up of a series of questions, with section A containing general information and a total of six questions from Gillian (2017). Section B1 contains five-question programs. B2 facilities and B3 entertainment are the next two parts, each with five questions from Cole (2009). Section C finishes the pull factors that drive millennials to attend cultural festivals (see Table 2.1). The questionnaires used in this study have four components that are used to measure the variable:

TABLE 2.1 Sections and Description of Questionnaires.

Section	Description	References	No. of questions
A	General Information	Gillian (2017)	6
B	General Questions for Citrawarna Attendees	Cihan (2016)	3
C1	Programs		5
C2	Amenities	Cole (2009)	5
C3	Entertainment		5
D	Influence Millennials to Visit Cultural Festival	Kesterson (2013)	5

2.4 FINDINGS

2.4.1 RELIABILITY ANALYSIS

According to Tavakol and Dennick (2011), Cronbach's alpha score above 0.70 is considered acceptable. Table 2.2 depicts the reliability analysis results based on the survey 350 set of questionnaires.

TABLE 2.2 Results of Cronbach's Alpha Analysis for Each Variable of the Study.

No	Variables	Cronbach's alpha	Number of items
1.	Programs	.719	5
2.	Amenities	.806	5
3.	Entertainment	.730	5
4	Visit cultural festival	.759	5

2.4.2 RESPONDENTS BACKGROUND PROFILE

There are five questions related to demographic profile were asked about the personal information in this questionnaire. These questions consist of gender, age, race, nationality, and qualification see Table 2.3.

2.4.3 GENERAL QUESTIONS

This section wraps up three generic questions about the Citrawarna festival that were distributed to the festival's millennial attendees. The purpose of this survey is to see if the respondents are aware of Citrawarna in Malaysia. In addition, respondents were asked if they liked or disliked the concept

Pull Factors That Influence Millennials 25

TABLE 2.3 RESPONDENTS PROFILE.

Background factor	Categories	Frequency	Percentage (%)
Gender	Male	159	45.4
	Female	191	54.6
Age	18–20	124	35.4
	21–23	142	40.6
	24–26	68	19.4
	27–29	16	4.6
Race	Malay	259	74.0
	Chinese	15	4.3
	Indian	62	17.7
	Others	14	4.0
Nationality	Malaysian	348	99.4
	Non-Malaysian	2	.6
Qualification	Diploma	179	51.1
	Degree	166	47.4
	Master	5	1.4

of the Citrawarna festival (see Table 2.4). Aside from that, the Citrawarna event, according to the respondents, involved all races in Malaysia.

TABLE 2.4 General Questions.

Questions	Answers	Frequency	Percent
Q1: Are you aware of Citrawarna Festival?	Yes	251	71.7
	No	99	28.3
Q2: Do you like the concept of Citrawarna Festival?	Yes	307	87.7
	No	43	12.3
Q3: Do you agree that Citrawarna festival involves all the races in Malaysia?	Yes	279	79.7
	No	71	20.3
	Total	350	100

2.4.4 CORRELATION ANALYSIS

This result demonstrates the intensity of the association between each variable and the likelihood of attending a cultural festival. The strongest correlation can be seen in entertainment, followed by programs, and finally amenities. As a result, all of the hypotheses H1 through H3 were found to be supported, as all of the independent variables had a significant link with attending a cultural event. Following the correlation analysis, regression analysis was used to determine which factors had a significant impact on the number of people who attend the cultural festival (see Table 2.5).

TABLE 2.5 Correlation Analysis.

		Programs	Amenities	Entertainment	Visit cultural festival
Programs	Pearson correlation	1			
Amenities	Pearson correlation	.456 **	1		
Entertainment	Pearson correlation	.485**	.528**	1	
Visit cultural festival	Pearson correlation	.479**	.463**	.547**	1

2.4.5 REGRESSION ANALYSIS

For this study, the correlation coefficient (R value) is .616. The R square shows how well the independent factors (programs, facilities, and entertainment) can explain the variation in the dependent variables in terms of percentage (visit cultural festival). Table 2.6 shows that the independent variable (programs, amenities, and entertainment) may explain 38% of the variation in the dependent variable (attend cultural festival).

TABLE 2.6 Regression Analysis.

Model	R	R square	Adjusted R square	Std. error of the estimate
1	.616	.380	.374	2.04932

2.4.6 COEFFICIENTS OF MODEL

According to the regression test, all of the independent variables have a significant impact because all of the significant values are less than 0.05. That is, programs, amenities, and entertainment have a big impact on whether or not people attend a cultural event. When all other independent variables are maintained constant, unstandardized coefficients show how much the dependent variable fluctuates with an independent variable. Table 2.7 shows the results.

Pull Factors That Influence Millennials 27

TABLE 2.7 Coefficients.

		Coefficients				
	Model	Unstandardized Coefficients		Standardized Coefficients	t	Sig.
		B	Std. Error	Beta		
1	(Constant)	5.320	1.107		4.804	.000
	program	.233	.050	.234	4.648	.000
	amenities	.172	.050	.177	3.414	.001
	entertainment	.347	.054	.340	6.455	.000

2.4.7 DESCRIPTIVE STATISTIC

To determine the variability and independence in this study, the mean and standard deviation for each factor were computed. Programs, amenities, and entertainment are independent variables in this study, while visiting a cultural festival is a dependent variable. To understand the variability and interdependence of subscales produced from the factor analysis, Table 2.8 shows the mean and standard deviation of both independent and dependent variables for each factor.

TABLE 2.8 Descriptive Statistics.

No	Item	Mean	Std. deviation
Program			
P1	Printed program	3.99	.777
P2	Children activity	3.97	.754
P3	Art and craft	4.12	.716
P4	Free gifts	4.12	.783
P5	Online information	4.26	.749
Amenities			
AM1	Event site	4.33	.730
AM2	Medics/medical room	4.33	.696
AM3	Information counter	4.27	.725
AM4	Washrooms	4.45	.682
AM5	Car park	4.49	.709
Entertainment			
E1	Participating inspire	4.18	.692
E2	Live shows	4.31	.709

TABLE 2.8 *(Continued)*

No	Item	Mean	Std. deviation
E3	Famous artist	4.34	.754
E4	Singing and dancing	4.21	.731
E5	Local artist	4.19	.770
Visit cultural festival			
D1	Promote Malaysia	4.27	.696
D2	Tourists attributed	4.26	.689
D3	Variety activities	4.19	.746
D4	Attendees	4.20	.726
D5	History	4.31	.770

2.5 CONCLUSIONS

This study was conducted to gain a better understanding and knowledge of millennials in terms of the importance of the program, entertainment, and amenities, and to determine which component has the greatest influence on these millennials' decision to attend the Citrawarna Festival. The findings revealed that all three independent factors, including program, entertainment, and amenities, have a positive significant link with millennials' willingness to attend the Citrawarna festival. It also mentions the value of cultural festivals in terms of making adjustments that would raise the pull factors of millennials attending cultural festivals in the future, based on the variables mentioned. Finally, the findings of this study show that entertainment is the most influential factor in millennials' decision to attend cultural events, particularly the Citrawarna fFestival. This study will provide a complete perspective and broaden the breadth of research into millennials' intentions to return. More related dynamics, such as the linkages between participants' self-images, perceived value, and place attachment, should be included in future research to expand the conceptual framework proposed in this study. Incorporating such variables could aid in identifying more outcomes of community-based heritage festival attendance.

KEYWORDS

- **Millennials**
- **Intention to Visit**
- **Pull Factors**
- **Citrawarna**
- **Cultural Festival**

REFERENCES

Akhoondnejad, A. Tourist Loyalty to a Local Cultural Event: The Case of Turkmen Handicrafts Festival. *Tour. Manage.* **2016,** *52*, 468–477.

Anrwar, S. A.; Sohail, M. S. Festival Tourism in the United Arab Emirates; First Time Versus Repeat Perceptions. *J. Vocation Market.* **2004,** *10*, 61–170.

Armstrong, K.; Slater, A. Understanding Motivational Constraints to Membership at the Southbank Centre. *J. Customer Behav.* **2011,** *10* (4), 353–373.

Baker, D. A.; Crompton, J. L. Quality, Satisfaction and Behavioral Intentions. *Ann. Tour. Res.* **2000,** *27* (3), 785–804.

Benckendorff, P. J. Planning for the Future: A Profile of Australian Tourist Attractions. Doctoral Dissertation, James Cook University, 2004.

Canadian Tourism Commission. Canada Millennial Domestic Travel Summary Report; CTC Research: Vancouver, BC, Canada, 2015. https://www.destinationcanada.com/sites/default/files/201611/Programs_MillennialTravel_DomesticReport_EN.pdf (accessed on 24 May 2017).

Coletto, D. *R U Ready 4 Us? An Introduction to Canadian Millennials*; Canadian Millennials: Ottawa, ON, 2012.

Duran, E.; Hamarat, B. Festival Attendees' Motivations: The Case of International Troia Festival. *Int. J. Event Fest. Manage.* **2014,** *5* (2), 146–163.

Fromm, J.; Garton, C. Marketing to Millennials: Reach the Largest and Most Influential Generation of Consumers Ever, 2013.

Gursoy, D.; Spangenberg, E. R.; Rutherford, D. G. The Hedonic and Utilitarian Dimensions of Attendees' Attitudes Toward Festivals. *J. Hospital. Tour. Res.* **2006,** *30* (3), 279–294.

Hernandez, J. M.-V. The Inter-Relationship Between Rural and Mass Tourism: The Case of Catalonia, Spain. *Tour. Manage.* **2016,** 43–57.

Huang, J.; Li, M.; Cai, L. A Model of Community-Based Festival Image. *Int. J. Hospital. Manage.* **2010,** *29*, 254–260.

Jackson, C. *The Lived Experience of the Popular Music Festival-Goer. Events and Festivals: Education, Impacts and Experiences*; Leisure Studies Association: Brighton, 2014; pp 131–145.

Kim, K.; Uysal, M. Perceived Socio-Economic Impacts of Festivals and Events Among Organizers. *J. Hospital. Leisure Market.* **2003,** *10* (3–4), 159–171.

Kinnunen, M. Total Festival Experience. A Mixed Methods Research Approach to Consumer Experiences in Finnish Cultural Festivals. Acta electronica Universitatis Lapponiensis, 2018; p 248.

Li, X.; Li, X. R.; Hudson, S. The Application of Generation Theory to Tourism Consumer Behavior: An American Perspective. *Tour. Manage.* **2013,** *37*, 147–164.

Litvin, S. W. Can a Festival Be Too Successful? A Review of Spoleto, USA. *Int. J. Contemp. Hospital. Manage.* **2006,** *18* (1), 41–49.

Mohammad, B. M. A.; Som, A. P. M. An Analysis of Push and Pull Travel Motivations of Foreign Tourists to Jordan. *Int. J. Busi. Manage.* **2010,** *5* (12), 41–50.

Prayag, G.; Ryan, C. The Relationship Between the 'Push' and 'Pull' Factors of a Tourist Destination: The Role of Nationality—An Analytical Qualitative Research Approach. *Curr. Iss. Tour.* **2010,** *14* (2), 121–143.

Rodrigue, J. P.; Comtois, C.; Slack, B. *The Geography of Transport Systems*; Routledge, 2016.

Sdnali, D.; Chazapi, K. Cultural Tourism in Greek Insular Community: The Resident's Perspective. *Tourismos: Int. Multi-Discip. J. Tour.* **2007,** *2* (2), 61–78.

Tavakol, M.; Dennick, R. Making Sense of Cronbach's alpha. *Int. J. Med. Educ.* **2011,** *2*, 53.

The Merriam-Webster. 2019. https://www.merriam-webster.com/dictionary/amenity

Throsby, D. *Economics and Culture*; Cambridge University Press, 2001.

United Nations. The Global Situation of Young People, 2003. www.un.org/esa/socdev/unyin/documents/worldyouthreport.pdf

Yan, Q.; Zhang, H.; Li, M. Programming Quality of Festivals: Conceptualization, Measurement, and Relation to Consequences. *Int. J. Contemp. Hospital. Manage.* **2012,** *24* (4), 653–673.

CHAPTER 3

Effects and Implications of Event Tourism on Sustainable Community Development: A Review

PARAG SUNIL SHUKLA[1] and SOFIA DEVI SHAMURAILATPAM[2]

[1]*Department of Commerce & Business Management, Faculty of Commerce, The M.S University of Baroda, Vadodara, Gujarat, India*

[2]*Department of Banking and Insurance, Faculty of Commerce, Maharaja Sayajirao University of Baroda, Vadodara, Gujarat, India*

ABSTRACT

The notion of community participation (CP) in the development process of emerging economies is a highly sought-after area of research and has its roots in diverse social, economic, and political theories developed by academicians and intellectuals from time to time. Given this backdrop, the participation of community in planning, decision-making, and allocation of resources, and with reference to needs/requirements of the community in particular holds sublime importance. The main premise of the research is built on the framework that CP has a significant role to play in the successful organization of event tourism through involvement, coordination by local authorities for proper allocation and distribution of available resources to bring maximum possible net social benefits that culminate into sustainable economic development. An attempt has been made in this study to review the implications of event tourism of a destination on sustainable community development. The main focus of the present study is that CP has a significant impact on sustainable community development, particularly in building good governance mechanisms, wherein the involvement of local authorities

Please note that few chapters were submitted during the peak of the pandemic. The long period of time to publish (due to supply chain and other issues) may have changed the perspectives presented in the chapter altogether.

Event Tourism and Sustainable Community Development: Advances, Effects, and Implications.
Ekta Dhariwal, Shruti Arora, Anukrati Sharma, Azizul Hassan (Eds.)
© 2024 Apple Academic Press, Inc. Co-published with CRC Press (Taylor & Francis)

is imperative for the successful implementation of all the planning for execution, organizing, and allocation of resources available in a given specific region/area. Further, if the role of private individuals is leveraged in the form of partnership in undertaking projects for the development of social and economic infrastructures in a given location or site, communities could be able to reap advantages in the form of cost-effectiveness and efficacy in operation through the scale economies.

3.1 INTRODUCTION

The travel industry has impacted various dimensions of economies, leading the economic forces to reckon with its potential as a catalyst for elevating the economy. Not exclusively does the travel industry lead development, but it additionally works on the nature of individuals' lives with its ability to make huge scope work of different kinds of economic activity at the micro and macroeconomic forefront. It upholds ecological security, champion's different social legacy, and fortifies harmony on the planet thereby making it more inclusive. Expansion just as reinforcing the travel industry in India is the fundamental goal of the Ministry of Tourism. The key areas are expanding the travel industry framework, facilitating the visa system, affirmation of value guidelines in administrations of the travel industry specialist organizations, projection of the nation as a 365 days' travel location, and technological advancement in the travel industry. These are the areas of strategic importance, which should be continually worked upon to augment the position of India as a traveling destination. Even the number of foreign tourist arrivals (FTAs) has increased to 10.89 million during the period 2019, a development of 3.2% over the previous year's records. Facilitation visa system is a pre-essential system for expanding inbound tourism. The Ministry of Tourism steps up to the plate with the Ministry of Home Affairs and Ministry of External Affairs for accomplishing something similar. As on December 2019, the e-visa service has been restored to the nationals of 169 Countries under five sub-classes for example "e-Tourist visa," "e-Business visa," "e-clinical visa," "e-Medical Attendant Visa" and "e-Conference Visa." The most recently added nation is the Kingdom of Saudi Arabia. "Swadesh Darshan" has a dream to develop traveler circuits with respect to the standards of high travel worth, seriousness, and supportability in an incorporated way by synergizing endeavors to enhance travel experience and improve destinations. Under the plan, 15 topical circuits have been distinctively identified for targeting tourism viz.,

North-East India Circuit, Buddhist Circuit, Himalayan Circuit, Coastal Circuit, Krishna Circuit, Desert Circuit, Tribal Circuit, Eco Circuit, Wildlife Circuit, Rural Circuit, Spiritual Circuit, Ramayana Circuit, Heritage Circuit, Tirthankar Circuit, and Sufi Circuit to name a few.

Since the commencement of the plan, a measure of Rs. 6035.70 crores has been endorsed for 77 ventures with an overall arrival of Rs. 3676.14 crores till December 31, 2019 under the aegis of Swadesh Darshan Scheme (SDS). This is an outstanding commitment to promote the travel industry (Ministry of Tourism, 2019).

Cultivating a genuinely comprehensive and coordinated approach to deal with tourist arrivals also calls for a comprehensive local area improvement as the local connection is of great importance for foreign travelers. Enabling "people-centric governance" by making systems will allow reciprocal relationships and economic growth through collaboration.

The second approach is for ensuring the Planet by cultivating aggregate endeavors to secure our house and the last target is to Shape New Frontiers by taking on long haul and intense techniques to use and share the advantages of advancement. It further creates associations developed to channelize by supporting governments and neighborhood networks to foster strategies and activity designs that form and upgrade public–private local area collaboration, making the travel industry a feasible instrument for comprehensive improvement through reasonable and proficient appropriation of the advantages of travel industry all through their regions. Leiper studied the industry framework, occasions, and events that have become a central component of the objective framework, where convenience, attractions, transport, and government administrations have been used or explicitly created. The purpose is to improve the convenience of visitors who particularly visit for attending an event, which may be of religious, social, recreational, adventure, or leisure in nature (Leiper, 1981).

A study by Connell, Page, and Meyer shows an integrative approach for occasions and tourist arrivals for guest attractions made by sightseers and the utilization of occasion marketing of local areas to attract tourists with collaboration with inhabitants of that area and home-grown guests. Peculiarly, place advertising is a mechanism toward "boosterism" and has arisen as a key element related to occasions to foster an extraordinary selling suggestion that separates the objective from one another (Connell et al., 2015). In this regard, occasions have a more extensive transmission than objective related to the travel industry albeit the focal point of this chapter is fundamentally on the objective-related issues of occasion in the travel industry and the investigations related to this space.

Arranged events in the travel industry are made for a reason, and what was once the domain of individual and local area drives the travel industry where regions are gaining popularity owing to the type of events that are held. Figure 3.1 shows a typology of the four fundamental classes of planned events. Business events are business-related activities that are generally held in cafés, inns, or resorts. Sports likewise require unique places including athletic parks, fields, and arena. Celebrations and other social festivals are less subject to offices and can utilize parks, roads, theaters, show lobbies, and any remaining public or private scenes. Amusement occasions like shows are by and large given by the private area and use many kinds of scenes. In the following section, the authors have given a brief overview of the key aspects of Event tourism and net social benefits and Events and Social Capital in Community Development (ibid.).

3.2 RATIONALE OF THE STUDY

Few studies on the extant literature about the impact assessment of event tourism on sustainable community development have so far been conducted particularly in the Indian context, and hence our study itself is no doubt, an exception. Our study entails an epigrammatic review of event tourism and sustainable community development.

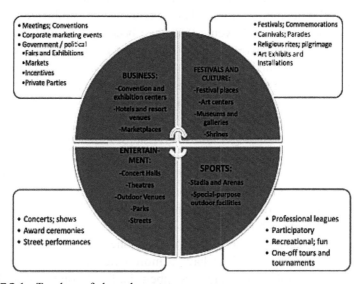

FIGURE 3.1 Typology of planned events.

Source: Compiled by Authors from Review of Literature

The research will be helpful in the policy framework of the analysis of impact assessment of event tourism on the community, population, and the place where it is organized and can be adopted as a model by other developing countries, under the given more or less similar kind of sociopolitical and institutional backgrounds.

3.3 THEORETICAL UNDERPINNINGS

The authors have made an attempt to understand the key linkages between event tourism and Net Social Benefits, events and their role in Community Development.

3.3.1 EVENT TOURISM AND NET SOCIAL BENEFITS

A holistic approach to understanding the diverse processes and outcomes in events is pertinent for the extension of strategic social leverage to all events organized on different occasions. The interconnectedness of social events with tourists needs to be understood to create, communicate, and deliver pertinent messages and thereby increases the footfalls of tourists. This can be done by promoting interactions of tourists with local communities so that the tourists not only understand the culture of the area but also become brand ambassadors and thus lead to net social benefits leading to reciprocal advantage for both the community and the tourists.

This will have greater scope for the researchers and policy makers as well to think toward varied dimensions and different types of events organized under scale and magnitudes to incorporate the aspects of SDGs alongside increasing the popularity of the tour destination. Another aspect to bring forth is the processes that lead to the cultural invention of events in terms of delivering a uniquely effective social experience to communities and tourists. In this respect, the strategic planning of events needs to identify the factors and mechanisms that allow the authentic creation of events that promote the local culture as well as to learn best practices of the traveler's home country by a meaningful dialogue between the two that leads to continuing social change that incorporates events in a host community's development agenda. In this regard, the essential arranging of occasions needs to recognize the components and systems that permit the real formation of occasions equipped for coordinating the assorted interests and implications that can drive enduring social change and fuse occasions in a host local area's advancement plan.

3.3.2 *EVENTS AND ROLE IN COMMUNITY DEVELOPMENT*

The study of social leverage needs to analyze how the dynamic processes and outcomes of events are interconnected with a host community's social fabric. To cite, Falassi (1987) has explained the social function and symbolic meaning of festivals that provide host communities the opportunity for the expression of overt values that are fundamental to their ideology and world-view, their social identity, their historical continuity, and their physical survival. Moreover, Quinn (2009) argued that the significance of festivals and events lies in the meanings they hold for both local and visiting populations, and in both their leisure and tourism functions, calling thus, for the need to align more closely different disciplinary ideas toward creating a holistic way to understand the nature, meanings, and management of event and tourism relationships. The event experiences and meanings attached to them vary as the interpretations of individuals, social groups, and communities are affected by several personal or sociocultural factors. This complicates the understanding of symbolic meanings and the design of appropriate event settings, program, and human interactions aimed at achieving social outcomes (Quinn, 2003).

Despite the fact that the "Community Driven Attitude" criticizes the commercialization of leisure practices, it suggests ways that events can be held in such a pattern that utilizes resources for the mutual benefits and social development of a host community. As event management is predominantly focussed on the commercialization aspects, the community-based concepts can be intertwined to achieve a striking balance between the two. To put forward, event management should be studied in a more integrated approach, wherein events be regarded as a means to build social capital for both economic and social development. Thus, it is important to consider the total benefits of the interconnectedness and the potential utility of events in creating a community-based tourism approach. In this sense, a host community's social development can be fostered in the focal practices of events, which connect groups of people who belong to different communities by providing opportunities to create shared meaning and build social networks.

The endeavor to foster the social value of events involves a set of complex processes because social heritage in the form of signs of aesthetic, regionalized cultural performances, and implementation of events, which need to be interwoven with the events according to the nature, size, and scale of the events keeping in mind the travelers' profile. For this reason, an understanding is required of the ways that the social, political, economic, and cultural context is intertwined with events. In other words, it needs a critical analysis of how event strategies will impact upon social processes within the host community. In this dimension, it is crucial that events are social constructions shaped by the negotiation of interests and exchange of resources. Consequently, the study of events' social utility is substantially illuminated by the social constructivist theory.

3.3.3   OUTCOMES AND IMPACT OF EVENTS

Getz (2008) defined as "important elements in the orientation of national societies to international or global society." In other words, countries across the globe used the term events as a mechanism to acquire or benefit legitimacy on the one hand and also reputation remarks which reflect connectedness. This will produce and incarnate a positive image of the destinations to tourists; no doubt there are choices against destinations for each tourist—the relevant question is why they need to select a destination. Therefore, it is the event that influences and creates a potential reason behind the choice and visit of a specific selected tour site. Events held in specific destinations have economic significance too above the social and cultural development of the location/sites, in that with the purpose of attending an event, it enables the sale and purchase of regional/local products offered in the destination. To conclude, events can fuel the local businesses, at the same time, can create a social bonding with the tourists leading to a feeling of "connect." The destination can add value by such emotional connect leading to patronage.

Given the economic, social, political, and institutional factors, many destinations are associated with seasonal problems, thereby making the inflow of tourists in this particular destination for a specific or short duration of time for the year. In this regard, events can play a significant role in getting the better off out of these problems and can help in attracting more tourists even during the off-season periods too. Ideally, events have substantial effects in building good identities of the destination, which can help them in promoting, positioning, branding of the location/sites for becoming a prosperous and potential tourist destination. Above these, for multiple destinations, it is through events which can be a source to expand the network and attention toward the public with the extensive coverage through media. A promotion and branding of events will have sociocultural benefits of the events to local community as well on the one hand,

and also increased different activities associated with the event, on the other hand, a way toward strengthening regional values and traditions of the destination. This becomes very effective particularly when tourists are in the process of searching for specific events when it comes across to the desired image of destination—may be either the reason for establishing the image of modern Indian city or preference of preserving the image of a traditional township.

To summarize, it is of utmost important to meticulously select the events assigned in the destinations, because we know that events have both positive and negative effects on destination image and identity. It is because a major event may bring menace, a threat to danger toward the image of the destination on one side of the same coin as the number of tourists will be more involved in the event than the destination itself, and on the other side, a major event cannot attract huge attention toward tourists when the destination is unfamiliar or unknown. Therefore, by perceiving all the expected outcomes of events, it is a fact that it can offer a mixture of benefits in terms of economic, social, and cultural dimensions for the destination and hosts should use events as a mechanism/instrument for the development of the tourism industry in each destination with long-term perspective to realize the full potentials of the destination.

3.3.4 FESTIVALS AND EVENT TOURISM

Ever since early human civilization, festivals are regarded as the building blocks of the communities in each region and the value of festivals has been demonstrated for political, social, and cultural dimensions from time to time. Festivals are unordinary times in the life of a community. Making celebration requires that people reach out from their usual routines and interest, go beyond themselves for the community good. The preparation for, and production of a festival makes people to cross-social boundaries and interact in different ways. No doubt, to organize a major festival in destinations, it may require proper arrangement of human resources and is a collective effort and involvement of the community in large. Generally, to perform such activities, the role of organizers is significant not in terms of devotion of time personally but also diligent efforts from "Volunteer" groups and support from NGOs.

It is considered that the term "Celebration" itself is a glue, which can bind a community and act as an elixir in keeping the community a novel part and perpetually renewing experience with a sense of responsiveness to the needs of times. Not only do annual festivals create a community of witness which marks the passage of time, but also it adds to the transition of the new power relations against the old ones. To bring forth, according to Dunstan (1994), celebration is the way humans integrate change.

Festivities held at the events can be a tool for co-creation wherein the local communities as well as tourists can collaboratively engage to make it a grand success in terms of a joyous and enjoyable event. This can be also used as a best practice as well as a promotional element to build and sustain new tourist arrivals. Festivals have their own significant dimensions, in that the more festivals in the destination, the more will be in creativity that fosters toward cultural changes. In its occurrence, in the cases of the more tolerant and embracing, the festivals may generate a more tolerant and embracing state in the community, a framework persists for better balance in the community. When it comes to acting locally on local issues, a common discovery of social activists is how unskilled most people are in the processes of collective action. The skills needed for a successful social action—meeting skills, goal setting, motivation and management of volunteers, conflict resolution, identification of resources, publicity and promotion, media management, strategy and tactics for achieving the goal—are the same skills as are needed to organize a successful festival. Events are not only meant to serve or to attract tourists, but it also has significant dimensions in the development or maintenance of the community or building regional identity and images (Getz and Frisby, 1987; Hall, 1992). They offer several reasons why communities organize events, "including enhancing or preserving the local culture and history and providing local recreation and leisure opportunities."

Cultural norms, as well as religiosity play a dominant role in attracting tourists, further, festivals act as a source of inspiration and build the identity of the destination that a particular group or a community will patronize to visit. In other words, it can work out as a tool to minimize the negative impacts of a large number of visits and to nurture better the association between host and guest. Further, the study adds that festivals in locations or destinations can extend the tourist seasons, making the tourist spot lively during off-seasons or to say introducing a new season into the life of a community at large.

Event tourism has substantial development perspectives toward the community in that it becomes a source and element of bringing community spirit and pride, cooperation, and coordination, empowering leadership, improvement in social and economic infrastructure, a capacity to control development through the enhancement of cultural and social traditions of the community. The ethnicities, as well as cultural norms of the local region, will have a profound impact as the identity of the community will pass on to the tourists.

It is about people having a good time and rarely requires massive infrastructure as it is generally organized around existing resources. Festivals offer a mechanism to foster the local organizational development, image and identity building, leadership and networking, and cultural and social heritage, all of which are vital support from the bottom of community-based tourism development. In the words of Getz (1991), the outcome of these processes is the development of tourism keeping with the fulfillment at the fundamentals in terms of community wishes, more authenticity, satisfying the residents as well as visitors for conscious sustainable living.

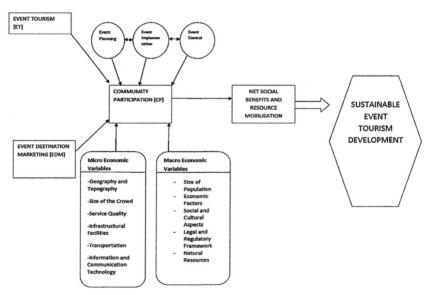

FIGURE 3.2 Conceptual framework of the research study.

Source: Prepared by the authors based on review of literature.

As shown in Figure 3.2, the concept of event tourism and event destination marketing has its advantages only if there is a higher degree of community participation (CP). The three concepts viz., event planning, event implementation, and event control exert a pressure on CP. Further,

Effects and Implications of Event Tourism on Sustainable Community 41

the extent of CP is also related to micro and macroeconomic variables, such as the magnitude, level, timing, and composition of the event depending on it. Community participation in any event results in net social benefits and resource mobilization in a given locality/region. The outcome is the sustainable event tourism development. Though there is no definite definition or approach the way to sustainability acceptable in general, it is recognized that the concept of sustainability is much higher and then simply "greening of events" relates tightly to the evaluation of values, significance for public–private intervention, continuity, and feasible solutions, considering population at large with a view to various lines of argument without any critical discourse.

3.4 INNOVATIVE STEPS TOWARD EVENT TOURISM IN INDIA: A BIRD'S EYE VIEW

Pursuant to budget announcements in 2018–2019 and 2019–2020, the Ministry of Tourism has composed "Development of Iconic Tourist Destinations Scheme," which is a scheme introduced at the Central sector level for the development of distinguished 19 iconic destinations in the country. A total number of 19 iconic destinations have been categorically classified for the period of FY 2020–2021 to FY 2025–2026. The proposal has now been processed for approval by the competent authority. The essence of this scheme is to promote the public–private partnerships (PPP) in tourism infrastructure development as the development of tourism infrastructure requires a huge amount of investments that cannot be individually undertaken out of the public financing alone, but requires to attract private capital as well as the techno-managerial efficiencies associated with it.

In this regard, the government has identified 15 circuits based on specific themes which include Krishna Circuit, Buddhist Circuit, Himalayan Circuit, Northeast Circuit, Coastal Circuit, wildlife circuit and tribal circuit. The annual budget of 2021–2022 envisages the notion of Swadesh Darshan to attract tourists to local places as per their preferences and for the marketing of the destinations, a mammoth budget of Rs. 1088.03 crore has been allocated. The government implemented different schemes from time to time to promote the tourism industry. National Mission on Pilgrimage Rejuvenation and Spiritual Augmentation was implemented by the Ministry of Tourism in order to enhance the basic infrastructures and facilities supplied to pilgrimage centers across the country. Under the

PRASHAD scheme for the development of tourist circuits, the government has allocated a sum of Rs. 207.55 crore (USD 29.70 million) during the budget plan 2020–2021 and at present, a total number of 28 projects have been sanctioned with an amount of Rs. 840.02 crore (USD 120.19 million) under the scheme. As a part of PRASHAD scheme, the Ministry of Tourism has facilitated "Tourist Facilitation Center" under the project development of Guruvayur, Kerala. In other words, as a promotional program, the Ministry of Tourism has taken up significant steps toward the development of tourism industry in India.

3.5 SUSTAINABLE DEVELOPMENT AND EVENT TOURISM: KEY LINKAGES

One of the profound attributes of the tourism sector is its ability to link the different segments of the economy, which acts as a thrust for mutual coordination and enhancement of sociocultural, economic, and ecological dimensions of sustainable development. Tourism has the power to act as a catalyst for the economic upliftment and preservation of the existing sociocultural heritage, environmental values, and economic point of view as a significant source of income to the locals/sites in region/destination, though it depends on the host communities and tourists visit in a destination. No doubt, there are advantages and disadvantages in that it can go beyond the tangible values of economic effects on the one hand, and non-economic intangible effects, breaking the chain in value systems in the destinations on the other hand. These may take the form of targeting only the revenue earnings from FTAs, income of the tourism industry and its contribution to GDP; and degradation in the sociocultural values attached, change in lifestyles of the people surrounding in particular, breakdown in family values, attributes in individuals and population at large, ceremonies and community organization at large. In other words, when the concept of sustainability is integrated with any development dimensions, it talks about the restoration of the existing values from the ethical point of view considering the demand from the present generation and also thinking for the future through proper management of scare resources, the mechanism for waste management, responsible and more accountable business operation with the core idea of ethics, etc. as dimensions to cover for, as it influences other industries too in the economy, particularly when the concept of sustainable development comes forth.

Effects and Implications of Event Tourism on Sustainable Community

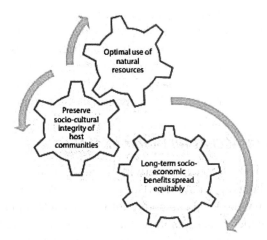

FIGURE 3.3 Pillars of sustainable tourism.
Source: https://jillonjourney.com/the-three-pillars-of-sustainability-in-tourism/

As shown in Figure 3.3, the tourism sector for achieving sustainability needs to reinvent the wheel and incorporate the fundamental principle of Sustainable Tourism, namely, optimum utilization of environmental resources, social, and cultural integrity for the preservation of heritage by theme-based events, and reaps the benefits of long-term economic and social equity among communities. As tourism sector has grown rapidly during the post-1950s period, researchers and policy makers have formulated models to identify and incorporate the dimensions of study in the area of tourism as a mechanism for pro-poor growth, inclusive growth, and sustainable development. In this chapter, an attempt has been made to review the seven key tools and mechanisms of the same.

3.5.1 CARRYING CAPACITY (CC)

The concept of carrying capacity (CC) is highly debated in disciplines, such as Geography and Environmental Science, though no exception to Environmental Economics as a course in the Economics discipline. The concept is basically used as an instrument to measure the overconsumption of natural, renewable, and non-renewable resources beyond their CC so that nature gets its way to preserve the quality though each development is associated with some high degree of degradation and destruction. For example, harvesting fish beyond its CC may harm the biodiversity of the ecosystem of water bodies, which may have ramifications for other species in the entire system.

The underlying concept is tourism, which is promoted in such a way that it should be well protected and it should not pass beyond the threshold of CC in each location/site in region/destination because this may cause the deterioration in the quality ecosystem in destinations. The focus to explore on environmental issues has expanded since 1960s. Harry Coccossis (2004) studied the same in light of over capacity utilization of tourist destinations.

3.5.2   LIMITS OF ACCEPTABLE CHANGE (LAC)

We know that every economic activity is associated with some sort of destruction and breakdown in the existing capacity. With the concept of CC, it is imperative that the local and communities must adopt planning perspectives the extent which is acceptable so that it can help in establishing toward immanent limitations to growth in the sector (Ahn, 2002).

3.5.3   SUSTAINABLE LIVELIHOODS APPROACH (SLA)

The cooperation of the rural population leads to community engagement with the tourists and thus can become an important source of poverty reduction, especially in the underdeveloped areas. The SLA as an approach envisages that the life of the rural populace revolves around the activities of tourism in that area thereby creating income generation opportunities. The findings of the study conducted by Macbeth (2004) also correlate that the creation of town or city infrastructure is an outcome of destination popularity. The value additions can be in the form of framing new attractions of sites, upgradation in existing social and economic capital, and directly linked among the stakeholders that can lead to development in the tourism sector.

3.5.4   SUSTAINABLE TOURISM BENCHMARKING TOOL (STBT)

A policy and decision-making tool based on quantifiable indicators, aims to compare, on a country-level, different destinations in terms of sustainability measures (Cernat, 2012).

3.5.5   TRIPLE BOTTOM LINE (TBL)

The concept of triple bottom line (TBL) is gaining traction in tourism as a sustainable practice as it connotes the far-reaching implications across

Effects and Implications of Event Tourism on Sustainable Community 45

geographies. The impact assessment of tourism practices on various sectors of the economy is a matter of concern (Vanclay, 2004).

3.5.6 INTEGRATED TOURISM YIELD (ITY)

The concept of integrated tourism yield (ITY) seeks to measure the holistic effect of the net benefits of tourism vis-à-vis the cost incurred across various dimensions in organizing any event or festival during the season and off-season periods in the destination. As mentioned by Jeremy Northcote (2006), the framework proposed that by incorporating the impacts of costs and benefits to evaluate the yield in terms of financial gains for business activity.

3.5.7 COST-BENEFIT ANALYSIS (CBA)

Though tourism sector produces significant contribution to the economy and restoration of sociocultural heritage, and helps in preserving destination images; on the other side, it has adverse impacts in terms of imbalance in biodiversity, environmental resources, erosion of the social values, overtourism, loss of cultural identity, aggression and frequency of crimes in destinations, etc. to cite for. In this regard, realizing the multiple aspects of the characteristics of tourism as a sector, a model to incorporate the externalities involved with appropriate methodologies inherent can help in measuring a wider scope of impacts in monetary units when both costs and benefits to society are analyzed by integrating tangible and intangible values added, then it can internalize the externalities assigned (Theobald, 2012).

3.6 CONCLUDING REMARKS

Our study focussed on the role of community as a collective agent in executing any sort of events/festivals during on and off-seasons organized at the destinations from time to time. We highlighted in this chapter how the involvement of communities can bring toward a good image or value of the destinations, impacting the economic, social, and cultural dimensions of the sites/region. In the context of outbreak of COVID-19, the tourism industry was seen as a major cause and carrier of the novel coronavirus that triggered across the globe, making the global tourism industry to a halt. In this regard, stakeholders in the industry need to collectively make an effort to work together to make the industry sufficiently resilient to deal with the crisis. A resilience-based framework is proposed for the sustainability of the sector and stakeholders, including—governments, market players, technology innovators, workforce employed in the industry, particularly during post–pandemic. In this situation, the involvement of local communities is significant, as at the regional and local level, it can undertake steps to restrict international travel and put restrictions to prevent the spreading of the pandemic. This will not only widen the base of the tourism industry but it also presents opportunities for less-developed tourism sites to grow further. To put it together, every destination that has a scope for improvement in its tourist attractiveness should make a detailed plan for the development of tourism sector with strategic planning of events including festivals with a view to realize the full potential of event tourism. Events which take place in certain location/sites/region should be well systematically planned and executed to attract tourists, image building, and catalysts for further development of the sector. Quality in terms of proper planning in such a way to make events differentiate from each other with the fact that product or service offered should provide recognition and status in the market, resulting in maximum satisfaction of the visitors and their loyalty is important to make repeated events at different point of time. The more recognizable events the destination has, the more it is attractive to the tourists. The key of their success lies in the support of accommodation facilities of an appropriate standard, the high level of cooperation between tourist agencies, the availability of specific information about events and follow-up activities, and most importantly, proper marketing activities.

The policy imperatives can be attributed to three major takeaways. Initially, tourism in the first phase can help the destinations to thrive balance thereby revitalizing and rejuvenating them. For this purpose, the destinations need to evolve a unique strategy, especially in COVID-19 pandemic-induced travel, where there are major setbacks to travelers as well as concern of health and safety takes the front seat. The most critical aspect is the effects of footfalls on local livelihoods. Secondly, the government as well as the local authorities need to support local artisans at the same time to promote tourism and that is the tightrope walk. The business health of the local entrepreneurs needs to be evaluated so that they can consolidate and partner with other small businesses that require financial handholding or start-up capital. Third, countries need to make strategic decisions regarding the future of tourism in their countries. Some tourism businesses will not survive even once travel restrictions are removed. Governments need to decide which to support and

Effects and Implications of Event Tourism on Sustainable Community   47

for how long-term, for example, the implications of the pandemic need to be considered.

To sum up, with the surge in the demand for tourism services and products assigned to conventional attributes of events and festivals as well as off-season non-conventional events organized from time to time, new destinations were being emerged with stiff competition among others to acquire larger amount, which calls for a constant development and progress in the sector for a sustainable business system. However, it is also true that in the processes of development of the sector, it may bring adverse impacts in terms of loss of competitive advantage of location/sites in region/destination thereby leading to overtourism, overcrowding, deterioration in the quality of the ecosystem and its CC, fading away the sociocultural fabrics, etc. among others to mention. In this regard, taking note of the significant advantages and the associated limitation, the challenge lies in coordination among different stakeholders, considering the size of the population, the speed of progress of the industry, and the pattern of investment planning for development perspectives to consider with. The reason is that it is only effective when successful execution of planning, programming, and investment to synchronize with a constant flow in resources that is assigned toward long-term success in any destination targets. The dimensions of community's role as a principal agent in the host destination, PPP along with the pros and cons from tourists/visitors are indispensable to look forward in the form of multifunctional ecosystem, posing an undeniable contribution from each party of the stakeholders in the ecosystem.

3.7 FUTURE SCOPE AND ROAD AHEAD

The researchers in this chapter have made an attempt to portray an epigrammatic view of the Effects and Implications of Event Tourism on Sustainable Community Development. It can be inferred that event tourism still needs a major attention to attract footfalls as well as needs specific policy framework from a regulatory as well governance point of view. One interesting finding that is yielded from the review of literature is that most of the researchers have focussed on the management of singular events. None of the studies have explained or forayed into making or planning of events with integration of local cultures as well as aligning the global cultural trends with the local areas. The globalization of tourism industry needs a thorough revamp by creating a unique and synergistic impact. This can be done by creating a unique set of discreet messages aimed at creating a unified appeal of the destination. Further, the application of portfolio concepts from the domain of finance and investment needs to be done for managing tourism events. There is a dire need to form an alliance with the government, private businesses, technocrats, and local entrepreneurs to evolve a strategy for event tourism and to enhance the tourist attractiveness of a town, village, or a city. The seasonal variation in the tourist footfalls as well as overtourism needs to be controlled by the government and by technological intervention. The events can also be interlinked with the celebrities that enjoy popularity in that area which will help to create a brand image and can also result in media buzz. The image improvement strategies that can be taken up through PPP models can also help tour destinations regain competitiveness.

KEYWORDS

- **community participation**
- **event tourism**
- **sustainable development**
- **net social benefits**

REFERENCES

Ahn, B. Y.; Lee, B. K.; Shafer, C. S. Operationalizing Sustainability in Regional Tourism Planning: An Application of the Limits of Acceptable Change Framework. *Tour. Manage.* **2002,** 1–15.

Annual Report of Ministry of Tourism-Government of India, 2020–2021. https://tourism.gov.in/sites/default/files/202103/Annual%20Report%202021%2021%20English.pdf assessed on 15/06/2021.

Cernat, L.; Gourdon, J. Paths to Success: Benchmarking Cross-Country Sustainable Tourism. *Tour. Manage.* **2012,** 1044–1056.

CII and YES bank Report on Sustainable Tourism in India. 2018. https://www.yesbank.in/pdf/sustainable_tourism_in_india_initiatives_and_opportunities.pdf (accessed on 15 May 2021).

Coccossis, H.; Mexa, A. *The Challenge of Tourism Carrying Capacity Assessment: Theory and Practice*; Routledge: New York, 2004.

Connell, J.; Page, S. J.; Meyer, D. Visitor Attractions and Events: Responding to Seasonality. *J. Tour. Manage.* **2015,** *46,* 283–298.

Dunstan, G. Sightseeing Tourists' Motivation and Satisfaction. *Ann. Tour. Res.* **1994,** *18* (2), 226–237.

Falassi, A., Ed. *Time Out of Time: Essays on the Festival*; University of New Mexico Press: Albuquerque, NM, 1987.

Frisby, W.; Getz, D. Festival Management: A Case Study Perspective. *J. Travel Res.* **1987,** *28* (1), 7–11.

Getz, D. Event Tourism: Definition, Evolution and Research. *J. Tour. Manage.* **2008,** *29* (3), 403–428.

Getz, D. Event Studies and Event Management: On Becoming and Academic Discipline. *J. Hospital. Tour. Hospital.* **1991,** *9* (1), 12–23.

Hall, M. *Hallmark Tourist Events: Impacts, Management and Planning*; Belhaven Press: London, 1992.

Leiper, N. Towards a Cohesive Curriculum in Tourism: The Case for a Distinct Discipline. *Ann. Tour. Res.* **1981,** *8* (11), 69–84.

Macbeth, J.; Carson, D.; Northcote, J. Social Capital, Tourism and Regional Development: SPCC as a Basis for Innovation and Sustainability. *Curr. Iss. Tour.* **2004,** 502–522.

Ministry of Tourism Report. 2019. https://tourism.gov.in/media/annual-reports (accessed on 20 Aug 2021).

Northcote, J.; Macbeth, J. Conceptualizing Yield: Sustainable Tourism Management. *Ann. Tour. Res.* **2006,** 199–220.

Quinn, B. Festivals, Events, and Tourism. In *The Sage Handbook of Tourism Studies*; Jamal, T., Robinson, M., Eds.; Sage: London, 2009; pp 483–503.

Quinn, B. Symbols, Practices and Myth-Making: Cultural Perspectives on the Wexford Festival Opera. *Tour. Geogr.* **2003,** *5* (3), 329–349.

Theobald, W. F. *Global Tourism*; Routledge: New York, 2012.

Vanclay, F. The Triple Bottom Line and Impact Assessment: How do TBL, EIA, SIA, SEA and EMS Relate to Each Other? *J. Environ. Assess. Policy Manage.* **2004,** 265–288.

CHAPTER 4

Rural Event Tourism and Community Development

KARABI KABIR[1] and MD. ASHIKUR RAHMAN AVI[2]

[1]Tourism and Hospitality Management at University of Dhaka, Dhaka, Bangladesh

[2]Department of Tourism and Hospitality Management, Pabna University of Science and Technology, Pabna, Bangladesh

ABSTRACT

While there has been a lot of work on rural tourism and community development in recent years, few studies focus on how rural events assist community development by ensuring sustainable development in the developing country perspective. Therefore, this chapter aims to explore the driving forces of rural event tourism in rural community development from the perspective of Bangladesh. In doing so, this research is guided by a qualitative research approach within a case study strategy. The data collection techniques comprise both primary and secondary methods. Using thematic analysis method, the collected data were analyzed. The findings reveal that rural event tourism fosters community development by enhancing the community status and image, rejuvenating the life stream of the community residents, improving social life, enhancing cultural values and destination development, and regenerating the economy. This is one of the first research attempts in Bangladesh that have covered up a very timely and unexplored research area, offering empirical evidence regarding how rural event tourism contributes to community development. This chapter will be helpful for tourism policy makers to formulate rural event tourism policy in Bangladesh.

Please note that few chapters were submitted during the peak of the pandemic. The long period of time to publish (due to supply chain and other issues) may have changed the perspectives presented in the chapter altogether.

Event Tourism and Sustainable Community Development: Advances, Effects, and Implications.
Ekta Dhariwal, Shruti Arora, Anukrati Sharma, Azizul Hassan (Eds.)
© 2024 Apple Academic Press, Inc. Co-published with CRC Press (Taylor & Francis)

4.1 INTRODUCTION

Cultural festivals and events are common phenomena in every culture. These events and festivals are most often termed as the jewels of culture for a community. Particularly, events are being used as a means of tourism and economic development for rural communities throughout the world (Butler et al., 1998; Higham and Ritchie, 2001; Roberts and Hall, 2001). The beneficial effects of rural events extend beyond profit generation (Janiskee and Drews, 1998; Xie, 2004). They often derive a social value by building social networks (Rao, 2001), extending the social capital of rustic communities (Arcodia and Whitford, 2007), and enriching the quality of rural life (Brennan-Horley et al., 2007). This usually takes place through the blending of sport, culture, tradition, and entertainment in events. This sort of event aims to provide a unique experience to local community which enhances the social bond, identity, and values of that particular community (Jonsson, 2003). For this reason, rural communities often rely on tradition (Ray et al., 2006) and organize cultural events under the guise of community development (Cameron, 1987). In recent years, a handful of works on rural tourism and community development are found but very few studies focus on how rural events assist community development by ensuring sustainability, in the context of developing countries. This chapter aims at exploring how the driving forces of rural event tourism contribute to rural community development from the perspective of Bangladesh.

Bangladesh is a developing nation having 87,182 villages (Bangladesh Bureau of Statistics, 2018) that host diverse tourism resources, that is, attractions, activities, events, festivals, and lifestyle, etc. Almost three-quarters population of this country lives in these country sides where most of them live below the poverty line and their livelihood mostly depends on agricultural activities. Because of the seasonal nature of agricultural employment, residents in these rustic areas are left unemployed during the off-season and forced to shift to the metropolitan areas in search of work, which in turn creates extra pressure for those cities (Rahman et al., 2018). In such a complex situation, the utilization of rural tourism resources can generate alternative livelihood, improve the quality of life, and contribute to community development.

The key objective of this chapter is to investigate how rural event tourism contributes to community development. In securing the research objective, the qualitative research approach is followed in this study where the data are collected by using both primary and secondary techniques. The

Rural Event Tourism and Community Development 53

in-depth interview technique is followed to collect the primary data and a range of journal articles, books, newspaper writings, and website materials are reviewed for collecting secondary data. The data are analyzed using the thematic analysis method. As there is no previous work regarding rural event tourism and community development in Bangladesh, the findings of this chapter set a cornerstone for future tourism researchers, academicians, and policy makers, and this is the novelty of this research.

There are three sections in this chapter. Firstly, the literature review section explores the conceptual relationship among sustainability, sustainable rural economic, sociocultural, rural community development, and rural event tourism. Then, the detailed research design, research context, sampling and data collection techniques, and data analysis methods are presented in the second section. Finally, the findings of this research as well as theme-based analysis results are portrayed in the third section, and the chapter concludes with some policy guidelines.

4.2 LITERATURE REVIEW

Events or festivals can play an obvious role in the tourism revitalization process by ensuring sustainable development. In reference, we can highlight the Shiosai festival which has taken place in Mitarai village in Japan which helped the community by improving their socioeconomic condition (Cheer et al., 2017). In this rejuvenation process, local cultural heritage plays a key role. This festival also increased community resilience and worked as an important social capital. Another notable facet of this festival is that it has been driven by the bottom-up approach without the help of any external bodies. However, this raises an issue whether the extent of future involvement of local level remains a critical success factor or not.

Sustainability and festivals raise debate among few researchers. Economics has been the central concern when they have featured it (O'Sullivan and Jackson, 2002). Whether festivals can provide an effective vehicle for sustainable tourism or tourism can enhance the sociable practice of feasibility remains a less discussed area. Quinn (2006) argued that to promote the socially and culturally sustaining activities of festivals and to encourage a sustainable approach in tourism development, festivals' affiliation with tourism needs to be managed carefully. An empirical study of two art festivals in Ireland demonstrates that tourism plays a vital role in promoting festivals' growth and expansion. The study also suggests that

54 Event Tourism and Sustainable Community Development

tourism helps to increase the year-round revenue, to enrich culture, and to improve venue infrastructure in both places.

4.2.1 SUSTAINABILITY

The terms sustainability, sustainable development, and sustainable tourism are used interchangeably most of the time, however, Liu (2003) explained the differences among the meanings associated with them. According to her, sustainability has been described as a "state—focused" condition, which involved long-term stability, whereas sustainable development (p. 460), focuses on the process which includes the management of something for both short term and long term. The McIntyre (1993) state that "sustainable tourism development meets the needs of present tourists and host regions while protecting and enhancing opportunities for the future." The World Commission on Environment and Development (WCED, 1987) in the Brundtland Report defined sustainable development as "development that meets the needs of the present without compromising the ability for future generations to meet their own needs" (p. 43). So here, the needs of tourists and host communities are in focus by protecting them for the future. Tourist satisfaction as a key dimension in developing sustainable tourism has been added by Cater in 1993. This idea was further developed by Liu (2003) and she argued that as a destination cannot assume the future growth of tourists, and that visitation numbers will grow, tourism demand must be part of any sustainable tourism development plan. Tourism is a vulnerable industry in which the preferences and motivations of tourists change frequently and most of them are subject to external forces, such as natural disasters, terrorism, and economic recession. To accompany these changes, it is important to view sustainable tourism development in a broader vision. This vision should acknowledge that tourism development is dynamic and it requires simultaneously meeting the needs of the tourists, the tourism businesses, the host community, and the needs for environmental protection (Liu, 2003, p. 467). Sustainable tourism has the dimension of the economy, environment, and sociocultural.

4.2.2 SUSTAINABLE RURAL ECONOMIC DEVELOPMENT AND RURAL EVENT

There are many evidences from different studies stretching back 30 years suggesting that tourism events hosted by rural community in rural arena tends to provide economic value to the community. In such events, most expenditures come from accommodation and food (Daniels and Norman, 2003; Horne, 2000; Veltri et al., 2009; Walo et al., 1996). All of these studies show that the economic benefits outweigh the costs. This is primarily because these events bring tourists to the area who visited the area only to participate in that particular event or festival. This provides an income opportunity for the local hotels and restaurants, and also benefits other businesses, such as petrol stations and retail outlets. To ensure the economic sustainability of these events, O'Brien and Chalip (2008) suggest developing an events portfolio for the community hosting events regularly, thereby ensuring a consistent flow of tourists and expenditures.

4.2.3 SOCIOCULTURAL DEVELOPMENT AND RURAL EVENT

The social benefits of hosting the events contributing to the quality of life (Walo et al., 1996) and increased community spirit and pride (Horne, 2000; Veltri et al., 2009; Ziakas, 2010) has frequently been cited by the authors of rural event literature. These studies also indicate the involvement of the community in the events as volunteers (Daniels and Norman, 2003; Horne, 2000; Walo et al., 1996; Wilson, 2006; Ziakas, 2010). Fyall and Jago (2009) suggested that to understand the concern of sustainability, the impact of rural event tourism needs to be understood in terms of the triple bottom line (sociocultural, economic, and environmental) and attention need to be paid over the influence of the external environment on rural events and tourism.

4.2.4 RURAL EVENT TOURISM AND COMMUNITY DEVELOPMENT

In rural areas, events whether it is big or small have economic and social impacts; however, studies suggest that the social impacts outstretch the economic benefits (Alves et al, 2010). According to Kotler et al. (2006), event-based tourism is a vital element to attract tourists. Small events and festivals require little investment as the infrastructure requirements already exist (Flognfeldt, 1999).

4.3 RESEARCH METHOD

This study uses the qualitative research strategy which is the most widely accepted and used method in tourism research (Ritchie et al., 2005; Jennings, 2004; Denzin and Lincoln, 2011). The "typical case sampling" strategy is prioritized in selecting the study region, in which key informants (at the central level) collaborated to determine the study area (Patton, 1990; Suri, 2011). As a part of this approach to identify a typical case, one government administrator and two stakeholders affiliated with the tourism industry were interviewed and finally, the researchers considered Lalon folk feast or Lalon Mela, a rural event at Chheuria, Kushtia, as the case of this study.

4.3.1 RESEARCH CONTEXT

The Lalon folk feast, also known as the Lalon Mela (fair), is an annual music celebration commemorating the death anniversary of Baul legend Fakir Lalon Shah (The Daily Observer, 2015; The Daily Star, 2013). The festival is held in Lalon's shrine in Chheuria, Kushtia, a small Bangladeshi village. Lalon first introduced this music festival. Lalon, also known as Fakir Lalon Shah, Lalon Shah, and Lalon Fakir, was a well-known Bengali philosopher, author, Baul saint, mystic, composer, social reformer, and thinker in present-day Bangladesh's Kushtia (Skoda and Lettmann, 2017). He established the Lalon Akhrah Institute in Chheuria, around 2 km (1.2 miles) from the Kushtia railway station. His followers are primarily found in Bangladesh and West Bengal. Thousands of his disciples and admirers from all over the world gather at Lalon Akhrah every year on the anniversary of his death to pay honor to him by celebrating and discussing his music and philosophy for a few days (Ahmed and Karim, 2012). The event is organized by the Lalon Academy in collaboration with the Ministry of Cultural Affairs. The Lalon fair, open discussion sessions, and cultural programs are all part of the festival.

4.3.2 SAMPLING, DATA COLLECTION, AND DATA ANALYSIS METHOD

This chapter adopted both primary and secondary data collection techniques to collect research data. Following Denzin and Lincoln (1994), the semi-structured in-depth interview technique is used for collecting initial data, and as a part of the secondary data collection strategy, a range of journal articles, books, book chapters, newspaper writings, and website materials are reviewed. The purposive judgmental sampling method is applied in this qualitative research to sample populations. The profile of the respondents is provided in the following Table 4.1

Rural Event Tourism and Community Development 57

TABLE 4.1 Profile of the Research Respondents.

Respondent no. and code	Identity	Age	Gender	Education	Interview length (minutes)
LC1	Teacher	30	Female	Postgraduate	40
LC2	Student	22	Female	Undergraduate	38
LC3	Student	23	Male	Undergraduate	30
LC4	Researcher	29	Female	Postgraduate	35
LC5	Businessman	36	Male	Primary	25
LC6	Student	24	Male	Undergraduate	20
T1	Student	23	Male	Undergraduate	30
T2	Student	21	Male	Higher Secondary	15
TO1	Businessperson	35	Male	Postgraduate	31
GO1	Administrator	38	Male	Postgraduate diploma	30
LAO1	Office staff	29	Male	Undergraduate	25

In total, 11 interview sessions were conducted. The respondent category covers Local Community (LC), Tourist (T), Tour Operator (TO), Government Official (GO), and Lalon Academy Official (LAO). The interviewer confirmed that all the respondents are well informed about the key research aim and objective before starting the interview session. The interviewer stopped interviewing when data saturation was observed. After conducting the interviews, selective transcription was employed to thematically analyze the data. Following Barun and Clarke (2006), the six stages thematic analysis method is applied for data analysis.

4.4 FINDINGS AND DISCUSSIONS

The participants in this research have provided insight into a variety of rural event tourism potentials to community development in Bangladesh which are summarized as key findings and thematically classified under three sub-themes (i) social, (ii) cultural, and (iii) economic contribution. The following exhibit 4.1 recapitulates the views of the research participants regarding how Lalon Mela as a rural event contributes to the local community (Chheuria village of Kushtia) development in Bangladesh.

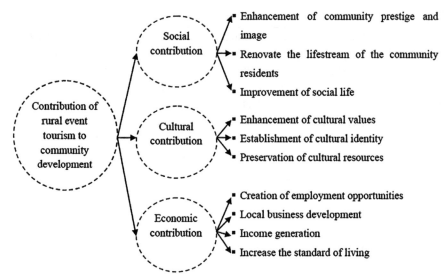

EXHIBIT 4.1 The key theme, sub-themes, and the contributions of rural event tourism in developing communities summarize the research findings.

Source: Developed by the authors.

The participants in this research have prioritized the sociocultural contribution of Lalon Mela to the community over economic contribution. They have identified that this rural event enhances community image and cultural values, renovates the lifestyle and improves the social life of the community residents, establishes a distinct cultural identity, as well as protects culture. A local community category participant mentioned that "Lalon Shah is the pride of Kushtia. Every day hundreds of people from all over the country congregate at Lalon's shrine and practice philosophical music introduced by Lalon. Added to this regular gathering, during Lalon Mela (held twice a year, one is on the Dol Purnima and the other is on the death anniversary of Lalon) thousands of Bauls, Lalon devotees, and tourists from home and abroad come here. The fair attracts around 4–5 lakh people, including 15–20 foreigners per day. Although Lalon enthusiasts are found in almost all countries of the world, their number is comparatively higher in neighboring India (especially the West Bengal part)". This viewpoint is equally endorsed and extended by two other participants from the local community category. Their comments are following:

> "Chheuria is a small village. Every year, this village wears a festive hue on the occasion of Lalon Mela. Despite the regular gathering of numerous

people here, the locals are seldom disgruntled rather considerably more welcoming to the visitors. Even, during the fair, the streets are congested and everyday life is disrupted, yet the people have no complaints. Because we believe that most of the tourists discover our culture through Lalon or Lalon Mela and return here again due to their devotion to our Lalon culture."

"Lalon is an integral part of Kushtia. Lalon Mela has brought Kushtia to the attention of a large number of individuals. In an essence, Lalon is our brand ambassador. Believing this fact, we protect Lalon culture and invite tourists."

The participants from the tourist category expressed similar opinions and stated that they come to Kushtia solely to attend Lalon Mela. Aligning to this finding, most of the local community category participants claimed that this rural event helps to protect the cultural values and makes them responsible to preserve. While interviewing, the interviewer also found that the local residents are very sensitive to Lalon culture. According to Prothom Alo (2021), the lifestyle and music introduced by Lalonis is a subject of research at the international level. The Daily Star (2018) reported that in 2017 Oxford University Press, New York, USA published a book of translated songs of Lalon Shah with original Bangla versions. The book titled *City of Mirrors: Songs of Lalan Sai* was translated by the US scholar Dr. Carol Salomon, and edited by Keith E. Cantú." Besides, Lalon Music is being practiced in many countries and when the name "Lalon" is uttered, everyone remembers the name of Chheuria village of Kushtia district of Bangladesh with respect (Prothom Alo, 2021). In describing the sociocultural contribution of Lalon Mela, one local community participant also added that "centering on Lalon's shrine, an auditorium, academy, museum, folk music center, and library have been established in our village."

In terms of the economic contribution of Lalon Mela to the community, most of the participants in this research claimed that this rural event creates job opportunities for the locals, develops local business, generates income, and eventually increases the standard of living. A local community category participant argued that "although the Lalon Mela lasts for 2–3 days, the souvenir shops, food stalls, furniture, and musical instrument retailer outlets, etc. operate their business for a month. Thus, the fair generates seasonal employment opportunities for the locals". In a similar tone, the official from Lalon academy also added that "....as there is no sufficient parking facility for the tourists, the locals arrange a parking zone in a large field

60 Event Tourism and Sustainable Community Development

nearby and charge a little in exchange, which provides them with additional income during the fair". This finding was also recognized by the participants from the "Tourist" and "Tour Operator" categories. Both tourist category participants stated that they participate in the Mela, stay a couple of days here, and locally spend a lot for their food, accommodation, and transport purposes. In this regard, the tour operator category participant shared his views as follows:

> "...we know that tourism generates 10% of employment around the world. In the case of Lalon Mela, the phenomenon is no exception. Through this rural event tourism, locals can be benefited financially. As a service provider, locals can engage themselves in business, offer services to tourists need, earn money in exchange, and with this additional income they can enjoy a better living"

Focusing on the multiplier effect of tourism, the participant from the government official category commented that this rural event tourism (Lalon Mela) has immense potential to boost up the local economy.

4.5 CONCLUSION AND SOME POLICY GUIDELINES

This study shows us that a rural event or festival whether it is big or small can significantly contribute to the community development of a small rural area. "Lalon Mela" is a distinguished example of how traditional rural events can vitalize the community development process of a small village. The study proposed a way to evaluate the contribution of a rural event in rural community development. Thus, it observes the contribution from three different perspectives—social, cultural, and economic. In sociocultural terms "Lalon Mela" increases the community image by bringing national and international recognition, improves the standard of living, and enhances cultural values. In the case of the economic contribution, this event is creating different sorts of opportunities, which are contributing to the local economy. By commemorating the legendary philosopher Fakir Lalon Shah, this event also preserves and promotes the local culture.

This research indicates the importance of local events in community development. This research further demonstrates that the more involvement of the population and local suppliers in terms of the provision of services, food, beverages, and attractions will eventually bring greater economic benefits to the region. In this sense, by building partnerships with local

Rural Event Tourism and Community Development

operator, the organizer can bring about the best benefit for them. Organizers should also consider the possible negative effects caused by these events, such as traffic congestion, environmental pollutions. In terms of future investigation, this approach can be replicated in other festivals to see whether the contribution to developing the local community is similar or not.

KEYWORDS

- **rural event tourism**
- **community development**
- **case strategy**
- **developing country context**
- **Bangladesh**

REFERENCES

Ahmed, W.; Karim, A. Lalon Shah. In *Banglapedia: National Encyclopedia of Bangladesh*; Islam, S., Jamal, Ahmed, A., Eds., 2nd ed.; Asiatic Society of Bangladesh, 2012.

Arcodia, C.; Whitford, M. Festival Attendance and the Development of Social Capital. *J. Conv. Event Tour.* **2007,** *8* (2), 1–18.

Alves, H. M. B.; Cerro, A. M. C.; Martins, A. V. F. Impacts of Small Tourism Events on Rural Places. *J. Place Manage. Dev.* **2010,** *3* (1), 22–37.

Bangladesh Bureau of Statistics. *2017 Statistical Year Book Bangladesh*, 37th ed.; Statistics and Informatics Division, Ministry of Planning, Government of the People's Republic of Bangladesh: Dhaka, 2018.

Braun, V.; Clarke, V. Using Thematic Analysis in Psychology. *Qual. Res. Psychol* **2006,** *3* (2), 77–101.

Brennan-Horley, C.; Connell, J.; Gibson, C. The Parkes Elvis Revival Festival: Economic Development and Contested Place Identities in Rural Australia. *Geogr. Res.* **2007,** *45* (1), 71–84.

Butler, R.; Hall, C. M.; Jenkins, J., Eds. *Tourism and Recreation in Rural Areas*; John Wiley & Sons; Chichester, 1998.

Cameron, C. M. The Marketing of Tradition: The Value of Culture in American Life. *City Soc.* **1987,** *1* (2), 162–174.

Cater, E. Ecotourism in the Third World: Problems for Sustainable Tourism Development. *Tour. Manage.* **1993,** *14* (2), 85–90.

Cheer, J. M.; Cole, S.; Reeves, K. J.; Kato, K. Tourism and Is Landscapes: Cultural Realignment, Social-Ecological Resilience and Change. *Shima: Int. J. Res. Island Cult.* **2017,** *11* (1), 40–54.

Daniels, M. J.; Norman, W. C. Estimating the Economic Impacts of Seven Regular Sport Tourism Events. *J. Sport Tour.* **2003,** *8* (4), 214–222.

Denzin, N. K.; Lincoln Y. S. *Handbook of Qualitative Research*; Sage: Thousand Oaks, 1994.

Denzin, N. K.; Lincoln, Y. S. Introduction. In *The Sage Handbook of Qualitative Research*; Denzin, N. K.; Lincoln, Y. S., Eds., 4th ed.; Sage: Los Angeles, CA, 2011; pp. 1–19.

Flognfeldt, T. Impacts of Short-Time Visitors on Local Communities in the Mountain Areas of Southern Norway. *Int. J. Tour. Res.* **1999,** *1* (5), 359–373.

Fredline, E. Host and Guest Relations and Sport Tourism. *Sport in Soc.* **2005,** *8* (2), 263–279.

Fyall, A.; Jago, L. Sustainability in Sport & Tourism. *J. Sport Tour.* **2009,** *14* (2 and 3), 77–81.

Higham, J. E.; Ritchie, B. The Evolution of Festivals and Other Events in Rural Southern New Zealand. *Event Manage.* **2001,** *7* (1), 39–49.

Horne, W. R. Municipal Economic Development via Hallmark Tourist Events. *J. Tour. Stud.* **2000,** *11* (1), 30–36.

Janiskee, R. L.; Drews, P. L. Rural Festivals and Community Reimaging. In *Tourism and Recreation in Rural Areas*; Butler, R., Hall, C. M., Jenkins, J., Eds.; John Wiley & Sons: Chichester, 1998; pp 157–175. .

Jennings, G. R. Interviewing: A Focus on Qualitative Techniques. In *Tourism Research Methods: Integrating Theory with Practice*; Ritchie, B., Burns, P., Palmer, C., Eds.; CAB Publishing: Wallingford, 2004; pp. 99–117.

Jonsson, H. Mien Through Sports and Culture: Mobilizing Minority Identity in Thailand. *J. Anthropol. Museum Ethnogr* **2003,** *68* (3), 317–340.

Kotler, P.; Gertner, D.; Rein, I. & Haider, D. (2006), Marketing of Places, How to Achieve Long-Term Growth in Latin America and the Caribbean; Pearson Education: Sã Paulo, 2006.

Liu, Z. Sustainable Tourism Development: A Critique. *J. Sustain. Tour.* **2003,** *11* (6), 459–475.

McIntyre, G. *Sustainable Tourism Development: Guide for Local Planners*; World Tourism Organization (WTO), 1993.

O'Brien, D.; Chalip, L. Sport Events and Strategic Leveraging: Pushing Towards the Triple Bottom Line. In *Tourism Management: Analysis, Behavior and Strategy*; Woodside, A., Martin, D., Eds.; CAB International: Wallingford, Oxford, 2008; pp 318–338.

O'Sullivan, D.; Jackson, M. J. Festival Tourism: A Contributor to Sustainable Local Economic Development? *J. Sustain. Tour.* **2002,** *10* (4), 325–342.

Patton, M. Q. *Qualitative Evaluation and Research Methods*; Sage: Beverly Hills, CA, 1990.

Prothom Alo *From Sadhusang to Lalon Mela.* https://www.prothomalo.com/special-supplement (accessed 29 June 2021).

Quinn, B. Problematising 'Festival Tourism': Arts Festivals and Sustainable Development in Ireland. *J. Sustain. Tour.* **2006,** *14* (3), 288–306.

Rahman, M. S.-U.; Muneem, A. A.; Avi, M. A. R.; Sobhan, S. Can Rural Tourism Promote Sustainable Development Goals? Scoping Rural Tourism Prospects in Rustic Bangladesh. *Rajshahi Univ. J. Busi. Stud.* **2018,** *11* (1), 131–144.

Rao, V. Celebrations as Social Investments: Festival Expenditures, Unit Price Variation and Social Status in Rural India. *J. Dev. Stud.* **2001,** *38* (1), 71–97.

Ray, N. M.; McCain, G.; Davis, D.; Melin, T. L. Lewis and Clark and the Corps of Discovery: Re-Enactment Event Tourism as Authentic Heritage Travel. *Leisure Stud.* **2006,** *25* (4), 437–454.

Ritchie, B. W.; Burns, P.; Palmer, C., Eds. *Tourism Research Methods: Integrating Theory with Practice*; CABI: Wallingford, Oxfordshire, 2005.

Roberts, L.; Hall, D., Eds. *Rural Tourism and Recreation: Principles to Practice*; CAB International, 2001.

Skoda, U.; Lettmann, B., Eds. *India and Its Visual Cultures: Community, Class and Gender in a Symbolic Landscape*; SAGE Publishing India, 2017.

Suri, H. Purposeful Sampling in Qualitative Research Synthesis. *Qual. Res. J.* **2011,** *11* (2), 63–75.

The Daily Observer. *Lalon Mela Begins at Cheuria.* https://www.observerbd.com/2015/10/17/115894.php (accessed 12 June 2021).

The Daily Star. *Five-Day Lalon Mela Underway.* https://www.thedailystar.net/news/five-day-lalon-mela-underway (accessed 12 June 2021).

The Daily Star. *On City of Mirrors: Songs of LalanSãi.* https://www.thedailystar.net/literature/news/city-mirrors-songs-lalan-sai-1649209 (accessed 29 June 2021).

UNEP. *UNEP Annual Report* 2002. https://www.unep.org/resources/report/unep-annual-report-2002 (accessed 28 June 2021).

Veltri, F. R.; Miller, J. J.; Harris, A. Club Sport National Tournament: Economic Impact of a Small Event on a Mid-Size Community. *Recreat. Sports J.* **2009,** *33* (2), 119–128.

Walo, M.; Bull, A.; Breen, H. Achieving Economic Benefits at Local Events: A Case Study of a Local Sports Event. *Fest. Manage. Event Tour.* **1996,** *4* (3–4), 95–106.

WCED. *Our Common Future*; Oxford University Press: Oxford, 1987.

Wilson, R. The Economic Impact of Local Sport Events: Significant, Limited or Otherwise? A Case Study of Four Swimming Events. *Manag. Leisure* **2006,** *11* (1), 57–70.

Xie, P. F. Visitors' Perceptions of Authenticity at a Rural Heritage Festival: A Case Study. *Event Manage.* **2004,** *8* (3), 151–160.

Ziakas, V. Understanding an Event Portfolio: The Uncovering of Interrelationships, Synergies, and Leveraging Opportunities. *J. Policy Res. Tour. Leisure Events* **2010,** *2* (2), 144–164.

CHAPTER 5

Growth and Development of Catamaran: A New Luxury Tourism Demand

ANUKRATI SHARMA and SHRUTI ARORA

Department of Commerce and Management, University of Kota, Kota, Rajasthan, India

ABSTRACT

The vacationers of the 21st century are searching for unique opportunities and have different needs. Catamaran trips are becoming increasingly popular all around the world for their exclusive ambiance, delicious cuisine, and exceptional experience. Catamaran tourism has fostered an assortment of entertainment opportunities that are not the same as conventional beach tourism. The sound of the sea and the appealing gentle wind can take anyone to a new height and make them closer to the sea. Earlier maritime sailing was considered as a somewhat noble hobby. However, in the recent years, the world of yacht racing has been modernized by the emergence of hydrofoil-supported catamarans, identified as "foilers." Catamaran market is unquestionably the quickest developing segment of the enjoyment boat sector. Catamaran excursions feature fantastic deals for its consumers, which will undoubtedly make their trip a memorable one. The plan of a catamaran is such that it feels appealing and secure on the water and to not move during the trip. The trends observed in this tourism market include increased spending on boating activities, technological advancements, and a rise in cruising events. But, the growth of this market is controlled by challenges such as natural issues and unfavorable climate conditions.

Please note that few chapters were submitted during the peak of the pandemic. The long period of time to publish (due to supply chain and other issues) may have changed the perspectives presented in the chapter altogether.

Event Tourism and Sustainable Community Development: Advances, Effects, and Implications.
Ekta Dhariwal, Shruti Arora, Anukrati Sharma, Azizul Hassan (Eds.)
© 2024 Apple Academic Press, Inc. Co-published with CRC Press (Taylor & Francis)

Hence, the point of this study is to review the concept of catamarans as a new luxury type of tourism in demand through conceptual study. Likewise, the advancement and kinds or types of catamarans are discussed with various marketing strategies adopted for promoting catamaran tourism.

5.1 INTRODUCTION

Derived from a Tamil word *kattumara, catamaran is a multihulled boat and a buzzing word of tourism industry. Catamarans* were primarily formed by the fishing group of people "Paravas" in Tamil Nadu in the 17th century. The major characteristic of these boats was that they had two hulls that had a great deal of steadiness and stability when contrasted with other fishing boats of that time. This thought of two-hulled boats was taken on by the British and afterward made admired across the world. A catamaran (popularly known as "Sports Cat") looks somewhat like a sailboat but has a broad beam, two hulls, and a powerful engine that allows more incredible speed. Rolling adaptation of sailing, cruising, water sports, and campaigning, these activities have become a major tourist attraction. Catamarans, invented by Austronesia people, are now one of the important contributors in tourists' decision making when it comes to spending their rising disposable income. Catamaran market is undeniably the highest growing segment. Catamarans are designed for their use in different aspects, like sports, cruising, and passenger transport, and military. The design of catamarans differ based on the applicability or its purpose of usage. Often catamaran tours are confused with boat tours and cruising. A boat tour is a short trip taken in a small boat, whose duration is of a few hours. Cruising is all about sailing in large ships that have cabins allowing travelers to stay aboard. However, catamaran tour is a day activity. Catamaran tourism is a new concept, which entails the fact that a particular destination is attracting tourist only because of its catamaran included activities, like sailing and water sports. The particular destination is a pro in offering a different experience, and hence the evolution of catamaran tourism is visible. Indeed catamarans are preferred because of their broader structure, offering people more space and agility of movement. Some of the key destinations offering catamaran tourism are Europe (Greece, Croatia,

France, and Spain), followed by Turkey, the Asia Pacific (Thailand, Australia, and India).

A recent trend observed is that catamarans have become popular for their existence in sailboat racing, which again is a major tourist attraction. The (Great Cup) GC32 Racing Tour held across southern Europe draws awareness from people around the globe. Aimed at pro and owner–driver teams, (Great Cup) GC32 racing tours allow contestants to fight on a five-event circuit, thereby providing them with venues with optimum conditions to sail their catamarans. The future scope of this tourism is to examine and evaluate how catamaran tourism can be equipped as a sustainable tourism, for example by introducing solar-powered catamarans.

5.2 LITERATURE REVIEW

As indicated by Grand view research (April 2021), Global Industry Report, 2021–2028, the global leisure time boat market size was estimated at USD 41.08 billion in 2020. It is projected to grow at a compound yearly extension rate (CAGR) of 4.5% from 2021 to 2028. The intensifying discretionary cash flow of citizens and prospering tourism sector in the rising economies, such as Brazil and China, are some of the main factors escalating the market development. Similarly, the increasing participation of people in leisure and competitive boating activities around the world is expected to boost growth. Furthermore, technological improvements that lead to the launch and adoption of connected boats are expected to drive market expansion throughout the forecast period. Boat builders, engine manufacturers, free dealers, service providers, and equipment manufacturers all compete in this sector.

Entertaining boating activities are getting recognition among tourists resulting in the rising number of boating events and trade shows facilitated in different parts of the globe. The growth and development in aquatic and coastal tourism have drastically attracted tourists across Europe, North America, and Australia because of an increase in per capita income of people in these countries. Outboard boats and yachts are broadly utilized by boaters for individual boating activities across the world and the prototype is relied upon to carry on over the supposition time frame. As marine coastal areas around the world face the pressure of tourism growth, fuel and oil-based vehicles are causing oil infectivity into the sea. These boats also make sound, vibrate, and emit smoke which annoy the tourists and release carbon to the atmosphere, which is one of the reasons that cause global warming (Amaechi and Godstime, 2015). Additionally, the of boats is a significant source of marine contamination that can veil biotic sounds, disrupting effective transmission between guest and recipient, and can cause bodily, physiological, and behavioral changes in some marine types (Holmes et al., 2017). In this manner, electric motors and solar cell catamarans were designed as the tool for promoting sustainable tourism.

Nonetheless, COVID-19 has negatively affected the tourism area worldwide with complete restrictions forced on international travel. Varied swiftness of water, from the vibrant drama of waterfalls to the peaceful creep of glaciers, is appreciated by tourists who welcome its erosive and artistic sway on landscapes. The omnipresence of water in tourism provides for a wide range of activities on, in, or close to lakes, rivers, pool, canals, seas, and oceans. (Rhoden and Kaaristo, 2020). Rise in income has increased traveling and tourism activities, rolling the adoption of sailing, cruising, and water sports. In combination with these recreational activities, exploring new places and spending quality time with loved ones and friends without outside interference is fueling the global catamaran market size from 2018 to 2024 (Bhutani, 2018). Vacations on catamaran are perfect for families as well as couples or friends who have passion for cruising. Once life becomes too tiring, dull, and boring, catamaran excursion is a tremendous way to get back one's lost strength and passion (Moor, 2012). The initiatives performed with the help of governments from various countries to expand marine tourism have encouraged the market's growth. In the coming years, ideas such as boosting investments in tourism, developing infrastructure, and changing convention are predicted to have a favorable impact on the tourism business. Boaters use outboard boats and yachts for personal boating activities all over the world and the trends are likely to continue over the projection period (Grand view Research, April 2021).

5.3 CATAMARAN TOURISM INDUSTRY

Without doubt, the catamaran market is the best-ever emergent division of the recreational boat industry. The vast number of players in this market is one of its most distinguishing features. World Cat, Robertson & Caine, Fountaine Pajot, Catana Group, Lagoon, and Outremer Yachting are some of the leading players with a global presence and significant industry dominance. Multihulled watercrafts have two equivalent hulls of identical size that provide excellent stability. Catamarans come in smaller and larger sizes, each with distinctive characteristics. On board, there is a music, drinks, and yummy meals for everyone's enjoyment. Tourists love to see the dazzling surroundings and sometimes, old shipwrecks. Increased spending on boating activities, technical developments, impending product introductions, and an increase in racing and cruising events are all important trends in this sector.

However, constraints such as environmental issues, harsh weather conditions, and regulatory effect limit the market's growth (Business wire, May 2019). Catamarans were originally intended as fishing boats, but their use and significance have grown in recent years. While they are more common in Europe, they are also becoming increasingly popular in the United States because of their greater comfort, stability, safety, and speed than monohulls. The following factors that are expected to contribute to the growth of the recreational boat market are the following:

- Development in marine technology
- Expansion in the electric boat industry
- High level of participation in leisure boating activities

In fact, *"the Catamaran market revenue was 1308 Million USD in 2019, and will reach 1704 Million USD in 2025, with a CAGR of 4.5% during 2020-2025."* (WBOC Delmarva's News Leader, 2nd June 2021).

However, in the first two quarters of 2020, the entire supply chain was disrupted, with several industrial units closing and firms facing a labor crisis. The COVID-19 pandemic had an influence on exports and imports, resulting in a lack of boat-building equipment and subassemblies. As a result, new customers faced lengthy wait times as manufacturers focused their efforts on guaranteeing timely delivery of pending orders. Along with boat sales, revenue from services took a blow, as tiny third-party merchants were forced to close their doors due to the financial difficulties brought on by the lockdown restrictions. However, the progressive reopening of economies, along with long-term limitations on people movement, has resulted in a desire among individuals to engage in recreational activities. As a result, over the forecast period, the market is expected to recover slowly.

5.4 TYPES OF CATAMARAN

Catamarans are now accessible in an extensive range of sizes, ranging from a 14-foot (4.5-m) modest catamaran to a 100-foot (30.5 m) racing/luxury catamaran boat (Mauritius catamaran). In coastal seas, catamarans (also identified as catboats) have been utilized for fishing and transportation. They were modified for racing around the turn of the 19th century. Catamarans are now mostly used for day sailing and entertainment trips. Like, evolution does not mean just alteration in the usage but additionally in the layout and production of these boats. There are two fundamental design types of catamarans. They are the following:

1. **Pontoon Catamaran Boat:** A two-hulled boat made of fiber and fiberglass that can be used to explore freshwaters, lakes, rivers, backwaters, and the sea adjacent to tourism-related waterfronts. It is capable of dragging a water skater as well as in paragliding. It has a type of fishing rod that is employed in lakes and rivers. This boat is used for cruise by honeymooners, corporate clients, and small families. In seawater, it has the capacity to go up to 45 miles. It is small and compact.

2. **Water-Plane Area (Small) Catamaran Boat with Twin Hulls (SWATH):** This is an upgraded variant of the catamaran, which is currently employed as cruise vessels in international tourism. Because it is durable enough to float in deep waters, it is elegant with luxury living space cabins. Its primary purpose is to maintain balance in places of the sea where the tides are erratic. As a result, SWATHs are available in medium-to-big sizes. Alaska, Canada, and Norway are home to the famed SWATH cruise boats. SWATH boats are also utilized as carriers, rescue boats, and by coast guards in the military and navy. They are favored because of their ability to balance hundreds of passengers at once.

In present times, all types of catamarans are motorized and engine-powered making them even more consistent than what they used to be before. Some of the main types of catamarans are as follows:

1. **Cruise Catamarans:** These ferries are also known as luxury catamarans or ferry catamarans since they provide the highest level of comfort to passengers. These catamarans operate within a country rather than across international borders.

2. **Sailing Catamarans:** This is a different type and utility of catamaran that is utilized for recreational purposes by people who desire to live like a sailor. Catamarans that are utilized as yachts are another name for them.

5.5 MARKETING STRATEGIES FOR CATAMARAN TOURISM

When an organization operates in market with many competitors, it is crucial to espouse an effective marketing plan or strategy. Today, personalization and customization in travel are among the growing trends in the industry. Catamaran tourism is more private, like with only family, couples, and friends, and it is an ideal outing during or after the pandemic. The demands for catamarans are also growing due to the services offered such as prewedding shoots, private parties, or experiencing deep sea fishing. Vacation time is especially meant to be enjoyed. After the COVID-19 pandemic, many people still look forward to have a unique and memorable experience, so, this is a good time to think of attractive promotions and marketing strategies. It is the time to design pull marketing strategy and reach out to potential tourists in new and creative ways.

Source: (Compiled by Authors) Sharma and Arora (2021).

It takes some time or even years for a business to reach its growth stage and achieve its targets. But with a sturdy or well-built marketing strategy, businesses can exceed their target and achieve success. Lastly, the tourism industry is looking up after months of a slump due to COVID-19 pandemic and the major applications of catamaran that can help this sector are as follows:

- Sport
- Cruising
- Ocean racing
- Passenger transport

Because there are so many boating and yachting companies that offer fantastic tours and activities, standing out with an efficient marketing strategy

72 Event Tourism and Sustainable Community Development

that is well-planned and readily reaches the target demographic may help the business run successfully. The growth of luxury tourism is outpacing that of general tourism.

5.6 CHALLENGES FOR SUSTAINABLE DEVELOPMENT OF CATAMARAN TOURISM

The main challenges found as a part for sustainable development of catamaran tourism in this study are the following:

1. Seasonality of demand.
2. Added value of offered services is low.
3. Sometimes outdated marketing approaches cause limited visibility of current offer.
4. Limited economic and societal returns for home communities.
5. High dependency on specific groups of visitors.
6. Proper monitoring mechanism to ensure that the boats or cruise do not discharge wastes into the water.
7. High taxation in few places is impeding the growth of catamaran tourism.
8. Rise in pollution levels and lack of port base are major challenges to growth.
9. Noise produced by cruise or boats or ships' engines, generators, and bearings can cause marine species such as whales to accidentally collide with vessels or abandon their natural habitat.

5.7 CONCLUSIONS

Even though catamaran tourism is accessible in several countries and has steadily been growing, COVID-19 pandemic had a huge impact on this market. Post COVID-19, a strong recovery is possible, providing an increase in consumer expenditure as a solo traveler or travel with limited number of people with a steady increase in extravagance lifestyle and leisure tour expenses. In this tech-driven generation, online processes have become an essential marketing tool for both big and small businesses. If there is no website or online information, chances may increase in missing out on a number of enormous opportunities for catamaran business. Social media such as Facebook, Instagram, or Twitter are digital platform tools where one can showcase the tour activities. Providing customers with a great sailing experience is good for repeat business. The new era of luxury tourism requires brands to continuously observe tourist expectations and acclimatize consequently. In other words, new lavishness is real time.

KEYWORDS

- **catamaran**
- **tourism**
- **boats**
- **marketing strategy**
- **luxury**

REFERENCES

Amaechi J. O.; Godstime T. C. Automotive Exhausts Emissions and Its Implications for Environmental Sustainability. *Int. Adv. Acad. Res. Eng.* **2015,** *1* (2), 1–11.

Bhutani A. Catamarans Market Size by Product (Sailing Catamarans [Leisure, Commercial], Powered Catamarans [Leisure, Commercial, Defense]), Industry Analysis Report, Regional Outlook, Growth Potential, Price Trends, Competitive Market Share & Forecast, 2018–2024, 2018. https://www.gminsights.com/industry-analysis/catamarans-market (accessed on 15 June 2021).

Business Wire. Global Catamaran (Multihull) Market: Industry Analysis & Outlook (2019–2023)—ResearchAndMarkets.com, 2019. https://www.businesswire.com/news/home/20190501006115/en/Global-Catamaran-Multihull-Market-Industry-Analysis-Outlook-2019-2023---ResearchAndMarkets.com. (accessed on 10 July 2021).

Grand View Research. Leisure Boat Market Size, Share & Trends Analysis Report by Type (New Leisure Boat, Used Leisure Boat, Monitoring Equipment), By Region (North America, Europe, Asia Pacific, South America, Middle East & Africa), And Segment Forecasts, 2021—2028, 2021. https://www.grandviewresearch.com/industry-analysis/global-leisure-boat-market (accessed 12 June 2021).

Holmes, L. J.; McWilliam, J.; Ferrari, M. C. O.; Maccormick, M. I. Juvenile Damselfish Are Affected But Desensitize to Small Motor Boat Noise. *J. Exp. Marine Biol. Ecol.* **2017,** *494,* 63–68.

Mauritius Catamaran—A Unique Cruising Experience. http://mauritiuscatamaran.com/about-catamarans.html (accessed on 4 August 2021).

Moor, R. Catamaran Tours Attract Adventurers and Families Alike, 2012. https://www.tourism-review.com/travel-tourism-magazine-catamaran-tours-for-the-love-of-sailing-article1868 (accessed on 15 June 2021).

Rhoden, S.; Kaaristo, M. Liquidness: Conceptualising Water within Boating Tourism. *Ann. Res.* **2020**, *81*. https://doi.org/10.1016/j.annals.2019.102854

WBOC Delmarva's News Leader, 2nd June 2021. https://www.wboc.com/story/44013417/catamaran-market-2021-2025-worldwide-industry-growing-at-a-cagr-of-45-and-industry-size-will-reach-1704-million-usd-in-2025 (accessed on 4 August 2021).

CHAPTER 6

Role and Importance of Event Tourism in Economic and Social Development

JEETESH KUMAR[1,2,3] and FARHAD NAZIR[4,5]

[1]*School of Hospitality, Tourism & Events, Taylor's University, Malaysia*

[2]*Centre for Research and Innovation in Tourism (CRiT), Taylor's University, Malaysia*

[3]*Sustainable Tourism Impact Lab, Taylor's University, Malaysia*

[4]*Institute of Cultural Heritage, Tourism, and Hospitality Management, University of Swat, Pakistan*

[5]*Department of Geography and Tourism, University of Coimbra, Portugal*

ABSTRACT

Tourism is travel for recreation and leisure and refers to providing services to achieve this goal. Events are an essential part of tourism, an inseparable part of human society, and essential motivators of tourism, which plays a more significant role in developing a host destination. The roles and impacts of events are well documented in tourism-related literature. Indeed, many countries have used events to gain legitimacy and reputation, highlight their achievements, support trade and tourists, or assist in the process of opening their countries to global influences. Events can help promote, position, and brand it, contributing to a more favorable perception as a potential tourist destination. For many destinations, events have provided comprehensive public attention through extensive media coverage. Sociocultural benefits of events on the local community, such as increased activity associated with the event and the strengthening of local values and traditions, are also significant.

Please note that few chapters were submitted during the peak of the pandemic. The long period of time to publish (due to supply chain and other issues) may have changed the perspectives presented in the chapter altogether.

Event Tourism and Sustainable Community Development: Advances, Effects, and Implications.
Ekta Dhariwal, Shruti Arora, Anukrati Sharma, Azizul Hassan (Eds.)
© 2024 Apple Academic Press, Inc. Co-published with CRC Press (Taylor & Francis)

The present study has addressed the considerate role of event tourism in socioeconomic development through archival analysis of the prior literature. Doing so has enabled the researchers to unveil the theoretical insights that prevailed in the happenings of event tourism at a specific destination. Additionally, several recommendations have also been drawn for shareholders of the event tourism.

6.1 INTRODUCTION

Events tourism shares a unique prospective outcome of economic development within a society or country in general (Frost and Frost, 2020; Kelly and Fairley, 2018; Lee, 2006; Sant et al., 2019). To contends the vastness of events tourism in monetary, communal, and environmental pros and cons. It is imperative to comprehend the etymology of events and tourism. Historically, events have been devised as ceremonies or celebrations by the societies, marked to specific dates and times having prevailed in religion, culture, and variation in climatic phases (Mair, 2009). The progressive development of humanity throughout history has further increased the numbers and celebrations charm of these events. In addition, the disparity in the racial classes of humanity has abundantly subsidized the events, displaying the national and cultural identities towards the outer global stage. On a similar avenue, traveling for trade and business exchange has been another major factor for events in the industry, allowing the trade and business representatives to organize trade shows and exhibitions of business. In the true essence, doing so mobilized the domestic and international inhabitants, eventually framing itself into an industry depending upon size and types of events (Mair, 2009). In contemporary times, the digitalization milieu has further paved for developing the event industry, providing temporary leisure escapes to the employed class. Similarly, tourism impermanent mobility of individuals or groups has engrained roots in medieval times under the hegemonic influence of religion, politics, education, and trade. Development paradigms have equally renovated the tourism to an industry and later denoting it as a compulsory supportive entity for the economic sustenance on the national, regional, and global stage.

To understand the blend of events and tourism, it is imperious to understand the semblances among these, equally motivating the mobilization of tourists. To this end, the facilitation or service sector has witnessed a great deal of development, satiating the expectations of incoming attendees, and tourists to these events. Such amalgamation has resulted in events and tourism as events tourism, categorically addressing the theoretical, managerial, and statistical dimensions. Events tourism is developing and marketing planned events as tourist attractions, catalysts, animators, image-makers, and place marketers (Jafari and Xiao, 2016, p. 352). In addition to these supply and demand-side definitions, Getz (2012) contends that tourism is inclined to travel by purposeful and casual event tourists to attend any specific event at a destination. Therefore, the present study has addressed the considerate role of event tourism in socioeconomic development through archival analysis of the prior literature. Doing so has enabled the researchers to unveil the theoretical insights that prevailed in the happenings of event tourism at a specific destination. Additionally, several recommendations have also been drawn for shareholders of the event tourism.

6.2 EVENT TOURISM: A SYNERGETIC RELATIONSHIP OF TOURISM AND BUSINESS

Considering the global economic status, there has been an essential inclusion of monetary factors while catering for the influx of tourists at a destination (Lee et al., 2017). Such inclusive patterns have linked the tourism and business sector of events eventually titled event tourism. Theoretically, the blend of event and tourism has been contested multiple times, equally highlighting the socioeconomic and socioenvironmental dimensions. However, Getz (2008) offered a very simplistic and understandable approach and presented event tourism. The model of event tourism and elaborating the subdimensions bridged together are shown in Figure 6.1.

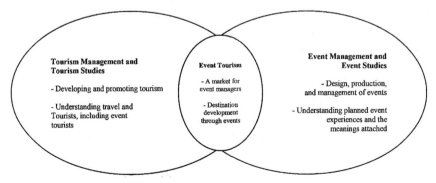

FIGURE 6.1 Event tourism model.
Source: Adapted from Getz (2008).

Such a synergetic relationship has been viewed as an opportunity by the shareholders of the industrial side of tourism and focused their attention on the development and investment in this market. Moreover, social media has further romanticized and eased event tourism in a globalized and digitally contracting arena. Pertinent to mention the Destination Management Organizations' (DMO) involvement in entwining event tourism through innovative business models and imprints of social media has become common in several countries (Mariani et al., 2016; Pino et al., 2019). Before this, it is imperative to understand the typologies and classification of event. As for the stakeholders, the variety and diversified nature of events in the globalized world have made it quite hard to understand its multidimensions. The events can be at a fundamental level based on size and limitations, maybe segregated into four main types (Getz, 2008, p. 407).

i. Mega Events.
ii. Major Events.
iii. Hallmark Events.
iv. Local/Domestic Events.

Mega-events are the largest and widely awaited events in the world. Their global recognition, prestige, identity, and broader economic and social impacts have been a keen reason for the national and regional stakeholders to participate and host them (Getz, 2008, 2012; Hall, 1992; Hiller, 1998). Urban regeneration has been witnessed as a significant outcome resulting from hosting such large-scale events (Sánchez and Broudehoux, 2013). Hosting such mega-events, including Olympics, FIFA, IIFA, Winter Olympics, Commonwealth Games, Asian Games, ICC Cricket World Cup, has amazingly developed the infrastructure of underdeveloped territories and slums conditional to community participation through collaboration. In the context of event tourism, the potential arrival and spending of domestic and inbound tourists have been a lucrative market for the Small Medium Enterprises (SMEs) and private sector to invest and excel.

Second, to this more significant type, significant events like the mega-events differentiate in the number of global attentions, media coverage, and the number of visitors, including Golf Championships, Women Rugby World Cup. Also, the geographical organizing of such events and participating limitations varies compared to large-scaled mega-events.

Hallmark events ranking at third are the types of events having a place attachment and distinctive program quality, including Rio Carnival Festival Brazil, Wimbledon Tennis Championship, Tour De France, and Bull Race

Spain. They may be any sporting or social event in a city and famed world-wide due to the quality of experience. Lastly, the local events are the ones that are organized on a domestic level and targeted for local audiences as well. Besides this typology of events and their importance in event tourism, another classification made based on apparent outlook and form. Getz (2008) has divided these forms of events as

i.   Cultural Celebrations,
ii. Political and State Events,
iii. Arts and Entertainment,
iv. Business and Trade Events,
v.   Educational and Scientific Events,
vi. Sports/Recreational Events,
vii. Private Events.

Among the forms above, the business and trade events or MICE (Meetings Incentives Conferences Exhibitions) and sporting events have been the significant chunk of event tourism, contributing visibly to economic and social development. However, the scope of event tourism has been inconsistent expansion, including sporting events, cultural events, and ceremonies. Purposeful development of destinations has been carried out in many countries regarding event tourism. To this end, certain countries have targeted specific events like Formula One Car racing in Malaysia, tour de France Cycling competition, Carnival Festival Brazil, and Shandur Polo Festival Pakistan.

6.3   DIRECT AND INDIRECT BUSINESS ASSOCIATED WITH TOURISM INDUSTRY—EVENT TOURISM

No doubt, event tourism through multiplier effect has an impact on the business sector, directly and indirectly, eventually channeling large sum of revenue in the national economy (Auld and McArthur, 2003; Hall, 1992; Hiller, 1998; Lee, 2006; Roche et al., 2013). The hospitality sector being beneficiary of direct and, up to some extent, indirect tourism business has witnessed a great deal of development, particularly in the last two decades. To the end of the direct and indirect business, prior consideration of the direct and indirect economic impacts is essential to be understood. Direct economic impacts denote the new money or new spending injected in the economy only due to particular business events (Kumar and Hussain, 2014), while indirect economic impacts represent the goods and services that tourism companies purchase from their suppliers, forming the tourism supply chain (Vellas, 2011). Other ancillary and backend businesses being indirect beneficiaries have also been entirely built-in event tourism. These intermediaries have been at the sole disposal of the demand side of tourism supply and frequently modify the nature of product and services consumed by the users. The large influx of tourists at an event tourist destination has been a profound source of activation of numerous frontline and backend industries. In addition, the entrepreneurship sector has also been observed to hook their financial share from the tourism cycle of event tourism. The entrepreneurial system and its efficacy have been determined as a major reason for the economic performance and sustenance of activity of event tourism (Spilling, 1996). Spilling (1996) analyzed the industrial changes after the 1994 Olympic Winter Games in Lillehammer, Norway. It revealed a series of failures, successes, and crises behind the curtain of successful gaming events and victories in a very complex entrepreneurial system. The completeness of this system is conditional to the economic growth of event tourism and postevent economic development.

6.4 COMMUNITY DEVELOPMENT THROUGH EVENT TOURISM

It is safe to say that event tourism has been a noticeable and apparent reason for community development. Generating employment, building infrastructure, cultural recognition, and opportunities for small-medium enterprises have been visible positive factors equally enhancing the socioeconomic graph of communities within an event tourist destination (Williams et al., 1995). In addition to these blended impacts of event tourism on the host community. Even though certain demerits and consequences during event tourism may be intensely focused while developing any event tourist destination, economic drainage, cultural abuse, and disturbance in daily social activities remained significant negative aspects of events tourism. The community has been quite aware of negative consequences and eager to collaborate with stakeholders, eventually making event tourism more inclusive and sustainable (Jackson, 2008). Community exclusion in developing and managerial phases may worsen the routine activities of tourists presenting a confronting situation with the host community by creating cultural distance and cultural shock.

6.4.1 ECONOMIC BENEFITS

Economic benefits for the host community in the existing global competition of event tourism may not be overlooked and neglected. DMOs and SMEs have injected huge investments and flow of capital in developing the stage for event tourism and extraction of enough revenue for the residing host populace. Return on Investment has been expected on a more increased level, specifically organizing mega-events including Olympics, FIFA, Winter Olympics, Commonwealth Games, and cost-benefit analysis before organizing events (Burgan and Mules, 2001; Hodur and Leistritz, 2006; Lee, 2006). It has been observed that the financial status of the host community has come across proactive progress, specifically in the postevent. The activities while the preparations and setting the stage for event tourism have also supported the financial conditions of the host community.

Moreover, specific (community) inclusive economic models have also been generated theoretically to adequately discuss the economic transactions during the ongoing event tourism (Roche et al., 2013). The MICE sector alone has been primarily developed and innovated at the corporate and business sectors, presenting a rivalry among countries to arrange and host events. To this end, though, comprehensive sustainable event marketing has been offered as an adaptative strategy to cope with the environmental and sustainability issues faced by the more extensive scale development of the event tourism industry (Bathing and Lai, 2017; Tinnish and Mangal, 2012). Developed countries have rapidly expanded the cityscapes through urban regeneration to have a more highlighted appearance among the global market. The sustainability concern may not be overlooked or neglected for the sole sake of economic valuation to the host community due to event tourism. Embarking on the same, event tourism has also sufficiently contributed to the economic up-grading of host community through revenue channelization at SME level and employments creation (Lamont and Dowell, 2008; Xie and Gu, 2015). In sum, event tourism is an affected typology of tourism to focus on and invest in, conditional to sustainability and a sense of responsiveness mutually beneficial for the host community's monetary, social, and environmental needs.

6.4.2 SOCIAL BENEFITS

Despite the attractive and lucrative outlook and results of event tourism on financial avenues, the social benefits and detriments prevailed. In contrast, the activities of event tourism have been a contested topic predominantly by anthropologists and social scientists. Additionally, in a more contracted global arena, social concerns have been side by side corroborated and, on several occasions, more valued and considered. Event tourism, in this case, pools up peoples from diverse cultures and ethnicities, shaping a fragmented milieu. Consolidation, harmony, and holism have been argued as the most critical situation during the happenings. Holism is the most compulsory critical situation during such events (Hall, 1992, p. 67). The social impacts have also been described very briefly as the changes in the standard of living of residents due to the celebration of such an event (Parra et al., 2017). On similar grounds, some severe attitudinal perspective of the host community prevails predominantly in the occurrence of any antisocial behavior, undermining all the positive social impacts an event tourism stage can provide (Deery and Jago, 2010).

Interestingly, understanding and considering the host community's culture has been argued as deemed necessary for the stakeholders of event tourism, enabling them to better plan for organizing and managing ongoing (Pavluković et al., 2017). Similarly, the perception of the host community is equally contested as necessary up to the extent that hosting of events has been considered conditional to the insights of locals (Yao and Schwarz, 2018). Moreover, studies have addressed the social impacts of events tourism and policymaking at a very minute level (Wallstam et al., 2020). Above all, in the current global stage, having more inclination toward the social impacts, event tourism has to have specific possible justifications and verifications. As the peoples are globally becoming more connected, social rights and privileges are considered more important than the financial impacts.

6.5 EVENT TOURISM AND INCLUSIVE DEVELOPMENT: GUIDELINES FROM SDGs

There has been a worldwide notion and plan to make tourism activities more inclusive and resilient, predominantly for the host community. Studies reflect that inclusive tourism growth and its models are presented to let the policymakers know this needed aspect to be heeded (Bakker, 2019; Scheyvens and Biddulph, 2018). Bakker (2019, p. 10) has posed the Tourism-Driven Inclusive Growth Diagnostic (T-DIGD) model and elaborated three essentials of inclusive growth strategy, (i) growth of tourism opportunities; (ii) equal access to tourism opportunities; and (iii) equal outcome of tourism opportunities. More specifically, the updated manifesto of Millennium Development Goals MDGs i.e. the Sustainable Development Goals SDGs 2015 have provided some guidelines that may be viable and adaptive for event tourism. SDG # 1 (No Poverty), #08(Decent Work and Economic Growth) and #11(Sustainable Cities and Communities), # 17(Partnership for

Role and Importance of Event Tourism in Economic and Social Development 83

Goals), and subtargets may be a foundational one to be focused on. Literature has contended the inclusive guidelines and strategies from the agenda of SDGs 2030 to develop tourism (Boluk et al., 2019; Hall, 2019; Scheyvens and Biddulph, 2018; Seraphin and Gowreesunkar, 2021; Tham et al., 2020). More fundamentally, in event tourism, a collaboration between the stakeholders or SDG # 17 has been corroborated as the sine qua noncondition for attaining sustainability (Seraphin and Gowreesunkar, 2021).

6.6 CONCLUSION AND RECOMMENDATIONS

The merger of business and tourism in the globalized milieu has introduced events tourism in the industrial and academic discourse. Of course, peoples' mobility has further impacted event tourism to have visible development and improvements. Besides the notable mega event of Olympics, FIFA, Winter Olympics, Commonwealth Games, the MICE sector alone has hatched the attention and investment of different levels of investors from SMEs to private and public sectors. Pertinent to discuss the preevent and postevent development has obliged the state actors to participate in the bidding and nominations draws. Cities have seen unmatchable transformation due to the tangible and intangible development for the stage and hosting of event tourism. On the side of human resource, event tourism has provided scores of employment slots as well.

Further charisma has been provided by the intention of regional and international sponsors to participate in the marketing campaigns actively. Several countries have seen this opportunity to promote their destinations and industrial products to the cross-bordered tourists and clients. Besides this, event tourism's occurrences also have another player—community, less theorized, and emphasized. However, considering the global appeal and stress for the social inclusiveness, stakeholders of event tourism have been quite alarmed and active about the potential social impacts of event tourism. Furthermore, the ethnocentric approach and even the riots and violence may erupt while the event tourism activities due to community participation and allocation of shares in the financial earnings. And in the postpandemic era, still, there is a long way to achieve a feasible and absorbing environment during the stage of event tourism. In addition, class structure and pre-eminence rooted in the society have been another barrier to this. To cope with these challenges of event tourism, the agenda of SDGs seems to have a credible answer and solution. The current study has corroborated this challenge and prevailing situations of event tourism through the archival analysis of secondary data.

For industries, the findings of this study imply that almost all the organizational and managerial plans may be executed with prior discussion with the local community. Even the decision-making process has to be mutually sketched with the consent of the local populace. For academia, the segment of social impacts of event tourism may be recognized as an individual subject or any diploma or crash course that may be useful for the graduates. Institutionally, this study is a blueprint for the state actors and players to review their policies and frame the new ones keeping in view the transitional appearance of event tourism. Deviation from the conventional approach in dealing with the event tourist at the state level may be another adaptative and proactive strategy. Above all, this study has only covered the secondary data for the archival analysis, leading to this scholarship's limitation. However, in the future, studies may be carried out to emphasize the analysis of primary data on the sole basis or in a mixed-method approach. This study reflects the sound argument that such studies may unveil some new perspectives over the issue under consideration.

KEYWORDS

- **event tourism**
- **economic**
- **social**
- **community development**

REFERENCES

Auld, T.; McArthur, S. Does Event-Driven Tourism Provide Economic Benefits? A Case Study from the Manawatu Region of New Zealand. *Tour. Econ.* **2003,** *9* (2), 191–201. https://doi.org/10.5367/000000003101298358

Bakker, M. A Conceptual Framework for Identifying the Binding Constraints to Tourism-Driven Inclusive Growth. *Tour. Plan. Dev.* **2019,** *16* (5), 575–590. https://doi.org/10.1080/21568316.2018.1541817

Boluk, K. A.; Cavaliere, C. T.; Higgins-Desbiolles, F. A Critical Framework for Interrogating the United Nations Sustainable Development Goals 2030 Agenda in Tourism. *J. Sustain. Tour.* **2019,** *27* (7), 847–864. https://doi.org/10.1080/09669582.2019.1619748

Buathong, K.; Lai, P.-C. Perceived Attributes of Event Sustainability in the MICE Industry in Thailand: A Viewpoint from Governmental, Academic, Venue and Practitioner. *Sustainability* **2017,** *9* (7). https://doi.org/10.3390/su9071151

Burgan, B.; Mules, T. Reconciling Cost—Benefit and Economic Impact Assessment for Event Tourism. *Tour. Econ.* **2001,** *7* (4), 321–330. https://doi.org/10.5367/000000001101297892

Deery, M.; Jago, L. Social Impacts of Events and the Role of Anti-Social Behaviour. *Int. J. Event Fest. Manage* **2010,** *1* (1), 8–28. https://doi.org/10.1108/17852951011029289

Frost, W.; Frost, J. Events and Tourism. In *The Routledge Handbook of Events*. Routledge, 2020; pp 76–92.

Getz, D. Event Tourism: Definition, Evolution, and Research. *Tour. Manage.* **2008,** *29* (3), 403–428. https://doi.org/10.1016/j.tourman.2007.07.017

Getz, D. Event Studies: Discourses and Future Directions. *Event Manage.* **2012,** *16* (2), 171–187.

Hall, C. M. Adventure, Sport and Health Tourism. *Special Interest Tour.* **1992,** 141–158. CABDirect. Retrieved from CABDirect.

Hall, C. M. Constructing Sustainable Tourism Development: The 2030 Agenda and the Managerial Ecology of Sustainable Tourism. *J. Sustain. Tour.* **2019,** *27* (7), 1044–1060. https://doi.org/10.1080/09669582.2018.1560456

Hiller, H. H. Assessing the Impact of Mega-Events: A Linkage Model. *Curr. Iss. Tour* **1998,** *1* (1), 47–57. https://doi.org/10.1080/13683509808667832

Hodur, N. M.; Leistritz, F. L. Estimating the Economic Impact of Event Tourism. *J. Conv. Event Tour.* **2006,** *8* (4), 63–79. https://doi.org/10.1300/J452v08n04_05

Jackson, L. A. Residents' Perceptions of the Impacts of Special Event Tourism. *J. Place Manage. Dev.* **2008,** *1* (3), 240–255. https://doi.org/10.1108/17538330810911244

Jafari, J.; Xiao, H. *Encyclopedia of Tourism*. Springer International Publishing. https://books.google.com.pk/books?id=ELmLngEACAAJ

Kelly, D. M.; Fairley, S. What About the Event? How Do Tourism Leveraging Strategies Affect Small-Scale Events? *Tour. Manage.* **2018,** *64*, 335–345. https://doi.org/10.1016/j.tourman.2017.09.009

Kumar, J.; Hussain, K. A Review of Assessing the Economic Impact of Business Tourism: Issues and Approaches. *Int. J. Hospital. Tour. Syst.* **2014,** *7* (2), 49–55.

Lamont, M.; Dowell, R. A Process Model of Small and Medium Enterprise Sponsorship of Regional Sport Tourism Events. *J. Vacation Market.* **2008,** *14* (3), 253–266. https://doi.org/10.1177/1356766708090586

Lee, C.-K.; Mjelde, J. W.; Kwon, Y. J. Estimating the Economic Impact of a Mega-Event on Host and Neighbouring Regions. *Leisure Stud.* **2017,** *36* (1), 138–152. https://doi.org/10.1080/02614367.2015.1040828

Lee, M. J. Analytical Reflections on the Economic Impact Assessment of Conventions and Special Events. *J. Conv. Event Tour.* **2006,** *8* (3), 71–85. https://doi.org/10.1300/J452v08n03_04

Mair, J. The Events Industry: The Employment Context. *People and Work in Events and Conventions: A Research Perspective* **2009,** 3–16.

Mariani, M. M.; Di Felice, M.; Mura, M. Facebook as a Destination Marketing Tool: Evidence from Italian Regional Destination Management Organisations. *Tour. Manage.* **2016,** *54*, 321–343. https://doi.org/10.1016/j.tourman.2015.12.008

Parra, D.; Calabuig, F.; Núñez, J.; Crespo, J. The Relevance of the Social Impact of Sports Events in the Context of Public Financing of Sport. En: *Sport Entrepreneurship and Innovation*; Ratten, V., Ferreira, J. J., Eds.; 2017; pp 118–141.

Pavluković, V.; Armenski, T.; Alcántara-Pilar, J. M. Social Impacts of Music Festivals: Does Culture Impact Locals' Attitude Toward Events in Serbia and Hungary? *Tour. Manage.* **2017,** *63,* 42–53. https://doi.org/10.1016/j.tourman.2017.06.006

Pino, G.; Peluso, A. M.; Del Vecchio, P.; Ndou, V.; Passiante, G.; Guido, G. A Methodological Framework to Assess Social Media Strategies of Event and Destination Management Organisations. *J. Hospital. Market. Manage.* **2019,** *28* (2), 189–216. https://doi.org/10.1080/19368623.2018.1516590

Roche, S.; Spake, D. F.; Joseph, M. A Model of Sporting Event Tourism as Economic Development. *Sport Busi. Manage.* **2013,** *3* (2), 147–157. https://doi.org/10.1108/20426781311325078

Sánchez, F.; Broudehoux, A.-M. Mega-Events and Urban Regeneration in Rio de Janeiro: Planning in a State of Emergency. *Int. J. Urban Sustain. Dev.* **2013,** *5* (2), 132–153. https://doi.org/10.1080/19463138.2013.839450

Sant, S.-L.; Misener, L.; Mason, D. S. Leveraging Sport Events for Tourism Gain in Host Cities: A Regime Perspective. *J. Sport Tour.* **2019,** *23* (4), 203–223. https://doi.org/10.1080/14775085.2019.1711444

Scheyvens, R.; Biddulph, R. Inclusive Tourism Development. *Tour. Geogr.* **2018,** *20* (4), 589–609. https://doi.org/10.1080/14616688.2017.1381985

Seraphin, H.; Gowreesunkar, V. Tourism: How to Achieve the Sustainable Development Goals? *Worldwide Hospital. Tour. Themes* (ahead-of-print). https://doi.org/10.1108/WHATT-08-2020-0086

Spilling, O. R. The Entrepreneurial System: On Entrepreneurship in the Context of a Mega-Event. *Entrepreneurship New Firm Dev.* **1996,** *36* (1), 91–103. https://doi.org/10.1016/0148-2963(95)00166-2

Tham, A.; Ruhanen, L.; Raciti, M. Tourism with and by Indigenous and Ethnic Communities in the Asia Pacific Region: A Bricolage of People, Places and Partnerships. *J. Herit. Tour.* **2020,** *15* (3), 243–248. https://doi.org/10.1080/1743873X.2020.1751647

Tinnish, S. M.; Mangal, S. M. Sustainable Event Marketing in the MICE Industry: A Theoretical Framework. *J. Conv. Event Tour.* **2012,** *13* (4), 227–249. https://doi.org/10.1080/15470148.2012.731850

Vellas, F. *The Indirect Impact of Tourism: An Economic Analysis.* Presented at the Third Meeting of T20 Tourism Ministers. Paris, France, 2011.

Wallstam, M.; Ioannides, D.; Pettersson, R. Evaluating the Social Impacts of Events: In Search of Unified Indicators for Effective Policymaking. *J. Policy Res. Tour. Leisure Events* **2020,** *12* (2), 122–141. https://doi.org/10.1080/19407963.2018.1515214

Williams, P. W.; Hainsworth, D.; Dossa, K. B. Community Development and Special Event Tourism: The Men's World Cup of Skiing at Whistler, British Columbia. *J. Tourism Stud.* **1995,** *6* (2), 11–20. CABDirect. Retrieved from CABDirect.

Xie, P. F.; Gu, K. The Changing Urban Morphology: Waterfront Redevelopment and Event Tourism in New Zealand. *Tour. Manage. Persp.* **2015,** *15,* 105–114. https://doi.org/10.1016/j.tmp.2015.05.001

Yao, Q.; Schwarz, E. C. Impacts and Implications of an Annual Major Sport Event: A Host Community Perspective. *J. Destination Market. Manage.* **2018,** *8,* 161–169. https://doi.org/10.1016/j.jdmm.2017.02.007

CHAPTER 7

The Terror, the Spectacle, and the Worker: The Role of Security Guards in the Organization of Mega Events and Festivals

MAXIMILIANO E. KORSTANJE

Department of Economics, University of Palermo, Buenos Aires, Argentina

ABSTRACT

Terrorism often targets leisure spots and tourist destinations because army forces and police are not taking a direct intervention in these pleasurable spaces. Tourists feel disgusted when they are subjected to countless obtrusive controls. Meanwhile, security officers play a leading role in mediating with foreign tourists while caring for them . Unfortunately, they are overexploited or subjected to indignant working conditions. As Professor Howie puts it, this happens because global capitalism expands according to the power of consumers, creating, in this way, some material asymmetries. The most important agents of capitalism are systematically left in a peripheral position. Quite aside from this, security guards play a leading role in ensuring the security and safety of global tourist destinations. Mega-events, such as festivals, sporting events, and royal weddings, are a fertile ground for terrorist attacks. The organization of mega-events includes the hiring of security guards to keep attendees safer. The present chapter synthesizes a part of an ethnography performed in security

Please note that few chapters were submitted during the peak of the pandemic. The long period of time to publish (due to supply chain and other issues) may have changed the perspectives presented in the chapter altogether.

Event Tourism and Sustainable Community Development: Advances, Effects, and Implications.
Ekta Dhariwal, Shruti Arora, Anukrati Sharma, Azizul Hassan (Eds.)
© 2024 Apple Academic Press, Inc. Co-published with CRC Press (Taylor & Francis)

agencies in Argentina. This chapter focuses on the importance and problems of security guards in the tourism industry. There is a clear dissociation between the importance security guards have and the real working conditions in Argentina. One of the limitations and problems of security guards include excessive working hours, low salaries, and alcoholism (only to name a few) without mentioning the monopoly of security-related agencies to regulate the labor market.

7.1 INTRODUCTION

It is tempting to say that mega-events are fertile ground for international terrorism (Giulianotti and Klauser, 2012; Peter, 2011). Terrorism as a main object of study has captivated the attention of scholarship worldwide. Since Munich Massacre, a terrorist attack perpetrated in 1972 by the radicalized group Black September where 11 Israeli coaches and athletes were killed, security management in festivals and sporting events posed as a major concern for authorities and policymakers (Schimmel, 2006; Jennings and Lodge, 2011). This was a foundational event that provided us with a before and an after in the history of event management. For some reason, a vast audience is expected to watch these types of events, whereas thousands of foreign visitors attend them. Terrorists do not want a lot of people dying; they want a lot of people watching! Emulating the logic of celebrities, terrorists are in quest of social recognition and fame. Their semiotic message is packaged and distributed by the mass media; mega-events exhibit a perfect place for terrorist attacks (Howie, 2012). Having said this, terrorism and event management are inextricably intertwined (De Albuquerque and McElroy, 1999; Tarlow, 2014; Toohey and Tarlow, 2008). As Korstanje puts it, terrorism operates in the shadows of clandestine life to ignite a climate of political instability for their claims to be unilaterally accepted by the nation-state (Korstanje, 2017, 2020). Particularly, one of the most troubling aspects of terrorism appears not to be the negative effects of the advertising of the event that is generated by the violence but a clear reminder the same event will repeat anytime and anywhere. In this vein, policymakers cautioned adamantly on the risks terrorism poses for the tourism industry worldwide (Ryan, 1993; Hall, 2010) as well as the pro and cons that often the specialized literature evinces revolving around the life of safety guards (Howie, 2014).

As the previous argument is given, even if specialists and academicians acknowledge that digital technologies help in surveillance and implementing efficient protocols of security as well as is a priority of extreme importance in event management, little attention was given to the financial and material conditions that precede mega-events of the caliber of Olympic Games or FIFA world cup. Recently, ISIS not only communicated its intention to seize and kill Leonel Messi—the Argentinean Football player superstar—but also serious alarms were issued for Rio 2016. Brazilian authorities assured to dismantle an emerging and dormant ISIS-related cell that planned an attack. Paradoxically, terrorism never took place in Rio but thousands of citizens went out to the streets to protest the economic downturn and Dilma Rousseff's administration. The interclass inequalities aggravated by an unparalleled economic crisis and the recent denunciation of corruption ultimately outraged Brazilians. This suggests that organizers of events should cope with internal and external risks. In context of economic emergency or poverty mega-events may potentiate or deteriorate authorities' social esteem. The success of mega-event organizations makes more resilient and sustainable destinations (Gaffney, 2013). Here, sustainability is understood as the capacity to protect the nonrenewable resources in favor of the next generations. Sustainability not only creates prosperous destinations but also resolves the glitches and economic problems of unjust wealth distributions. At the same time, sustainability helps to placate the interclass conflict and discrepancies among stakeholders (Bramwell, 1997; Hall, 2012; Ma et al., 2011). Terrorism harms sustainability, affecting the organic image of the destination. Countries that are dependent on foreign tourists are particularly hurt by the action of terrorism (Somnez et al., 1999; Brondoni, 2017; Araña and Leon, 2008). Furthermore, mega-event management overlooks the significance of the internal agency, a gap that the present study case intends to fill out. Although in many cases the external macrostructural variables are successfully addressed, the local humor as well as the expectances, fears and problems of lay citizens are misjudged (Korstanje et al., 2014). As stated, this chapter dissects the difficulties and substantial changes the event-management teams face given the rise of radicalized and extreme forms of conflicts as terrorism, or even the civil riots in London (2011) or Rio (2016) without mentioning the acts of vandalism and hooliganism in the last Euro Cup between Russians and Britons. Sociologically speaking, although the organization of mega-events is originally to revitalize psychological frustrations, fostering in-group social cohesion (Dayan and Katz, 1992) it is vital to note how events engender a serious risk for hosting a city because of the attraction for radical cells. Keeping on Luke Howie's legacy (2014), this chapter debates hotly the challenges and problems security guards face in Argentina to contain the internal or external levels of violence in the society.

This chapter is divided into three parts. The first section introduces readers to the sociology of mega-events. As rites of passages, mega-events catalyze social discontent and frustration creating an atmosphere of cooperation and social cohesion. The second section discusses the intersection of mega-events and terrorism. Terrorist cells look to create political instability through the articulation of violent acts or crimes in these sacred spaces. The third last section gives some insights on the labor conditions of security guards who care for attendees in these mega-events. With the concentration of a case study based on Argentina, we continue the debate left by Professor Luke Howie. Security guards play an important role in caring for the consumers but paradoxically they are exposed to indignant working conditions. In a global and hyper-capitalized society, citizens are ranked and valorized by what they can consume, and not for what they produce daily.

7.2 THE ORGANIZATION OF MEGA-EVENTS

In a seminal book entitled *Media Events: The Live Broadcasting of History, Dayan & Katz* define mega-events as rituals oriented to enhance social cohesion and citizens' loyalties. These mega-events include aristocrat and royal weddings, celebrations, and sporting events. The legitimacy of authorities depends on the success of performing the rite. Lay citizens are daily subjected to social frustrations and discontent. These negative feelings are redeemed through common rituals. Mega-events catalyze to activate the necessary channels to foster social trust and reciprocity (Dayan and Katz, 1992). As R. Tzanelli (2016) eloquently notes, mega-events are politically manipulated not only to domesticate the lay citizen but also to protect the status quo. Hence events are packaged and performed according to two main forces: artificial economy and the economy of the imagination. While the former refers to the needs of stability and normalcy, which associates with home, the latter signals to the reproduction of externally fabricated allegories. To put things in other terms, the artificial economy orchestrates the interclass inequalities with a sense of security strictly given by the nation-state. The games represent a communal act of cohesion where the relegated classes are temporarily accepted. Paradoxically, the economy of imagination molds the borders of ideology introduced by the exploited groups in Eden. With a focus on a study case mainly based in Rio de Janeiro 2016, Tzanelli toys with the belief that the tourism industry gives marginalized favelados (slum dwellers) a happier (but emptied) future to dream while a westernized

The Terror, the Spectacle, and the Worker 91

landscape of Brazil is internalized. To some extent, as Tzanelli adheres, Rio 2016 exhibits the archetype of an outlaw territory that was widely colonized by a White Elite. At the same time, the games define the dangerous presence of the "other" culturally ingrained in the discourse of a multiethnic nation. "The state of poverty and the experience of radicalization and criminalization remove the act of futurising from these communities, whereas their displacement in an informal (tourism or otherwise) economy, suggests a sort of phenomenological disappearance from future urban possibilities." (p. 21)

The above-cited excerpt marks a paradoxical situation simply because the same ruling elite that displaced the blacks, slaves, and mulattos to a peripheral position is now boasting a type of melting-pot culture. Mega-events are always festivals reserved for only a small portion of the population. The mobilities of minorities are feasible through the immobilities of the rest. Favelados are immersed in fabricated identities that integrate them to be sold as a commodity to foreign tourists (Tzanelli, 2018). Tzanelli's book sheds light on the mega-events as sacred spaces of consumption and exclusion where host–guest relations turn practically unpredictable. Although consumption unites commoditizing citizens and consumers, exclusion divides expulsing the foreign element from the core of society. Everything can happen in these liminoid spaces. For that reasons, these spaces are often targeted by terrorist (radicalized) groups (Korstanje, 2017).

7.3 TOURISM, EVENTS, AND TERRORISM

Over the recent years, some voices claimed that terrorists are far from being hatred-filled maniacs psychologically deprived or frustrated persons looking for a form of sublimating their resentment (Victorov, 2005; Kruglanski and Fishman, 2006; Corner and Kendall, 2007). Centered on the alienation theory, terrorism studies focus on urban areas as spaces of low interaction and competence. Because of this, lay people feel distressed and frustrated due to constant demands. Urban westernized cities are fraught with social maladies and maelstrom. These pathologies, which include drug addiction, criminality, and high rates of suicides, characterize urban life. Louis Wirth (1938) was a pioneer in showing how cities are fertile grounds for the decline of social bonds. Citing Durkheim and Mauss, Wirth elaborates that urbanism, which is derived from the expansion of industrialism, created substantial changes in the capitalist means of production. Urban city formation is proportional to the corrosion of social ties. As a result, thousands of impoverished farmers migrated to overcrowded cities. Citizens were transformed into workers and consumers. To keep ideological control over the workforce, lay citizen was subjected to a much deeper process of depersonalization. In consonance with this, Dean MacCannell (1976; 1992) argues convincingly that tourism consumption revitalizes the social discontent and frustration provoked by the climate of labor exploitation in urban areas. Through tourism consumption, the society is not only united but also protects its interests. For Enders and Sandler (2011), the attractiveness of mega-events for radicalized groups links to a type of economy of terror. Terrorists are economic agents who maximize profits while minimizing costs. Their political goals are finely calculated to move in rational logic. Mega-events offer a ground to call the attention of authorities while the demands are finally met. Mega-events are liminoid spaces of flexibility where security forces are constrained to act. Attacks perpetrated in these sacred spaces are low-cost enterprises with major psychological effects on social imaginary. In recent years, international terrorism targeted the tourism industry as well as mega festivals and celebrations such as the FIFA World Cup and the Olympic Games (Baker and Coulter, 2007; Korstanje et al., 2014, 2018). Raj et al (2018) introduce readers to the complexity of events and risk perception. Risk perception theory has gained an imprint in the field of tourism just after 9/11 and the War on Terror declared by the Bush administration. Though it was widely used in applied psychology, no later than 2001 the theory arrived at the constellations of tourism research. Terrorism is considered today one of the major risks—but not the only one—that threatens the tourism industry and event management. In this respect, Alan Clarke (2018) calls attention to the role of ideology as the set of shared cognitions and narratives that explain the external world. Terrorists want to destroy tourism because we—the westerners—venerate it as a religion. The cult of tourism—as well as its so-called prosperity—paves the ways for the rise of a radicalized sentiment of hostility against the western tourist in the Middle East. They look to redefine the society to the inversion of its cultural values. At the same time, we often legitimize racist discourses mainly based on Islamophobia as usual. As Cyril Peter (2018) explains, terrorism seems rarely selective, at least nowadays. Terrorism selects its victims in equal conditions and little information is known about them. Policymakers should cultivate the needs of security consciousness which means more than being aware of the dangers. Security consciousness gives the lead to mitigate the negative impacts of terrorism in destination advertising. After 2001, incidents and terrorist attacks in the tourism industry have notably increased worldwide. The fragility of tourism varied on country and culture but it makes harder for those destinations, which are dependent on tourism consumption. Peter Tarlow (2014) laments that the scourge of terrorism not only posited a great challenge for the industry but also a world that changed after 9/11. He remarks that policymakers should shorten the gap between practice and theory. They should work actively to offer all-encompassing diagnoses that mitigate the effects of terrorism. As a rite, the act of traveling needs security to be performed. This happens because political stability provides tourists with certain trust. Tourists are psychologically motivated by two contrasting forces: the urgency to discover something new, and the needs of resting safely at the destination. Novelty and protection are two key forces that shape tourism consumption. Several mythical texts like the Bible speak of the importance of honoring hospitality and protecting outsiders while their sojourn. Hospitality activates a human sentiment of solidarity that nears hosts and guests. As Tarlow (2014) observes, it is safe to say tourism and security are inevitably entwined. At the same time, the world expands in a more globalized version, security is situated as the top priorities of governments. Although foreign tourists are often harmed or killed by locals, specialists should distinguish terrorism from local criminality. Criminals attack tourists for their profits, but terrorists are not moved by commercial interests. At a closer look, terrorism appeals to political violence to instill terror in society. Through violence, these groups look for creating an atmosphere of political instability (Tarlow, 2014). What is equally important, it is vital to know that risk perception offers a model that helps policymakers to understand the steps of terrorism. Besides, risk perception theory gives professionals an efficient platform to improve the communication process to mitigate the devastating effects of terrorism. Mega-events take different meanings and pursue different aims. Tarlow says that athletic games, celebration, and sporting events captivate the attention of a vast audience. As something more complex than sporting events, they should be defined as anthropological rites of communion where the self is sacrificed by social cohesion. Lay citizens enthusiastically embrace the mainstream cultural values of their societies while depositing their legitimacy in authorities. For that reason, harming the game's reputation is a useful instrument to harm authorities (Tarlow, 2017). Athletes embody the mythical archetype of the ancient hero who confronts the Gods' wills. Whether these heroes are killed or attacked, the society is panicked (Tarlow, 2017). Sociologists of mega-events suggest that these rites bestow to citizen the pride of belonging to the in-group, abiding the law and authorities, but at the same time they erect a barrier for those who do not belong to the group. In Ancient Rome, the role of gladiators emulated the different historic enemies of the empire. At the same time, hundred animals were sacrificed in the games. These games symbolized not only the power and glory of Rome, but also how the human character dominates the natural world. Unlike the animals, the human spirit defies the Gods and their arbitraries. In these games, all Roman citizens were equal. Most certainly, thousands of poor citizens attended while suppressing temporarily their frustrations (Korstanje, 2009).

Lastly, Skoll and Korstanje (2014) enumerate a set of risks tourists often face in public festivals and event management. Terrorism coordinates efforts to promote uncertainness and surprise factor. Terrorism seems to be one of the major problems for the tourism industry. Events and festivals are primary targets for terrorism because of the negative message distributed to the audience. The main goals of terrorism are associated with undermining the authority emanated from the nation-state. As Skoll and Korstanje write, the effects of terrorism in public spectacles depend on four variables: , *The Threshold of Control*: This factor shows the degree of control the society may bear or at the best exerts to predict disasters. Society orchestrates techniques of surveillance to create a steady sense of security but when this is altered, panic emerges. While bombing and terrorism can be easily monitored, there are other risks as food contamination or virus outbreak that interrogate the ontological security of society.

The probability of repetition: It signals to the probabilities traumatic events can be repeated on a later day. This point operates in short or long runs, paving the ways the society moves all material and symbolic resources for citizens to feel secure.

Targeted victims: The victims often send a message to survivors. Depending on the status of the victims or the circumstance of their death, societies are prone to valorize some groups over others. For the sake of clarity, when the terrorist attack involves youth, children, or women, society reacts more energetically than soldiers are shot. The status of the victims is a key factor in how the risk is communicated and finally perceived.

7.4 EXPECTANCIES AND DAILY LIMITATIONS OF SECURITY GUARDS IN TOURISM

Despite the abundance of literature on security and safety issues for tourism and hospitality, it is frustrating to say that only a marginal number of studies focused on the expectations of security guards. Paradoxically, while security

The Terror, the Spectacle, and the Worker   95

guards are discursively valorized as the first agents to struggle against terrorism, no less true is that they are subjected to countless deprivation such as lower paid wages, higher levels of uncertainty, and excessive working hours (Howie, 2014). This led to pathologies such as alcoholism, addiction, or even insomnia among many others problems, without mentioning the possibility to receive bribes from the terrorist cells to abandon the target temporarily (Goodrich, 2002; Dobson and Sinnamon, 2002).

Citing Guy Debord (2012) in The Society of the Spectacle, citizens are passively commoditized on consumers. The authentic daily life is replaced by a representation where the lived events become a simple representation. The gradual decline of self crystallizes when the being sets the pace to the having, and then having to "the appearing." In the capitalist system, history witnesses how the visual commodity colonizes social life. Therefore, the spectacle seems to be an invention designed not only for domesticating the citizen but also to mediate between people and their institutions. While citizens are degraded, they look for consuming authentic experiences. Ultimately, the worker who is an active producer becomes a commoditized consumer. The spectacle culture—which is amplified by the mass-media—obscures the understanding of the past situating the person in a dark never-ending present.

As the previous argument is given, Luke Howie (2014), who has published an interesting manuscript in the *International Journal of Religious Tourism and Pilgrimage,* paid heed to the working conditions of the security forces—with an emphasis on guards—as a significant aspect of counterterrorism responses. In his viewpoint, the private sector, as well as the tourist enterprises, looks to minimize costs, hiring unprepared and uneducated security guards, in which case cements the possibility to conduct more efficient steps against terrorism. Howie reminds us how in this post-9/11 context, security guards intervene not only in helping the first victims but also in preventing future attacks. However, society shows certain indifference regarding their well-being. Though it is a matter of public discussion, it remains uncovered or tangentially addressed by the executive branches of almost all nations. Security guards play a major role in the tourism security issues. Fussey and Coaffe (2012) explain that organizing a mega-event represents an exceptional effort for hosts devoting much time and financial resources. Having said this, discontent citizens take the opportunity to show their claims in these types of events, or what are worse separatists or radicalized groups target mega-events such as the Olympic Games or FIFA world cup to perpetrate their attacks. Mega-events are ephemeral episodes that have direct and profound consequences for hosting society. If athletes are harmed or killed it creates serious geopolitical tensions for the hosting state. For policymakers, it is important to decipher the intersection of sport and terrorism. Although terrorist cells operate domestically in their respective communities, no less true seems to be that they have not only global connections sometimes working together in different countries but also move freely worldwide. Terrorist acts take place in the event but are very well planned earlier. As the authors agree, this posits an interesting dilemma between the global and the local. Terrorist groups claim localized demands but overcoming globalized models of security. There is a powerful symbolic connection between hosting sporting mega-events and terrorist violence. One of the quintessential features of mega-events is the presence of military forces. Urban militarization is a fresh landscape we are accustomed to watching during mega-events. The second point of interest is the security guards or private security. Security personnel are not only subjected to a climate of labor instability and exploitations they work excessive hours and poor conditions. These workers are replete with ephemeral and temporal contracts in which case significant questions around the figure of national security surface. Sports events represent valuable symbolic targets for international terrorism. Spaaij and Hamm (2015) draw a comparative analysis of the attacks on the 1996 Atlanta Olympic Games and the 2013 Boston Marathon in the United States. Their research shows how lone wolves target these types of public events which are densely crowded to generate further impacts at lower costs. Terrorism moves and inspires through a copycat phenomenon that is packaged and disseminated by the mass media. The credibility of authorities is ultimately damaged once the attack is successfully perpetrated. What seems to be more important, terrorism is mutating into new forms where lone wolves or small groups perpetrate devastating attacks. While the attacks are politically motivated, these lone wolves feel grievance and social frustration.

Last but not least, Toohey and Taylor (2008) offer a clear diagnosis to understand the securitization process during mega-events. Attendees often are passively in acceptance of obtrusive surveillance techniques and technologies when their ontological security is in jeopardy. The importance of security guards in security management has been overtly valorized by authorities and scholars, but private security companies pay lower wages than other sectors. There is a gap between the paid salaries or the poor working conditions and the significant role of security guards worldwide. Of course, national security is in charge of military forces or the police, but organizers are prompted to contract private security companies. The following lines contain 40 interviews performed with over 50 security guards and five

The Terror, the Spectacle, and the Worker   97

private companies. The real names of the involved participants have been changed because of privacy and security issues.

7.5 SECURITY GUARDS IN ARGENTINA

In this section, we describe part of a set of 50 interviews administered to security guards between 2010 and 2019. The sample was drawn by 40 male and 10 female workers serving important private security companies. This represents a labor niche occupied preferably by men. Most of them have worked for the tourism industry though rarely were involved when there were terrorist attacks. The selected method was the snowball technique, which means each interviewee recommends the next worker to consult. Since the chosen method is not statistically representative, obtained results cannot be extrapolated to other universes. One of the aspects present in almost all interviews is the excessive working hours and lower salaries. Though the market offers plenty of jobs in the field, security guards are not valorized as they want.

Marcelo (male, 27 years old) said "I am working as a security guard since 2001 when I lose my job. I have taken several courses and occupied different positions in the organization and always I met with the same problem, we earn lower salaries while working more than 8 hours. I know there are a lot of agencies where security guards are recruited, but all paying the same wages. It is like a paradox, you know will have a future job if you are fired, but always it is a low pay." This coincides with Jose who claims "I have a family and 4 children, I cannot be the only support with this wage. Security guard agencies exploit their workers creating a unique monopoly … at the same time, private companies or even organizers look cheaper their costs contracting phantom companies in some cases offering unregistered jobs." Samantha (female, 29 years old) says "this job is not forever, I have a lot of debts and bills to pay. Agencies play a major role in security management and earn considerable profits for their service, these profits are amassed by a small portion of private companies. The generated wealth is not justly distributed to workers." In other cases, the excessive working hours lead security guards to alcoholism or drug abuses. As Carlos (male, 35 years old) notes "I am alcoholic and this caused me some health problems in the past. I have lost many jobs because I cannot stop drinking. It all started when I was alone caring for a museum for more than 12 hours at the night. I did nothing to do and opted to drink to spend my time." Marcelo (male, 30 years old) goes in a similar direction when he highlights "I lost my wife because of my alcoholism. I worked for several hours and suffered great distress and depression. To my daily burdens, I experienced a much deeper depression. The excessive working hours aggravated my situation. I found in alcohol and other drugs a pain reliever. I began several drug abuse treatment but without any result. "

Another interesting point of the debate is the worries of security guards being selected to cover a sporting event. The problem of terrorism interrogates interviewees and their inner worlds. Juan (security manager, male, 35 years old) assured he worked as a security guard at an important hotel. In his view, terrorism is not the only major, threat security guards are also not trained to deal with counterterrorism protocols: "we are not being trained to cope with terrorists. They are well-trained people who plan their attacks for months. Security guards feel fear to cover mega-events that may be a potential target of international terrorism. We are not police officer, we can guide attendants but we are legally unable to carry weapons. Figure out, if terrorists perpetrated the attacks to World Trade Center in the safest country, what they can do in Buenos Aires?" For Alicia (female, 45 years old) "terrorism reveals one of the contradictions of our capitalist societies. We are encouraged to play a leading role in the mega-events caring people but we are low paid. If you ask me, it is very odd that terrorists bribe security guards to turn a blind eye. When this happens, terrorists have the time to put the bomb or planning the attack better. " Carlos—ultimately—acknowledges that "the problem of labor exploitation associates with two major forces. On one hand, the monopoly of security-related agencies amass greater profits … this monopoly is based not only on labor exploitation but also on tacit (invisible) rules shared by all private companies. If you give up on a job, you have no further possibilities with other agencies. The payment is the same, the labor conditions too. On another, there is a gap between the over-valorization of the sector and the real salaries. We play a leading role in the prevention and security managers but it does not lead to better working conditions."

The obtained interviews reveal two important things.

At a closer look, security guards manifest a clear discontent for the working conditions as well as the lower salaries. At the same time, they contend to have problems with alcohol and drug abuses. Security guards are subjected to a climate of psychological distress and depression which usher them in a state of vulnerability. Second, terrorist groups can very well bribe security guards to plan their attacks. Lastly, there is the dissociation between the importance of security guards—claimed by authorities—and the paid wages the market offers. Echoing Howie, this contradiction that

The Terror, the Spectacle, and the Worker 99

is culturally proper of the capitalist system is the blind point from where terrorism successfully operates.

7.6 CONCLUSIONS

Terrorism often target leisure spots and tourist destination because army forces and police are not taking a direct intervention in these pleasurable spaces. Tourists feel disgusted when they are subject to countless obtrusive controls. Meanwhile, security officers play a leading role mediating with foreign tourists while caring them. Unfortunately, they are overexploited or subjected to indignant working conditions. As Professor Howie puts it, this happens because global capitalism expands according to the power of consumers creating in this way some material asymmetries. The most important agents of capitalism are systematically left in a peripheral position. Quite aside from this, security guards play a leading role in ensuring the security and safety of global tourist destinations. The present book chapter synthesizes a part of an ethnography performed in security agencies in Argentina. This study focuses on the importance and problems of security guards in the tourism industry. There is a clear dissociation between the importance security guards have and the real working conditions in Argentina. One of the limitations and problems of security guards include excessive working hours, low salaries, and alcoholism (only to name a few) without mentioning the monopoly of security-related agencies to regulate the labor market.

KEYWORDS

- **mega-events**
- **sustainability**
- **security guards**
- **tourism**
- **terrorism**
- **fear**

REFERENCES

Araña, J. E.; León, C. J. The Impact of Terrorism on Tourism Demand. *Ann. Tour. Res.* **2008,** *35* (2), 299–315.

Baker, K.; Coulter, A. Terrorism and tourism: the vulnerability of beach vendors' Livelihoods in Bali. *J. Sustain. Tour.* **2007,** *15* (3), 249–266.

Bramwell, B. A Sport Mega-Event as a Sustainable Tourism Development Strategy. *Tour. Recreat. Res.* **1997,** *22* (2), 13–19.

Brondoni, S. M. Global Tourism and Terrorism. Safety and Security Management. *Symphonya Emerg. Iss. Manage.* **2017,** 2, 7–16.

Clarke, A. Religion, Ideology and Terrorism. *Risk and Safety Challenges for Religious Tourism and Events*; Korstanje, M., Raj, R., Griffin, K., Eds.; CABI: Wallingford, 2018; pp 8–19.

Comer, J. S.; Kendall, P. C. Terrorism: The Psychological Impact on Youth. *Clin. Psychol. Sci. Prac.* **2007,** *14* (3), 179–212.

Dayan, D.; Katz, E. *Media Events: The Live Broadcasting of History*; Cambridge University Press: Cambridge, 1992.

De Albuquerque, K.; McElroy, J. Tourism and Crime in the Caribbean. *Ann. Tour. Res* **1999,** *26* (4), 968–984.

Debord, G. *Society of the Spectacle*; Bread and Circuses Publishing: New York, 2012.

Dobson, N.; Sinnamon, R. A Critical Analysis of the Organization of Major Sports Events. In *Sport in the City*; Routledge: Abingdon, 2002; pp 75–89.

Enders, W.; Sandler, T. *The Political Economy of Terrorism*; Cambridge University Press: Cambridge, 2011.

Fussey, P.; Coaffee, J. Balancing Local and Global Security Leitmotifs: Counter-Terrorism and the Spectacle of Sporting Mega-Events. *Int. Rev. Sociol. Sport* **2012,** *47* (3), 268–285.

Gaffney, C. Between Discourse and Reality: The Un-Sustainability of Mega-Event Planning. *Sustainability* **2013,** *5* (9), 3926–3940.

Giulianotti, R.; Klauser, F. Sport Mega-Events and 'Terrorism': A Critical Analysis. *Int. Rev. Sociol. Sport* **2012,** *47* (3), 307–323.

Goodrich, J. N. September 11, 2001 Attack on America: A Record of the Immediate Impacts and Reactions in the USA Travel and Tourism Industry. *Tour. Manage.* **2002,** *23* (6), 573–580.

Hall, C. M. Crisis Events in Tourism: Subjects of Crisis in Tourism. *Curr. Iss. Tour.* **2010,** *13* (5), 401–417.

Hall, C. M. Sustainable Mega-Events: Beyond the Myth of Balanced Approaches to Mega-Event Sustainability. *Event Manage.* **2012,** *16* (2), 119–131.

Howie, L. Witnessing Terrorism. In *Witnesses to Terror*; Palgrave Macmillan: London, 2012; pp 155–175.

Howie, L. Security Guards and Counter-terrorism: Tourism and Gaps in Terrorism Prevention. *Int. J. Religious Tour. Pilgrimage* **2014,** *2* (1), 38–47.

Jennings, W.; Lodge, M. Governing Mega-Events: Tools of Security Risk Management for the FIFA 2006 World Cup in Germany and London 2012 Olympic Games. *Gov. Opp.* **2011,** *46* (2), 192–222.

Korstanje, M. E. Reconsidering the Roots of Event Management: Leisure in Ancient Rome. *Event Manage.* **2009,** *13* (3), 197–203.

The Terror, the Spectacle, and the Worker

Korstanje, M. E. The Commoditization of Security Guards in the Tourism Industry: The Case of Argentina. In *Post-Disaster and Post-Conflict Tourism*; Palm Beach, Apple Academic Press, 2020; pp 197–212.

Korstanje, M. E. *Terrorism, Tourism and the End of Hospitality in the West*; Springer Nature: New York, 2017.

Korstanje, M. E.; Raj, R.; Griffin, K., Eds. *Risk and Safety Challenges for Religious Tourism and Events*; CABI: Wallingford, 2018.

Korstanje, M. E.; Tzanelli, R.; Clayton, A. Brazilian World Cup 2014: Terrorism, Tourism, and Social Conflict. *Event Manage.* **2014,** *18* (4), 487–491.

Kruglanski, A. W.; Fishman, S. The Psychology of Terrorism: "Syndrome" Versus "Tool" Perspectives. *Terror. Polit. Violence* **2006,** *18* (2), 193–215.

Ma, S. C.; Egan, D.; Rotherham, I.; Ma, S. M. A Framework for Monitoring During the Planning Stage for a Sports Mega-Event. *J. Sustain. Tour.* **2011,** *19* (1), 79–96.

MacCannell, D. *The Tourist: A New Theory of the Leisure Class*; University of California Press: Berkeley, 1976.

MacCannell, D. *Empty Meeting Grounds: The Tourist Papers*; Psychology Press: London, 1992.

Peter, C. 13 Hospitality, Tourism, Terrorism: Creating a Security-Conscious Culture. In *Risk and Safety Challenges for Religious Tourism and Events*; Korstanje, M., Raj, R., Griffin, K., Eds.; CABI: Wallingford, 2018; pp 123–133.

Peter, C. R. *Implications and Impacts of Terrorism on Sporting Events: Is the Hospitality Industry Prepared and Equipped to Host Mega Events?* Doctoral dissertation, Auckland University of Technology, 2011.

Raj, R.; Griffin, K.; Korstanje, M. E. 1 Risk and Safety Challenges Facing Religious Tourism–An Introduction. In *Risk and Safety Challenges for Religious Tourism and Events*; Korstanje, M., Raj, R., Griffin, K., Eds.; CABI: Wallingford, 2018; pp 1–7.

Ryan, C. Crime, Violence, Terrorism and Tourism: An Accidental or Intrinsic Relationship? *Tour. Manage.* **1993,** *14* (3), 173–183.

Schimmel, K. S. Deep Play: Sports Mega-Events and Urban Social Conditions in the USA. *Sociol. Rev.* **2006,** *54* (2_suppl), 160–174.

Skoll, G. R.; Korstanje, M. E. Terrorism, Homeland Safety and Event Management. *Int. J. Hospital. Event Manage.* **2014,** *1* (1), 95–110.

Sönmez, S. F.; Apostolopoulos, Y.; Tarlow, P. Tourism in Crisis: Managing the Effects of Terrorism. *J. Travel Res.* **1999,** *38* (1), 13–18.

Spaaij, R.; Hamm, M. S. Endgame? Sports Events as Symbolic Targets in Lone Wolf Terrorism. *Stud. Conflict Terror.* **2015,** *38* (12), 1022–1037.

Tarlow, P. *Tourism Security: Strategies for Effectively Managing Travel Risk and Safety*; Elsevier: Oxford, 2014.

Tarlow, P. *Sports Travel Security*; Elsevier: Oxford, 2017.

Toohey, K.; Taylor, T. Mega Events, Fear, and Risk: Terrorism at the Olympic Games. *J. Sport Manage.* **2008,** *22* (4), 451–469.

Tzanelli, R. *Mega Events as Economies of the Imagination. Creating Atmospheres for Rio 2016 and Tokyo 2020*; Routledge: Abingdon, 2018.

Victoroff, J. The Mind of the Terrorist: A Review and Critique of Psychological Approaches. *J. Conflict Resol.* **2005,** *49* (1), 3–42.

Wirth, L. Urbanism as a Way of Life. *Am. J. Sociol.* **1938,** *44* (1), 1–24.

CHAPTER 8

Advancing Women's Roles and Empowerment in Event Tourism in Rajasthan

EKTA DHARIWAL

Social Activist, India

ABSTRACT

Event tourism is one of the stress busters that change the mindset of an individual completely. Traversing around the world is considered the greatest experience a human being can ever experience especially when it is done for participating in an event of festival. From the prehistoric period to the present day, man has exhibited undue interest in traveling for attending and organizing events. It is a multifaceted fast-growing economic and industrial activity of immense global importance. It has become one of the effectual tool for generating employment, improving infrastructure, earning foreign exchange, helping regional development, and thereby facilitating the overall development of an economy in the recent years.

Rajasthan is a state of artisans and craftsman that has a lot of traditional arts and crafts, which have been carried forward through generations. The event tourism industry in Rajasthan is found growing by leaps and bounds over the years due to its rich and diverse range of unique tangible and intangible cultural, unique environmental, and scenic beauty with which it has been endowed as well as the historic role it has played as a symbol of chivalry for the nation. In recent years, the silver lining is seen that this industry has become a priority sector for the women also as they contributed immeasurably to the development of culture, education, art, architecture, and glamour.

Please note that few chapters were submitted during the peak of the pandemic. The long period of time to publish (due to supply chain and other issues) may have changed the perspectives presented in the chapter altogether.

Event Tourism and Sustainable Community Development: Advances, Effects, and Implications.
Ekta Dhariwal, Shruti Arora, Anukrati Sharma, Azizul Hassan (Eds.)
© 2024 Apple Academic Press, Inc. Co-published with CRC Press (Taylor & Francis)

To enhance the employment opportunities, women are participating in tourism empowerment programmes together with several hand on training in specific skills in the hospitality industry. These programmes have open the doors for women's employment and opportunities for generating self-income through small and medium activities. Keeping the traditional touch in view, thousands of women in Rajasthan are manufacturing Rajasthani traditional handicrafts and textiles for national and international markets. Each and every such design and pattern is unique to influence the tourists. In Rajasthan, the culinary culture is shaped by its particular available resources such as climate, geography, and natural vegetation. The culinary basket includes hardy crops and grains together with various kinds of herbs, green vegetables, different kinds of breads and rich butter oil. Foods with greater self-life are preferred in this state.

The particularly designed folklore musical instruments and traditional dances along with the regional songs are benchmarked as a thrilling part of entertainment. Kalbeliya and Ghoomar are traditional folk dances performed by the women of Rajasthan. Rajasthani men and women are also interested in imitating the splendor of the jewelry meant for the royal dynasties earlier. Hence the business of ornaments is one of the key earners here which is a combination of trendy style and authentic traditional design. This all combines into building this province into one of the major destinations for different sought of events such as wedding events, cultural and traditional events, and education events. The role of women in traditional to modern events is very well recognized in Rajasthan.

When measured through the scale of the Global Tourism Industry it is ironical to grasp the reality that this business producing tenth part of global World's Gross Domestic Product is still shaping women as a part of gender inequality. To add fuel to injury the data speaks that 70% tourism sector is connected by the women. The women are paid sometimes only one-tenth honorarium when compared to their male counterpart especially in the informal work related to this industry. Hence it is a formidable message to potentize the industry to uproot the gender inequality by the women empowerment.

8.1 INTRODUCTION

In the recent past, the women empowerment has put forth a silver lining for the carrier advancement of women in all dimensions. However, the managing and leading skills inherited by women have not produced satisfactory results in the tourism industry in particular. Combining a major part in this sector, women are less paid and are engaged in low-profile works. It imprints a psychological depression on the entire women society. The present study aims to understand the preference of tourists in Rajasthan as a place for spending their leisure time and to refresh and rejuvenate themselves particularly in the rural and agriculture-based communities. The recent surveys state that the financial, traditional, and technologically advanced scenario of Rajasthan awes largely to the contribution of women. Also the glory of a rustic Rajasthani culture is managed and transmitted by the women more enthusiastically than their male counterparts.

Of course the sustainable tourism plays an important role as a key factor, which generates income to the local communities and other businesses related to tourism. There are many evidences that have shown many tourist destinations that reduce environmental effects have generated more profit and become more competitive.

8.1.1   WOMEN'S ROLE IN PROMOTING ECOTOURISM CULTURE

Rajasthan is one of the rapid growing industry of the sustainable tourism, which helps in shielding environment, socioeconomic development, wildlife preservation, and poverty palliation. It also affects the social, economic, and environmental elements of all the sections of the society as well as the whole country. Wearing and Larsen (1996) showed how ecotourism can empower local communities by giving them a sense of pride and awareness of the importance of their natural resources and control over their development, on a contrary note Scheyvens (2000) argued that women do not benefit significantly from ecotourism projects. Beside women are playing a leading role for conservation and enhancement of environment by earning more honorarium also for themselves.

In Rajasthan, women have a close connection with the physical environment of their community. They have a special knowledge of walking routes, craft production, and useful indigenous plants and herbs all of which are related to the development of rural tourism products and services, which shows that women are capable in managing tourism projects. It is remarkable to state that being devoid of formal education, women in Rajasthan are capable enough to maintain eco-friendly culture and transmit it to their family members as well as to tourists also with great patience. However, with the lack of resources even they have been skilfully protecting their raw houses and craftsmanship. By this virtue, women have attained a key role in their families to earn the livelihood and projecting the varieties of items to the tourists.

Source: Clicked by the Author.

8.1.2 WOMEN'S ENTERPRISES FOR CULTURE TOURISM

It is understood that cultural tourism is one that helps the tourists understand perfectly the regional cultural aspects like religious objects, architectural modules, social festivity, and sources of entertainment. It is historically proven factor that since the dawn of Mesolithic era the development of human civilization is witnessed growing neck to neck with its counterpart in Rajasthan. Viewing the historical importance of Rajasthan all in all in the Indian context, it is advisable that the tourism promoters must uplift and boost up the women participation in different sectors of tourism on equal terms with man. Also the minute survey of the regional peculiarity can also support to heighten the tourism faculties. In addition to increase the export, import market the development of regional handicraft, culture, tradition, and cuisine involving women by creating small businesses and jobs are found fruitful now. Through this tourism, it is evidently an empowering factor for women and to bring them out to overcome mainly the social-cultural constraints that have kept them in back doors for centuries.

Source: Clicked by the Author.

8.1.3 CONTRIBUTION OF WOMEN IN MEDICO TOURISM

It is a growing factor that not only in Rajasthan but in the entirely reputed hospitals across India the medico tourism is an intensively growing business. It is noticeable that the expenditure in India is more affordable and the facilities are of international level. This type of tourism appears to be instantaneous earning source within highly prestigious pursuit also. This industry is experiencing >10% growth earning in India. The various estimated size of the Indian medical tourism industry at $3 billion in 2015, which is expected to grow to $7–8 billion by 2021. Rajasthan is blessed to be more empowered by the tourism because of its historical glory connected with digital media as of now. Mainly, it is observed that the greater number of medico tourism is formed by women due to cosmetic or reproductive requirement. On a contrary note, this industry has projected numerous opportunities and challenges also for female healthcare providers, which makes them run their private clinics to attract local and overseas patients. Presently the increasing consumerism has globally enhanced the importance of women on ethnic level.

It is surprising to note that Rajasthan does have a specular package of absolutely ingenious healing therapy, mostly managed by local women which helps generating handsome amount from medico tourists. It is also pleasant to say that this kind of treatment is still unknown to various parts of world. Especially skilled women work for peculiar kind of massage and prick therapy to relieve pain of different body organs. Henceforth it is high time to manage an infrastructure of managing force to work in intraoperative system and to establish Human Resource Management Policy guideline also.

8.1.4 RADIANT BEAUTY IN RELIGIOUS TOURISM

Religious tourism is one of the branches of tourism and it is in fact the oldest form of tourism which came into being almost with the creation of humanity. It is perhaps in India one of the most earning form of indigenous tourism especially for the people belonging to all parts of society. Rajasthan is an emerging domestic religious tourism destination in India where religiousness is a keystone of Rajasthani culture and is the foundation of social values and cultural phenomenon.

The ancient iconic religious sites of Rajasthan are booming markets for both for national and international tourism. The temples in Rajasthan have identified several groups of women that are seen thrilled and overpowered with spiritual emotions and performing different gesture in the shape of dance, which helps them to attract and earn through religious tourism down the centuries. Even in the Rajput states, there were the departments entitled as Gunijan Khana to manage the livelihood of these artists on behalf of the state. The chronicles nourish the facts that those flawlessly dressed artists have been breathing sensational, mythological stories and events in the different temples. In the terminology of modern tourism it is not less than a sustainable religious tourism which has its untold myth and spiritual fervor. Also the colorful flower jewelry selling women have a constant source of income at each big and small temples in Rajasthan earning by their wit from the tourists.

This kind of tourism is added gloriously and colorfully by the accessory requirements with the prayer in the temples like candles, sandal sticks, different types of fragrant oils, fruits, grains, butter oil, saffron, gold and silver leaves, and many types of sweets along with coconut and perfumes. This whole scenario is a bread and butter for a large number of families not only in Rajasthan but across India. The most reputed temples in this direction are reckoned as Dilwara Temple Ranakpur, Govind Dev Temple in Jaipur, and Khatu Shyam Temple in Sikar.

Source: Clicked by the Author.

It is a peculiar and remarkable module of worship in Rajasthan to potentize the religious importance of some of the small living creatures like monkeys, snakes, and mouse in particular temples only. Such temples are benchmark as Karni Mata Temple at Bikaner, Dard Devi Temple in Kota, etc.

8.1.5 COVID-19: FIRE FOR WOMEN

The impact of Covid virus has decimated the hospitality industry. The recent Covid-19 pandemic has grapples with market instability and business slowdown worldwide which triggered not only the unorganized sectors but micro, small, and large business groups across the world. Unprecedented travel restrictions and stay-at-home and lockdown orders are exacerbating the world's greatest disruption since the Second World War. This change in the current system has led to the beginning of the recession and depression, seeking a transformational change in society. Worldwide travel restrictions impacting >90% of the travelers. So the sustainable tourism is now awaiting the elimination of the restrictions, taking place gradually.

As Rajasthan is known for its uniqueness in its tradition, culture, history, chivalrous, events, artistic modules, and fabulous folk culture, which has been adversely effected in the field of tourism in the present scenario. That is why it seems an earnest need of the hour to enhance the measures of hospitality for international tourists in different destinations and creating several employment opportunities. However, the tourist influx since March in the desert state has been considerably low. The data on tourist arrivals from the Rajasthan tourism department, shared with The Wire, shows that in 2020, the state has seen a fall of 69.3% in Indian tourist arrivals. Last year, 39,685,822 Indian tourists had visited various places in Rajasthan while this year, the number stood at 12,175,524.

Rajasthan that had been enjoying huge income through tourism, has now been suffering depreciation of tourism and the income of male and female service providers too. As a result, it seems difficult for them to earn the required livelihood even at a micro level. Before the coronavirus, many women were involved in tourism sectors like tour guides, tour operators, housekeepers, hotel owners, restaurant owners, service providers in malls and emporiums, but they lost their jobs overnight due to the lockdown and travel restrictions. Contrary to add fuel to injury appeared in the shape of family violence, sexual abuses, misleading in medical sectors, adverse effects of social media, raising the number of suicides, lack of non-Covid medical facilities leading to the rise of psychological disorder and unprecedented panic buying, hording of necessary consumable items, etc. This wholesome adversity on one hand damaged the supply line in the market and on the other hand the lower income trailed behind the haves largely.

8.2 CONCLUSIONS

The tourism sector definitely has the potential to assist women empowerment and development in adjacent areas and beyond this initiating socioeconomic development projects, employment, boosting the country's foreign reserves, and buying of farmers produce for use in local hotels. However, the pandemic situation has hindered the total packaging of tourism badly not only to minimize the income of man but for their female counterparts too, heading to the loss of self-reliance, self-confidence, and self-motivation in women. Now one must aware each opportune time to avail the skill to revive and regenerate the income opportunities neck to neck with the relaxation of restrictions to survive.

KEYWORDS

- **tourism empowerment programme**
- **global tourism industry**
- **world's gross domestic product**
- **human resource management policy**

REFERENCES

http://videa.ca/wp-content/uploads/2015/08/Women-empowerment-through-Ecotourism.pdf

https://thewire.in/economy/rajasthan-tourism-covid-19-lockdown

https://www.longdom.org/open-access/the-impact-of-covid19-in-the-indian-tourism-and-hospitality- industry-brief-report.pdf

https://www.researchgate.net/publication/311533595_Women's_participation_in_environmental_management_and_development_Promotion_Culture

https://www.researchgate.net/publication/331521808_MEDICAL_TOURISM_IN_INDIA_STRENGTHS_AND_WEAKNESSES

https://www.researchgate.net/publication/342400250_MANAGING_WOMEN_EMPOWERMENT_THROUGH_PARTICIPATION_IN_SUSTAINABLE_TOURISM_DEVELOPMENT_IN_KAMPONG_PHLUK_SIEM_REAP_CAMBODIA

https://www.sciencedirect.com/science/article/abs/pii/S1751485118301065

Scheyvens, R. Promoting Women's Empowerment Through Involvement in Ecotourism: Experiences from the Third World. *J. Sustain. Tour.* **2000,** *8* (3), 232–249.

Wearing, S.; Larsen, L. Assessing and Managing the Sociocultural Impacts of Ecotourism: Revisiting the Santa Elena Rainforest Project. *Environmentalist* **1996,** *16* (2), 117–133.

CHAPTER 9

Collaborative Involvement of Major and Minor Stakeholders for Organizing Community Events

MONIKA BARNWAL[1,] and VIJAY KUMAR[2]

[1]*Jamia Millia Islamia (Central University), New Delhi, India*

[2]*Department of Tourism and Hospitality, Jamia Millia Islamia Central University, New Delhi*

ABSTRACT

The management of local events and festivals depicts a destination's culture and lifestyle, depending majorly on the involvement of various stakeholders. Whether it is local government, tour operator, or local stall-seller, everyone has their own role in making a local event/festival appealing and successful. The PPP model states that there needs to be active participation from stakeholders to provide financial resources (manpower, materials, budget, etc.) and human resources (knowledge, networks) and to be aware of their sustainable responsibilities, information exchange, and societal norms. This creates major gap of understanding and a lack of awareness between major and minor stakeholders. The chapter aims to analyze the involvement of the local major and minor stakeholders (micro-entrepreneurs) in community events. An exploratory study is conducted on a local festival where role and participation of stakeholders are analyzed by examining their understanding through Social Capital, and Social Network parameters, and a theoretical Collective Responsibilities Model is proposed for the involved stakeholders.

Please note that few chapters were submitted during the peak of the pandemic. The long period of time to publish (due to supply chain and other issues) may have changed the perspectives presented in the chapter altogether.

Event Tourism and Sustainable Community Development: Advances, Effects, and Implications.
Ekta Dhariwal, Shruti Arora, Anukrati Sharma, Azizul Hassan (Eds.)
© 2024 Apple Academic Press, Inc. Co-published with CRC Press (Taylor & Francis)

9.1 INTRODUCTION

The first InstaMeet, an event organized in Spiti, India brought the inspiration of Plastic ban to the destination by the active involvement of the local NGO Spiti-ecosphere along with support from local community, social influencers, home-stay owners, and tourists who acted as volunteers present a good example of sharing responsibilities together in order to develop a positive destination image. When speaking regarding service industry, the principle of working side by side becomes more effective for better performance. As Atkinson et al. (1997) state, the "modern organization is a web of contracts," and its need for planning and development plays an important role in finding ideas among the organization's stakeholders. Stakeholders of an organization can be any local/individual or identified group who can bring effect or who can get affected by any initiative or achievement of public and private objectives (Glicken, 2000; Bryson and Crosby, 1992; Ryan, 2002). The principles applied regarding the tourism system, where it is pressured into more partnership particularly in the marketing and planning areas. Three potential benefits, as Bramwell and Sharman (1999) identify derived from consensus-based collaboration. First, any price-related conflicts need to be avoided (Healey, 1996). Second, the involvement of stakeholders in decision making needs to be legitimate, which affect their group activities (Benveniste, 1989). Third, the coordination of policies, schemes, and related services would be enhanced through the willingness to collaborate. As Pearce (2001, p. 51) points out, "Rather than go it alone, individual countries collaborate to create a more attractive single destination area than each is able to achieve its own." During the nineties, authors and researchers started to evaluate and explore different kinds of stakeholders involved in destination planning, development, management, and marketing (Sheehan and Ritchie, 2005). They also studied partnerships as a key factor for destination competitiveness (Gill and Williams, 1994; Ritchie, 1993; Selin and Beason, 1991). There is a need in destination planning of involving public and private sectors to gather data, figures, establish institutions, organizations implementing strategies to attain a common goal (Pforr, 2006; Bramwell and Lane, 2000; Bramwell and Sharman, 1999; Healey 1996; Jamal and Getz, 1994; Gill and Williams, 1994). Gunn (1994) describes that continuous planning in tourism is necessary and must be involved with all other planning for socioeconomic development. Inskeep (1991) advocated the need of a proper and working tourism structure and continuous planning. Achieving coordination among different stakeholders needs a new approach in the tourism system. It is necessary to have a regional approach to, and regional analysis of, tourism (Pearce, 2001). Alliance with regional level will help these less developed countries to generate revenues from the areas having low economic activities or are far from main economic areas through connectivity. From a stakeholder's perspective, the local event can be seen as an open system of interdependence (the action of one stakeholder impacts on the others) and involvement of multiple (private and public) stakeholders. The networks act as platforms for academic, private, and public bodies to share, exchange and access information while getting benefits to create, integrate and modify innovative ideas. These collaborations help in different sectors harness their potential sustainably. Here, local communities, experts, tourism destinations, academics, private and public sector stakeholders share a common goal to develop socioeconomic order in the tourism sector. This chapter will give an overview of how a partnership between major and minor stakeholders through analyzing with the concept of Social network Analysis and Social Capital, interrelationships can be maintained and flourished for all the stakeholders in a sustainable way.

9.2 PUBLIC–PRIVATE PARTNERSHIPS BETWEEN MAJOR AND MINOR STAKEHOLDERS

The Public–Private Partnership stands on three keywords: First is Partnership for action and relation formed when different parties come together having common objectives, and organize any event and festival. Second is Public, which constitutes local, regional, and national government resources, funding, etc. Third is Private, which belongs to big, medium, and small business operators as well as individual property owners, and sellers. The amount of understanding, and sense of collaboration between major and minor stakeholders reflects the outcome of any event. The major stakeholders constitute local/regional/national government, big private tour operators, hotel chains, restaurant owners, and transport providers who are directly responsible for planning and organizing a mega festival or event. The minor stakeholders also referred as tourism micro-entrepreneurs are usually constitutes individual stall owners, craftsmen, street food stall owners, tour guides, homestay owners, performers, and camel/horse owners who provide rides in name of giving touristic experiences. During the macroeconomic era of the 1980s with an increment of public debt, a sense of cooperation between state and private organizations arose. According to De Lacy et al. (2001), partnerships are the basic element of sustainable tourism development, which is the current need of every destination. During the First, Seventh, and then, Ninth five

Year plan, the Indian government advocated for getting community support and acknowledged the role of the private sector including, NGOs for social, and economic development. So, PPP is regarded as long-term relationship model for overall community growth, greater efficiency, and better source of employment and better execution of government regulations through sharing responsibilities. The PPP model depicts different perceptions:

First perception: The PPP model in this perception focuses on the process of organizational arrangements and sharing of risks. It is considered important for Public and Private Sectors to share risk to provide better quality services and products and organize a better event/festival by working together.

Second perception: The PPP model focuses on the financial aspects of organizing an event or festival. The partnership between the two sectors would give much leverage to the funding and allocation of resources. Thus, sharing of profits and investments can bring economic development for both sectors through joint ownership.

Third perception: As per World Bank, PPP is considered Joint collaboration of the Public and private sectors. In the partnership, every responsible stakeholder provides resources like workforce, utilities, investment, information, technical support, and many more. Also, they need to participate in the roles they have been given, or allotted from decision making to selling of products and services. The perception stands for how the organizational structure is managed by different actors involved in carrying out community festivals/event.

Fourth perception: The perception depicts the strategies undertaken for carrying out of the whole involvement and collaboration of different sectors together. From the process of having vision, goals, objectives, directions, cooperation model to the allocation of roles and responsibilities and sharing of benefits, collaboration is needed at all levels.

The two very important features of PPPs are, first is heavily focused on service delivery with a good rate of investment, and second is shifting of risk factor from government to private sector. Some major characteristics of the PPP would be:

- Sharing of responsibility for development of adequate infrastructure and having investment risks in designing and construction by public and private sectors.
- The partnership can be valid for a longer period of time in order to provide quality facilities, service, and products to people/tourists through contractual agreement between public and private sectors.

- The distribution of risk factors and benefit from the outcome of a successful organized event/festival by involving and public sector skills leads to better community development.

The Ministry of Finance adopted an overall definition of PPP as "Public Private Partnership means an arrangement between a government/statutory entity/government owned entity on one side and a private sector entity on the other, for the provision of public assets and/or public services, through investments being made and/or management being undertaken by the private sector entity, for a specified period of time, where there is well-defined allocation of risk between the private sector and the public entity and the private entity receives performance-linked payments that conform (or are benchmarked) to specified and predetermined performance standards, measurable by the public entity or its representative."

9.2.1 COLLABORATION BETWEEN MAJOR AND MINOR STAKEHOLDERS

The Public and Private sector holds numerous stakeholders directly and indirectly involved in organizing a community event/festival. The major and minor stakeholders in this partnership may differ in many issues from different objectives to different outcomes. Micro-entrepreneurs also refer as minor stakeholders, generate an alternative source of income by participating in any event/festivals (Nicholson, 1997) by offering their services as local food-seller, guiding tours, offering animal rides/safaris, offering trekking, hiking, adventure activities, local handicraft seller, performing local art, music or dance, providing home-stays, cooking classes, and many more. These Minor stakeholders usually work as an individual or in a very small group but act as an important element in carrying out the whole project of community event. For example, in Pangadaran, many boat owners in time of community event/festival switch their daily fishing to offering transport to carry tourists to different sites. The role of major stakeholders who are actively involved from planning to execution of community event/festival needs to include the interest of minor stakeholders as they are the ones whom tourists interact directly while enjoying different amenities and services. Often, in decision making and development of strategies, minor stakeholders are ignored and this later creates a raft and confusion of what is promised to the tourists and what they actually witness on the ground level. In Rural India, women are encouraged to start their own B&B, home-stays, and indulge in handicraft and cooking classes. The role of women micro-entrepreneur is coming into the picture who are getting help from government schemes. The government scheme offers funds, skill development training, marketing assistance, infrastructure, and many more as per need. There is a constant need for the Major and Minor stakeholders to work together in order to create a distinctive image of the event/festival. Proper sharing of information with good communication about different events is needed. The sharing of responsibilities would bring more innovation and new ways of offering products and services to the tourists, like promoting local products in festival by involving local traders and local people in the organization process. The operation of Minor stakeholders often lacks experience, funding, and required resources which could be managed by collaboration with major stakeholders like tour operators, government funding, etc. This partnership would make the community and local people more engaged in the event bringing more acceptance towards tourists and more creativity on the ground level. The system would then follow a bottom-top arrangement where the local community would feel the importance of touristic activities for their growth and reliability towards local/regional/national government. For major and minor stakeholders, there are some crucial aspects to be considered for every stage of collaborations.

9.2.1.1 MAJOR CHALLENGES

There are significant challenges that create barriers among stakeholders while working together during managing of event:

- Transparency: Being transparent while working together is a big challenge when there is a difference among the major and minor stakeholders about their work.
- Project Appraisal: Before the execution of PPP, it is required to pass the project through appraisal to check its technicality.
- Risk Allocation: In collaborating and organizing of an event, several risk factors emerge from social risks to financial risks proving a major challenge.
- Government guarantee: Support from local government through various funds, schemes, policies, taxation, etc. is needed.
- Regulatory Independence: There is a need to have freedom of doing work. Excessive scanning and direction from the government hamper creativity and innovation.

Collaborative Involvement of Major and Minor Stakeholders 119

- Corporate governance: A proper administration is needed to regulate work without discrimination.

9.2.2   COLLABORATION PROCESS

There is a process to follow for the planning to execution of the event with the collaboration of Major and minor stakeholders. In the six stages of the collaboration process described below in Table 9.1, different stakeholders play their role with certain responsibilities.

Stage 1 of the process is about precondition, which varies differently for major and minor stakeholders. For major stakeholders, strategic planning is needed to be done while for minor stakeholders, there is need to plan about their products and marketing tactics while keeping an eye on relative competitions.

Stage 2: Problem: There is need to identify different problems and issues that could arise at any stage of planning and organizing of an event for different stakeholders and alert them for any unwanted disturbances and be quick to come with alternatives.

Stage 3: Direction Setting: The major stakeholders need to be aware of their goals and objectives during their planning process, which would guide them to follow certain instructions. Minor stakeholders take these instructions as direction in order to maintain proper management of the event. In this stage, it is very required to have proper communication setup along with different stakeholders' group and channels. The information flow and its validity are very much needed to be checked and coordinated.

Stage 4: Implementation: Major stakeholders are needed to be creative and innovative in their approach in order to implement the planned event properly. For this, they require loyalty and trust of minor stakeholders.

Stage 5: Evaluation: This is a very important stage of collaboration process between major and minor stakeholders. The evaluation of attained objectives, goals, sales, arrivals of tourists, etc is needed to be analyzed to know involved stakeholder's performances, mistakes, and area for improvement for future purposes.

Stage 6: Outcomes: For future work, this stage is very important to act on the evaluation made on the performances of major and minor stakeholders in the organized event. The outcome will give a clear picture on the actual result of the event.

120 Event Tourism and Sustainable Community Development

TABLE 9.1 Collaboration Process for Community-Based Events.

Stage	Action	
	Major stakeholder	**Minor stakeholder**
Stage 1: Precondition	Crisis/competition/organization network influencing current brand strategy	Profiling of destinations Selection of organizing sites Organizing tourism products and services
Stage 2: Problem	Indentify convener Convene stakeholders Define problems/issues Formulate Brand strategies Legitimate stakeholders Building collaboration Addressing stakeholders' issues Ensure availability of resources	Assessment of existing problems at ground level Proving feedback to Major stakeholders Building collaboration at destination level Address issues at ground level related to resources, finances, disputes etc.
Stage 3: Direction Setting	Collect & Share information Appreciate shared value Distribution of roles Organizing subgroups Establish rules & regulations Discuss various alternatives Sharing common goals Stream detail brand strategy	Formulation of union and subgroup Setting goals, rules, and guidelines Ensuring enough funding, resources, and manpower Ensure regular supervision and work progress
Stage 4: Implementation	Formalize legal structure Implement assigned roles & responsibilities Discuss solutions, strategies, plan, and vision Design, Monitor, and Control	Collective implementation of resources at gourd level Collaboration at horizontal and vertical level Ensure maximum output
Stage 5: Evaluation	Assess predefine objectives Evaluate planning strategies Evaluate responsibilities Document evaluated results Follow up Benchmark	Evaluate and analyze routine work daily Ensure fair and impartial evaluation Provide proper feedback to organizers
Stage 6: Outcomes	Programmatic outcome Collaborative outcome Benefits to stakeholders Capital-oriented outcomes Return of investment (human, financial, social, and sustainable)	Match outcomes with preconditions Prepare further strategies as per outcomes Establish Feedback –outcome base communication channel

Source: Author; Adapted from Simons and Groot (2015)

9.2.3 SHARED RESPONSIBILITIES AMONG STAKEHOLDERS

There are three levels where stakeholders of a tourism destination share responsibilities, co-operation, coordination, and collaboration. As the major stakeholders are involved in the partnership process actively, they get direct benefit from the exposure while the minor are just acts as spectators without much involvement and concern of their needs and demands. It is acknowledged that the community participation varies across places, particularly in developing countries. One factor that inhibits community participation is having the top-down approach to planning or decision-making, where decision-making power lies with government or stakeholders with "official" standing (e.g., NGO), leaving little role for local communities (Wall and Mathieson, 2006, Wilkinson and Pratiwi, 1995). The limitations of a top-down approach is that it diminish the role of minor stakeholders. Thus, a bottom-up approach is needed to be in literature, which guides the potential benefit of less involved stakeholders as well (Narayanan, 2003). The approach will make the involvement of stakeholders on major and minor scale more controlled with distributions of responsibilities, information, and benefit properly managed. This will make the planning process smoother with more control in any crisis in future (Wall and Mathieson, 2006). This is necessary to lower the negative attitudes among major and minor stakeholders to improve their quality of life (Sofield, 2003; Komppula, 2016). There is need to identify different roles and responsibilities of major and minor stakeholders according to their capacities in order to develop tourism communities and help interaction between all stakeholders (Lima, 2021).

9.3 COLLABORATION IN ORGANIZING COMMUNITY EVENTS

The activities conducted by stakeholders create four frameworks of power in the empowerment process namely power over, power to, power with, and power within (Knight and Cottrell, 2016). The result indicated that the tourism organization empower by working collectively.

9.3.1 THROUGH SOCIAL CAPITAL

Social capital connects individuals through social networking and their trustworthiness of each other (Putnam, 2000, p. 19). As per Rohe (2004), new relationships lead to greater trust, and trust leading to efficient collective action upbringing social benefits. Putnam (2000) argued that social capital is the modification of social networks. Defragmenting Capital means any resource that can be used as investment to create value. Social capital emerges from social structure. Social structures and their relationships are termed as multifaceted. The initial motives among stakeholders can be to solve a destination problem but overtime can be developed into more partnerships and more dealings with each other according to level of involvement, directionality, and trust. The initiative of multistakeholder partnership, around 300 public–private partnerships under the UN ground (WSSD, 2002). The two types of social capital make the relationships among stakeholders more fruitful. Strong tie social capital is referred to as cohesion as well as closure though their meaning is bit different. Weak ties social capital is the process of defragmenting information within a structure. It exists by social networks, reacting with information and resources that will not process through formal way (Koput and Broschak, 2010).

9.3.2 THROUGH SOCIAL NETWORKS

As the tourism structure becoming more and more volatile with increase in categorical fragmentation, the everyday tourism business keeps evolving in order to let proper planning and marketing. The benefits of this collaboration can be following (Bramwell and Sharman, 1999):

- The collaboration would help in reducing the cost of solving problems among stakeholders;
- Collective decision making will help in fueling active involvement and carrying out collective actions more profoundly; and
- The level of trust and willingness to work together would increase the policy coordination and activities related to it.

The central position at first glance is taken by stakeholders at management level who are national travel associations, regional governments, travel agencies, local tourism associations, and local communities. Today the world is more and more becoming as virtual world. The reference groups are mostly active with their recommendations and reviews in online networking. Individuals getting registered with various social networks get their required social capital and networking as well as customers from online and use them in enhancing their real business setup. The concept of people-first tourism system supported by cloud and social media technology was developed as web-based and phone-enabled social network system, which connects micro-entrepreneurs with their potential markets and targets.

Collaborative Involvement of Major and Minor Stakeholders

9.3.3 *SHARED RESPONSIBILITIES THROUGH SOCIAL NETWORK AND SOCIAL CAPITAL*

The Shared Responsibilities table shows collaboration among major and minor stakeholders through the method of social network and social capital. Major stakeholders in order for getting a good social network relies on establishing large network of categorical and subcategorical networks, works together in an organization for a common goal, and relies on different departments for proper management. In social capital, the major stakeholders need to possess good brand value, reputation, competitive advantage, and building trustworthy relationships all along. Minor stakeholders' responsibility in social network is to work as a group for maximum output and providing ground level authentic products and services connective to the event. In social capital, minor stakeholders build their brand image by interacting with big stakeholders, maintaining proper communication, and actively participating as per their assigned responsibilities with the rest of the management as depicted in Table 9.2.

TABLE 9.2 Shared Responsibilities Through Social Network and Social Capital Among Stakeholders

Shared responsibilities in stakeholders	Major stakeholders	Minor stakeholders
Social Network	Establishing large scale social network Work as an organizational level towards collectives' vision Working towards connective and establishing social cooperation among major tourism stakeholders	Establishing small scale social network Work as an individual and group level towards collective's goals Working at ground level through connecting local tourism stakeholders towards organizing community events
Social Capital	Building Goodwill and Branding of tourism destination Creating destination image and attractiveness Ensuring shared responsibilities with minor stakeholders and fellow stakeholders Maintaining destination sustainability, authenticity and uniqueness.	Building trust among local stakeholders Establishing effective communication and cooperation at ground level Ensuring shared responsibilities with major stakeholders and local communities about local events Maintaining ethnicity and cultural values of community events Seeking active participation and cooperation with local residents

Source: Author.

9.4 COLLECTIVE RESPONSIBILITY MODEL (CRM)

With the need of making the different stakeholder at different levels to come together and deliver their products and services through shared responsibilities, which is described in Table 9.1 with the six stages of collaboration planning process and how the planning divides responsibilities through social network and social capital in Table 9.2. From Tables 9.1 and 9.2, a joint framework of CRM is proposed that defines how major and minor stakeholders perform their responsibilities and bear the profit and feedback for the event together. The model in Figure 9.1, also describes the involvement of stakeholders as per their roles toward social network and social capital in different stages of planning process.

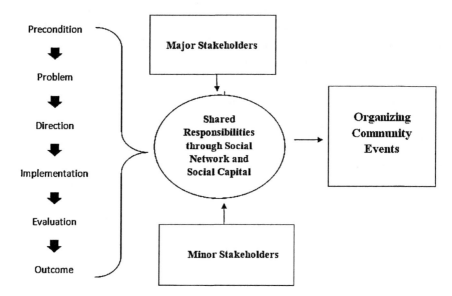

FIGURE 9.1 Collective responsibilities model (CRM) for stakeholders towards organizing community events.

Source: Author.

9.5 CONCLUSIONS

The study shows that there needs to be a proper collaboration management system, which would analyze and evaluate stakeholders' performance and how willing they are to collaborate as well as cooperate in order to organize a successful event or fair. The collaboration process is constituted with six divided stages which would be applied to major as well as minor stakeholders. Also, these stakeholders needed to be sharing responsibilities with each other on the basis of social network and social capital. Collectively, a CRM model is proposed to understand the system in more efficient manner and how connected they are with each other. The CRM depicts that is by following different six kinds of process from planning to organizing an event with the cooperation of major and minor stakeholders to work together and share information easily along with their separate assigned roles.

KEYWORDS

- **public–private partnership**
- **stakeholders**
- **community events**
- **collective responsibilities model (CRM)**
- **social network**
- **entrepreneurs**

REFERENCES

Atkinson, A. A.; Waterhouse, J. H.; Wells, R. B. A. Stakeholder Approach to Strategic Performance Measurement. *Sloan Manage. Rev.* **1997,** *38*, 25–37.

Benveniste, G. *Mastering the Politics of Planning*; Jossey-Bass: San Francisco.

Bramwell, B.; Lane, B. *Tourism Collaboration and Partnerships. Politics, Practice and Sustainability*; Channel View Publications: Clevedon, 2000.

Bramwell, B.; Sharman, A. Collaboration in Local Tourism Policymaking. *Ann. Tour. Res.* **1999,** *26* (2), 392–415.

Brunet, S.; Bauer, J.; DeLacy, T.; Tshering, K. Tourism Development in Bhutan: Tensions between Tradition and Modernity. *J. Sustain. Tour.* **2001,** *9*. DOI: 10.1080/09669580108667401.

Bryson, J.; Barbara C.; Stone, M. The Design and Implementation of Cross-Sector Collaborations: Propositions from the Literature. *Public Admin. Rev.* **2006,** *66*, 44–55. http://www.jstor.org/stable/4096569 (accessed June 5, 2021).

Getz, D. Resident Attitudes towards Tourism: A Longitudinal Case Study in Spey Valley, Scotland. *Tour. Manage.* **1994.**

Getz, D.; Jamal, T. The Environment-Community Symbiosis: A Case for Collaborative Tourism Planning. *J. Sustain. Tour.* **1994.**

Gill, A.; Williams, P. Managing Growth in Mountain Tourism Communities. *Tour. Manage.* **1994,** *15* (3), 212–220.

Gray, B. *Collaboration Finding Common Ground for Multi-Party Problems*; Jossey-Bass: San Francisco, CA, 1989.

Gunn, C. A. *Tourism Planning*, 2nd ed.; Taylor and Francis: New York, 1988.

Gunn, C. A. *Tourism Planning: Basic Concepts Cases*, 3rd ed.; Taylor and Francis: Washington, DC, 1994.

Healey, P. The Communicative Turn in Planning Theory and its Implications for Spatial Strategy Formation. *Environ. Plan. B* **1996,** *23* (2), 217–234. https://doi.org/10.1068/b230217

Inskeep, E. *Tourism Planning: An Integrated and Sustainable Development Approach*; Van Nostrand Reinhold: New York, 1991

Knight, D. W.; Cottrell, S. P. Evaluating Tourism-Linked Empowerment in Cuzco, Peru. *Ann. Tour. Res.* **2016,** 56(C), 32–47.

Komppula, R. The Role of Different Stakeholders in Destination Development. *Tour. Rev.* **2016,** *71* (1), 67–76. https://doi.org/10.1108/TR-06–2015–0030

Koput, K. W.; Broschak, J. P. *Social Capital in Business*; Elgar Research Collection, 2010.

Lima, V. Collaborative Governance for Sustainable Development, 2021. DOI: 10.1007/978–3-319–71066–2_2–1.

Mor, S.; Archer, G.; Madan, S. Gender and Entrepreneurial Activities: Microentrepreneurs in Rural India, **2018,** *7*, 55–74.

Narayanan, P. Empowerment through Participation: How Effective Is This Approach? *Econ. Polit. Wkly.* **2003,** *38*, 2484–2486. DOI: 10.2307/4413702.

Nicholson, B. From Migrant to Micro-Entrepreneur: Do-It-Yourself Development in Albania. *SEER: J. Labour Soc. Affairs Eastern Eur.* **2001,** *4* (3), 39–41. http://www.jstor.org/stable/43291881 (accessed June 5, 2021).

Pearce, D. G. Towards a Regional Analysis of Tourism in Southeast Asia. In *Interconnected Worlds: Tourism in Southeast Asia*; Teo, P., Chang, T. C., Ho, K. C., Eds.; Pergamon: Amsterdam, 2001; pp 27–43.

Pforr, C. The Makers and the Shakers of Tourism Policy in the Northern Territory of Australia: A Policy Network Analysis of Actors and Their Relational Constellations. *J. Hospital. Tour. Manage.* **2002,** *9* (2), 134–151.

Pforr, C. Tourism Policy in the Making: An Australian Network Study. *Ann. Tour. Res.* **2006,** *33* (1), 87–108.

Putnam, R. D. Bowling Alone: America's Declining Social Capital. *J Democr* **1995,** *6*, 65.

Putnam, R. D. *Bowling Alone: The Collapse and Revival of American Community*; Simon & Schuster: New York, 2000.

Ritchie, J. B.; Crouch, G. I. *The Competitive Destination: A Sustainable Tourism Perspective*; CABI, 2003.

Rohe, W. Building Social Capital Through Community Development. *J. Am. Plan. Assoc.* **2004,** *70*, 158–164.

Ryan, C. Equity, Management, Power Sharing and Sustainability-Issues of the 'New Tourism'. *Tour. Manage.* **2002,** *23* (1): 17–26.

Selin, S.; Beason, K. Interorganizational Relations in Tourism. *Ann. Tour. Res.* **1991,** *18* (4), 639–652.

Sheehan, L. R.; Ritchie, J. R. B. Destination Stakeholders, Exploring Identity and Salience. *Ann. Tour. Res.* **2005,** *32* (3), 711–734.

Simons, I.; Groot, E. D. Power and Empowerment in Community-Based Tourism: Opening Pandora's Box? *Tour. Rev.* **2015,** *70*, 72–84.

Sofield, T. *Empowerment for Sustainable Tourism Development*; Emerald Group Publishing, 2003.

Sofield, T.; Li, F. M. S. China: Ecotourism and Cultural Tourism, Harmony or Dissonance. *Crit. Iss. Ecotour.: Understanding A Complex Tourism Phenomenon* **2007**.

Turnley, J. Getting Stakeholder Participation 'Right': A Discussion of Participatory Processes and Possible Pitfalls. *Environ. Sci. Policy* **2000**, *3*, 305–310. DOI: 10.1016/S1462–9011(00)00105–2

Wall, G.; Mathieson, A. *Tourism: Change, Impacts, and Opportunities*; Pearson Education: Essex, 2006.

Wilkinson, P. F.; Pratiwi, W. Gender and Tourism in an Indonesian Village. *Ann. Tour. Res.* **1995**, *22*, 283–299.

CHAPTER 10

Promoting Events and Festivals Through Digital Marketing Tools: A Conceptual Framework

BETÜL KODAŞ

Department of Tourism Management in Faculty of Tourism, Mardin Artuklu University, Artuklu/Mardin, Turkey

ABSTRACT

In the digitalization of marketing, digital marketing tools are the best way to advertise and promote the products and services. In the context of events and festival, digital media is better than traditional media to promote the events using digital marketing tools such as social media networks, content marketing, search engine optimization, search engine marketing, web portal, mobile marketing, e-wom marketing, etc. To illustrate, event's organizers use the social media applications like Facebook, Instagram, and YouTube to advertise and promote events they organized at the stage of pre and during events. Parallel to advent of information and communication technology, every destination must adopt their management and marketing practices to the changed world and changed consumer behavior. In this context, tourism destination try to look for new communication way and new marketing approaches in order that they could satisfy their consumers, advertise, and promote their product. Digital marketing tools are appropriate way to reach targeted audience to announce and marketing the events by creating effective promotional strategies. Thus, the aim of this chapter to present the usage of digital marketing tools for event and festival promotions conceptually.

Please note that few chapters were submitted during the peak of the pandemic. The long period of time to publish (due to supply chain and other issues) may have changed the perspectives presented in the chapter altogether.

Event Tourism and Sustainable Community Development: Advances, Effects, and Implications.
Ekta Dhariwal, Shruti Arora, Anukrati Sharma, Azizul Hassan (Eds.)
© 2024 Apple Academic Press, Inc. Co-published with CRC Press (Taylor & Francis)

10.1 INTRODUCTION

Events and festivals that can be considered as important destination attractions for the tourist can attract to the destination. They are used to improve tourism and hospitality supply and support tourism development, accordingly, expanding alternative tourism products (Connell et al., 2015). For this reason, destination can attract their current and potential targeted customers to their region with some special events using both traditional and digital media. For example, reviewing UGC in social media can be important tools for promoting events and festivals as it allows to understand the characteristic of consumers who use digital communication channel (Leung et al., 2013). Thus, through social media as an extended web.2.0, events and festival organizers have an ability to manage targeted consumers engagement (Hudson et al., 2013; Kodaş, 2021). Understanding which media is more important to both consumers and festival organizer needs to be answered firstly. Today, although traditional media is useful for product advertising and develop promotional strategies for tourism and event industry, marketing digital media era is becoming more dominant for business. In this chapter, it will be examined with benefit of digital marketing for event and festival organizer and tourism destination and how digital marketing tools will be used for promoting tourism events and festivals by giving some examples. In this line, in this chapter, the integration of social media within integrated marketing communication and various digital marketing tools which can be used in the advertising and promoting events and festivals will be discussed conceptually by making comprehensive literature review and reveal digital marketing tools used by events industry. So, the aim of this chapter is to analyze in depths relation between digital marketing tools and events promotions, advertisement and reveal how digital marketing tools applications can be used effectively to promote tourism events and festivals. In the end of chapter, some practical examples will be presented to events marketers about digital marketing tools used effectively.

10.2 EVENTS CONCEPT AND IMPORTANCE FOR TOURISM DESTINATIONS

Festivals and events have become an essential component of every destination and are considered beyond tourist attractions because they assist in sustaining tourism destination by creating awareness, building image, and promoting destination (Prentice and Anderson, 2003; Lee et al., 2004: Getz, 2008; Kim et al., 2010). Festivals and events remark among different tourism destinations by increasing the awareness of the region where they are held (McClinchey, 2008; Lee et al., 2012, 2013). For example, a destination staging a mega event such as the Olympic Games, the World Cup, can expect much media coverage and resulting visitor's awareness of destination (Dimanche, 2002).

Events and festivals are crucial elements of tourism industries and playing an important role in destination familiarity and branding. (Getz and Page, 2016). Additionally, as events and festivals which are held in a particular destination, are enhancing the positive brand image of destination and destination brand loyalty, they can be considered as a way of promoting tourism destinations (Kodaş, 2021).

Shone and Parry (2004, p. 4) defined *"events" as "non-routine events other than normal events that people have in their daily lives."* According to Getz (1997, p. 16) event tourism as the *"planning, development and marketing of events as primary or secondary tourist attractions to maximise the number of tourists participating in events."* Event is defined as a notable activity taking place in a specific place and a period of time (Getz, 2007, p. 19). As it is seen that event and events tourism are defined according to various researcher but in the context to types and features of events, these definitions may be changeable in terms of classification. For example, the aim of events is different in terms of types of events such as politic events or educational and scientific events. It is derived from classification of event types and purpose. As a part of destination tourist attractions, events are classified in the scope of its size, types, and features. According to sizes of events, it is classified as mega, hallmark, special and local (Hall, 1989, p. 265). There are some various events that are classified by Getz (2008, p. 404). According to Getz (2008) cultural celebrations, (Festivals, Carnivals, etc), recreational activities (such as entertainment events) political events, art and entertainment (concert, exhibitions, etc), business trade, educational, and scientific (conferences, congress, symposium, etc) sport competitions and special events are considered the most widely accepted event types in the literature.

Events that hold in a destination in a specific date and theme give some important contributes to the destination. Firstly, events are important facilities for the destination because they make contribution to regional economic development by increasing visitors' number and tourist expenditures (Koba, 2021). Also, events build strong positive image for the host destination, create competitive advantage, and extend tourism season (Tassiopoulus, 2005; Koba, 2021). While the organized festivals increase the perceived image of the attendees toward to the region, they also positively affect the revisit intention of the attendees (Morais and Lin, 2010, p. 193). Being an integral part of human society, with events and festivals, the awareness of the local history and culture is increased, especially among the local people, and it also plays an important role in the development of local industries (Ngeryuang and Ying Wu, 2020). Therefore, it can be noted that events provided some advantages for any destination in the context of social, economic, and cultural development (Koba, 2021). For example, cultural interaction between event or festival attendee and local resident may occur during events and enable tourist to gain cultural knowledge about regional culture such as consuming local food when participating gastronomy festival. As revealed in study of Kim Goh and Yuan (2010), knowledge and learning is a dominant tourist motivational factor in the food events to which tourists attend. To state that events and festival's importance for destination, Getz (2016) have presented some core propositions for event tourism. These assert that event tourism is attractions for tourist, can create positive images for any destination toward they want to improve loyalty level of tourist, and assist brand or re-position cities; contribute to place marketing by making cities more livable and attractive for targeted audience; animate some elements of city (such as resorts, parks etc.), making them more attractive to visit and re-visit, and drawing advantage from them more efficiently; and finally acts as a catalyst for other forms of desired development, thereby generating a long-term or permanent legacy (Getz, 2016, p. 597). When considered that events have so many advantages for development of tourism in a destination, every destination tries to make events and festivals, which is organized in their destination, more attractive and to promote them in an efficient way using digital media. The fact that usage of digital media is better than traditional media as it provided them two-way communication way to reach eventgoers and persuade them to attend the events or festivals.

10.3 DIGITAL MARKETING AND ITS TOOLS TO PROMOTE EVENTS

Digital marketing is a kind of marketing that uses technology to make promotional activities more effective, comprehensive and target large populations (Merisavo, 2006, p. 6). *Digital marketing uses the Internet and Information technology to extend and improve traditional marketing functions* (Urban,

2004, p. 2). The main goal of digital marketing is attracting customers and allowing them to interact with the brand, business, and organization through digital media tools and utilizes electronic media to promote products (Yasmin et al., 2015). In terms of tourism organizations and destinations beyond the traditional marketing, digital marketing and its tools are important ways to communicate with targeted customers efficiently as they enable two-way communication between business and consumers. Therefore, tourism organization should pay attention to opportunity of internet if they want to have good interactions with their customer and reach to the potential customers. Being as a part of destination promotion polices, events, festivals, or special events are now vital for contributing to the destination branding studies. In the scope of events and festivals which is a form of events, event organizer could use internet marketing especially digital marketing with its tools such as social media networks, mobile networks, search engine optimization etc., to promote products and services regarding to events and festivals which they organized and offered. As significant development in the evolution of the internet and technology in the world, the information and communications technologies (ICTs) play a major role in development of tourism industry and destination (Bethapudi, 2013). Parallel to these developments in the information and communication technologies, digital marketing has been considered more importantly in various service business.

Digital marketing, which has been developed since the 1990s and 2000s, has changed the way brands and businesses used technology with digital media for their marketing (Carter et al., 2007). There are some tools of digital marketing that business utilizes to contact with customers such as content marketing, influencer marketing, social media marketing, online advertising, and business websites (Suryawardani and Wiranatha, 2016). So, it is stated that digital marketing tools such as social media marketing, viral marketing, e-Wom, search engine marketing, online marketing, mobile communication, and many others of digital media, are commonly used in business and destination marketing facilities such as hotels, accommodation, travel agency and events, etc. In the events marketing and management, especially social media tools are used frequently.

Social media is defined by Brake and Safko (2009, p. 6) as *"activities, practices, and behaviors among communities of people who gather online to share information, knowledge, and opinions using conversational media."* Allowing individuals to contribute their thoughts, opinions and creations to the internet via technology has radically changed the way in which information is created and spread (Buhalisand Law, 2008; Xiang and Gretzel, 2010).

Many researchers examined that the usage of social media applications in the tourism and hospitality literature including event and festival studies (Paris et al., 2010; Hudson and Hudson, 2013; MacKay et al., 2017; Wong et al.,2020). So, it can be said that social media platforms are beneficial to developing different marketing and management strategies to promote the tourism events. (Cobanoglu et al., 2021). For example, Paris et al. (2010) revealed that how the influence of trust, expected relationships and perceived enjoyment forming consumer attitudes toward Facebook and consumers attending intentions to the event and using Facebook "events" as a way for promoting special events for customers. Mintel (2013) and Hudson et al. (2015) indicated that tourists are using social media networks like Facebook, Instagram, and YouTube to look for needed information about festivals. In the study of Suryawardani and Wiranatha (2016), digital marketing is found that it is an effective promotional tool for Sanur Village Festival 2015 via different forms of digital media. Therefore, marketing through social media is vital for event's organizers to reach and attract targeted potential customer for promotions events. To do this, it is required to use digital marketing tools effectively, especially social media marketing (using various social media platforms (Facebook, Twitter, YouTube, and blogs etc.), which provide mutual communication between event organizer and customer. Besides social media marketing which is one of the important tools of digital marketing (Chaffey, 2011) and with the advent of internet, various digital marketing tools are started to have been used to promote events by event organizer.

Considering that social media marketing is the dominant digital communication channels (Hudson et al., 2015), social media platform is a good source for E-wom, which is seen as a reflection of word-of-mouth marketing in the digital world. E-wom is considered as a sharing information and with this information sharing, the recommendations of other consumers, who experienced with the product or service, which they consumed, should be taken into account by tourism and event practitioner.

With content marketing (digital) events practitioners can give information to customer by preparing contents and sharing about events facilities. So, content marketing is significant information source for eventgoers by gaining deep knowledge from various contents created about events by event marketers. Tourist can draw advantage from the experiences and thoughts of other tourist in their purchasing decision processes against any product.

Web portal is a good way to give information and announce the events to the events or festival attendees. Event's organizer can improve their visibility and attractiveness if they design a good web portal by providing needed information. To illustrate, the whole information about congresses, festivals, cultural, and artistic events to be held on certain dates in the destination should be given on the destination web portal. The portal has different language options, and information on promotions of businesses and applications such as 360 virtual tours which can make contribution to the promotion of the events or festivals (Unurlu, 2021).

Another digital marketing tool is *mobile marketing* which is considered as a digital marketing communication strategy, and it can be an effective promotional tool that lead to communication between events and festival organizer-goers mutually. Friedric et al. (2009) stated that the mobile phone is the best tool ever made for building an effective customer relationship management. So, with mobile marketing, event organizer and marketers can communicate with their current and potential customer, provide some valuable information about events with mobile apps. Mobile advertising offers marketers the potential to promote tourism products in a personalized and interactive way (Smutkupt et al., 2010).

E-mail marketing is one of the fundamental of digital marketing tools to announce information event content such as participating date, scope of events, or festivals. By sending mail, event organize can give all information about events to reach and persuade eventgoers to attend. It is used for sharing information, promoting products, and interacting with customers (Simmons, 2007). In terms of event and festival organization, e-mail can assist in reaching existing and target specific communities to announce and promote their product and service regarding events activities, which are held in a specific destination or venue. Via direct digital marketing, event's organizer sends ads to attract their customer easily (Yasmin et al., 2015).

Search Engine Optimization (SEO) is one of the important digital marketing tools. SEO plays a very important role in designating the website traffic (Kaur, 2017), and it is used to promote product digitally. SEO not only attracts many visitors toward the tourism destination but also allows the visibility of the destination or business website to increase (Oklobdžija, 2015). As for Search Engine Marketing (SEM), it is defined as *a process of marketing a business, brand, product, or service through paid advertisements that appear in the search engine results pages* (Rajkumar et al., 2021, p. 4269). Events are held in destination, could be investigated in the search engines like Google by visitors via keyword. With keyword planner, searched keywords related to events and festivals can be identified, thereby assisting in positioning the website in the first page of the search engine results pages by paying a fee like Pay Per Click (PPC) or Adwords (Rajkumar et al., 2021).

Thus, destination may have a competitive advantage between other destination which organized the similar event or festivals. SEO and SEM provide for the improvement of the visibility of the website. Through SEM, which is considered as a valuable part of a media plan, when they organized any kinds of events or festivals, destination advertisers can benefit from direct communication with consumers (Kelley et al., 2015).

10.4   FINAL CONSIDERATION

Generally speaking, consumers are now dramatically being more and more involved in the digitalization world when they want to purchase products and services. The internet revolution has altered the consumer behavior, demands, and business management practices. In the context of marketing practices, the importance of digitalization has increased after web revolution in terms of both consumer and business (Drummond et al., 2020). With regards to the events industry, event organizer must analyze their status and develop strategies of marketing in digital world. Rapid development of digital media tools for the marketing and management of any tourism business and destination, many studies including bibliometric research were conducted in the tourism and hospitality literature in the context of ICT and social media (Law et al., 2014; Mirzaalian and Halpenny, 2019; Harb et al., 2019; Ip et al., 2020; Türkmendağ, 2021). While consumers or tourists are seeking valuable information regarding products or establishment through digital platform, business is trying to engage them to their business to enhance their loyalty using internet marketing. For the event or festival management, this effort is the same. For this, destinations use both traditional and digital media to advertise and promote their tourism product to their current and potential customer. For instance, an event organizer must use social media to build successful events and announce the required information before the events, so as to encourage current and potential attender to attend the event (Kodaş, 2021). If event organizers want to promote events or festival via social media, they should learn current and potential customers' preferences and event-related personality to fulfill their request and demand (Moise and Crucero, 2014).

Consumers feel more engaged with products, services, and organizations when they have given feedback (Mangould and Faulds, 2009). For example, congress and symposium organizers are trying to respond the attendee's question before and during congress and to engage them by giving feedback to satisfy the congress attendees. Congress organizers use social network applications and give them to submit feedback regarding to products or services, which offered to them. During the outbreak's periods, especially in the COVID-19 pandemic, some of congress, symposium, festivals are held online environment. These events try to be in contact in their participants with digital media and use to digital marketing tools to them by giving all information that they needed. In the other events organization such as festivals, festival organizer can design a website by which current and potential goers can take information all about festivals and make comment or provide feedback. To attract current and potential customers, event's organizers use digital media channels (social media marketing, mobile marketing, e-mail marketing, etc.), and through digital engagement (Hudson et al., 2015; Kodaş, 2021), they could build customer loyalty toward their organized events.

Today, digital marketing provides businesses with significant advantages in reaching out to their customers. Event and festival practitioners, who adopt marketing practices made with digital media, can reach their customers quickly, respond to their requests and demands, promote their products easily and with the least cost, ultimately affect the decision-making processes of the participants thanks to digital marketing. For example, an effective and well-designed website, digital advertisements containing promotional information, advertisements in social media applications, MMS, SMS, etc. sent with mobile marketing, and information about the event by sending direct mail to the customers are some forms of digital marketing which are effective in the marketing of event and festival. Finally, it can be stated that these digital marketing tools offers remarkable advantages to event organizers in terms of creating, building images, and enhancing loyalty of customer. To conclude, this chapter hopefully contributes to improve the usage of digital marketing tools in the event industry.

KEYWORDS

- **digitalization**
- **digital marketing**
- **event and festival promotion**

REFERENCES

Bethapudi, A. The Role of ICT in the Tourism Industry. *J. Appl. Econ. Busi.* **2013,** *1* (4), pp. 67–79.

Brake, D.; Safko, L. The social media bible. John Wiley and Sons, Inc.Newyork.

Bu, Y.; Parkinson, J.; Thaichon, P. Digital Content Marketing as a Catalyst for E-WOM in Food Tourism. *Australasian Market. J.* **2021,** *29* (2), 142–154.

Buhalis, D.; Law, R. Progress in Information Technology and Tourism Management: 20 Years on and 10 Years After the Internet—the State of eTourism Research. *Tour. Manage.* **2008,** *29* (4), 609–623.

Carter, B.; Gregory, B.; Frank, C.; Bud, S. *Digital Marketing for Dummies*; John Wiley & Sons, 2007. ISBN 978.

Chaffey, D. *E-Business and E-Commerce Management*; Pearson Education: Harlow, 2011.

Cobanoglu, C.; Doğan, S.; Güngör, M. Y. Emerging Technologies at the Events. In *Impact of ICTs on Event Management and Marketing*; IGI Global: Communication Corporation, 2021; pp 53–68.

Connell, J.; Page, S. J.; Meyer, D. Visitor Attractions and Events: Responding to Seasonality. *Tour. Manage.* **2015,** *46*, 283–298.

Dimanche, F. The Contribution of Special Events to Destination Brand Equity. In *City Tourism 2002: Proceedings of European Cities Tourism's International Conference*; Wöber, K. W., Ed.; Springer: Vienna, 2002; pp. 73–80.

Drummond, C.; O'Toole, T.; McGrath, H. Digital Engagement Strategies and Tactics in Social Media Marketing. *Eur. J. Market.* **2020,** *54* (6), 1247–1280.

Friedrich, R.; Grone, F.; Holblin, K.; Peterson, M. The March of Mobile Marketing: New Chances for Consumer Companies, New Opportunities for Mobile Operators. *J. Advert. Res.* **2009,** *49* (1), 54–61.

Getz, D. *Event Management and Event Tourism*; New York: Cognizant, 1997; p 251

Getz, D. *Event Studies: Theory, Research and Policy for Planned Events*; Elseiver Butterworth-Heinemann: Oxford, 2007.

Getz, D. Event Tourism, Definition, Evolution and Research. *Tour. Manage.* **2008,** *29*, 403–428.

Getz, D.; Page, S. J. Progress and Prospects for Event Tourism Research. *Tour. Manage.* **2016,** *52*, 593–631.

Hall, C. M. The Definition and Analysis of Hallmark Tourist Events. *Geo J.* **1989,** *19* (3), 263–268.

Harb, A. A.; Fowler, D.; Chang, H. J. J.; Blum, S. C.; Alakaleek, W. Social Media as a Marketing Tool for Events. *J. Hospital. Tour. Technol.* **2019,** *10* (1), 28–44.

Hodeghatta, U. R.; Sahney, S. Understanding Twitter as an e-WOM. *J. Syst. Inf. Technol.* **2016,** *18* (1), 89–115.

Hudson, S.; Hudson, R. Engaging with Consumers Using Social Media: A Case Study of Music Festivals. *Int. J. Event Fest. Manage.* **2013,** *4* (3), 206–223.

Hudson, S.; Roth, M. S.; Madden, T. J.; Hudson, R. The Effects of Social Media on Emotions, Brand Relationship Quality, and Word of Mouth: An Empirical Study of Music Festival Attendees. *Tour. Manage.* **2015,** *47*, 68–76.

Joy, J.; Dadwal, S. S.; Pryce, P. A. Innovative Trends in Technology for Marketing of Events. In *Handbook of Research on Innovations in Technology and Marketing for the Connected Consumer*; IGI Global, 2020; pp 374–400.

Kaur, G. The Importance of Digital Marketing in the Tourism Industry. *Int. J. Res-Granthaalayah* **2017**, *5* (6), pp. 72–77.

Kelley, L.; Sheehan, K.; Jugenheimer, D. W. *Advertising Media Planning: A Brand Management Approach*, 4th ed.; Routledge: New York and London, 2015.

Kim, S. S.; Prideaux, B.; Chon, K. A Comparison of Results of Three Stastical Methods to Understand Determinants of Festival Participants' Expenditures. *İnt. J. Hospital. Manage.* **2010**, *29* (2), 297–307.

Koba, Y. Internet Marketing Communication in Event Tourism Promotion. In *The Emerald Handbook of ICT in Tourism and Hospitality*; Emerald Publishing Limite,2 2020; pp 149–164.

Kodaş, B. Web Revolution and Events: Development and Progress. In *Impact of ICTs on Event Management and Marketing*; IGI Global, 2021; pp 18–32.

Law, R.; Bai, B.; Ip, C.; Leung, R. Progress and Development of Information and Communication Technologies in Hospitality. *Int. J. Contemp. Hospital. Manage.* **2011**, *23* (4), 533–551.

Law, R.; Buhalis, D.; Cobanoglu, C. Progress on Information and Communication Technologies in Hospitality and Tourism. *Int. J. Contemp. Hospital. Manage.* **2014**, *26* (5), 727–750.

Lee, I. S.; Lee, T. C.; Arcodia, C. The Effect of Community Attachment on Cultural Festival Visitor's Satisfaction and Future İntentions. *Curr. İss. Tour.* **2013**, *17* (9), 800–812.

Lee, I.; Arcodia, C.; Lee, T. J. Benefits of visiting a multicultural festival: The Case of South Korea. Tourism Management, 33, pp: 334–340

Lee, Y. K.; Lee, C. K.; Lee, S. K.; Babin, B. J. Festivalscapes and Patron's Emotions, Satisfaction, and Loyalty. *J. Busi. Res.* **2004**, 56–64.

Leung, D.; Law, R.; Van Hoof, H.; Buhalis, D. Social Media in Tourism and Hospitality: A Literature Review. *J. Travel Tour. Market.* **2013**, *30* (1–2), 3–22.

MacKay, K.; Barbe, D.; Van Winkle, C. M.; Halpenny, E. Social Media Activity in a Festival Context: Temporal and Content Analysis. *Int. J. Contemp. Hospital. Manage.* **2017**, *29* (2), 669–689.

Mangold, W. G.; Faulds, D. J. Social Media: The New Hybrid Element of the Promotion Mix. *Busi. Horiz.* **2009**, *52* (4), 357–365.

McClinchey, K. A. Urban Ethnic Festivals, Neighborhoods, and the Multiple Realities of Marketing Place. *J. Travel Tour. Market.* **2008**, *25* (3–4), 251–264.

Merisavo, M. *The Effects of Digital Marketing Communication on Customer Loyalty: An Integrative Model and Research Propositions*; Helsinki School of Economics Working Papers. Finland, 2006.

Mintel. *Music Festival Tourism Worldwide. Travel and Tourism Analyst*, 10; Mintel Group Ltd: London, 2013.

Mirzaalian, F.; Halpenny, E. Social Media Analytics in Hospitality and Tourism: A Systematic Literature Review and Future Trends. *J. Hospital. Tour. Technol.* **2019**, *10* (4), 764–790.

Moise, D.; Cruceru, A. F. An Empirical Study of Promoting Different Kinds of Events Through Various Social Media Networks Websites. *Procedia: Soc. Behav. Sci.* **2014**, *109*, 98–102.

Morais, D. B.; Lin, C. H. Why Do First Time and Repeat Visitors Patronize a Destination? *J. Travel Tour. Market.* **2010**, *27* (2), 193–210.

Müller, B.; Florès, L.; Agrebi, M.; Chandon, J.-L. The Branding Impact of Brand Websites: Do Newsletters and Consumer Magazines Have a Moderating Role? *J. Advert. Res.* **2008**, *48* (3), 465–472.

Ngernyuang K.; Wu, P Using Social Media as a Tool for Promoting Festival Tourism. *Int. J. Comput. Sci. Inf. Technol (IJCSIT)* **2020**, *12*, (3), 17–32.

Oklobdžija, S. The Role and Importance of Social Media in Promoting Music Festivals. In *Synthesis 2015-International Scientific Conference of IT and Business-Related Research*; Singidunum University: Belgrade, Serbia, 2015; pp 583–587.

Paris, C. M.; Lee, W.; Seery, P. The Role of Social Media in Promoting Special Events: Acceptance of Facebook 'Events. In *Enter 2010 eTourism Conference*, 10–12 February **2010**, Lugano, Switzerland, 2010.

Prentice, R.; Andersen, V. Festival as Creative Destination. *Ann. Tour. Res.* **2003**, *30* (1), 7–30.

Rajkumar, S. G.; Joseph, C. S.; Sudhakar, J. C. Digital Marketing Communication Strategies and Its Impact on Student Higher Education Decision Making Process–A Review of Relevant Academic Literature. *Psychol. Educ. J.* **2021**, *58* (2), 4267–4279.

Shone, A.; Parry, B. *Successful Event Management: A Practical Handbook*; Thomson Learning: London, 2004.

Simmons, G. I-Branding: Developing the Internet as a Branding Tool. *Market. Intell. Plan.* **2007**, *25* (6), 544–563.

Smutkupt, P.; Krairit, D.; Esichaikul, V. Mobile Marketing: Implications for Marketing Strategies. *Int. J. Mob. Market.* **2010**, *5* (2), 126–139.

Suryawardani, I. G. A. O.; Wiranatha, A. S. Digital Marketing in Promoting Events and Festivities. A Case of Sanur Village Festival. *J. Busi. Hospital. Tour.* **2017**, *2* (1), 175–183.

Tassiopoulus, D. Events: An Introduction. In *Event Management: A Professional and Developmental Approach*; Tassiopoulus, D., Ed.; Juta Academic: Cape Town, 2005; pp. 2–36.

Türkmendağ, Z. A Bibliometric Analysis of Information Technology Research in Tourism and Hospitality Journals in the SSCI. *J. Yasar Univ.* **2021**, *16* (Special Issue on Managing Tourism Across Continents), 94–110.

Unurlu, C. The Integration of Social Media into Event Tourism. In *Impact of ICTs on Event Management and Marketing*; IGI Global, 2021; pp 69–85.

Urban, G. L. Digital Marketing Strategy: Text and Cases; Prentice Halls: New Jersey, 2004.

Wong, J. W. C.; Lai, I. K. W.; Tao, Z. Sharing Memorable Tourism Experiences on Mobile Social Media and How It Influences Further Travel Decisions. *Curr. Iss. Tour.* **2020**, *23* (14), 1773–1787.

Xiang, Z.; Gretzel, U. Role of Social Media in Online Travel Information Search. *Tour. Manage.* **2010**, *31* (2), 179–188.

Yasmin, A.; Tasneem, S.; Fatema, K. Effectiveness of Digital Marketing in the Challenging Age: An Empirical Study. *Int. J. Manage. Sci. Busi. Admin.* **2015**, *1* (5), pp. 69–80.

CHAPTER 11

Events Create a Successful Destination Imaging: Case of Kirkpinar Oil Wrestling Festival

KAPLAN UĞURLU[1] and AYDEMIR AY[2]

[1]Faculty of Tourism in Kırklareli, Kırklareli University, Turkey

[2]Tourism Consultant at the Municipality of Edirne, Edirne, Turkey

ABSTRACT

More visitors have recently attended local and national events. The majority of visits consist of private, unique interactions, and amusement. Events not only provide social, cultural, and economic benefits to local residents and domestic and international travelers, but also enhance the image of the destination by increasing tourism. However, inadequate event management and marketing might damage your brand. As long as the events are successful, they can offer the destination an edge in the national and international tourism markets. Events can extend the tourist season, increase the variety of marketable tourism products, and encourage people from around the globe to visit a location. Local administrations and visitors appreciate the fact that a regional event stimulates tourism and regional development. The events attract tourists, advertise the location, and strengthen the destination's brand. In this study, the Kirkpinar Oil Wrestling Festival, which has been held in Edirne for 661 years, will be transformed into the image of the province of Edirne, and its contributions and concepts will be presented. Numerous national and international events have made Edirne a destination for tourists. The Kirkpinar

---

Please note that few chapters were submitted during the peak of the pandemic. The long period of time to publish (due to supply chain and other issues) may have changed the perspectives presented in the chapter altogether.

Event Tourism and Sustainable Community Development: Advances, Effects, and Implications.
Ekta Dhariwal, Shruti Arora, Anukrati Sharma, Azizul Hassan (Eds.)
© 2024 Apple Academic Press, Inc. Co-published with CRC Press (Taylor & Francis)

Oil Wrestling Festival is the greatest entertainment and sports festival in Southeast Europe and the Balkans. According to the study, the Kirkpinar Oil Wrestling in Edirne province will influence the destination's image.

11.1 INTRODUCTION

People travel to different destinations for very different reasons. Tourists, even if the main purpose of travel to the destination is not cultural, necessarily participate in various activities at the destination. In this study, Kirkpinar Oil Wrestling, a sports event that has been taking place in Edirne, a city in Turkey—which was the second capital of the Ottoman Empire for 92 years and where many civilizations flourished—will be discussed, and the contribution of this sports event to the city of Edirne and the image of the city within the framework of event tourism will be examined. The study's goal is to propose ideas for Edirne's tourism growth by addressing the contributions and shortcomings of Edirne city from the event and sports tourism, based on the idea that sports and event tourism can contribute to the image of the city if it succeeds.

11.2 CONCEPT AND TYPES OF EVENTS

According to the dictionary, the synonyms "event" includes "occurrence," "happening," "incident," or "experience" (Dictionary.com). The main criterion that defines any type of "event" is that they are temporary. All events have a limited length, and for scheduled events, this is usually fixed in advance and publicized. Perhaps the greatest attraction of the events is that everyone knows and expects that every event will be over. Periodic events take place regularly, as in festivals held in the same place every year, or regularly always, but in different places. By dividing the concept of an event into a temporary event and a planned event, Getz (1994: 27) describes the event as events that begin and end at a predetermined time.

Today, there are many big and small events in every city, region, and village. Some of these activities can be defined according to their newness and some according to their historical value. Some of such activities may contribute to local culture and economy. Some destinations copy some activities and replicate them for reasons such as economic contribution and keeping traditions alive. The events evolve to provide multiple different aims. Tourism is a part of one of these aims. The events support raising the community's local pride, expanding the tourism season, and improving the image of the destination (Özdemir, 2016: 142). Festivals, for example, are being pushed and organized as tourist attractions due to their social and cultural significance. They are also valued for their capacity to revive locations such as cities, resorts, and attractions, and as instruments for destination marketing and image construction (Andersson and Getz, 2008: 200).

The relationship between tourism and events was established in the 1980s with the introduction of "the sights of events, as image builders' catalysts and strategically planning, promotion, and marketing," (Getz, 1997) which is described as "event tourism" (Wicks and Getz, 1993: 2). Tourism has fuelled much of the interest in special events, as cities recognize the value of unique events in attracting visitors from other areas. For example, at the 2015 Formula One Grand Prix in Hungary, spectators ranged from 10 to 30%, with hotel occupancy reaching 96% (David et al., 2018). It's vital to realize the relevance of unique events involving indigenous residents, as they're frequently reliant on local marketplace patronage to flourish. Despite this, participation in special events activity continues to be an important goal in part because tourists spend a day on average, however, this varies based on the sort of activity and spending habits (Brown et al., 2004: 280–283).

According to Getz's (2008) portfolio approach, events are possibly categorized according to the event's size as a mega event, hallmark event, regional event, and local event (Getz, 2008: 405). The *mega event* is an organized event that has an impact on the entire economy and the community's economy and is closely monitored by the media. (Allen et al., 2005: 13). Due to the policy impact of public finance regulation and media coverage of target markets, the number of visitors (including the audience) is classified as mega. A *hallmark event* is the symbol of a city or region, even synonymous events that have become the brand of the event (e.g. Munich Oktoberfest). They are programmed for one or more times a limited period; however, they are principally developed to increment the attractiveness and profitability of the targets (the brand) and profitability in a short and/or longer period. The *regional event* is significant in terms of attracting enormous crowds of people in relation to the scope and media interest, as well as achieving a significant economic impact (Mihajlovic and Vidak, 2017). *A local event* is a cultural event held inside the host town primarily for the amusement of the local population, as well as to contribute to the location's economy, celebrate diversity, and foster sports participation. Local events are those that make people feel like they belong where they live, regardless of whether they reside in a city or a town, and this event reflects the features of that location. As part of their social and cultural initiatives, municipal governments

144   Event Tourism and Sustainable Community Development

fund local events. Volunteers frequently join the host community in their organization. They typically occur in public areas such as schools, streets, and parks. An event is organized with the help of the local government. Allen et al. (2011) suggest that the local festival may become a hallmark event, attracting additional tourists to the community.

11.3   EFFECTS OF EVENTS ON DESTINATION TOURISM

Events should be classified as the planning process, implementation, and promotion of physical and natural tourist sites as an energizing, appearance, and tourist attraction in locations where events are hosted (Getz and Wicks, 1993: 1–3). In addition to attracting tourists to the destination or region where the events are held, they also help maintain and develop social identity (Derrett, 2004: 39). Events are a major generator of tourism and are heavily incorporated into most destinations' planning and marketing plans. Planned activities' functions and impacts in tourism are widely established, and they are becoming increasingly important for a destination's competitiveness (Getz, 2008: 403). For this reason, every society, institution, and destination can use these events effectively in the field of tourism, as they ensure integration in economic, social, cultural, and environmental areas. As one of the most important and rapidly increasing categories of events in the tourist industry, events play an important part in advertising and branding a region or location (Peters and Pikkemaat, 2005). On the other hand, marketing these events may affect increased public and tourist participation. As a result of successful marketing, the number of domestic and foreign visitors is possibly to increase. It is possible to measure the impact of events from increased media attention or tourism demand in an area or destination. Furthermore, in addition to creating a tourist attraction, the events also help to maintain tourists in the region, preventing revenue loss (Getz, 1997: 52).

Depending on the tourist season, events can be used as a remedy for low tourism and income in the tourism sector. Especially in the winter season, sports events, local cultural events, festivals and fairs, business meetings, academic seminars, camps of sports clubs, weddings, etc. events, meetings, and celebrations are effective in reviving tourism's off-season. Destination managers have started to resort more to revitalizing tourism with activities during the off-season. Climate change has successfully implemented event management in destination management to diversify tourism activities and extend the tourist season. Music festivals, film festivals, car races, various sports tournaments, industrial and agricultural fairs, etc. thanks to events, destinations find solutions to both the problem of seasonality, they can distribute the demand for tourism to different times and places, and benefit the promotion, image, and development of the region.

The positive effects of the events, which have become an economic and mass phenomenon, on the economies of destinations, regions, and countries have brought their economic effects to the forefront. On the other hand, the fact that the event sector combines other service industries such as entertainment, lodging, catering, and travel, as well as having direct and indirect connections with other sub-sectors of the economy, further increases its importance. Events held in various countries and cities in recent times have greatly contributed to the economy of the region in which they are organized (Tokay Argan and Yenci, 2015: 27). Thanks to events, new investments are realized in destinations and employment is increasing. The multiplier effect of the participants, the visitors, and tourists' income has a positive impact on the level of prosperity and peace of the local population is increasing, and the expenditures of the organizers of events in the region are again used in the development of the destination. Events can have positive effects on local people living in tourist destinations. Interacting with foreign tourists and visitors coming to the destination will allow people to develop their self-confidence and express themselves. They will meet different cultures and gain different cultural experiences, especially in foreign languages. Events are an opportunity to promote the culture, art, history, faith, entertainment, folklore, gastronomy, customs, etc. characteristics of the region or even the country. It evokes a desire in people to participate in tourism and travel. Local people take pride in being a host. Events also have negative social aspects, such as the commercialization of personal and private values and the corruption of social values (Delamere, 2001). Other negatives that the events cause to the region and destination where they are held are damage to the natural environment (air and water pollution, destruction of the ecosystem, etc.) and damage caused by building and crowding, disrupting the physical fabric and visuality of the region.

11.4 TYPES AND DEFINITIONS OF WRESTLING WITHIN THE SCOPE OF SPORTS EVENTS

Sporting events in numerous cities and nations, in a variety of sports, have strengthened global competitiveness between countries and cities to this point. Participating in intercontinental sports events such as the Olympics,

Europe, or World Football Cups is prestigious for cities and countries, and it also helps to promote sports, athletes, and sports clubs as well as cities and countries. As a result of increasing competition, countries and cities have begun to develop new strategies to attract tourists, investors, companies, and residents to their regions, and ensure the development and promotion of their regions. The financial success of sporting events in the region plays a crucial act in increasing public authorities' interest in sports events, with cities and countries creating strategies to host sports events. Some of the sports events strategies developed by local governments to deal with the growing rivalry between regions have decayed into public policy in the 2000s (Pinson, 2014: 127). Therefore, regions have started to focus on sporting events in their development and promotion strategies. The philosophy in the back of the tactics of hosting these sporting events is to increase tourism mobility in the region and enable these international one-off events to initiate or enhance local development. Sports tourism will be created by combining sports events held in the host country with the cultural resources of the region.

According to Gibson (1998: 10), sports tourism is a complicated topic, with much of its complexity stemming from challenges in describing it. For example, sports tourism is defined as "a journey that temporarily removes individuals from their homes to engage in various activities, play games, watch games, or enjoy attractions, or in other words, to have fun." Gibson proposes that sports tourism is comprised of three fundamental behaviors, namely, "attending an event, watching an event, and visiting the event's venue." Neirotti (2003: 2) defines sports tourism as "taking advantage of leisure time, traveling away from one's residence to participate in a sporting event for recreational or competitive purposes, traveling to observe sports activity at the amateur or elite level, and visiting sports areas that are widely considered attractions." These definitions covered sports tourism only with sports activities. However, those who participate in sports tourism participate in other activities of the region (such as accommodation, food, and drink, travel, entertainment and recreation, museums, festivals, and fairs) as well as sports events, and benefit from the social, cultural and physical fabric of the region by experiencing it. Therefore, it seems unlikely to separate sports events from tourism.

Every nation has had traditional games and sporting events throughout its history. These traditional folk games and sports events are full of rituals that demonstrate the society's own culture, lifestyle, knowledge, abilities, achievements, heroism, valor, courage, will, and desires. Every nation has

Events Create a Successful Destination Imaging 147

a cultural knowledge of sports that is rooted in the past, stems from society and living, and incorporates some physical location elements. Wrestling is a collection of physical and mental activities in which two people try to excel at each other without using any tools or similar elements. Wrestling has been one of the sports events that have come to the present day in the culture of many nations throughout history, necessitating the coexistence of distinct physiological and motoric characteristics (Türkmen and Şener, 2020: 438). Wrestling is regarded as an "honor form" in Turkish and related communities from Greater Asia to the Balkans, was formed from the combination of the word "eş," which means struggle and competition, with the word "kür," which means strong, unshakable, heartfelt. "kür-eş-mek" (Turkish: Güreş = wrestling) refers to a wrestling match with another person. The person who wrestles is called "the wrestler" (Turkish: Pehlivan/Güreşçi). As is obvious, wrestling means a truthful and courageous competition (Korkmaz, 2020: 4). The exact time of the emergence of the sport of wrestling is not known. But it is rumored that it came from Asia to the Balkans, and today it is almost everywhere in the world (including international tournaments) and continues to exist as a traditional and modern sports event. Wrestling is a cultural heritage that has come from very ancient times to this day. Wrestling is a self-contained activity that also serves as a kind of physical education for young people. Wrestling is widely lived as a sports culture nowadays as a sport in modern Turkey, Bulgaria, Greece, Moldova, Ukraine, Russia, Kazakhstan, and other nations. National wrestling tournaments are held in every village, and wrestling events are organized in the mood of a festival and fair, by the tradition that exists among the people of the Balkans and Asia, notably in Turkey.

Some notable wrestling types known around the world include the following:

The Greco–Roman form of wrestling is one of the first Olympic sports. Greco–Roman wrestling is one of the original nine Olympic sports, having made its debut at the inaugural modern Olympic Games in Athens in 1896. Greco–Roman wrestling's fundamental objective is to pin both opponents' shoulders to the mat to win the bout or accrue more points under a specified time limit. Genuine takedowns, including grips, locks, and throws, can score points for wrestlers. The number of points awarded for moves and holds is based on how difficult they are to perform (Nag, 2021).

Schwingen is a type of Swiss wrestling that originated in the Tirolese Valley. Wrestlers wear Schwinghosen (wrestling breeches) with thick belts that they use to take holds. Lifting and tripping are common, and the bout is won by the first guy down. Tournaments in Schwingen have been held since 1805 (Encyclopedia Britannica, 2021).

The *Cornish wrestling* contest took place in London early in the 13th century. Jacket wrestling, also known as Cornwall and Devon, has been practiced in England and Brittany since the fourth or fifth century (Encyclopedia Britannica, 2021).

Glima is Icelandic wrestling. An ancient kind of wrestling derived from the Viking Age combat traditions introduced to Iceland by its inhabitants and performed by their descendants for the last 11 centuries (Einarsonn, 2021).

Sumo is a Japanese wrestling style in which size, strength, and weight are the most important factors, however, quickness and suddenness of attack are also important. The goal is to either throw the opponent out of a ring with a circumference of 15 feet (4.6 m) or cause him to hit the ground with any portion of his body other than his feet's soles. The wrestlers are simply dressed in loincloths and hold each other's belts (Encyclopedia Britannica, 2021).

The *Pehlwani* wrestling style incorporates elements of the traditional Mall–Yuddha and Koshti Pahlavani wrestling styles in India and some other South Asian countries. Pehlwani contains most of the moves that are used in modern wrestling, such as pins, locks, throws, and submission grips. Strikes and kicks are strictly forbidden. The shoulder throw and strangling pin are the most regularly employed maneuvers (Elias-Varotsis, 2006).

11.5 EFFECT OF KIRKPINAR OIL WRESTLING ON EDIRNE PROVINCE'S DESTINATION IMAGE

Festivals and other traditional events are an indispensable part of Edirne's cultural identity. Because Edirne was known as the city of the festivals in the Ottoman Empire. There were six circumcision and marriage festivals in Edirne throughout the era of the Ottoman Empire and a few of them are one of the most important festivals of the Ottoman period (Ay, Kocadogan 2021: 22–24). Edirne currently hosts three international festivals. These are Kirkpinar Oil Wrestling Festival, Kakava and Hidirellez Festival, and Marching Band and Liver Festival. These festivals increase Edirne's local and national awareness to the highest level.

Organizing Kirkpinar Oil Wrestling in Edirne allows local and foreign sports fans and tourists to come to the city. The UNESCO-registered, countrywide-known major sporting events such as Kirkpinar Oil Wrestling attract international media and social media influencers' attention. According to Guinness World Records, Kirkpinar Oil Wrestling is the oldest continuously organized sports competition in the world. In 2010, UNESCO added the Kirkpinar Oil Wrestling Festival to its Representative List of Intangible Cultural Heritage of Humanity (UNESCO, 2021). The Kirkpinar Oil Wrestling tournament and festival are excellent instruments for the promotion of the city and its attractions. Every year, the press from many countries of the world follows Kirkpinar wrestling and its festival. News and articles appear on social media and media. It would not be wrong to think that the city has increased the image of the destination with the news. The TV and social media live broadcasts of wrestling and festival activities increase interest. The existence of Kirkpinar Oil Wrestling and Festival in Guinness World Records and UNESCO can be said to have contributed positively to the image of Edirne's destination.

Throughout the Kirkpinar Oil Wrestling Festival, Sarayiçi (today, the people of Edirne named this palace area, where Kirkpinar wrestling is also held, as Sarayiçi) evolved into the eyewear of local culture. It is an awful excellent opportunity to grab local's performances for the tourists. During the festival, all of Edirne's and the surrounding cities' lodging establishments are completely booked. During the Kirkpinar Oil Wrestling Festival, over 300,000 people visit the Sarayiçi festival area. Kirkpinar Oil Wrestling and its festival attract not only the attention of Turks. Many international well-known originations have been interested in Kirkpinar Oil Wrestling and Festival. Sarayiçi is turned into a local cultural extravaganza during the Kirkpinar festival. Over 2,000 oil wrestlers, over 300,000 tourists, visitors, and locals flock to Edirne to be a part of history. There are many local restaurants, and mini shops for spectators and tourists representing Turkish culture. Picnicking and camping around the stadium are common in the festival area, Turkish folk-dance groups and nationally renowned pop vocalists take place, and a gypsy band can always serenade you while eating lamb on the spit close by to the Tunca River. The untouched spectator's and local's habits make it unique.

11.5.1 EDIRNE CITY AS A TOURIST DESTINATION

With a population of 142,000, Edirne is located 245 km (152 miles) northwest of Istanbul. The city, situated in the north-western corner of Turkey, can be easily reached from Istanbul via a 2.5-h drive along the Trans European

Motorway. The city has always been an important junction between Europe and the Occident. Edirne is situated at a crossroads between Asia and Europe. Edirne is home to the busiest border crossings with Greece and Bulgaria. Greece is only 7 km away, while Bulgaria is 17 km away. According to 2020 statistics; Edirne has 28 hotels licensed by the Ministry of Tourism, with 1255 rooms and 2453 beds. In Edirne, the number of municipal-certified hotels is 98, the total number of rooms is 2598, and there is a total of 6007 beds (yigm.ktb.gov.tr, 2021). In Edirne, according to accommodation data since 2015, there is a growing trend in the number of arrivals to hotels and overnight stays in Ministry of Tourism-certified and municipal-certified hotels. Both certified hotels made 3,049,000 overnight stays for a total of 2,073,000 people between 2015 and 2019. The average stay during this period is 1.4 nights and hotels show a 31.5% occupancy rate.

Edirne is a city dating back to Orestes, the son of Agamemnon (Kayıcı, 2013). The original inhabitants of the city were the Odrysians and Bettegers of the Thracian tribes in the region. Later, the Macedonians turned the city into a colony of Orestes. The Roman Emperor Adrian built the city in 117–137, however, as a result of the Roman Empire's division, it remained on the border of Eastern Rome. The city was raided by the Goths, Huns, Avars, Pechenegs, and Bulgarians for a long time and then it was the first part of the Byzantine Empire followed by the invasion of the Pecheneg Turks. All of these tell us about the richness of Edirne's history (Ay and Secim, 2021: 11).

Edirne is a treasure trove of historical, natural, and cultural relics. Edirne, formerly known as Hadrianopolis, was built by Hadrian and served as the Ottoman Empire's second (some historians argue third) capital city for 92 years. Edirne is one of the cities numbered with cultural and historical riches in Turkey. Edirne is home to several ancient sites from various civilizations and religions, including Islam, Christianity, Judaism, and Bahaism. Apart from the Selimiye Mosque in Edirne, which was listed on the UNESCO World Cultural Heritage List in 2011, the city also has the second largest synagogues in Europe, particularly in Kaleiçi, which is densely populated by Turkish Jews. There are three churches in Edirne which names are the Bulgarian Church (Sv. Georgi), Sv. Konstantin Elena Church, and Italian Church. Edirne has many historical sites in Kaleiçi, such as the Bahá'í House, as well as numerous temples belonging to different faiths (Uca Özer et al., 2014: 4). Edirne's another significant cultural feature is The Complex of Sultan Beyazit II Health Museum, located within the University of Thrace and awarded the European Museum Award by the Council of Europe in 2004. This award is considered to be one of the most distinguished in the

Events Create a Successful Destination Imaging

field of museology. Besides, Edirne is an interesting city for both domestic and foreign visitors with its activities. Edirne hosts three international very knowable festivals such as Kirkpinar Oil Wrestling Festival, Kakava and Hidirellez Festival, and Marching Band and Liver Festival. Edirne has historic bazaars, caravanserais, mosques, bridges, fountains, a clock tower, palaces, mansions, houses, sea, rivers, nature, festivals, celebrations, etc.; it is a city with tourist attractions with its features. All of these aspects combine to make Edirne a lively and potentially very appealing tourist destination for a wide range of visitors.

11.5.2 KIRKPINAR OIL WRESTLING FESTIVAL AS A TOURISM EVENT

Wrestling is one of Turkey's most prestigious ancestral sports. Traditional wrestling tournaments with different names such as Oil Wrestling, Karakucak, Aba, and Alvar are organized in different regions of Turkey. The 661st edition of Kirkpinar Oil Wrestling, one of the historical Turkish heritages, was held on July 1–3, 2022. In the 661st Historical Kirkpinar Oil Wrestling, a historical record was set on the first day of wrestling, which was attended by a total of 2,475 wrestlers in 14 categories. The 661st Kirkpinar Oil wrestling is held in Sarayiçi and the audience capacity is 13,600 people. However, due to COVID-19, only 4,300 spectators watched wrestling tournaments in 2021 (Hurriyet.com.tr.:2021). The wrestling tournament was broadcast live on national TV channels during the 3-day tournament. It is said that the number of participants in festival events other than the spectators is at least 100,000 visitors a week (no exact figure can be given as entrances to the festival area are free). Kirkpinar Oil Wrestling and others, the traditional sport in the Turks, pass in a festive mood. People follow and participate in various celebrations, religious and national holidays, and sports events such as fairs and festivals in large open spaces to be together, have fun, and spend time. People from surrounding provinces or even remote regions participate in these events, which are attended by people from the region, as tourists. Traditional wrestling, such as Kirkpinar Oil Wrestling, is an essential cultural folkloric value that reveals the traditions and customs of the Turks and is a living example of Turkish culture that has lived for many years. Kirkpinar Oil Wrestling is a traditional kind of wrestling that dates back to the centuries to this day and is still ongoing, was placed on the "Intangible Cultural Heritage List of Humanity" by UNESCO on 16 November 2010.

Kirkpinar Oil Wrestling can be traced back to the Ottoman Empire's beginnings and is now considered part of Turkey's cultural heritage. In case of fiction or fact, the Kirkpinar is thought to have begun in 1361, when Süleyman Pasha, son of the second Ottoman ruler, attempted to capture Domuzhisar, Thrace from the ruling Byzantines in Samona, his 40 troops began wrestling (now in Greece), two brothers, Ali and Selim had been wrestling for a long time, each attempting to overcome the other. They died of weariness on a field near Edirne, Ahırköy. According to legend, forty springs formed beside Ali and Selim's tombs, commemorating the original 40 wrestlers. According to another legend, the conqueror of Edirne Murat Bey gave the order to organize wrestling matches. Ali and Selim wrestled for so long that they died of exhaustion. It was named Kirkpinar for the forty brave soldiers, it remains within Greece's borders. Modern wrestling was relocated to Virantekke near Edirne after the Balkan War and World War I. In 1923, the Turkish Republic was established, and the boundary with Greece was established at the current location of Sarayiçi (Ay, 2010). Kirkpinar Oil Wrestling is more than just a wrestling tournament; it's a 661-year-old cultural tradition and custom. In the transformation of the Kirkpinar sports event into a festival, historical customs, religious values, folklore, clothes, music, shopping, eating, and drinking, and entertainment rituals in a sports tradition are undoubtedly having a great effect. In this regard, the fact that Kirkpinar Oil Wrestling is based on a legendary story and that there are different religious and cultural practices distinguishes Kirkpinar Oil Wrestling from other sports and festivals.

11.6 CONCLUSIONS AND RECOMMENDATIONS

Recently, the growing competition in sports and cultural tourism between cities and countries is developing new strategies for developing the image of the city and country and paying decency to destination marketing. In urban tourism marketing for cultural and sports purposes, the goal is to attract tourists to their destinations, cities, or countries in a strong competitive environment. To accomplish this goal, it is essential to generate interest in the location and to create or develop the destination's image through the use of the appropriate tourist resources (attractions). The main and most important reason for visiting a destination is that the natural, historical, cultural, and recreational resources of that destination match the motives of tourists to travel. In this study, Edirne has (Selimiye Mosque, Kirkpinar Oil Wrestling, etc.) it can be easily said that natural and cultural resources provide a competitive advantage in terms of cultural tourism. Edirne, Istanbul is 2.5 h by road,

Events Create a Successful Destination Imaging

and borders with Greece and Bulgaria, so the day is easily accessible to even tourists can visit. Although Edirne has the characteristics of a strong tourism destination, to be a competitive tourism destination and the image of the city to be much better, its shortcomings also need to be improved. For example, Edirne's infrastructure and superstructure problems related to tourism should be solved by the growing demand for tourism. Also, the following are some suggestions:

- As part of tourism and culture, the commodification and degradation of the originality of Kirkpinar Oil Wrestling and festival events should be thoroughly studied. To remain traditional, the municipality of Edirne must legislate to preserve the traditional culture of the festival and the oil wrestling.
- The budget should be allocated for the promotion of all tourism activities, including the border city of Edirne and Kirkpinar Oil Wrestling, where the historical and cultural heritage is the most intense.
- Cooperation with domestic and international travel agencies and tour operators (particularly in the Balkans and major cities such as Istanbul) should be sought to promote Edirne and increase visitor numbers.
- Mainly central government and local government stakeholders (hotels, transport companies, agencies, restaurants, professional chambers, universities, Chambers of Industry and Commerce, professional chambers, etc.) management of the city, marketing, finance, planning, etc. they should consult and cooperate on their issues.
- From digital marketing techniques (websites, virtual media, kiosks, augmented and virtual realities, etc. in the promotion of the city and its events) should be employed.
- Leaders of the city should get professional support in public relations.
- Historical traditional rituals should be preserved, and importance should be given to educating and informing the public and organizers on these issues.
- Selimiye Mosque, Kirkpinar oil wrestling, especially the cultural fabric and essence of the city should continue to be transferred to future generations without being corrupted and no concessions should be made.
- Festival organization, activities that visitors and tourists who come to festivals and athletes can participate in sporting events together with

local people (local games, local dances, local music, local cooking, etc.) should be organized; visitors and tourists should experience different experiences.

- Gift, shopping, organic product sale, etc. shopping diversity should be ensured, and artisans should be encouraged.

KEYWORDS

- **Kirkpinar oil wrestling festival**
- **destination marketing**
- **destination image**
- **destination brand**
- **Edirne**
- **Turkey**

REFERENCES

Allen, J.; O'Toole, W.; Harris, R.; McDonnell, I. *Festival and Special Event Management*, 3rd ed.; John Wiley and Sons: Australia, 2005.

Allen, J.; O'Toole, W.; Harris, R.; McDonnell, I. *Festival and Special Event Management*, 5th ed.; John Wiley and Sons: Australia, 2011.

Andersson, T. D.; Getz, D. Stakeholder Management Strategies of Festivals. *J. Conv. Event Tour.* **2008,** *9* (3), 199–220. https://doi.org/10.1080/15470140802323801.

Ay, A. *Kirkpinar Oil Wrestling*; Amazon, 2010.

Ay, A.; Kocadogan, S. *Edirne Sarayı Sunnet Senlikleri ve Mutfagi*; Municipality of Edirne Publications: Edirne, 2021.

Ay, A.; Secim, Y. *Jewish Cuisine of Edirne*. Edirne: Municipality of Edirne Publications.

Brown, G.; Chalip, L.; Jago, L.; Mules, T. *Developing Brand Australia: Examining the Role of Events.* In *Destination Branding: Creating the Unique Destination Proposition*; Morgan, N., Pritchard, A., Pride, R., Eds.; Elsevier Butterworth-Heinemann: Oxford, 2004; pp 279–305.

David, L.; Remenyik, B, Molnar, C.; Csoban, K. The Impact of The Hungaroring Grand Prix on The Hungarian Tourism Industry. *Event Management* **2018,** *22*, 671–674.

Delamere, T. A. Development of a Scale to Measure Resident Attitudes Toward the Social Impacts of Community Festivals, Part II. Verification of the Scale. *Event Manage.* **2001,** *7* (1), 25–38.

Derrett, R. Festivals, Events and the Destination. In *Festival and Events Management: An International Arts and Culture Perspective*. Yeoman, I., Robertson, M., Knight, J., Eds.; Elsevier Butterworth Heinemann: Amsterdam, 2004.

Dictionary.com. Event Definition & Meaning. Dictionary.com, n.d. https://www.dictionary.com/browse/event.

Einarsonn, T. History of Glima, 2020. https://www.vikingmartialarts.com/history-of-glima.

Elias-Varotsis, S. Festivals and Events—(Re)Interpreting Cultural Identity. *Tour. Rev.* **2006,** *61* (2), 24–29. https://doi.org/10.1108/eb058472

Encyclopædia Britannica, Inc. Cornish Wrestling. Encyclopædia Britannica, n.d. https://www.britannica.com/sports/Cornish-wrestling

Encyclopædia Britannica, Inc. Schwingen. Encyclopædia Britannica, n.d. https://www.britannica.com/sports/Schwingen

Encyclopædia Britannica, Inc. Sumo. Encyclopædia Britannica, n.d. https://www.britannica.com/sports/sumo-sport

Getz, D. Residents' Attitudes Towards Tourism: A Longitudinal Study in Spey Valley, Scotland. *Tour. Manage.* **1994,** *15* (4), 247–258.

Getz, D. *Event Management and Event Tourism*; Cognizant Communication Corporatison, USA, 1997.

Getz, D. Event Tourism: Definition, Evolution, and Research. *Tour. Manage.* **2008,** *29* (3), 403–428.

Getz, D.; Wicks, B. Editorial. *Fest. Manage. Event Tour.* **1993,** *1* (1), 1–3.

Gibson, H. Sport Tourism: A Critical Analysis of Research. *Sport Manage. Rev.* **1998,** *1*, 45–76.

Hurriyet.com.tr. Son Dakika: 660. Tarihi Kirkpinar Yagli Guresleri icin seyirci kararı!, 2021. https://www.hurriyet.com.tr/sporarena/son-dakika-660-tarihi-kirkpinar-yagli-guresleri-icin-seyirci-karari-41846834

Kayıcı, H. *Salnamelere gore idari, sosyal ve ekonomik yapisiyla Edirne Sancagi* (Birinci baskı). Edirne Kitapligi, Vol. 12; T.C. Edirne Valiligi: Edirne, 2013.

Korkmaz, S. Fair Play in Kirkpinar Tradition as an Intangible Cultural Heritage, *Eur. J. Phys. Educ. Sport Sci.* **2020,** *6* (2), 106–114.

Mihajlovic, I.; Vidak, M. The Importance of Local Events for Positioning of Tourist Destination. *Eur. J. Soc. Sci. Educ. Res.* **2017,** *4* (4), 228–239.

Nag, U. What İs Greco Roman Wrestling: From Rules to Olympic History. Greco Roman Wrestling: Rules, Scoring, and All You Need to Know, 2021. https://olympics.com/en/featured-news/what-how-greco-roman-wrestling-style-rules-scoring-techniques-olympics

Neirotti, L. D. Sport and Adventure Tourism. In *An Introduction to Sport and Adventure Tourism*; Hudson, S., Ed.; Haworth Hospitality Press: Binghamton, 2003; pp 1–25.

Özdemir G. Festivals as a Short-Duration Tourism Attraction in Turkey. In *Alternative Tourism in Turkey*; Egresi, I. Ed.; GeoJournal Library, Vol. 121; Springer: Cham, 2016. https://doi.org/10.1007/978-3-319-47537-0_9

Peters, M.; Pikkemaat, B. The Management of City Events: The Case of Bergsilverster in Inssbruck, Austria. *Event Manage.* **2005,** *9* (3), 147–153.

Pinson, J. Heritage Sporting Event: An Old Recipe for a New Problem. In *Heritage, Tourism and Hospitality International Conference HTHIC*; Turkey Boğaziçi University Publication: Istanbul, 2014; pp 127–138.

Tokay Argan, M.; Yenci, D. *Etkinlik Pazarlama Yönetimi*. Detay Yayıncılık: Ankara.

Türkmen, M.; Şener, O. A. Traditional Wrestling of Gagauz Turks and Its Role in Strengthening of Nation's Cultural Traditions. *Turk. J. Sport Exer.* **2020,** *22* (3), 438–443.

Uca Ozer, S.; Cavusgil Kose, B.; Kucukaltan, D. Edirne as a Cultural Destination a Forecast for Foreign Tourists to Determine Potential Analysis, *Soc. Sci. Res. J.* **2014,** *3* (1), 1–11.

UNESCO. Kırkpınar Oil Wrestling Festival, 2021. https://ich.unesco.org/en/RL/krkpnar-oil-wrestling-festival-00386

Yigm.ktb.gov.tr. Konaklama Istatistikleri, 2021. https://yigm.ktb.gov.tr/TR-201120/konaklama-istatistikleri.html

CHAPTER 12

A Feasibility Study of Resurrecting Elephant Marriage Ceremonies in Mondulkiri, as a Tourism Event: Case Studies of Pu Trom and Pu Tang Villages

ORN KIMTEK

Royal University of Phnom Penh, Major Tourism Management, Cambodia

ABSTRACT

Bunong indigenous communities in Mondulkiri province have a unique and remarkable culture with their elephants in captivity. The traditional event, Elephant Marriage Ceremony, has been neglected to call for urgent cultural revitalization and preservation. Using tourism as a means of resurrecting indigenous culture, it would be necessary to investigate the feasibility of restoring the Elephant Marriage Ceremony as a tourism event. The study aims at investigating the feasibility of resurrecting the Elephant Marriage Ceremony as a tourism event with four objectives: (1) to determine the cultural background, processes, and culturally significance of the Elephant Marriage Ceremony, (2) to identify interest and capacity of local communities in restoring the ceremony, (3) to identify key stakeholders' interest on and support for using the ceremony as a tourism event, and (4) to analyze the challenges and opportunities for resurrecting ceremony as a tourism event.

Focus group discussions were employed with villagers from Pu Trom and Pu Tang villages, and semi-structured interviews were conducted with key stakeholders including government departments, the private sector, and non-governmental organizations (NGOs). A total of 187 national and

Please note that few chapters were submitted during the peak of the pandemic. The long period of time to publish (due to supply chain and other issues) may have changed the perspectives presented in the chapter altogether.

Event Tourism and Sustainable Community Development: Advances, Effects, and Implications.
Ekta Dhariwal, Shruti Arora, Anukrati Sharma, Azizul Hassan (Eds.)
© 2024 Apple Academic Press, Inc. Co-published with CRC Press (Taylor & Francis)

international tourists were surveyed to assess their perception and interest in the event. Content analysis was used to analyze qualitative data, and quantitative data were analyzed using the Statistic Package for Social Science (SPSS).

Findings indicated that Elephant Marriage matched two criteria of event feasibility by Goldblatt (2014): fulfilling financial viability to support the event and accomplishing the politics as usual. The Elephant Marriage did not fulfill the human dimension criterion since indigenous villagers did not dare to revive and celebrate the event due to their strong beliefs and taboos. Although the elephant marriage was not feasible to be transformed into a tourism event, a celebration for the elephant baby would be an alternative and promising event that has all the feasibility criteria for the sustainability of domesticated elephants.

12.1 INTRODUCTION

In response to the rapid growth in the tourism industry, the Ministry of Tourism (MoT) has given priority to this sector. The MoT had set the Tourism Development Strategic Plan 2012–2020. In this strategic plan, MoT analyses six important strategies one of which focused on tourism product development. It aimed to promote, diversify the existing product, and innovate new tourism products while enhancing the service quality standard to meet the need of tourists. Within this strategy, the focus on cultural and natural resources was the major foundation for tourism sustainability. Mondulkiri is one of the northeastern provinces of Cambodia which is rich in natural and cultural resources. The natural resources could be counted from panorama mountain views, waterfalls, grassland, river, wildlife, and domesticated elephants. The cultural resources include traditions and cultural diversity of ethnic minority groups. One of the prioritized strategies for tourism development of the province had also focused on tourism product development such as the establishment of community-based ecotourism sites and organizing tourism events. Tourism events can be counted from elephant festivals, mountain festivals, dance, and performance of ethnic, ethnic cuisine exhibitions, ethnic traditional festivals, and other potential sports activities (PDoT, 2012). According to Arcodia and Whitford (2006), the festival is an emerging and growing sector of the leisure and tourism industry, and it contributes significant sociocultural, economic, and political impacts on the host community and destination.

12.1.1 BACKGROUND OF THE STUDY

Mondulkiri is one of the ecotourism destinations in the northeastern part of Cambodia which also consists of indigenous people and their culture that should be preserved. Pu Tang and Pu Trom villages are located near the town area and they are home to the indigenous Bunong minority group with up to 90% of the total population (Heng et al., 2016). Both villages had a total domesticated elephant 18, 10 in Pu Tang village and 8 in Pu Trom village. Villagers owned domesticated elephants collectively, 10 households per elephant on average in which each household took turns to look after the elephant (Heng et al., 2016). Most of the elephants from the two villages are under control and support from the Elephant Livelihood Initiative Environment organization (ELIE). These two villages are being taken as study areas in this research.

12.1.2 PROBLEM STATEMENT

One of the core values of Bunong culture is their elephants in captivity. Bunong people have shared their lives with elephants therefore, elephants are treated like their family members. Bunong people believed that if elephants had a baby, the spirit would get angry. So, they must arrange marriage ceremonies for those elephants (Vater, 2006). One important thing, Bunong people believe that baby elephants will bring bad luck to villagers. Therefore, they put male and female elephants separately not to have a baby. Having a domestic elephant baby without marriage is taboo. This raises the issue that if Bunong still prohibits their elephants not to have babies, it is likely that domestic elephants will disappear from the villages of Mondulkiri in the next 20 years. Since law enforcement on conservation in the mid-1990 forbids people to capture wild elephants from the forest, capturing elephants is illegal. On the other hand, the price of the domesticated elephant is about 30,000 USD per elephant if they buy from another province or country. More importantly, there is not yet a research study assessing the possibility of conducting the ceremony to deal with the existing barrier of belief as well as to appeal to tourists.

12.1.3 AIM, OBJECTIVES, AND RESEARCH QUESTIONS

12.1.3.1 AIM AND OBJECTIVES

The research aims to investigate the feasibility of resurrecting elephant marriage ceremonies as a tourism event. Four objectives are taken into the investigation. (1) to determine the background culture, processes, and importance of the elephant marriage ceremony (2) to identify the interest and capacities of local communities for the event celebration (3) to identify key stakeholders' interest in and support for the ceremony (4) to analyze the challenges and opportunities of conducting the ceremony as a tourism event.

12.1.3.2 *RESEARCH QUESTIONS*

From the objectives above, five research questions need to be answered to achieve the objectives.

1. What are the background culture and processes of elephant marriage celebration?
2. Are local people interested in celebrating the ceremony?
3. What are their capacities for ceremony celebration (in case they are interested)?
4. Are key stakeholders interested and willing to support the celebration?
5. What are the opportunities and challenges of conducting ceremonies as tourism events?

12.1.4 *CONCEPTUALIZATION AND OPERATIONALIZATION*

TABLE 12.1 Conceptualization and Operationalization of Research Key Terms.

Key term	Conceptualization	Operationalization
Feasibility study	"An examination of a situation to decide whether a suggested method, plan or piece of work is possible or reasonable" Cambridge Advanced Learner's Dictionary, third edition.	A study of conducting an elephant marriage ceremony as a tourism event involving various key stakeholders and based on the three criteria of event feasibility raised by Goldblatt (2014).
Tourism event	From a tourism perspective, it is inclusive of all planned agendas or activities, with tourism-oriented, in the combined approach to marketing and development (Getz, 2007).	The event is transformed from the tradition of indigenous Bunong culture of domestic elephant marriage to serve tourism purposes.

A Feasibility Study of Resurrecting Elephant Marriage Ceremonies in Mondulkiri   161

TABLE 12.1 *(Continued)*

Key term	Conceptualization	Operationalization
Stakeholders	Stakeholders are defined as people or groups who influent the firm or organization (Getz, 2007).	In this study, stakeholders refer to government bodies from two ministry departments in Mondulkiri, the Provincial Department of Tourism (PDoT) and Provincial Department of Cultural and Fine Art (PDoCFA), local authorities, NGOs such as ELIE and Local Environmental Awareness Foundation (LEAF), and visitors.
Challenges	According to the Macmillan dictionary, challenges refer to something that needs a lot of skill, energy, and determination to cope with or achieve, especially something that we have never done before and will enjoy doing.	Something that causes difficulties, problems, or threats that will emerge from the celebration of the event if it is conducted. This will raise the perception of villagers and key stakeholders.
Opportunities	An occasion or situation that makes it possible to do something that we want to do or must do, or the possibility of doing something (Cambridge advanced learner's dictionary).	Positive things, advantages, benefits, favorable situations for local people, stakeholders, elephant conservation, and tourism development will happen in case the event is celebrated.

Source: Conceptualization and Operationalization were cited from various sources including:

1. Getz, D. Event Tourism: Definition, Evolution, and Research. J. Tour. Manage. 2007, 29,403–428.

2. Goldblatt, J. Special Events: Creating and Sustaining a New World for Celebration; John Wiley & Sons, Inc; New Jersey, 2014.

3. Cambridge Advanced Learner's Dictionary, third edition, and Macmillan dictionary.

12.2   LITERATURE REVIEW

12.2.1   TOURISM PRODUCT AND TOURISM EVENT

Tourism product is defined as a combination of tangible (product) and intangible (service) products that tourists will experience upon their traveling to the tourism destination (Cooper and Hall, 2008). Swarbrooke (2001), cited in BPP Learning Media, categorized tourism attraction (main products) into two main parts, namely, site attraction and event attraction. Site attractions include a wide range of natural attractions and man-made attractions. Event attractions contain sports events, major music or art festivals, business trade conference, religious or cultural festivals, historic pageantry, and so on. Getz (2007) gave a definition to the planned event from the event viewpoint as an essential motivator in the tourism sector and is a phenomenon that is spatial-temporal, and special due to the interaction between audiences, the theme of the event, and management systems. Richards and Palmer (2010) provided a simple definition for events as the occurrences which are important, exciting, and interesting or extraordinary. According to Bowndin et al. (2006), an event is categorized into two main features—based on the size and based on the content and form of the event. *Size:* events are categorized based on their size and scale. *Form and content:* another simple way of categorizing the events is by their form and contents. There are cultural events, sports events, and business events.

12.2.2   KEY STAKEHOLDERS AND DECISION OF THE EVENT

Bowndin et al. (2006) focused that one of the essential components in creating the event is the knowledge of the event environment. The environment in which the event takes place plays a major role in its success. There needs to be the identification of major players referring to the stakeholders, individuals, or groups who affect the event, the interest, and objectives of these players. This can involve various key elements including stakeholders in the events, their objectives as well as the challenges and opportunities which will emerge. Stakeholders include the audience and spectators, the host community, the host organization, sponsors, coworkers, and the media (Bowndin et al., 2006). In this regard, they stressed the importance of the community expectation and other requirements for the success of the event that it is not enough for an event to meet only the needs of the audience. Yeoman et al. (2004) figured out that a more achievable event can happen once the needs of stakeholders are met and satisfied. They mentioned that it is not only about finances but also public acknowledgment, in-kind support, shared expertise, and so on.

12.2.3   EVENT FEASIBILITY

Bowndin et al. (2006) described the significant considerations that are needed to look at in conducting a feasibility study. The elements of feasibility can be varied according to the event. These include a budget requirement, managerial skill, venue capacity, host community, destination impact, sponsor and support, project visitation, and availability of public and private sector financial and infrastructure requirements. However, a feasibility study was also raised by Goldblatt (2014). In his masterpiece, he has determined three main components when assessing or analyzing a feasibility study.

(1) financial considerations: refers to available or sufficient financial resources to implement the event. It also includes what resources could be counted on for an immediate infusion of cash.
(2) the human dimension: event assessors must know where human resources are from and how they work together effectively. More importantly, how they will be rewarded and benefit financially and through intangibles should be also considered.
(3) politics as usual: refers to the support of politicians and their bureaucratic staff to make sure the cooperation for the event is smooth. Moreover, it also counts on the permitting process to determine if the event is feasible.

12.2.4 *INDIGENOUS CULTURE AND CULTURAL EVENTS*

McCracken (1986) stated that each culture constructs its special sense of the world. Thus, the understanding, norms, and traditions that a group in one cultural context considers appropriate may be inappropriate for another group. He added that for a set of terms in one culture, the members consider virtually nothing weird or unintelligible and advantageous for that culture. Culture has a back-and-forth beneficial relationship which helps add up to the attractiveness and competitiveness of the destination (Organization for Economic Cooperation and Development [OECD], 2009). Australian Heritage Commission (AHC) (2002) raised that indigenous heritage is dynamic. It can be counted from the tangible and intangible manifestation of culture which is passed on from generation to generation of the indigenous group. The way indigenous people demonstrated their culture was through the person. According to AHC (2002), indigenous heritage value consists of knowledge, traditional resources, practical experience, and other belief. The definition of traditional owners was given as those people who belong to a group and have accountability for caring the heritage. In tourism, culture is very much defined as a product and a process. According to Richard and Palmer (2010), cultural events consist of many activities such as art, music, and community tradition in their agenda. They added that these kinds of events are normally recurrent and are limited in duration. From Bowndin et al. (2006) view, the cultural event can contender as major events. More importantly, this kind of event, along with tourism, can generate economic benefits for the host community.

12.2.5 CAPTIVE ELEPHANT AND ELEPHANT FESTIVAL

According to Asian Elephant Rang State Meeting Final Report (2017), each state provided the numbers of wild and captive elephants as in the summary Table 12.2:

TABLE 12.2 Asian Elephant Statistic 2017.

Country	Number of wild elephants	Number of captive elephants
Bangladesh	268 (estimated)	96
Bhutan	513 (estimated)	09
Cambodia	400–600 (estimated)	70
China	300 (estimated)	243
India	29,391–30,711	3467–3667
Indonesia	1724 (estimated)	467
Lao PDR	600–800	454
Malaysia	1223–1677	92
Myanmar	2000 (estimated)	approx. 5000
Sri Lanka	5879 (estimated)	230
Thailand	3100–3600	3783
Vietnam	104–132	88

Source: Asian Elephant Rang State Meeting Final Report (2017), pp 13–22.

There were some issues with the domesticated elephants such as no breeding facilities, no government registration system for captive elephants, and no monitoring for transfer of ownership. The capacity for managing elephants was still low and elephants were facing the issue of disease transmission.

12.2.5.1 ELEPHANT FESTIVAL IN LAO PDR

The Elephant Festival was initiated in 2006 by one non-government organization, called ElfantAsia, which worked closely with elephants and their mahouts (the elephant rider, trainer, and keeper) in response to the endangering of Asian elephants. (Elephant festival, 2018). The aim is to raise awareness of elephant protection and conservation as part of the cultural and natural heritage of Lao People's Democratic Republic (PDR) and countries in the region. More than 60 elephants were showcased in

A Feasibility Study of Resurrecting Elephant Marriage Ceremonies in Mondulkiri   165

the festival and more than 100,000 audiences participated in the event, generating approximately 28 billion kips to the local economy (Vilaysack, 2014). The festival has been celebrated for 3 days annually since 2007 and is scheduled for February.

12.2.5.2   ELEPHANT FESTIVAL IN THAILAND

In Surin province, the Elephant Festival called Elephant Roundup is held in November yearly according to Tripadvisor (2017). This event aimed to increase tourism development and preserve the local culture between people and elephants. Three hundred domesticated elephants match the food and have a feast of a lifetime (Surin's Elephant Roundup, 2017). The event also contained a cultural performance, fun and food, and a presentation of ancient elephant warfare techniques. It was held within the Buddhist beliefs. The Elephant Festival has appealed to many national and international visitors (Buddhist Tourism, 2007).

12.2.6   CONCEPTUAL FRAMEWORK

The following diagram demonstrates the inputs and criteria to determine the possibility to conduct the event. To investigate the feasibility of the event, there needs to be input from the local community and all concerned stakeholders. First and foremost, the input from local indigenous people who were the owners of tradition is needed. Apart from this, perception and support from stakeholders must be investigated. With these inputs from two main groups of players, the challenges and opportunities could be analyzed and utilized to measure the three feasibility criteria of the event. There are three main criteria for event possibility (Goldblatt, 2014). First is the budget or financial dimension referring to financial resources available to conduct the event. Second, the human dimension reflects the possibility of human resources and human participation in the event to be celebrated. Finally, politics as usual means the interest of stakeholders, government, and policy makers. In other words, political dimension here can mean that events meet the government's interest. Once the three considerations are investigated, there could be decision making on the event whether it is feasible or not. If it meets all three criteria, the event should be feasible to keep on planning.

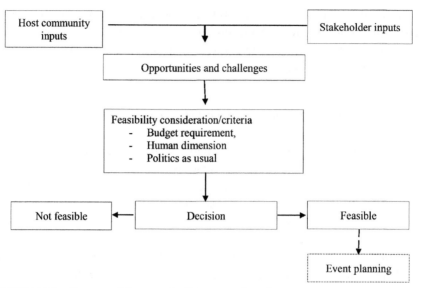

FIGURE 12.1 Conceptual framework of the research study.

Source: Conceptual framework was cited from Goldblatt, J. Special Events: Creating and Sustaining a New World for Celebration; John Wiley & Sons, Inc; New Jersey, 2014.

12.3 METHOD

12.3.1 RESEARCH DESIGN

The study is exploratory research. According to Neth (2017), exploratory research is used to explore the area of study which is new or not being investigated more clearly. Qualitative and quantitative methods are the major ground for this study. For the quantitative method, the researcher used a questionnaire paper as a data collection technique to describe the perception and interest of visitors regarding the ceremony celebration. In the qualitative approach, the researcher applied semi-structured interviews and focus group discussions to gather an in-depth understanding of the phenomenon from various stakeholders and local people, respectively.

12.3.2 DATA COLLECTION TECHNIQUE

12.3.2.1 PRIMARY DATA

The semi-structure interview was utilized to collect information from various stakeholders including government departments PDoT, PDoCFA of Mondulkiri, NGOs such as Elephant Livelihood Initiative Environment (ELIE) and LEAF, key informants in the villages, local tour operator. The focus group was employed to gain insight information from villagers who were involved mainly in the event celebration. The topic of discussion was their livelihood connecting to elephants, the background culture of the elephant marriage ceremony, their perception of the celebration, the capacity of making the celebration happen, the challenges and opportunities that would emerge from the event as well as the ethical issue with elephants. The survey was utilized to gain some information from both national and international visitors who visited Mondulkiri regarding their pattern of visitors, especially their perception, interest, support, and willingness to join the event if it takes place.

12.3.2.2 SECONDARY DATA

Secondary data was collected and reviewed before the primary data. Importantly, books chapter, international journals, previous research papers, case studies, news, social media, and websites are the main source of secondary data.

12.3.3 SAMPLE SELECTION AND SAMPLING TECHNIQUE

Two hundred visitors were planned to survey utilizing convenience sampling. However, the researcher managed to survey only 190 visitors, but three questionnaires were error, thus 187 questionnaire papers could be used to analyze. Two villages of indigenous people and elephants, namely Pu Trom and Pu Tang were selected. Between 10 and 15 villagers from each village participated in separate focus group discussions. Semi-structured interview was utilized with some key stakeholders. A purposive sampling technique was applied for both focus group and semi-structured interview.

12.3.4 DATA ANALYSIS

Content analysis was applied to analyze the collected qualitative data while quantitative data collected was analyzed using statistical analysis, SPSS to present data numerically. The researcher employed two steps of coding to analyze data collected from the interview and focus group discussion. Initially, analysis by respondents was applied to group various main themes of data, and, second, analysis by objectives of the study was employed in addition to the first analysis. Different categories of generated data were quoted and used in report writing.

12.3.5 DATA VALIDATION TECHNIQUE

The researcher validated qualitative data by conducting a workshop with some informants especially villagers from the two villages. The workshop was conducted with support from PDoT Mondulkiri and the presence of the deputy director of PDoCFA, village chiefs, elder people, and key informants. The researcher represented the primary results that were collected during fieldwork. After that, there was a further discussion between villagers and chief villages under the facilitation of the researcher.

12.3.6 SCOPE AND LIMITATION OF THE STUDY

The researcher has a period of five months to finish counting from early February to June 2018 to conduct the study. Two villages, Pu Tang and Pu Trom, in Mondulkiri were the study sites. The research explored both the supply and demand sides, simply the local host community, local authority, NGOs relating to elephant conservation, and tourists. The limitation of the research included lacking secondary documents on the research area focusing on indigenous tradition and background of the celebration, conducting field-work during the holiday limiting the availability of some respondents due to the time constraint, some national visitors were not opened to spend their time doing the survey, and the time and budget constrain of the researcher.

12.3.7 RESEARCH ETHICS

The participation of the individual is voluntary. The consent letter was given to participants before conducting the interview. The researcher kept the right for the individual to refuse or withdraw from the research at any time during the process. Finally, the received information was kept confidential and just used for the specific purpose of this research.

12.4 FINDINGS

12.4.1 RESULTS FROM VISITOR SURVEY

12.4.1.1 PROFILE AND PATTERN OF VISIT

A total of 187 (101 women, 54%) national and international visitors were surveyed, with the majority of age groups between 15 and 24 (36% of total respondents) and 25–34 (42%). National visitors came from different

A Feasibility Study of Resurrecting Elephant Marriage Ceremonies in Mondulkiri   169

provinces and cities of Cambodia, especially the capital Phnom Penh (24%). International visitors were mainly from France (13%), Australia (12%), the USA (7%), UK (6%). The average length of stay was between two and three nights for both types of visitors, and 35% of them visit Mondulkiri more than once (repeated visit) and the other 65% of them were first-time tourists. The purposes of visit were mainly for holiday (55%) followed by study trip (27%) and visit friend and relative (VFR) (9%). The major tourist destinations respondents would like to visit were natural tourism sites, community ecotourism sites, indigenous tourism sites, wildlife sanctuary sites, and cultural tourism sites.

12.4.1.2   TOURIST INTEREST IN AND SUPPORT FOR THE EVENT

Tourists were narrated in the questionnaire about the issue of domesticated elephants and indigenous (Bunong) people so that they know the clue to decide whether they should support the celebration of the event or not. Through the analysis, among 187 respondents surveyed, 141 (75.4%) of them support the event to happen. Almost one in four the respondents (24.6%) did not support this kind of event, which shared 46 of all respondents.

Some tourists surveyed gave their comments on the event which could be contradicted by two different points of view. Supported tourists seemed to feel positive about the tradition and they would like domesticated elephants to be able to reproduce so that the next generation can witness this. More importantly, they thought that this was the opportunity which indigenous people could dig up, conserve, and promote their culture while sustaining the domesticated elephants in the village. In contrast, non-supported visitors see this event as a bad idea. They seemed to be negative about the culture of indigenous Bunong which did not allow domesticated elephants to breed. Moreover, some tourists are concerned about elephants' rights when conducting events like this. They thought elephants should not adhere to people's traditions and they should live naturally. Among 141 visitors who supported the event, 121 of them intended to join the event if it was celebrated. This represents 85.8% of tourists who supported or 64.7% of all visitors surveyed.

12.4.1.3   TOURIST PERCEPTION OF THE PROPOSED EVENT

Out of 121 visitors who supported the event, 60% (73) of them commented that the event was very interesting and unique. Some viewed it as a wonderful event to be celebrated and they would like to know about indigenous people, domesticated elephants, indigenous culture, and tradition, especially the process of conducting the ritual. "This event helps to care for elephants, tourism attraction and promote indigenous culture," "(We should) promote elephant marriage and show next generation about culture event" (Respondents' comments). Supported visitors see the event as an opportunity to help both villagers and domesticated elephants. "Elephant marriage is elephant conservation"; "…it can help elephants in reproducing." "Elephant marriage is good for elephants because they need to breed and produce their next generation."

However, 19 out of 46 visitors who did not support the event showed their opinion that elephants had the right to reproduce and should be free if they wanted to have a baby, they should not be forced to adhere to the people's tradition. Some said they did not need elephants in captivity to reproduce anymore. Below are some noticeable quotes from non-supported tourists. "Does not seem correct to force animals to adhere to custom at culture just to reproduce" (A male tourist). "An elephant is not human but an animal! I do not believe in marriage at all (neither for humans), so it is not ok for me they need to have a ceremony before getting babies" (A male tourist). "I think it's natural for animals to reproduce and have babies why humans wanted to change what is natural? It is weird". "We do not need more captive elephants" (A female tourist).

12.4.1.4 TOURISTS 'RECOMMENDATION FOR ELEPHANT MARRIAGE

Supported visitors recommended that if the event were to take place it should be respectful of elephants' indigenous people. Elephants should be treated well; no jumping, or touching, and tribal villagers should be protected from becoming too touristic. A respondent commented,

It needs to be well advertised on travel forums and explained that it's a cultural traditional. (We should) also protect the tribal villages from becoming too touristic maybe build another place to do the ceremony to keep the village privacy.

One of the recommendations was that there should be an organization that is responsible for the event. "(We should) create a specific NGO dedicated only to weddings, use the money to help elephants have babies or they will go extinct and at the end, the Bunong people would also suffer."

Non-supported visitors showed their ideas that they would like the fund to be for indigenous people's well-being and elephant conservation rather than spending on the ceremony. Some recommended that this tradition should be eliminated because elephants need to have babies. Some thought that elephants should be treated well and not used as an objective of tourism. Other visitors commented that this event should be organized in only a village or community when it is needed, if not it would become a commercialized attraction, thus it is dangerous for indigenous people.

12.4.2 *RESULTS FROM SEMI-STRUCTURE AND FOCUS GROUP INTERVIEW*

The researcher was able to interview five institution representatives including government bodies such as PDoT, and PDoCFA of Mondulkiri, NGOs including ELIE and LEAF, and one local tour operator which represented the private sector. Two focus group discussions were held in both villages individually. In addition, the workshop was conducted to validate data from interviews and focus groups. The data were transcribed and analyzed in two steps, by respondents, and by objectives.

12.4.2.1 *STATUS AND BIOLOGICAL FACTORS OF DOMESTICATED ELEPHANTS*

Captive elephants in Mondulkiri have been mostly owned by indigenous Bunong people because they had the tradition of capturing wild elephants to live in their village for helping with their daily work, especially because elephants were the easiest mean of transportation in the mountainous areas. However, domesticated elephants in Mondulkiri are facing the problem of the decreasing year on year due to the health factor, aging and problem when they are in musth (male elephants). According to the ELIE director, 5elephants died in 2017 because of these problems. There are a total of around 40 (28 female) domesticated elephants in Mondulkiri which represents about 59% of the total population of domesticated elephants in Cambodia. The status of elephants was also a concern for their existence of them in the future. Bunong tradition is the main barrier for elephants to reproduce their next generation. There were still some problems relating to domesticated elephants such as the breeding facilities and transmitting diseases. Indigenous people kept elephants in the traditional way, and they had a low capacity of managing and taking care of their elephants.

Like human beings, elephants can reproduce between the age of 16 and 45 years. This applied to female elephants and for males the starting ages are the same, but they can reproduce for the rest of their lives. When they can reproduce, male elephants are in musth (a periodic condition in bull (male) elephants, characterized by highly aggressive behavior and accompanied by a large rise in reproductive hormones). This condition happens two times a year for each mature male elephant. For female elephants whenever they reach the age of reproducing, they have a period once every three months. Elephants spend 24 months to pregnant for a male baby and 18 months for a female baby. The gap from one baby to another is 5 years long. Based on the interview and focus group, elephants, like other animals, would have various relationships among their group or other elephants. According to villagers, elephants were believed to have a special sense can know when the mahout did anything wrong. For instance, elephants would sleep in the morning, which was abnormal. Villagers believed that elephants know this by asking the earth. Villagers in Pu Trom explained that,

In case, they (the mahouts) betray their wife or husband or break our culture (has love without marriage), the elephant will be angry with them, hits them, and it sleeps in the morning. The way elephants know/notice this is through eating or asking the earth.

12.4.2.2 INDIGENOUS BUNONG TRADITION WITH ELEPHANTS

Indigenous people have a tight connection with their elephants. So far elephants still help people in their daily work, but less intensive than before since now people have alternative transportation. Villagers told similarly that domesticated elephants had been helping them to pull wood to build houses, transport people to visit relatives, and carry goods such as bananas and so on. Besides helping people do their daily work, elephants have also related to villagers' beliefs and traditions. According to focus group discussions in each village, there were some customs that indigenous people had with their elephants. Indigenous people put their beliefs with their elephants. A representative from LEAF said, "there are the traditions of praying with (domesticated) elephants; they have the tradition of sacrificing animals. When people get married, the lady got a miscarriage or people die, they also have to pray with the elephants".

12.4.2.3 NON-BREEDING TABOO AND THE REASONS BEHIND

One of the taboos for elephants was forbidding domesticated elephants to breed in the village of Bunong since it was considered bad luck. Villagers mentioned that male and female elephants were not allowed to live together and had a baby, except in the case that villagers did not know. "In general, villagers do not let elephants to be together and have baby" (Villagers in PuTrom).

Villagers also stated that if elephants had a baby in any case, they believed that bad things would happen in the village, for instance, the villager got sick, had accidents, or died. To prevent these things, if an elephant had a baby, the elephant owner or mahout had to celebrate a ritual in which they would spend a lot to pray and sacrifice for happiness in the village. The reason for praying and sacrificing was to prevent unluckiness. This ritual happened in Pu Tang village almost 20 years ago when an elephant delivered a baby. In the interview with one local tour operator representative who was close to Bunong and lives in Pu Tang village interpreted that the possible reason behind this taboo was that in the old time, elephants were a very important means of transport for indigenous people. Therefore, if elephants had babies, people wasted a lot of time and assistance from elephants. It was not only the time when the elephant was pregnant and delivered the baby but also when they started to love each other. So, people thought that it was a waste of time and resources to let elephants reproduce. Moreover, because in the previous time, they could capture elephants from the wild, there was no reason why they let domesticated elephants breed. This statement aligned with what the village chief of Pu Tang mentioned during the workshop.

[..] and for the taboo of not allowing elephant to breed was because in the past indigenous people had only elephant as their mean of transportation. So, if elephant love each other and have a baby, they will spend time for elephant not to work since they started to be together until they deliver baby, especially for female elephants (Village chief in Pu Tang).

Local tour operators added that after the elephant delivered the baby, it may become aggressive and would protect its baby, thus it may cause danger to people or mahout. This can be the possible assumption that the taboo was from the old time and passed from generation to generation. The local tour operator said, "I think this belief has been passed on from generation to generation. They believe that". The village chief mentioned that since elephants were not intensively used for helping people doing a daily task, but they gave people economic benefits from tourism, the tradition of not allowing elephants to breed was less strict. A villager in Pu Tang said, "but now people have machines instead of elephants; they don't need elephants mainly to help their work. Elephants become interesting for tourists, and tourist does not want to see the machine. Therefore, people now are less strict about this".

12.4.2.4 ELEPHANT MARRIAGE CEREMONY

Based on the results from semi-structured interviews and focus group discussions, not all informants knew about the ritual or elephant marriage. However, the ELIE director also used to hear and discuss elephant marriage. He stated that he used to bring one provincial officer who was also from Bunong to the elephant place. The provincial officer told him about elephant marriage:

> For me, the idea of conducting elephant marriage, I heard only from H.E Rang Chan but he died already… I used to bring Provincial board of director (Mr. Rang Chan) to the place that elephants stayed. He said that elephant baby which is born in the village is aggressive. In addition, if elephant breed baby in the village, it causes diseases or illness to villagers. However, he said if we get married to elephants, they will be legal so there will be no problem (man respondent, ELIE).

Only some people in Pu Trom village used to hear and discuss about elephant marriage. One of the villagers also described the process of celebrating the marriage. A village in Pu Trom mentioned, "we only heard about the marriage, but we never celebrated it…previously one of the provincial officers who was also from ethnic minority group intended to conduct marriage for the elephants and he knew the process from elder villagers." There was another mahout who also knew about elephant marriage, and he used to tell Pu Trom village chief that the celebration of elephant marriage was like the celebration of indigenous Bunong people's marriage. Based on this, it can be assumed that elephant marriage existed in the past. In contrast, people in Pu Tang village responded that they had never heard of or conducted this celebration. Thus, for the questions about elephant marriage, they were not able to answer. However, people in both villages knew about the ritual when the elephant delivered a baby.

12.4.2.5 PROCESS OF ELEPHANT MARRIAGE

The process of elephant marriage was described by some villagers in Pu Trom village. To celebrate the marriage, it was when people knew that male and female elephants love each other and there was a possibility that elephants would have a baby. First elder people in the village needed to meet and discuss to arrange the celebration. Once they agreed, the marriage can be celebrated. More importantly, they must pray for ancestors and spirits to inform them about the marriage. To pray for this, they need one chicken and one jar of wine praying at the house of the female elephant owner and one chicken with one jar of wine praying for ancestors and spirits. After elder people discussed and prayed to the spirit, they choose the date to celebrate the ritual. On a ritual day, there must be two matchmakers (one for each side of the elephant owner) to act on behalf of each side of the elephant. Each love consultant would need sacrifice from the elephant owner such as one pig, two chickens, and two jars of wine. During the marriage, they had to sacrifice one buffalo, one cow, ten small pigs, one mature pig, one white chicken, one black chicken, one dog, one duck, rice and food, ten jars of rice wine, some money (depending on ability), two dishes of rice, two candles which are made from bee wage. The process of sacrificing was that people took all animals mentioned earlier to get their blood to mix with wine and started to pray with the rice and candle which claimed to inform the marriage of elephants and may pray for happiness for both people and elephants.

12.4.2.6 PROCESS OF CELEBRATION FOR ELEPHANT BABY

Villagers mentioned that they all knew about the celebration when the elephant delivered a baby in the village. However, people in each village told the ritual in a bit different process.

- Pu Trom Village

Requirements for sacrificing to conduct the ritual included one buffalo, one dog, four small pigs, one duck, five jars of wine, one dish of rice, a candle (made from bee wage), and some money. To sacrifice, all animals were taken blood to mix with wine and put in the jar. After that mahout, owners, elder people, and villagers took the mixed blood and wine by putting the jar on their forehead and start to pray for happiness in the village and make sure that the new elephant baby would live well with people. Participants were from both sides of the elephants, mahouts, and elder people. The celebration took place one day at the owner of the female elephant's house starting in the morning when villagers arranged and managed to sacrifice an animal and then gathered to pray.

- Pu Tang Village

The ritual had to be conducted two times, when the elephant was pregnant and when it delivered a baby, but there was the same process and requirement for praying. Requirements for sacrificing and praying included one duck, one chicken, one dog, two jars of wine, two pigs (one black and one white), one cow, one buffalo, one dish of rice, and one candle. The process was quite like that of Pu Trom. However, villagers mentioned that they rarely celebrate this ritual since elephants were not easily allowed to breed. The last ritual celebration was almost 20 years ago, and the process of the ceremony can be forgotten if elephants were not able to breed in the village.

12.4.2.7 LOCAL PEOPLE'S INTEREST AND CAPACITY TO CELEBRATE THE EVENT

The researcher discovered two different concepts. It was noticeable that when asked about the disappearance of elephants, villagers said they were worried about this issue, however; they did not have any solution. Some villagers seemed neutral about letting elephants breed. Some villagers in Pu Trom felt positive about the elephant marriage because they would like to see elephants breeding in the village. However, they needed further discussion with other elder people in another village. Elephant owners or villagers did not have any financial ability to conduct the event. They could just participate and involve in the event. In contrast, villagers in Pu Tang village said they never heard of or knew about elephant marriage, so they would not dare to celebrate it although there would be support from various government bodies, and private and NGO sectors. They worried about the bad effects that they believed would happen after the marriage.

During the validation workshop, the researcher invited some villagers from both villages and directors of PDoCFA and PDoT. Primary results were presented to participants and after their discussion under the facilitation of the researcher, the result saw that elephant marriage was known by only two villagers who may have known it from other elder people from the previous generation. One of them was the provincial officer and one was the elephant mahout who had just died a day before the workshop because of suicide. Two more people discussed about that. One of them was the village chief in Pu Trom and another one is the ELIE director. Based on this, the researcher assumed that the tradition of elephant marriage was abandoned a long time ago and was forgotten for several generations. Since indigenous people believed in superstition and celebrated only the tradition that we were sure of in the process, they decided that they did not dare to celebrate the ceremony. Therefore, this can conclude that elephant marriage cannot be conducted because there was no specificity of the celebration.

However, villagers in both villages seemed to feel positive about celebrating rituals when an elephant delivered a baby if there were support from any stakeholder and if an elephant had a baby. According to people in Pu Tang village, there was still hope that in the future there would be elephant baby in the village due to the fact that female elephant was still in the age of breeding. Villagers also told that provided there would be support for them to conduct rituals when the elephant delivers a baby, they will let elephants live together. Moreover, during the focus group discussion, villagers in both villages seemed to show positive concepts on tourists and would like to show and share their culture and tradition with visitors to see their village and explore their culture and livelihood.

12.4.2.8 STAKEHOLDER INTEREST AND SUPPORT FOR THE EVENT

All stakeholders would like the event to happen, but it should depend on indigenous people to decide by them because that is their tradition. Based on the semi-structured interview, all key informants see the event as two useful ways can benefit Bunong people and tourism in Mondulkiri province. The first one is about keeping the numbers of domesticated elephants sustainable which continues to generate benefits for local people and the environment. The second one is about digging up and conserving indigenous culture and tradition.

There would be various support from government bodies, NGOs, and private sectors for local people if elephant marriage were celebrated. Government bodies from the two departments would cooperate with provincial authorities, NGOs, and especially local people to organize the event. Furthermore, PDoT, for example, would work with PDoCFA to facilitate the event and propose for any possible financial budget to support the event. In addition, NGOs and projects which were focusing on elephants like LEAF and ELIE stated that they had a prepared budget for the marriage or any ritual, provided that indigenous people let their elephants reproduce.

12.4.3 CHALLENGES AND OPPORTUNITIES

There were both opportunities and challenges for the elephant marriage ceremony to be conducted.

TABLE 3.3 Opportunities and Challenges of the Event.

Opportunities	Challenges
• Revitalization of tradition/culture	• Mindset of indigenous people (feeling doubtful and worried after celebration)
• Sociocultural benefit	
• Building destination image	• Elephants might be uncontrollable
• Economic opportunity	
• Conservation benefit	
• Further attention and research in this area	

Source: Opportunities and challenges of the event: this was analyzed from the primary data (interviews, focus group discussion, and survey).

- **Cultural revitalization:** Indigenous people's tradition and culture of elephant marriage celebration would be dug up again. Since most people did not know about the process of celebration and there had been no written documents for the next generation. Both written and live documents would be passed on to the next generation.

- **Sociocultural benefit:** From a cultural perspective, some respondents viewed the event as an opportunity to showcase indigenous culture, art, performance, and so on to other people, especially tourists.

- **Building destination image:** The other opportunity is to build a destination image of the villages and Mondulkiri province. This can attract more attention from visitors.

- **Economic opportunity:** Celebrating the event can generate opportunities for the host community and for people within that destination. The possible positive economic from the event will be both direct and indirect impact.

- **Conservation opportunity:** Informants considered such a celebration to be a key for domesticated elephant conservation since the number of elephants is decreasing year on year. They also raised concern that villagers do not allow elephants to reproduce and said that elephant marriage would be a solution for the increasing number of elephants in Bunong villages.

- **Further attention and research in the area:** The possible opportunity from the event is that it will attract more attention from researchers who are interested in indigenous culture and tradition. Moreover, if elephants can reproduce, there will be also attention from experts for elephants' caretaking and conservation.

However, the challenges which can be the barrier to the feasibility of elephant marriage as well as a problem that would happen afterward.

A Feasibility Study of Resurrecting Elephant Marriage Ceremonies in Mondulkiri   179

- **People mindset:** The first and foremost challenge is about indigenous people's mindset. Because they have a strong belief in superstition, villagers were afraid of the problems which would happen afterward.

The representative from PDoCFA said, "this will be the mindset of the people that they may feel worried after conducting this event because they haven't conduct in generation to generation. So, if they conduct this, they may doubt/worry afterward." There was also a concern that if elephant marriage were celebrated without any specific reference, villagers would assume that all the problems that may happen were from the celebration. Based on the interview with the LEAF representative, there was also the same concern relating to this matter. The representative from LEAF stated, "there can be challenges after we finish this event. All the problems that will happen after marriage, they will assume that it is because of the marriage." This was also confirmed by the response from villagers during the validation workshop. Elder persons and village chief in Pu Trom mentioned: "thing that we are not sure, we should not conduct because we are afraid that serious things could happen from this."

- **Elephants might be uncontrollable:** There was also concern about elephants when taking them to participate in ceremonies where there are many people, and elephants might be staggered during the celebration of the event. However, if it was well planned, there should not be any problem regarding this as the ELIE representative mentioned the organization has methods to control this.

From all the findings, especially qualitative findings, the study had bridged the community/local people to various stakeholders to consider the issue and strive to find out a solution for indigenous culture and the sustainability of captive elephants. Since all partners had never been together to deliberate on the case. Individual players of the event stayed on their side and just noted the issue. Only the two NGOs interviewed mentioned that they had tried to explain and persuaded indigenous people to let elephant breed, but they had not agreed. The study made all relevant stakeholders and villagers understand each other and led to the understanding of each side more precisely.

12.5   DISCUSSION

12.5.1   STAKEHOLDERS' PERCEPTION OF BUNONG TRADITION AND PROPOSED EVENT

Stakeholders had rather a similar perception of the Bunong belief regarding forbidding their domesticated elephant to breed. Government departments,

180   Event Tourism and Sustainable Community Development

NGOs, and the private sector surveyed viewed the taboo as strange, but they understood that is because indigenous people have different traditions and ways of life from the majority of Khmer. Most visitors surveyed were very interested in the Bunong tradition and culture and they would like the event to happen so that captive elephants would have the next generation in the village. However, some non-supported visitors suggested that the tradition should be forgotten. According to McCracken (1986), each culture constructed its special sense of the world. The belief, norms, and traditions in one cultural context in which a group is regarded as appropriate may not be appropriated or acceptable for another. Based on this, each culture has its value which a group found it is acceptable. Thus, the majority of the other group could not eliminate or tell people in that cultural context to forget about it. AHC (2002) stated that indigenous culture was dynamic and consists of tangible and intangible manifestations of tradition. The way the indigenous culture was transmitted is through "the person." Along with this, the findings showed that from the perspective of villagers, the tradition of not allowing the elephant to breed had been strictly followed by the elder generation. This belief was passed on from generation to generation. However, based on the current situation, elephants were not so intensively used to help with the daily work of people, but now elephants have become more popular in the tourism sector and generate income for them. Because culture is dynamic and needs to be adapted following the times and living conditions of people, indigenous people turn to be less strict on the taboo. The majority of respondents were interested and supported financially and politically for the event to take place, yet they stressed the importance of indigenous people as the ones who make a decision. Based on Bowndin et al. (2006), for an event, it is not sufficient to achieve only the audience's needs. Taking into consideration the importance of each player who involves in the event, it is not appropriate just to celebrate any event without clarification and involvement from any player especially the owner or host of the event which is the Bunong people.

12.5.2 *EVENT FEASIBILITY CRITERIA*

Goldblatt (2014) stated there were three main criteria to assess the feasibility study of the event. As presented in the conceptual framework, the first consideration was a financial dimension, the second was a human dimension, and finally politics as usual. The findings from primary data matched only two of the three criteria of Goldblatt. The first criterion, the financial dimension, there was support from stakeholders including government bodies and NGOs. There would be various supports from other related organizations and individuals. Furthermore, ELIE and LEAF, which work relating to elephant conservation and protection, reserved a budget for celebrating the ritual which leads to the possibility for elephants to reproduce. Second, the human dimension, which included various human resources involved with the event. The local villagers, known as the host or owners of the culture, were the main player throughout the event. The others can include the management board of the event, stakeholders, and volunteer groups. Since the indigenous people felt insecure to make the event happen and they would not involve with such an event because they did not have enough proof about the process of celebrating, the second criterion was not applicable to the feasibility of the event. Finally, the politics as usual. Assessing the perception of all stakeholders, especially the government body, there was no disapproval from any of them regarding the event. They all considered the event as a key for elephant conservation and protection, and importantly it matches the interest of all sides including tourism, culture, and environment. Along with this, the perspective of the event was already aligned with the Tourism Strategic Development Plan (2012–2020) of the government.

12.5.3 ALTERNATIVE TO ELEPHANT MARRIAGE

The final decision of villagers in the workshop showed the disagreement of celebrating elephant marriage since they did not clearly know how to perform it and importantly indigenous people felt doubtful about bad things that might happen after the celebration. Alternatively, they were clear about the process and requirement of conducting rituals when an elephant delivered a baby. One villager who was the elephant mahout used to experience conducting the ritual. According to this, villagers felt secure about celebrating the ritual when the elephant baby was born. From the perspective of villagers, there were also worries about the disappearance of domesticated elephants in their villages, thus if there were financial and mechanism support, villagers would not separate male and female elephants anymore so that there were chances for elephants to have babies. Moreover, it was noticeable from the perspectives of stakeholders and the audience that the major reason for their support and interest in the event was for elephants to be able to reproduce. As the deputy director of PDoCFA mentioned at the end of the workshop that whatever celebration relating to indigenous and leading to the possibility for elephants to breed, the department would still support it. Therefore, if reflecting on the criteria for event feasibility by Goldblatt (2014), the celebration of the baby elephant was highly possible. Therefore, an alternative to the celebration of elephant marriage was the celebration of an elephant baby.

12.5.4 *CHARACTERISTICS OF THE ALTERNATIVE CELEBRATION*

Whether conducting elephant marriage or celebrating of ritual for elephant baby, there was still the possibility of including indigenous culture in the event according to villagers. Yeoman et al. (2004) stated that the cultural process could aim to encourage local participation in increasing awareness of a tradition, place, and the value of the social and culture of a destination as well as to satisfy the demand of special interest group. The celebration of the elephant baby when it is born is concerned with the process of performing rituals and praying in an indigenous cultural context. In addition, it was appropriate to include other forms of culture and art, and show how to add more value to the event. The characteristic elephant baby celebration should aim to promote captive elephant conservation, and caretaking, and attract more attention to elephants. The event should be a combination of natural and cultural heritage, especially indigenous culture. However, the event would not happen annually or follow any fixed calendar as the Elephant Festival in Lao, since it depends fully on the nature of elephants. If it happens, the celebration will take place irregularly depending on the where elephants are. It would become special that everyone is going to look forward to participating and hearing good news from the elephants when they have a baby.

12.6 CONCLUSION AND RECOMMENDATION

12.6.1 *CONCLUSION*

Three-fourth of both national and international visitors surveyed supported elephant marriage to happen. Over 60% of all visitors intended to participate in the event if it took place. From the perspective of stakeholders, there were various supports both financial and mechanism for the process of the event. They found the celebration beneficial, and it would generate opportunities for local people, domesticated elephant conservation, NGOs, the private sector, and general tourism in Mondulkiri. Results from the focus group interview indicated that the tradition of elephant marriage was not widely known among indigenous people. Only some people in Pu Trom village used to hear and discuss it. Two people mentioned about elephant marriage passed away. That was why there was not sufficient proof of the celebration process although some people in Pu Trom village described the process and requirements, they just heard from those who died. Considering the components for event feasibility of Goldblatt (2014), the researcher found that elephant marriage could fulfill only two of the three criteria. First was the financial dimension and second was politics as usual. The third criterion, the human dimension, was not applicable since villagers who were considered traditional owners did not show approval and were willing to celebrate it. Villagers from both villages reached a consensus on the celebration of ritual for elephant babies to provide the opportunity for elephants to reproduce. Since villagers agreed on the celebration for elephant baby alternative to elephant marriage, this celebration matched the three elephants for feasibility criteria as mentioned above. The consensus of the village indicated that the human dimension criteria were fulfilled. The celebration of the elephant baby is characterized mainly as a cultural event since it demonstrated the process in the culture, indigenous, belief, and ritual performance.

12.6.2 RECOMMENDATION

12.6.2.1 POSSIBLE CELEBRATION OF THE FEASIBLE EVENT

Considering the feasible celebration for the elephant baby, the management committee of the event would need to be formed. This committee for the event should include various stakeholders such as government departments, non-government organizations which work closely for elephant conservation, the private sector, and especially elder indigenous people from villages who know about the process of celebrating the ritual. The committee should play important role in decision making of what could be included and what could not be included to show to the audience. The process and requirements of the ritual need to be documented for the next generation of indigenous people.

The community may have limited capacity to welcome visitors. To minimize the negative impacts which might occur from the event, there should be a study on the capacity of the event, and how resistant is the local people to host a large number of tourists. Attracting mass tourism can generate great financial advantages but may not be appropriate for sociocultural factors. Too many tourists can spoil the destination, so there must be clear consideration of the number of visitors to be attracted.

12.6.2.2 CAPACITY BUILDING OF CAPTIVE ELEPHANTS MANAGEMENT

The findings showed that indigenous people still managed their elephants via the traditional way of feeding. Domesticated elephants still faced some health issues since indigenous people strongly believed in superstition. There should be training for elephant mahouts or elephant owners on technical management and caretaking for elephants. The knowledge of elephant management, especially when elephants are in, must be improved among indigenous people. The breeding facilities should be prepared in advance in order that elephants can breed their babies safely. Moreover, in Cambodia's context, there was no formal government registration system for domesticated elephants, and the monitoring of transfer of ownership. Therefore, the government should register captive elephants in the system and monitor the transfer of ownership, in order the government can manage and give assistance for elephant conservation. The monitoring of ownership will help manage the trading of domesticated elephants in and outside of the country.

12.6.2.3 FURTHER STUDY

The next study should pay attention to discovering the tradition of elephant marriage in other villages or areas where Bunong people live. Future research may focus on the planning of the feasible event. Good planning will help the event flow smoothly and gain fruitful results. Moreover, future research should pay attention to benefit sharing generated from the event so that all stakeholders and local people can get equitable benefits. Lastly, further study should also focus on other forms of indigenous heritage including tangible and intangible to be included in the event; this should also consider the impact of transferring those heritages into tourist attractions.

KEYWORDS

- **feasibility study**
- **tourism event**
- **stakeholders**
- **challenges**
- **opportunities**

REFERENCES

Arcodia, C.; Whitford, M. Festival Attendance and the Development of Social Capital. *J. Conv. Event Tour.* **2006**, *8* (2), 1–18.

Asian Elephant Range States Meeting. *Final report*; Ministry of Environment and Forestry, Government of Indonesia: Jakarta, 2017.

Australian Heritage Commission. *Ask First: A Guide to Respecting Indigenous Heritage Place and Value*; National Capital Printing: Canberra, 2017.

Bowndin, A. J.; Allen, J.; O'Toole, W.; Harris, R.; McDonnel, I. *Event Management*; Elsevier Ltd: Great Britain, 2006.

BPP Learning media. *CTH Diploma in Tourism Management: Travel Geography*; Singapore: Author, 2011.

Cooper, C.; Hall, C. M. *Contemporary Tourism: An International Approach*; Butterworth-Heinemann: Oxford, 2008. http://www.eventscouncil.org/Files/APEX/APEX_Event_Specifications_Guide.pdf

Elephant Festival and Stay at Tong Tarin Hotel, Surin, Thailand. In *Tripadvisor*, 2017. https://www.tripadvisor.com/ShowUserReviews-g303923-d600709-r541950348-Thong_Tarin_Hotel-Surin_Surin_Province.html

Elephant Festival. In *Everything about Luangprabang-Laos.com*. https://www.luangprabang-laos.com/Elephant-Festival

Getz, D. Event Tourism: Definition, Evolution, and Research. *J. Tour. Manage.* **2007**, *29*, 403–428.

Goldblatt, J. Special Events: *Creating and Sustaining a New World for Celebration*; John Wiley & Sons, Inc; New Jersey, 2014.

Heng, N.; Ngin, C.; Yin, S.; Thatt, R.; Dork, V.; Nop, S.; Men, P.; Seang, P. *Indigenous Tourism Strategic Plan for the Northeast of Cambodia Mondulkiri*; Phnom Penh: RUPP, 2016.

McCracken, G. Culture and Consumption: A Theoretical Account of the Structure and Movement of the Cultural Meaning of Consumer Goods. *J. Consumer Res.* **1986**, *13*, 71–84.

Ministry of Tourism. *Tourism Development Strategic Plan 2012–2020*; Author: Phnom Penh, 2012.

Mondulkiri Department of Tourism. *Mondulkiri'sdevelopment strategic plan for tourism 2014-2018*. Mondulkiri: Author.

Neth, B. *Research Methods Toward a Thesis Preparation*; Author: Phnom Penh, 2017.

Organization for Economic Cooperation and Development. *The Impact of Culture on Tourism*; OECD Publishing; France, 2009.

Richards, G.; Palmer, R. *Eventful Cities: Cultural and Urban Revitalization*; Butterworth-Heinemann, Oxford, 2010.

Southeast Asia. In *Aseantourism*, 2015. http://www.aseantourism.travel/event/detail/wedding-ceremony-on-elephants-back.

Surin's Elephant Roundup. In *ilikevents*, 2017. https://ilikevents.com/event/3057-surin-elephant-roundup.

Swarbrooke, J. *The Development and Management of Visitor Attractions*; Butterworth-Heinemann: Oxford, 2002.

Vilaysack, S. Elephant Festival Readies for Over 100,000 Visitors. *Vientiane Times*, Feb 15, **2014,** p 2.

Yeoman, I.; Robertson, M.; Ali-Knight, J.; Drummond, S.; Beattie, U., Eds. *Festival and Events Management: An International Arts and Cultural Perspective*; Elsevier Butterworth-Heinemann: Oxford, 2004.

CHAPTER 13

Antecedents and Challenges of Sustainable Event Management Practices in Sri Lanka

A. M. D. B. NAWARATHNA[1] and R. S. S. W. ARACHCHI[2]

[1]*Department of Tourism Studies, Faculty of Management, Uva Wellassa University of Sri Lanka, Badulla, Sri Lanka*

[2]*Faculty of Management Studies, Sabaragamuwa University of Sri Lanka, Belihuloya, Sri Lanka*

ABSTRACT

Sustainable event management continues to grow in popularity in recent years in the world, and it is not yet common practice in the Sri Lankan context. Hence, the study examines the antecedents and challenges of sustainable event management practices in Sri Lanka. Primary data was collected through structured interviews from 15 event managers who have membership of the Sri Lanka Association of Professional Conference, Exhibition, and Event Organisers using the purposive sampling technique. In addition, the Qualitative data analytical method was employed, and the collected data were transcribed and analyzed by using content analysis. The findings of the study reveal that economic influence, social and political influence, and psychological factors influenced to move sustainable practices and cost, limited infrastructure facilities, lack of government support, and customers' mentality were the challenges of implementing sustainable event management practices in Sri Lanka. Further, implications and recommendations are discussed based on the generated codes and categories.

Please note that few chapters were submitted during the peak of the pandemic. The long period of time to publish (due to supply chain and other issues) may have changed the perspectives presented in the chapter altogether.

Event Tourism and Sustainable Community Development: Advances, Effects, and Implications.
Ekta Dhariwal, Shruti Arora, Anukrati Sharma, Azizul Hassan (Eds.)
© 2024 Apple Academic Press, Inc. Co-published with CRC Press (Taylor & Francis)

13.1 INTRODUCTION

The event industry is rapidly developing and makes a significant contribution to business and leisure-related tourism (Ranasinghe and Nawarathna, 2020). It has a range of impacts, both positive and negative, on their host communities and stakeholders. Globally, more and more events are hosted in an environmentally, socially, and economically responsible way. However, due to global warming, most event organizers rethink their attitude toward the environment and resources. Therefore, sustainable management practices have been applied using more advanced techniques at various international festivals and events. In addition, many international companies are making event greening a part of their tender process (Ahmad et al., 2013).

Sustainability in event management integrates socially and environmentally friendly decision making into event planning, organizing, and implementation processes. The British Standards Institution (2012) defined sustainable event management as an enduring balanced approach to economic activity, environmental responsibility, and social progress. Maguire and Hanrahan (2013) stated festivals and events generate the vast majority of negative impacts in different areas, and the urgency of sustainability is clear, and society should acknowledge this. Further, they mentioned an apparent need for festivals and events to be sustainably managed and therefore utilize and adopt new sustainability technologies to minimize costs and plan and manage for cleaner and more sustainable festivals and events. Moreover, it is necessary to identify appropriate strategies to maximize the benefits of events for the interest of different communities in the scale of sustainability (Schulenkorf et al., 2018).

MICE arrivals have been increasing in Sri Lanka in the last three years, continuing to grow. Around 11% of the total visitors into Sri Lanka represent the MICE segment, and currently, it stands over 119,000 with a 5–10% increase annually. Further, Sri Lanka Tourism recommended actions and implementation mechanisms with a long-term view toward Tourism Vision 2025 and achieving the United Nations Sustainable Development Goals.

Moreover, Sri Lanka has identified a number of opportunities that can be created through the effective promotion of business tourism and MICE tourism. The sustainability of the tourism industry is strongly linked with the environmental and sociocultural aspects of a destination (Wickramasinghe, 2018). And also, to the best of the author's knowledge, there is no research on this topic in the Sri Lankan context. Therefore, the purpose of this study is to identify the antecedents and challenges of implementing sustainable event management practices and provide an opportunity to manage and reduce the impacts, while improving the quality of events.

13.2 LITERATURE REVIEW AND THEORETICAL BACKGROUND

13.2.1 SUSTAINABLE EVENT MANAGEMENT

Sustainable event management has evolved over many years and is not a term that emerged from policy, policies, or academic posturing. A natural advance is a recent proposal to convert past and present systems to a known standard. A conceptual framework that has evolved over the last 10 years from event planning and management is an essential requirement for a responsible professional event throughout the 21st century. Sustainability and event management are relative concepts when combined to make sustainable event management (Jones and Scanlon, 2010). Still, if we want to achieve the best results, both need to be managed responsibly. Sustainability and event management are currently gaining increasing popularity among academic and professionals (Getz, 2009; Holmes et al., 2015; Jones and Scanlon, 2010).

The concept of sustainability has three components as environmental, economic, and social, which are classified as the Triple Bottom Line. The word sustainability has become an important topic in today's community, especially within the tourism industry (Byrd, 2007) and the event industry. Thus, sustainable practices include removing harmful substances produced by the environment and gaining benefits to the community and economy.

Sustainable event management is a collection of tools, processes, and procedures that event organizers and operators use to make events greener. The British Standards Institution (2012) described the sustainable event as a means to cope with economic activity, climate responsibility, and social progress. According to Tzla (2007), sustainable event management is the convergence of sustainability with the project planning process of event management. The combination of sustainability and events management creates a better future for the community, the economy, and the rest of the environment. As a result, event organizers increasingly seek to improve sustainability, and the sustainable event is a popular event with the media and the public (Laing and Frost, 2010).

For events to contribute to sustainable development, there must be a balance between economic, social, and environmental objectives with strategies to optimize positive and minimize negative impacts. Therefore, it is vital to recognize the unique features of events and the events industry and develop operational strategies whereby event stakeholders act responsibly and contribute to development.

13.2.2 ANTECEDENTS AND CHALLENGES OF IMPLEMENTING THE SUSTAINABLE EVENT MANAGEMENT PRACTICES

The event industry caters to diverse types of events and different industries while serving the views and choices of different people in society. With further illustration of the critical areas of antecedents, there was limited literature available on this topic. For example, Etiosa (2012) highlights events have the ability in creating brand loyalty with respect to particular organizations image and durability. Also, the reviews of Sustainable Event Planning Guide Denver Convention Host Committee Greening Initiative Fall (2008) indicate organizations' movement to sustainable practices would guide them to reduce the cost on larger scales. Further, the studies of Maguire and Hanrahan (2013) emphasize the requirement in adopting new sustainability technologies that transit the higher number of costs to lower numbers generated from events both in the long run and short run.

The literature enriches another element in identifying social movements which are directly or indirectly influenced the event industry to turn into new sustainable adaptation within themselves while encouraging the employees to innovate with sustainable practices and events at work (Edwards, 2005; Holmes et al., 2015; Stettler, 2011; Sustainable Event Planning Guide Denver Convention Host Committee Greening Initiative Fall, 2008). Most of the above studies predict the utilization of diverse aspects and antecedents in implementing sustainable event management practices diverse factors.

In refereeing to the challenges in sustainable events management, limited researches have investigated by scholars. Herciu and Ogrean (2014) illustrate the facts on the increased costs of sustainable initiatives, which causes issues in handling the sustainable events since these causes diverse and complex barriers for the prevalence of the sustainability approaches in the event industry with also emphasizing the facts on its rare application in the market.

Herciu and Ogrean (2014) discuss environmentally friendly events usually contribute to higher budgets with more indirect and additional costs and efforts that ultimately result in and influence the organizations' planning process. Stettler (2011) studies identified cost-prohibitive sustainability solutions, implementation of sustainability practices and methods, festival viability, attendee engagement, internal support, commitment and priority, infrastructure and local resources, and government support as the challenges of implementing the sustainability practices in the event industry.

13.2.3   THE NEED FOR SUSTAINABLE EVENTS MANAGEMENT PRACTICES IN SRI LANKA

Sri Lanka's Tourism Vision 2025 and Sri Lanka's Roots Philosophy emphasize eco-friendly practices and green principles for tourism and tourism institutions should work closely with the relevant authorities and existing national plans and strategies to achieve the sustainable goals and mitigate the effects based on the national economic objectives and guiding principles for the tourism industry in Sri Lanka. Therefore, the event sector is specified in reaching the above principles in attaining sustainability goals in 2025.

Further, the initial requirement is there to examine the facts that create the event industry in Sri Lanka reachable in a sustainable approach as this study predicts and dictates in an upscale manner. Then, building on the evidence of social and environmental impacts generated by events, there is a need for research to identify strategies suitable for maximizing event benefits for disparate communities' interest in the scale of sustainability (Schulenkorf et al., 2018).

Moreover, Chiu et al. (2020) cited; despite many sports tourism events have been organized globally, the understanding of the event greening practices is reasonably low, and there is still a lack of related studies pertaining to green events. Therefore, the roles of the event organizers or planners are vital to ensure that the ecological-friendly or environmental-friendly events are engaged. Therefore, this research aimed to fulfill this gap and identified antecedents and challenges to implementing sustainable event management practices to ensure the development of the Sri Lankan events industry.

13.3   METHODOLOGY

This study is mainly based on the primary data collected via structured interviews selected from the events companies, which are members of the Sri Lanka Association of Professional Conference, Exhibition, and Event Organizers (SLAPCEO) in Colombo, Sri Lanka (2020). Hence, the purposeful sampling technique was used for this research and 15 events companies were interviewed who were the members of SLAPCEO in Sri Lanka for this study as the sample size.

An interview guide was created after the research objectives and goals were established. Usually, this guide consists of 11 main questions, and several subquestions are included wherever necessary for this study. The interview guide itself was developed, including general questions about the company background and questions about the antecedents and challenges of implementing sustainable event management practices in Sri Lanka. General questions aimed to get background information about the company and the motivations for organizing a sustainable event. Interview participants were contacted via phone, e-mail, in-person, or a combination of the previous. All 15 interviews held via phone and person. The length of each interview ranged from 45 to 60 min. Firstly, the background of the study and the purpose of the interview have been explained to the participants to get an idea about the study. Then, interview participants were asked to discuss their perceptions of sustainable event management, antecedents, and challenges in implementing sustainable events. After the interview, each conversation was transcribed and reviewed again by the researcher. Every transcript was sent to the respective respondent to get confirmation that the information recorded is correct. The revised transcripts were then analyzed.

According to the research, the researcher has used content analysis as the data analysis method. It is the most widely used method of qualitative data analysis that focuses on identifying patterned significance across a dataset. It aims to identify meaning patterns across a dataset that provide an answer to the research question to be dealt with. Patterns are defined by a comprehensive data familiarisation process, data coding, and categories creation and revision.

13.4 RESULTS

The event industry contains many different types of events and various industries, and each event draws different kinds of people with different reasons to participate. Therefore, the first objective of the research was to examine the antecedents of sustainable event management practices in Sri Lanka. Analyzing the respondents' interview responses, the researcher has identified seven key antecedents of sustainable event management and these antecedents, based essentially on economic influence, social and political influence, and psychological factors.

The first category of the antecedents was the economic influence, and it influenced the organizations and people who were in the society to engage in sustainable event management practices. According to the research, most of the respondents stated that brand loyalty influenced them to move sustainability. Doing any business aims to increase productivity and earned more profits at the short run and long run stages. This was similar to the event industry also. In order to achieve those objectives, it is essential to have a positive attitude in the customers' mind toward the event. The customer has the perception that the event has the qualities that meet their expectations. Most of the event management companies were focused on short-term earnings, and it was not easy to sustain the long run in the event industry. Therefore, they have realized the importance of becoming sustainable and building a solid customer base in the event industry.

Sustainable event management concept is new to the Sri Lankan context, and it has the greater awareness that we can make our event locally and internationally. Moreover, the positive publicity creates loyal customers towards the event and less likely to get influenced by the marketing efforts of the competitors. Then, we can market our event in the long run, and brand loyalty has motivated us to move sustainable practices.

(Participant 06: Personal communication, 2020)

According to the research, the researcher has identified most of the respondents mentioned that cost reduction had influenced them to move sustainable event management practices. A small country like Sri Lanka focusing on large events may create an imbalance in economic, social, and environmental sustainability and directly impact the organization's financial strength. Further, they have stated that operational cost was high in organizing events and adopting sustainable practices lends itself to efficient operation, conserving resources, enhancing employee productivity, and reducing cost. This overall impact could be more expensive to implement, but the long-term results justify the investments.

Yes, we thought adopting sustainable practices will be a cost. But, in reality, it will be differing. We have not incorporated sustainable practices into our company earlier. But later, we are used to adopt it because we want to reduce our cost of the event operations.

(Participant 07: Personal communication, 2020)

And also, some of the event management companies moved to sustainable event management practices to generate income. According to the perspectives of the event managers, they have used sustainability as a viable economic solution. However, in the event industry, the usage of resources and amount of wastage was high. Therefore, it is crucial to minimize the use of resources and reduce the amount of waste produced from event activities.

As an industry, we have to face a global crisis in different ways. But, on the other hand, the wastage generated by events has also enormously increased. Therefore, we started to use sustainable event management practices to generate a better income while surviving within the industry.
(Participant 10: Personal communication, 2020)

And also, due to high competition, employees encouraged to adopt sustainable practices at work by reducing energy and resources usage, enhancing recycling efforts, and contributing ideas for additional ways to apply sustainable practices in the workplace. Further, it creates a sustainable competitive advantage. It is the force that enables an event to have a greater focus, better profit margins, and higher customer and staff retention than competitors.

The second category of the antecedents was a social and political influence. It influenced the performance of the organizations and behavior of the local community to engage in sustainable event management practices. According to the research, most respondents stated that law and ethics influenced them to move sustainability. Further, they have mentioned that there has been a rising demand for environmental-friendly event management practices with increasing awareness of environmental issues. Finally, it built managers' confidence and trust rather than damage society and the environment.

Further, there was a criticism that events create short-term benefits and generate long-term unsustainability. As a result, social groups worked toward a common goal and provided a voice to the unethical behavior and activities generated from the events. This has influenced them to do their operations sustainably, mainly with less impact on society and the environment.

Social communities are mainly concerned about the green concept adaptions events in Sri Lanka. Therefore, in order to reduce the pollution, the event management companies have been pressured to provide solutions or event concepts which support sustainable event management practices.
(Participant 12: Personal communication, 2020)

The third category of the antecedents was psychological factors, and it motivated the organizations and the society to implement sustainable event management practices. The top organizational management motivates to adopt such practices within the company to provide opportunities to improve an organization's reputation by supporting a good cause and publicizing this involvement with many prospective clients, customers, and media. Society motivates to gain the maximum benefits and improve their quality of life. According to the findings, the researcher has stated that most of the event managers' moved to implement sustainable event management practices to motivate their employees to achieve their organizational goals and retained their employees of the organization. Further, this mindset toward events motivates employees to feel more considered and respected. They think that sustainable events are more focused on the wellbeing of their people compared to other businesses. Therefore, they encouraged their employees toward active engagement in sustainable initiatives.

Moving sustainable practices create us the positive reputation and improve the image of the organisation, and it helps to attract foreign participants that are becoming increasingly aware of sustainability issues. In addition, this has led to more strengthen bonds between suppliers and customers and increase the morale of the employees.
(Participant 11: Personal communication, 2020)

It is essential to motivate employees and society to create a competitive advantage and increase the organization's long-term financial growth. Further, this makes pride and satisfaction work in prestigious organizations and increase pressure to meet high standards of corporate and ethical behaviors. Therefore, motivation directly influences to move of sustainable event management practices in Sri Lanka.

The second objective of the research was to the challenges moving toward sustainable events management in Sri Lanka. Analyzing the respondents' interview responses, the researcher has identified four challenges as cost, limited infrastructure facilities, lack of government support, and customers' mentality.

The first challenge that occurs in implementing sustainable event management is cost. It becomes the delaying factor of any organization which contemplates sustainability initiatives in the events industry. Although Sri Lanka is not famous for sustainable events yet, even other developed countries are still finding various processors and methods to make their events green. However, when we market a sustainable event, the first interpretation that anyone would make is more expensive than a formal event. Also, a sustainable event gives the understanding of an eco-friendly event forgetting the economic and social aspects. Therefore, overcoming the above first impressions and carrying forward a successful sustainable event is a challenge.

Cost is the biggest factor as the latest high-efficiency equipment is always more expensive............

(Participant 13: Personal communication, 2020)

The second challenge of implementing sustainable event management is limited infrastructure facilities. The available venue does not fulfill the capacity requirements for larger-scale exhibitions or conferences in the exhibition and conference industry. Due to this, most of the event companies are made to temporary construct facilities to serve events which reduce the profitability and increases environmental waste and other unwanted practices. If Sri Lanka has large-scale venues for events, they can save the cost. And also, Sri Lanka being a hub in South Asia is an ideal hub for regional events to take place. But due to the above-stated factors, most of the companies are unable to host any large-scale exhibitions or conferences, unlike in India, Thailand, Singapore, and Dubai.

The local government plays a vital role in promoting sustainable tourism development. They are responsible for providing the required infrastructure facilities, promoting the host area, and the significant economic benefits it can bring to the event industry. In addition, they can support the event industry through build event venues, funding grants, and promoting local events. And also, they are responsible for overseeing the conduct, and safe staging of events and these bodies have an integral relationship with the industry. However, according to the research, the third challenge of implementing sustainable event management is the lack of government support in Sri Lanka. Some of the respondents suggested that the sustainable concept would be improved by implementing rules and regulations from the government authorities. There are no sustainable initiatives for the event industry from the government. Still, they have sustainable initiatives for other sectors in Sri Lanka.

The fourth challenge of implementing sustainable event management is customers' mentality. Customers are the key to the events industry. Most people want to live and make choices without sacrificing the world to meet their present needs. Customers want to carry out something physically, and filling something on paper cannot be changed. Their mentality and perception of being sustainable are challenging to achieve, but it is a critical element that influences the effectiveness of sustainable event management.

We try to do a sustainable event. But people must be adopted. Because they still need to carry out something physically, and they still want to fill in the form.

(Participant 08: Personal communication, 2020)

To address the above issue, it is crucial to educate and engage clients in sustainability awareness. It encourages the development of the expertise, skills, understanding, values, and actions needed to create a sustainable world that safeguards and conserves the environment, promotes social equity, and economic sustainability.

13.5 DISCUSSION

This research is regarding the antecedents and challenges of implementing sustainable event management in Sri Lanka. In this section, it discusses the findings according to the research objective.

The first objective was to examine the antecedents of sustainable event management practices in Sri Lanka. According to the findings, the researcher has identified three antecedents, namely, economic influence, social and political influence, and psychological factors. Brand loyalty, cost reduction, income generation, competition, law and ethics, social movements, and motivation influenced them to move sustainable event management practices. The study showed that positive publicity creates loyal customers toward the event and is less likely to get influenced by the competitors' marketing efforts. Etiosa (2012) mentioned events could be used to create the brand loyalty toward the organizations. Similarly, Sustainable Event Planning Guide Denver Convention Host Committee Greening Initiative Fall (2008) cited, adopting sustainable practices in events, enhanced the organizations' image and generated loyal customers. And also, the findings indicated that organizations moved to sustainable practices to reduce the cost of events. Maguire and Hanrahan (2013) mentioned, there was a requirement to adopt new sustainability technologies in order to minimize costs generated from events. Further, event management organizations moved to sustainable practices to retain the competitiveness of the market. This encourages employees to adopt sustainable practices at work by reducing energy and resources usage, enhancing recycling efforts, and contributing ideas for additional ways to apply sustainable practices in the workplace. Edwards (2005) argued the same, and this creates a competitive advantage in the event industry. Moreover, social movements influenced them to adopt sustainable practices and encourage their employees to implement sustainable initiatives.

The second objective was to explore the challenges moving toward sustainable events management in Sri Lanka. According to the findings, the researcher has identified four challenges, namely; cost, limited infrastructure facilities, lack of government support, and customers' mentality. The findings showed that an increased cost of sustainable initiatives was the biggest issue of handling the sustainable event in Sri Lanka. Herciu and Ogrean (2014) cited that the organization of environmentally friendly events is usually associated with additional costs and additional efforts. This is the main reason that deters companies from planning one. And also, Stettler (2011) mentioned, increased costs of sustainability initiatives and limited resources was the most significant barrier associated with sustainable event management of music festivals.

Further, limited infrastructure facilities put backward to the sustainable initiatives in the Sri Lankan events industry. The results indicated the available venue does not fulfil the capacity requirements for larger-scale exhibitions or conferences. As a result, organizations moved to unsustainable practices and increased environmental waste. Limited infrastructure and local resources within the host region restricted the event's sustainable opportunities (Stettler, 2011). Moreover, lack of government support is another challenge associated with the implementation of sustainable event. It was the least discussed and referenced barrier but was still described as quite a significant challenge and a critical need. Maguire and Hanrahan (2013) cited that local authorities must plan and manage events to sustain the process of sustainable event management.

Further, he explained that the government could approve and disapprove of events based on various aspects of the events planning process. Additionally, customers' mentality was an issue of being sustainable at the events. The client is the final decision maker, and their requirements mainly affect the implementation of an event. Stettler (2011) mentioned it was difficult to adopt customers and change their behavior toward sustainable event management practices.

13.6 CONCLUSION AND IMPLICATIONS

Events have been recognized as a vital factor in the development process as well as in the decision-making of business strategies. Sustainability practices have begun to take hold in all kinds of events. There are very few forces or mechanisms driving the widespread adoption and expansion of sustainable event management to become a common practice throughout the community in Sri Lanka (Nawarathna and Arachchi, 2021). Brand loyalty, cost reduction, income generation, competition, law and ethics, social movements, and motivation influenced them to move sustainable event management practices. However, cost, limited infrastructure facilities, lack of government support, and customers' mentality were the challenges to implement sustainable events management in Sri Lanka. The potential of developing Sri Lanka as a MICE destination is blocked due to these challenges. Hence, it is essential to address them immediately to get a competitive advantage in the event tourism sector.

The findings elucidate compelling managerial implications for event organizers, government, and residential communities where events are held (Nawarathna and Arachchi, 2021). Maximizing the awareness of attendees with sustainable education, developing a sustainable event model, adapt to green-related technology, introduce green venues and promote sustainable events, government involvement of making policy framework and public–private partnership create long-term and sustainable legacies for host communities and development of sustainable event management in Sri Lanka.

KEYWORDS

- **event tourism**
- **sustainable event management**
- **antecedents**
- **challenges**

REFERENCES

Ahmad, N. L.; Rashid, W. E. W.; Razak, N. A.; Yusof, A. N. M.; Shah, N. S. M. Green Event Management and Initiatives for Sustainable Business Growth. *Int. J. Trade Econ. Finance* **2013,** *4,* 331.

Byrd, E. Stakeholders in Sustainable Tourism Development and Their Roles: Applying Stakeholder Theory to Sustainable Tourism Development. *Tour. Rev.* **2007,** *62* (2), 6–13.

Chiu, L. K.; Ramely, A.; Abdul Wafi, A. Make Green Growth a Priority: Issues and Challenges in Organising Green Sports Tourism Events. *Malaysian J. Sustain. Environ.* **2020,** *7* (1), 53. https://doi.org/10.24191/myse.v7i1.8910

Edwards, D. *Incorporating Sustainability in Meetings and Event Management Education.* **2005,** *1* (1), 30–45.

Etiosa, O. *The Impacts of Event Tourism on Host Case: The City of Pietarsaari Thesis Degree Programme in Tourism, April,* 1–63, 2012.

Getz, D. Policy for Sustainable and Responsible Festivals and Events: The Institutionalisation of a New Paradigm. *J. Policy Res. Tour. Leisure Events* **2009,** *1* (1), 61–78. https://doi.org/10.1080/19407960802703524

Herciu, M.; Ogrean, C. An Overview on European Union Sustainable Competitiveness. *Procedia Economics and Finance* **2014,** *16,* 651–656. https://doi.org/10.1016/s2212-5671(14)00853-3

Holmes, K.; Hughes, M.; Mair, J.; Carlsen, J. Events and Sustainability. In *Events and Sustainability*, 2015. https://doi.org/10.4324/9781315813011

Jones, X.; Scanlon, M. *Signing to a Greener Tune; Current Status of the Music Industry in Addressing Jonas, M Scanlon, X. (2010). Signing to a Greener Tune; Current Status of the Music Industry in Addressing Environmental Sustainability*, 2010. https://docplayer.net/8420054-Singing-t. https://docplayer.net/8420054-Singing-to-a-greener-tune-current-status-of-the-music-industry-in-addressing-environmental-sustainability.html

Laing, J.; Frost, W. How Green Was My Festival: Exploring Challenges and Opportunities Associated with Staging Green Events. *Int. J. Hospital. Manage.* **2010,** *29* (2), 261–267. https://doi.org/10.1016/j.ijhm.2009.10.009

Maguire, K.; Hanrahan, J. Sustainable Event Management in Ireland: A Local Authority Perspective. *Hospitality Research in Ireland.* http://cual.openrepository.com/cual/handle/10759/346270

Mair, J.; Jago, L. The Development of a Conceptual Model of Greening in the Business Events Tourism Sector. *J. Sustain. Tour.* **2010,** 77–94. https://doi.org/10.1080/09669580903291007

Nawarathna, A. M. D. B.; Arachchi, R. S. S. W. A Study on Sustainable Event Management Practices in Sri Lanka; Event Managers' Perspective. *Tour. Sustain. Dev. Rev. J.* **2021,** *2* (1), 49–64. ISSN 2722-2152.

Ranasinghe, J. P. R. C.; Nawarathna, A. M. D. B. Antecedents of Residents' Support for Mega-Events: A PLS Path Model Based on Perceived Event Impacts and Quality of Life. *Travel and Tourism: Sustainability, Economics, and Management Issues*; Springer: Singapore. https://doi.org/10.1007/978-981-10-7068-6_20

Schulenkorf, N.; Giannoulakis, C.; Blom, L. Sustaining Commercial Viability and Community Benefits: Management and Leverage of a Sport-for-Development Event. *European Sport Management*, 1–18. https://doi.org/10.1080/16184742.2018.1546755

Stettler, S. L. Sustainable Event Management of Music Festivals: An Event Organiser Perspective. *Vasa* **2011,** 144. http://pdxscholar.library.pdx.edu/cgi/viewcontent.cgi?article=1256&context=open_access_etds

Sustainable Event Planning Guide Denver Convention Host Committee Greening Initiative Fall. *Sustainable Event Planning Guide Greening Initiative*, 2008.

The British Standards Institution BSI Standards Report to the Department of Business, Innovation and Skills Use of BIS funding for the financial year 1 April 2011 to 31 March 2012. 2012.

Tzila, C. *Event Greening: Is This Concept Providing a Serious Platform for Sustainability Best Practice? This Thesis Uses a Proposed Rating System to Measure the Sustainability Factor of Event Greening Projects and in So Doing Remove the 'Greenwash' Syndrome A. March.* 200.

Wickramasinghe, K. Millions of Tourists, Millions of Opportunities. *The Island News Paper*, Aug 20, 2018. http://www.ips.lk/talkingeconomics/

CHAPTER 14

Event Organization Issues and Challenges of Disabled Youths

SHARALA SUBRAMANIAM[1], THILAGAVATHI SHANMUGANATHAN[2], ANG PEI SOO[2], and JEETESH KUMAR[3,4,5]

[1]*Faculty of Social Science & Leisure Management, Taylor's University, Lakeside Campus, Malaysia*

[2]*Faculty of Languages and Linguistics, University of Malaya, Kuala Lumpur, Malaysia*

[3]*School of Hospitality, Tourism & Events, Taylor's University, Malaysia*

[4]*Centre for Research and Innovation in Tourism (CRiT), Taylor's University, Malaysia*

[5]*Sustainable Tourism Impact Lab, Taylor's University, Malaysia*

ABSTRACT

The government's target to receive 36 million tourist s by 2020 requires about 497,000 manpower in the tourism sector. Of that number, 65% of the workforce are required to be certified. The Ministry of Higher Education, Malaysia, introduced the Polytechnic Special Skills Certificate program in event organization in 2002. This descriptive study examines the marketability of hearing-impaired graduates in the hospitality industry in Malaysia by studying the impact of special skills education on the careers of hearing impaired in event organization, level their interests, and study the barriers that limit these graduates' opportunities to work in the event organization. Article 23 (1) of the Universal

Please note that few chapters were submitted during the peak of the pandemic. The long period of time to publish (due to supply chain and other issues) may have changed the perspectives presented in the chapter altogether.

Event Tourism and Sustainable Community Development: Advances, Effects, and Implications.
Ekta Dhariwal, Shruti Arora, Anukrati Sharma, Azizul Hassan (Eds.)
© 2024 Apple Academic Press, Inc. Co-published with CRC Press (Taylor & Francis)

Declaration of Human Rights of 1948 explains that the right to work is a human right. According to the "World Health Survey 2010," of the 28 million total population, estimated at 10% or 2.8 million people are disabled and the Malaysian government has allocated 5.8% opportunities for persons with disabilities to each sector employment including event organizations . However, < 2% of the quota was met. Therefore, this chapter identifies issues and challenges that disabled people facein getting opportunities in event organizations even if they were from their own vocational special education. Art activities were given to 26 students with disabilities at Pusat Latihan Perindustrian Dan Pemulihan PLPP , Bangi, which has special drawing classes for students between the ages 19 and 31 . This chapter reviews a number of issues and challenges faced by the disabled youths and conclude that the need is to be more focused for further improvement of youths with disabilities. These findings are also supported by the findings from the interviews conducted. Overall, although special skills education helps graduates improve their skills and knowledge as well as having an interest in working in the industry, the obstacles and constraints that exist cause not all graduates have the opportunity to work in the event organizations. Employers in the event organizations are expected to change their perceptions for this group because they are qualified and are able to work in the event organizations if opportunity is provided.

14.1 INTRODUCTION

People with disabilties (PWD)or individuals with special needs are one of the target groups in social development programs and the Malaysian government is committed to helping them to live lives like ordinary people, get same jobs economically and socially, and enjoy the result of the development of the country. One approach taken to help these groups is to encourage them to venture into employment that will not only enable them to be independent but also not have to rely entirely on government assistance but allow them to jointly contribute to national development (Ministry of Education Malaysia, 2011).

From the perspective of the Department of Health and Human Services (2001), a person with disabilities has hindered movement function that requires specially designed facilities such as buildings, equipment, and supplies as well as outside the structure to overcome the obstacles of their movement (Reuter, 2001). Persons with Disabilities Act in 2007 define disabilities as those who have long-term physical, mental, intellectual, or sensory impairments, which in interaction can restrict their participation in society. Samuel et al. (2001) viewed individuals with disabilities who require special services due to physical or mental disabilities to enable them to live independently in the community. There are six categories of disabled enrolled in the PLPP, that is, cerebral palsy, learning disability, speech impairment, and spina bifida. Various programs have been introduced by the government to the PLPP students to upskill the disabled youths. However, this could drain the government investment, unless necessary action is been taken to solve the problem faced by the disable youths who have graduated from PLPP. Table 14.1 shows the number of admissions and completed training of PLPP trainees by ethnic group and sex in 2016.

TABLE 14.1 Number of Admission and Completed Training of PLPP Trainees by Ethnic Group and Sex, 2016.

Institution	Malay	Male Chinese	Indian	Others	Total	Malay	Chinese	Female Indian	Others	Total
Admission	72	1	1	1	75	47	0	1	0	48
Completed	45	1	1	1	48	30	0	1	0	31
Unemployed	40	1	1	1	43	28	0	1	0	29

14.2 STATEMENT OF THE PROBLEM

There is a problem of unemployment of graduates including graduates with disability in the field of event organization but at the same time, there are vacancies in this industry. The growth of this industry is also hampered and slightly disrupted due to the high layoff rate in this sector. This industry has difficulty retaining employees when they are unable to identify the factors that contribute to employee satisfaction and subsequently loyal employees (Abdullah, 2007).

Malaysia has a population of 31.62 million (2017). The registered Person with Disabilities (PWD) at the Department of Social Welfare, Malaysia, in 2017 were 453,258. PWD in physical category recorded the highest number which was 35.2%, followed by learning disability category (34.8%) and visually impaired category (8.9%). Speech category recorded the lowest registration of 0.5%.

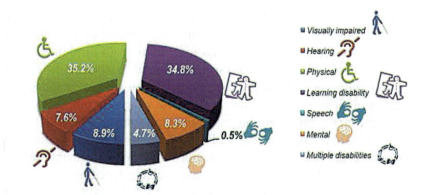

CHART 1 Percentage of registration of Persons with Disabilities (PWD) by category of disabilities, Malaysia, 217.

Source: Department of Social Welfare, Malaysia

The Malaysian government has allocated 5.8% of jobs in the public sector to the disabled (circular nos. 10/1988). As of May 15, 2012, only 20.7% of registered PWDs managed to get jobs in event organizations and received assistance to disabled workers (EPC) involving anallocation of RM 6.0 billion (Jessica, 2012). Although there are provisions for the disabled employment quota of 5.8% in the public sector, most of the disabled in Malaysia has received special education and vocational education centers either in government or private practice, positive attitudes of disabled people to focus more work than normal, malleable and never breaks, but, until now, PWD have yet to be fully accepted in the job market in event organizations and they cannot find jobs (Zinaida Ariffin, 2006). Based on the difficult issue of getting career opportunities in event organizations for PWD, a study was conducted to identify issues and challenges among arts class students with disabilities (cerebral palsy, learning disability, speech impairment, spina bifida) in PLPP in Malaysia. The variables studied were the alignment between the skills learned by students with disabilities (cerebral palsy, learning disability, speech impairment, spina bifida) in PLPP compared with the skills required by the industry, the family, on the job training, skills and attitudes of students with disabilities involved itself in the choice of career in event organizations. It is also important to understand that the event organizations does not stop at hiring but the youths with disabilities also must receive equal opportunities similar to the individual without disabilities. According to De Jonge et al. (2007), advances in various skills reduced barriers to the youths with disabilities participate in across type of jobs and professions.

14.3 PURPOSE OF THE STUDY

This study aims to identify the issues and challenges of the arts class students with disabilities (cerebral palsy, learning disability, speech impairment, spina bifida) in PLPP of the alignment of the skills learned in PLPP compared with the skills required by the event organizations, the family, at the workplace, skills in which training and attitude of students with disabilities themselves in career selection.

14.4 METHODOLOGY

This survey involved the entire population (26 students) of arts class students with disabilities (cerebral palsy, learning disability, speech impairment, spina bifida) in PLPP as the sample. This chapter draws on qualitative data comprising interview transcripts. In qualitative research, researchers use the data-gathering techniques such as in-depth interviews and observations, through source documents and records or artifacts. But in this study, the main data is the primary data and the results of in-depth interviews with a sample-to-face. Primary data in this study is through in-depth interview techniques, the main purpose of the interview is to get specific information. Semistructured in-depth interviews were conducted five times with 26 students with disability in PLPP in event organizations.

The aim was to identify employment issues and challenges. Purposeful sampling was used to identify and recruit participants. The established organizations this chapter refers to, PLPP, are comprised of five different categories of disabled people. In qualitative research, data analysis is an ongoing process from the start of the study. This enables the design of qualitative research to develop and give direction to the next data collection (Patton, 1990). Therefore, the qualitative data was analyzed as an activity that simultaneously with data collection, data interpretation, and report writing narrative. Content analysis approach was used by researchers to systematically analyze the text. Transcript of interview was analyzed for its contents and researchers calculated the frequency of words or themes that arise from the text and run the frequency analysis. According to Merriam (2001), giving meaning to data involving multiple listing data and classification of data by category or theme is appropriate and accurate data. To this end, interviews were conducted on 29th March 2019, 10th May 2019, 17th May 2019, 25th July 2019, and 27th Sep 2019. The questions focused more on the objectives

206   Event Tourism and Sustainable Community Development

of this research and recorded transcription and code along with the collected data helped develop a deeper understanding of the objectives of this research.

14.5 FINDINGS AND DISCUSSION

The results show that students with disabilities (cerebral palsy, learning disability, speech impairment, spina bifida) in the art class at PLPP had difficulty getting jobs because of the constraints due to the absence of facilities for them in the workplace in event organizations, lack of skills in the field of endeavor, and the attitude with disabilities (cerebral palsy, learning disability, speech impairment, spina bifida) itself in the career selection. Constraints at a moderate level are also due to the inconsistency between the arts class taken by disabilities (cerebral palsy, learning disability, speech impairment, spina bifida) in PLPP with the skills required by industry and the influence of family. Both null hypotheses were accepted that there was no significant difference between the level of constraint career choices occupations with disabilities (cerebral palsy, learning disability, speech impairment, spina bifida) by specialization taken by them in the PLPP. There was no significant difference between the level of constraint in career choices of students with disabilities (cerebral palsy, learning disability, speech impairment, spina bifida) by gender. This finding is consistent with the findings Azlina (2005), who found the needs of the disabled in the workplace is not complete and safe to keep on working because there is no perfect facilities such as free accommodation, food allowance, bank service, location near the hospital, a mini gymnasium, prayer room, and canteen. According to Abdul Halim (2004), the employer needs the employee will lead to workers interested in working while Shertzer and Stone (1992) also found nothing interesting at a job such as the wage, social, employment assessment, and the opportunity to progress in event organizations.

This study also demonstrates the disabled (the employer needs the employee will lead to workers interested in working) could not find employment because they were poorly versed in the field of endeavor. Esah (2003) stated that skills that are not followed by students with special needs can reduce their interest in a career with the skills learned at the institute. The findings by Mohd Hanafi (2009) also showed that the disabled are not able to work effectively due to lack of skill and the lack of teachers who are highly skilled in the technical field and at the same time can use sign language. Zainolrin Saari, (2005) found that the cause of PWD employed by the

Event Organization Issues and Challenges of Disabled Youths

event organizations is difficult because there is no work experience and low skill levels. Review from Ramlee and Ramziah (2002) found that the manufacturing industry in Malaysia sighted students with disabilities in . In Malaysia, the disabled students have the skills but they do not have additional skills of self-motivation, communication skills, interpersonal skills, critical thinking, problem solving, and entrepreneurship. This study also found students with disabilities (cerebral palsy, learning disability, speech impairment, spina bifida) did not find work in event organizations because of the constraints of their own attitude and felt inferior, did not like a new challenge, are easily discouraged, are not interested in the job skills-based, are embarrassed to find a job, and did not like to venture into new areas. Loo (2004) also found PWDs are difficult to explore new challenges and situations. Cynthia's study (2008) found that most students with disabilities in accordance with their peers working in the same place even if they have no skills in the work. This shows that there is no significant difference between choosing a career field and work constraints the disabled students (cerebral palsy, learning disability, speech impairment, spina bifida) c h o s e a s specialization in PLPP. The study found that PWD (cerebral palsy, learning disability, speech impairment, spina bifida) choose a specialization to be learned at school because they are interested in this specialization. However studies by Gordon (1992) found that gender, race, parents, work experience and course work influence the students, and career choices affectthe course work. For some jobs, the gender factor is a matter of priority for a company to hire workers. Male workers are more inclined and interested in heavy industry, while women are more inclined toward delicate and creative skills. Review of Chew (1992) also shows the factors that influence the students in choosing a job related to vocational skills are friends, interests, jobs, parents, and counselors, while mass media, natural talent, and teachers are factors that are less influential.

14.6 CONCLUSIONS

This study shows the limitations of career choices among students with disabilities (cerebral palsy, learning disability, speech impairment, spina bifida) in arts class at PLPP is at a high level due to the lack of facilities at the workplace, lack of skills in their respective fields in event organizations. The attitude of the disabled themselves is less self-reliant while the inconsistency between the skills that followed during the training institutions with the skills required by industry and constraints affecting families at a moderate level. The study also showed that there is no significant difference between choosing a career field and work constraints the disabled students (cerebral palsy, learning disability, speech impairment, spina bifida) chose as specialization in PLPP and there was no significant difference between students' career choice and constraints disabilities (cerebral palsy, learning disability, speech impairment, spina bifida) based on their gender. These constraints need to be overcome to help raise the economic level of PWD. If the constraint is allowed, it will be difficult for them to be at the same level and these people will not be taken care of. Opportunities must be seized to show the skills of the disabled despite their lack of belonging.

KEYWORDS

- **event organizations**
- **disabled youths**
- **event**
- **learning disability**
- **government**
- **issues**
- **challenges**

REFERENCES

Abdul, H. *Analisis Investasi (Belanja Modal) Sektor Publik-Pemerintah Daerah*; Upp Stim Ykpn: Jakarta, 2004.

Azlina, A. Demand for Fresh Graduates In Malaysia: The Importance of Experience, Level of Education and Training. In Proceedings: International Conference on Quantitative Sciences and Its Applications 2005; Icoqsia, 2005; Penang, December 6–8.

Chew; Moy, H. *Faktor-Faktor Pemilihan Sekolah Vokasional: Satu Tinjauan. Projek Sarjana Muda*; Universiti Pertanian Malaysia: Serdang.

Cynthia, K.; Mei, Y. *Faktor-Faktor Yang Mempengaruhi Penyertaan Tuisyen Berbayar Di Taman Universiti, Skudai*; Penerbitan Universiti Teknologi Malaysia: Johor, 2008.

De Jonge, D.; Scherer, M.; Rodger, S. *Assistive Technology in the Workplace*; St. Louis, Mo: Mosby, 2007.

Esah, S. *Asas Pedagogi*; Universiti Teknologi Malaysia: Johor Bahru, 2003.

Gordon, V. N. *Handbook of Academic Using*; Greenwood Press: Westport, CT, 1992.

Jessica, J. *Bangunan Harus Mesra Oku*; Terbitan Borneo Post Online Sarawak: Malaysia, 2012

Loo, R. Relationship Between Attitudes Toward Euthanasia and Attitudes Toward People with Disabilities. *Soc. Sci. J.* 2004; *41* (2), 295–299.

Merriam, S. B. *Qualitative Research: A Guide To Design And Implementation*; Jossey-Bass: San Francisco, 2001.

Mohd Hanafi Mohd Yassin. *Pendidikan Teknik Dan Vokasional Untuk Pelajar Berkeperluan Khas;* Universiti Kebangsaan Malaysia: Bangi, 2009.

Patton, Q. M. *Qualitative Evaluation and Research Methods*, 2nd ed.; Sage Publication, Inc: Newbury Park, CA, 1990.

Ramlee, M.; Ramziah, H. *Perancangan Pendidikan Untuk Pembangunan Sumber Manusia Dalam Era Globalisasi Dan K-Ekonomi. Jurnal Teknologi 37(E) Disember* 2002, 47–56. Utm.

Reuter, N. Department of Health and Human Services, Texas: Federal Register **2001,** *66* (11).

Samuel, L. O.; Robert, H. H.; Martha, E. S.; Jan, B. *Handbook of Developmental Disabilities*; Guilford Press: New York, 2001.

Shertzer, B.; Stone, S. C. *Asas-Asas Bimbingan*; Dewan Bahasa Dan Pustaka: Kuala Lumpur, 2000.

The Office of Chief Statistician Malaysia, Department Of Statistics, Malaysia, 31 October 2017.

Zainolrin, S. *Keberkesanan Pendidikan Serta Latihan Teknik & Vokasional Di Kalangan Golongan Orang Kurang Upaya Dalam Melahirkan Keperluan Sumber Guna Tenaga Negara, 2005*; Universiti Teknologi Malaysia: Disertasi Sarjana.

Zinaida, A. *Kerjaya Untuk Orang Kurang Upaya. Ed Ke-2*; Pts Professional Publishing Sdn. Bhd: Kuala Lumpur, 2006.

CHAPTER 15

Case Study of Tripura as a Destination Brand with Post-Pandemic Perspectives

MANISHANKAR CHAKRABORTY

Higher Colleges of Technology, United Arab Emirates

ABSTRACT

The chapter presents the case study of Tripura as a new destination brand in the Northeastern part of India. It discusses the change in approaches from being a laid-back one to that of proactive one since the time the new state government joined office in 2018. The leadership has been putting on extra thrust on the tourism sector and that has started to bear the fruits. In a competitive tourism market, where most of the Northeastern neighbors are established as tourist destinations, the steady start of the state of Tripura was possible through a planned branding initiative launched by the ministry of tourism, Government of Tripura. The chapter also highlights various competitive advantages the state enjoys as a destination, along with the possible challenges that ought to be overcome not only for the state, but also for the region, in the postpandemic scenario. Leveraging the inherent strengths of the state based on nature, culture, history, art, literature, climate, handicrafts, Tripura has been able to differentiate itself on planks, which also resonates in the strategies crafted by her competitors in the region, owing to some commonalities existing in that region. The infrastructural and connectivity-related push given by the new central government since 2014 has enabled tourist to reach out for this destination that was considered far-flung and unreachable no so long ago. The railway connectivity of the state to Kolkata via Bangladesh is also on the verge of being completed. This will be yet another avenue for the tourist to reach out to this destination.

Please note that few chapters were submitted during the peak of the pandemic. The long period of time to publish (due to supply chain and other issues) may have changed the perspectives presented in the chapter altogether.

Event Tourism and Sustainable Community Development: Advances, Effects, and Implications.
Ekta Dhariwal, Shruti Arora, Anukrati Sharma, Azizul Hassan (Eds.)
© 2024 Apple Academic Press, Inc. Co-published with CRC Press (Taylor & Francis)

15.1 INTRODUCTION

Tourism play a very important role in presenting the various uniqueness possessed by a place. Some of the tourist destinations have been famous for a long time, while others are gradually coming to the fore, with many unknown specialties being highlighted by those, off late. Researchers have emphasized that the emergence of tourism, including "mass tourism" has not been a new phenomenon, but has been continuing for centuries. Furthermore, in order to understand the significance of tourism-related research with respect to a destination, it is imperativeto fully review what has gone before, along with the influences of factors, including technology, innovation, social as well as economic changes in the societies (Butler, 2015). Tripura as a tourist destination came into the limelight once a new government took charge of the state in the year 2018. It has continued with the same party's government winning the election for the second time in 2023. The thrust and focus of the new government on tourism was given to leverage the huge potential the state had in terms of resources, diversity, nature, art, crafts, culture, while generatingemployment for the local youth. A structured and unified approach was visible since that time with tourism getting adequate attention by the regulators. Government of various developing countries has been active in destination management and development as compared to the past. The challenges, however, present in the form of determining an appropriate level of involvement and even research have pointed out toward the fact that government play a critical role in tourism development (Marketa, 2016). In fact the central government of India since 2014 have complimented very well with the respective state government to provide adequate support in order to develop tourism ecosystem in several states, by highlighting the distinct advantages each of the destination possessed. Tripura government since 2018 under the leadership of Chief Minister, Mr. Biplab Kumar Deb and Tourism Minister, Mr. Pranajit Singha Roy, has not only ensured that the major highlights of the state those were completely unknown to the world are being highlighted extensively, but have also developed a strong philosophy and standing of the state as a tourism destination. This has been continued with the new leadership team under Prof. (Dr.) Manik Saha as the Chief Minister as well. The significance of marketing tourism destination by ridding piggy on unique sellingpropositions, which are competitive in nature, is of paramount importance. There are studies that have highlighted that lack of steadiness, unexplained deficiencies, absence of a tradition in tourism or even building a marketing strategy for travel destination based on artificial planks, devoid of substantial issues and perceptions of real and potential tourists have led to places not getting their fair share of the tourism pie (Gabriela and Paul, 2012). This was evident for Tripura as a tourist destination before the new government took over in 2018. Once the new leadership realized the inherent potential the state possessed in terms of harnessing the resources and abilities of the people, fast decisions and support were provided not only to government entities, but also to private bodies to develop the tourism standing of the state. The chapter tries to put across the transformation that has been brought into the state of Tripura, since 2018 that has catapulted it into one of the emerging tourist destination in Northeastern India.

15.2 BACKGROUND

Tripura is one of the most beautiful, unexplored states of the eight Northeastern sisters of India. The state shares borders with neighboring Bangladesh, Mizoram, and Assam. The northern, southern, and western border encompassing 856 km that is almost 84 percent of the total border is linked to Bangladesh. To put the particulars in specifics, Tripura as a state has $10.491.69$ km^2 of area, with Agartala as the capital. The population as of census 2011 is 3,673,917. The official languages of the state includes Bengali, Kokborok, and English, while several other languages like Mogh, Chakma, Halam, Garo, Bishnupriya Manipuri, Hindi, and Oriya are also spoken by the people. The temperature during summer ranges between 20 and 36°C, whereas, the winter witnesses 7–27°C. The recent data on literacy rate makes the state as one of the highest in the country with 96% literacy (Tripura State Portal, 2020).

15.3 RICH CULTURE AND TRADITION

The state has exquisite mix of natural beauties, rich cultural tradition of tribal, and nontribal populace. The diverse set of culture in the state is evident from the "Hoza Giri" dance of the Reang tribesman, the collective musical recitation of "Manasa Mangal" or "Kirtan" of the nontribals. Even the "Garia" dance of the tribals, "Dhamial" dance of the nontribals during familial occasions provides a rich blend of culture and tradition for the tourists. The periodical evolution of the cultural presentation has happened with the passage of time. The traditional touch has been retained while adding a

214   Event Tourism and Sustainable Community Development

modernity in the form of western musical instruments like guitar, mandolin, to blend with the traditional indigenous drums and flutes to name a few. Songs and recitations while celebrating birth anniversaries and other major events of great poets and lyricists like Rabindra Nath Tagore and Kazi Nazrul Islam bring in more color and charm by enmeshing many streams of the subculture seen in the state (Tripura State Portal, 2020).

15.4   PRISTINE NATURAL BEAUTIES AND HISTORICAL MARVELS

In addition to the aforementioned art and cultural uniqueness, the state also presents myriad offerings of destination, fairs, and festivals to attract tourists of all hues. Despite the small geographical area that the state possess, it can be safely said that small is indeed beautiful. This is evident from attractions ranging from palaces of historical significance like Ujjayanta Palace, Kunjaban Palace, Neermahal-Lake Palace, splendid rock-cut carvings, and stone images of Unakoti, Debtamura, Pilak, important temples and monasteries, including Tripureswari, one of the 51 Pithasthans as per Hindu mythology. Natural beauties in the form of Dumboor lake, Rudrasagarlake, Jagannath Dighi, and Kalyan Sagar, along with the beautiful hill station of Jampui, wildlife sanctuaries of Sepahijala, Gomati, Rowa, and Trishna make it one of the vibrant and diverse tourist destination. Furthermore, the capital city of Agartala provides many unique attractions in the form of Ujjayanta Palace State Museum, Tribal Museum, Sukanta Academy, M.B.B. College, Laxminarayan Temple, Uma Maheswar Temple, Jagannath Temple, Benuban Vihar, Gedu Mian Mosque, Malancha Niwas, Rabindra Kanan, Heritage Park, Purbasha, Handicrafts Designing Centre, Fourteen Goddess Temple, and Portuguese Church to name a few (Tripura State Portal, 2020).

15.5   UNIQUE FAIRS, FESTIVALS, AND EVENTS

Tripura celebrates plethora of events, fairs, and festivals that are the cynosure for all the tourists visiting the state. The rich blend of tribal and nontribal populace, along with their unique set of events makes the diversity a perfect topping for the tourism package. Some of the major ones are as follows:

(1) Garia Puja—The presence of a bamboo pole symbolizing Lord Garia, the deity of livestock and wealth is worshipped during the event. The celebration comprises of unique ingredients that forms the

foundation of the event, notably among them are cotton thread, rice, riccha, fowl chick, rice beer, wine, earthen pots, and eggs. As per the tradition, a fowl is sacrificed before the deity and the blood is then strewn to seek lord's blessings. Garia carnival happens in agreement with the Ochai instructions. At this point in time no one is allowed to cross the shadow of the symbolic god Garia, with the fear of making him annoyed. The children play drums, sing, and dance before the lord to solicit their prayers. The puja is held during the seventh day of the month of Baisakh (April) and continues for a period of 7 days (Tripura Tourism, 2020).

IMAGE 15.1 Garia Puja.
Source: http://www.tripuratourism.gov.in/festvalfair/.

(2) Unakoti Festival or Ashokastami Festival—The historical beauty of huge rock-cut images of gods and goddesses in a natural setting makes Unakoti one of the most important attraction for the tourists. The place forms an ideal combination of history, hill station, or a holy place possessing "Sitakunda" or "Ashtamikunda," a natural reservoir having spring of crystal water. Taking a holy tip in the chilling winter forms the basis of Maghi Sankranti in February along with Ashokastami. The passage of time witnessed the transformation of Raghunandan Parvat of the past paving way for Unakoti. The nature at its best provides exquisite experience of god-gifted landscaping along with sculptor's beauty. All these miraculous presence made Archaeological Survey of India link these with the famous scriptures of Mahabalipuram. In fact, it is considered the largest bas-relief sculptures carved on the face of a hill in India. The event is held every year in the month of February (Tripura Tourism, 2020).

216   Event Tourism and Sustainable Community Development

IMAGE 15.2   Unakoti festival.
Source: http://www.tripuratourism.gov.in/festvalfair/

(3) Pilak archaeological and tourism festival—The place possessing vast collection of Hindu and Buddhist images dating back to the eighth and ninth centuries presents scriptures spread across 10 square kilometer. The archaeological findings have images and terracotta plaquesreminiscing the survival of both heterodox sects and creeds representing both Hinduism and Buddhism. The grand stone images of Avolokiteshwar and Narasimha were found here and the Pilak archaeological and tourism festival happens for 3 days in the month of February or March. Several cultural programs displaying the rich cultural diversity is show cased during these events (Tripura Tourism, 2020).

IMAGE 15.3   Pilak archaeological and tourism festival.
Source: http://www.tripuratourism.gov.in/festvalfair/

(4) Kharchi festival—One of the famous festival of Tripura, the celebrations witnessed transcend participations from all the communities of the state as well as the tourists. The event is said to have the influence of Brahmanical Hindus and is associated with the indigenous tribal deities held in the month of June or July. The head images worshipped are identified by various Brahmanical names like "Hara," "Uma," "Hari," "Maa," "Bani," "Kumar," "Ganesh," "Brahma," "Pritthi," "Ganga," "Abdi," "Kamesh," and "Himadri." Even Hindus have accepted the head images as popular deities and there are several legends about these fourteen deities circulating in the state. The ceremonial worship starts a day before the actual day of the festival. The rituals need Buffalo, riccha, he-goats, eggs, bamboo poles and pipes, umbrella, earthen pot, duck, pigeon, bamboo stick, thread, cotton, turmeric, vermilion, wine, banana leaves, and rice. "Chantai" or the chief priest chants mantras, while his deputy assists in the sacrifices of the animals. The event is a symbol of peace, harmony, and fraternity while people descent representing diverse caste, creed, and religion. This is generally held in the month of July (Tripura Tourism, 2020).

IMAGE 15.4 Kharchi festival.

Source: http://www.tripuratourism.gov.in/festvalfair/

(5) Neermahal tourism and water festival—The water palace is a picturesque royal mansion built by Maharaja Bir Bikram Kishore Manikya in 1930 AD as his summer residence. Built on the inspiration gathered from Mughal style of architecture, the palace witnesses the water festival in the month of August. The 3 days extravaganza consists of

boat racing, swimming competition, and cultural events in the attractive winter season (Tripura Tourism, 2020).

IMAGE 15.5 Neermahal festival.

Source: http://www.tripuratourism.gov.in/festvalfair/

(6) Diwali festival—This festival happens in Tripura Sundari Temple, one of the fifty-one Hindu Pithas that is considered as a holy and sacred places by Hindus. Devotees throng the place and after taking a holy plunge in the adjoining lake, situated next to the temple, they worship goddesses Kali. There is a grand fair that is also spread across the vicinity of the temple and people enjoy the 2-day event with grandeur. It is generally held in the month of October/November (Tripura Tourism, 2020).

IMAGE 15.6 Diwali festival.

Source: http://www.tripuratourism.gov.in/festvalfair/

(7) Pous Sankranti Fair or Tirthamukh Mela—This is marked with the assembly of people of all backgrounds to take a holy dip the Gomati River at its place of origin, known as Tirthamukh. The day marks the starting of the Sun's northern course, the last day of the month of Pousa coinciding with the mid of January. Located in a beautiful surrounding of high hills, Tirthamukh, the place witnesses several religious events along with a 2-day fair (Tripura Tourism, 2020).

IMAGE 15.7   Pous Shankranti fair.
Source: http://www.tripuratourism.gov.in/festvalfair/

15.6   DESTINATION BRANDING AND TRIPURA

Destination branding is akin to the branding of any other products and services. "Destination brand' as a national identity has received attention with a strategy of building a unique identity of destination, which makes differentiation (Morrison and Anderson, 2002). In this regard, the state government of Tripura has been making extraordinary efforts to brand Tripura as one of the tourist destination of national identity by displaying the culture, history, art, literature, handicraft, and the like. There are elements of tangibles as well as intangibles that form the elements of the destination brand. The major component in destination brands includes the element of services with the right usage of slogan (Pike, 2005). Tripura too presents both the tangible as well as the intangible aspects through structures, locations, cultures, festivities, history, and several other events. Furthermore, the state also promotes its tourism vertical with a similar slogan, "Tripura Tourism-Where Culture meets Nature," intertwining the significance of natural beauty with the diverse cultural aspect of the state. Five components form the cornerstone of destination branding. These are vision and stakeholder management, target customer and product portfolio matching, positioning and differentiation strategies using branding components, communication strategies, and feedback and response management strategies (Melodena, 2009). Tripura tourism as seen in the information provided to reach out to the stakeholders talks about the uniqueness in terms of the origin and history of Tripura, population, tribes, cultural heritage, food habits, Rabindra Nath Tagore, Sachin Dev Burman, thereby, blending both the cultural as well as the historical aspect in optimum proportion. The vision of Tripura tourism is to present a perfect mix of the past, both from the cultural as well as the historical significance, in a natural setting, and therefore, the tagline too resonates it while saying, "Where Culture meets Nature" *(http://www.tripuratourism.gov.in/)*. Tripura provides a wide range of touristic options right from heritage tourism sites, religious destinations, archaeological tourism, eco and wildlife destination, art and crafts, fairs and festivals, as well as nature and adventure tourism. All these points toward the fact that the target customer comprises a diversified segment of youth, senior citizens, nature lovers, art and craft connoisseur, and historians to name a few. This makes the destination provide a wide spectrum of avenues for the prospective segments to consider the destination as a tourist hotspot. The product portfolio matches with the target customer to a nicety as each of the aforementioned segment can select one or more reasons to visit the destination as a tourist. Tripura as a tourist destination has significantly differentiated and positioned itself from neighboring competitors as the other eight sisters comprising of states like Assam, Meghalaya, and Arunachal Pradesh thriving on nature-based tourism mainly, with culture playing a second fiddle. While most of the regional competitors positioned themselves as nature-based ones, Tripura blended nature with the culture, especially with a wider range of diversity present amongst the populace of the state. The major branding components Tripura uses to market the destination, includes nature, culture, history, events, fairs, and physical evidences to name a few. The communication strategies, feedback, and response management strategies as is evident from Tripura tourism websites shows extensive presence in social media platforms with dedicated handles for each. Furthermore, the portal provides comprehensive insights along with pictures related to the state in general; destination in particular, along with accommodations, bookings, galleries, tourist corners, and the department-related information. A glance through the portal, as seen below in Image 15.8 clearly depicts what has been mentioned above. Moreover, one can also witness customized offerings in line with the requirements of different consumer segments. Notably among those are Explore Tripura package for 8 days and 7 nights, meant for the ones willing to explore the whole state as a destination. The packages being fragmented into coach and car options provide even more alternatives to the consumer to select as far as the type and mode of transportation is concerned. Then there is a pilgrimage tour that is planned for 4 days and 3 nights, comprising of visits to the major pilgrimage sites in the state of Tripura. The eco-tourism package is targeted to those who wish to enjoy the pollution-free environs and the greens of the state, and is planned for 5 days and 4 nights. The other options are weekend package tours and archaeological tours for 3 days, 2 nights, and 4 days, 3 nights, respectively *(http://www.tripuratourism.gov.in/pack)*. From the offerings, it is evident that the packages targets not only the local consumers but also those who wish to travel from various parts of India and also from other overseas destinations. One can handpick according to his liking or the objective of the visit to that destination as the packages are providing flexibility, hereby going a long way in converting suspects into prospects and then into actual consumers. The new hotels that have come up in the capital city of Agartala as well as in various tourist sites have added to the convenience of the customer.

IMAGE 15.8 Portal of Tripura tourism.
Source: http://www.tripuratourism.gov.in/

There has been a complete shift in the branding strategies as everything has been evolving constantly (Zikmund, 2003). There is a definite need to look into destination branding from a new perspective post-Covid pandemic. This can be attributed to altered market conditions, loss in customer confidence, changed economic conditions, and the like. Organizational systems today rely a lot on market behavior. Therefore, it is imperative for the practitioners and planners to look for suitable way of shaping the branding strategy, in order to move up the performance pyramid while tapping into diversified segments of customers (Kapferar, 2008). From this perspective Tripura as a branding destination need to have a relook into the market dynamics not only from the customers and environmental perspective, but also from the internal standpoint to satisfy all the stakeholders, culminating in making the necessary tweaks in the offerings.

A study conducted in Mexico highlighted that there were key factors those influenced the perception of city branding. The researchers conducted an exit pool survey from a selected sample of 601 tourists. The factors those influenced the perception of the tourists were wide offer and connectivity, urban environment, historical and cultural heritage, monuments, traffic safety, friendliness, and security. The study further corroborated that the opinion of tourist's matters a lot as their incorporation into branding of a tourist destination, makes it easier for the place to develop a unique personality for the place and contribute toward the long-term vision for the marketing activities related to the tourism sector (Onsimo and Arley, 2017). If one is to implement the findings with destination Tripura, one can safely say that tourists visiting the destination have good connectivity through air, road, and train, which was probably not a reality just a few years back. Presently, a tourist can fly in and fly out into Agartala from any part of India, either through a direct or a hopping flight within a few hours. The dream of connecting this Northeastern state of India with the rest of the country through rail network also became a reality after the new government took over at the central level in 2014 and the push increased even further with new state government taking over in 2018. Even the connectivity through neighboring Bangladesh has opened a lot of opportunities for international tourists who might also be interested to come over for medical tourism. This connectivity through road and rail via Bangladesh will also lessen the time taken for tourists from other parts of India to reach Tripura via road and rail. The urban environment of Agartala might not resemble that of an Indian metropolis; however, there are enough opportunities for the tourists to spend their leisure time, owing to the latest initiatives and thrust given to the sector, after the new state government took over in the year 2018. Historical, cultural heritage, and monuments are strong pillars for Tripura as a tourist destination and even the traffic safety, friendliness, and security of the state is impeccable for the tourists visiting the state with diverse objectives. One big advantage is a pollution-free environment that is green in most of the places, would make a tourist sit back and ponder. It would be interesting to see the findings of a similar kind of survey being done for the tourists visiting the state, in order to check if the speculative thoughts described above, actually matches with

Case Study of Tripura as a Destination Brand with Post-Pandemic Perspectives 223

the real finding or not. The success of destination branding hinges on factors like the hosts, policy objectives, and tourist's demands coming on the same based on a perfect alignment. Presence of multiple stakeholders and little or no management control in destination branding possess some additional challenges (Morgan and Pritchard, 2004). Tripura as a tourist destination has been able to understand the fact that the hosts being courteous and friendly toward the tourists, along with the policies laid down by the government bodies and regulators that bodes well for the people visiting the destination play a significant role. The fulfillment of the demands of the tourists too has gone a long way in developing Tripura as a new destination in the North-eastern part of India. The ability of the new state government since 2018 to manage everything under the ministry of tourism has enabled a coordinated effort, thereby, leaving no avenues of multiple stakeholders being in charge, leading into chaos and confusion. The pointed and focused approach by the department of tourism has exponentially increased the standing of the state as an eco-friendly and economic tourist destination, providing extensive value additions to the customers.

15.7 POSTPANDEMIC TOURISM PERSPECTIVES

Covid pandemic has brought in a new uncertainty into all the industries. The impact on travel and tourism has been the most serious. From a national perspective tourism sector contributes ~9.2% of the country's GDP and employ 42.7 million Indians directly and indirectly. The Indian Association of Tour Operators has forecasted that hotel, aviation, and travel sector in combination would incur a loss of INR 85 billion due to travel restrictions. Furthermore, Indian hospitality industry would miss 38 million-employment opportunities that tantamount to 70% of the overall workforce. A further detailed analysis reveals that the overall loss in revenue in the branded or organized hotel rooms that is only 5% of the total availability will reach to the tune of 1.3 to 1.55 billion dollars. The other 95% comprises of the B&B's, Guesthouses, and the unbranded and the unorganized sectors. The national loss is also reflected in the Northeastern figures that are also on the similar lines (Talukdar, 2020). This means that all the stakeholders involved in the travel and tourism industry has to pull up their socks, think out of the box and bring in changes that would not only ensure safe inflow of tourists, but would also put the industry back into the track. Tripura and Northeastern part of India have been resilient owing to the hardships they had faced over the years, especially when the geographies does not resemble the plains. This resilience can now be leveraged by all the eight states to bring together a collective positive change that would inject fresh blood into the tourism industry.

Studies have revealed that there has to be wholesale changes in approaches and strategies pertaining to the tourism to get back the sheen that was existing during the prepandemic days. Some of the suggestions highlighted in studies showed that players should avoid price competition, as 15% of the respondents declined to travel for leisure owing to budget deficit. Furthermore, opinions were also shared showing a preference for less crowded tourist destination with a better healthcare system. Price competitions in such a scenario is a strict no-no and players should think of other competitive advantages to draw the attention of the market, vis-à-vis the competitors. Pointers have also indicated to the fact there is a need for redesigning and redefining tourism as tourist behaviors and preferences have undergone a change due to the pandemic. New expectations of attributes related to safety are very crucial, along with other attractions offered by the destination. Sustainability of the tourism business would henceforth depend on health, hygiene, safety, less inflow of crowds, and ability to handle uncertainties akin to that of the pandemic. Government actions and handholding destinations until they are established as a reputed brand in line with the new normal-related expectations also holds the key. Therefore, using data analytics, interpretation, and making the necessary support to the industry during these challenging times holds the key for the future. Crisis management and ability to ensure safety of the customers would also play a crucial role in making tourist destinations attractive, post-pandemic (Bloom, 2020). Tripura as a tourist destination has to make only minor changes pertaining to the new dynamics. The state already has benefits in terms of cost as compared to the neighboring competitors. Furthermore, the place is also not that crowded unlike many of the competing markets in the adjoining Northeastern India. A slight enhancement of the healthcare system would do the trick and with the supportive government, always in the lookout to bring in private investors in the healthcare as well as the tourism industry, the destination is well-placed to handle the challenges and convert those into opportunities. Some other studies too have highlighted several changes that is expected to happen in the travel and tourism industry post-Covid pandemic. The changes could be country borders may not be open to all for some time, some geographies could be a strict no-no for tourism for quite some time, business travel will decrease significantly, events related market would be in a coma for some

Case Study of Tripura as a Destination Brand with Post-Pandemic Perspectives 225

time as big events would be shelved, group travel will shrink, leisure travel will dwindle for some time to come, matured travels like retirees would also decrease significantly, religious tourism would drop, tourism may be domestic directed, destination weddings would stop, school trips would dry up, nature will triumph, and road traveled would be preferred (Economic times, 2020). Tripura as a branding destination mostly benefit from the challenges mentioned in the report above and especially when the target market comprises of domestic audience, who prefer to travel by road, the inbound travelers would embrace up the destination wholeheartedly. The economic situation that has nosedived globally would take sometime to recover. The analysts pointed out to the faster recovery of the Indian economy based on various measures taken by the government of India. This will also push the travel and tourism industry as has been witnessed with the central government employees cashing on the Leave Travel Concession and several other stimulus measures offered by the central as well as the state governments. The atmanirbhar or self-reliance scheme started by the government of India can also nurture a whole new breed of *travelpreneurs* (entrepreneurs interested in travel and tourism business), resulting in generation of employment.

Articles published on the revival of the tourism sector post-Covid pandemic, in the Northeastern part of India pointed toward several other support that the industry is looking forward to from the government. The stock-taking deliberation on the state of tourism that was held in the city of Guwahati, capital of the state Assam, as part of North East festival brought in private and government stakeholders together. There was a call for the formulation of an integrated policy forthe whole of the Northeastern region so that the revival can happen faster. They pointed out what has been highlighted in another study that was mentioned earlier in this chapter, whereby, emphasis was to be given more to domestic tourism rather than having tourists from far-flung areas. It is from this perspective an integrated policy for the whole of the region would be handy to revive the industry from the post-Covid pandemic shock. The need for having horizontal collaboration between the state tourism of all the eight states, along with the tourism associations, transport associations would result in seamless travel across the whole region. Uniformity,collaboration, standard operating procedures, and sharing of resources as a one-tourist destination, inclusive of all the eight states would be the need of the hour (Barooah Pisharoty, 2020). In that regard, Tripura has to join hands with the neighboring states to finalize the contours made by other states in an integrated manner. Any single service provider or a single manufacturer cannot fight Covid pandemic-related challenges being faced by the universe, and therefore, it is extremely important to join hands and convert the challenges into business opportunities. The common enemy of covid pandemic has brought in competitors to share their resources and abilities. Coordinated strategies that is forward looking and one which creates employment for the local population would go a long way in bringing in the desired participation from the local stakeholders that in turn would have a beneficial impact on the end users (read tourists). The government of Tripura has been very smart in doing that while promoting various local masterpieces under the vocal for local initiative.

The measures that has been cited by experts and forecasted by the author, in order to bring back the tourism sector of Northeastern part of India into tracks, including Tripura could be the following:

1. Enhancement of regional connectivity of all the eight Northeastern states with Assam beingthe hub. However, that might change with a proposed Special Economic Zone coming up in Sabroom in Tripura and with extensive connectivity happening between India and Bangladesh through several corridors in the state of Tripura. From Assam, Tripura can takeup the onus to be the hub of tourism for all the eight sisters of Northeastern India.

2. A hub and spoke model that can connect all the eight states for the tourists to explore the region, rather than having standalone approaches individually by each of them. Economies of scale would help while value adding into the customers palate.

3. Massive spending on infrastructure like, roads, hotels, and motels by roping in private players and if necessary adopt the private–public partnership model in such projects.

4. Air transportation should be made affordable to enhance tourist inflow, as the other means of transportation remains a challenge owing to the mountainous terrains.

5. Advanced landing grounds in various states should be activated to facilitate air transport culminating in roping in high-end domestic and international tourists.

6. A strong digital presence with state-of-the-art technology and experts who can digitally market the destinations to the international tourists by highlighting the inherent benefits, would go a long way in making these international tourist hotspots.

7. Pushing the Small and Medium Enterprises to take up entrepreneurial opportunitiesfor providing economies of scale to the industry while ensuring local employment.

Case Study of Tripura as a Destination Brand with Post-Pandemic Perspectives   227

8. Preparing for contingencies by learning the lessons from Covid pandemic so that the industry can withstand future man-made and natural disasters better.

15.8 CONCLUSIONS

Tripura as a tourist destination has caught the attention since the new government took charge in the state from the year 2018. The government has optimized the usage of cultural, natural, and historical masterpieces present and has leveraged them beautifully to shape-up the tourism industry. The proactive approaches of the government are evident from several measures and marketing initiatives that has been taken from time to time, to ensure attraction of local, regional, and even international tourists. Furthermore, the benefit of the development of the sector on the generation of employment has also been felt. The government has been proactive in aligning with the central government, while using the stimulus measures, vocal for local initiatives to boost up the industries, including that of tourism. The enhanced connectivity with neighboring Bangladesh and a proposed road with the South East Asia would further enhance the industry from the global perspective. The situation is ripe for making the next big move to make Tripura one of the best regional tourist destination, not only for the domestic audience, but also for the global market.

15.9 ISSUES FOR DISCUSSION AND ANALYSIS

1. Conduct a comprehensive Strength, Weakness, Opportunity, and Threat analysis of destination Tripura and reflect on the branding strategies followed by the state.
2. If you would be made the head of the tourism department of Tripura, what changes would you bring about in the destination branding post-pandemic. How do you think that those changes would have brought you the desired results?
3. Highlight the Unique Selling Propositions of destination Tripura and comment on their sustainability especially from the post-pandemic perspective.
4. If you are hired as a consultant to advise the government on making Tripura an international tourist destination, what advice would you

KEYWORDS

solicit to the decision maker to convert Tripura from a domestic to that of an international tourist hub?

- **Tripura**
- **tourism**
- **branding**
- **destination**
- **post-pandemic**
- **fairs**
- **festivals**

REFERENCES

Arionesei, G.; Ivan, P. Marketing of Tourism Destination from the Public Relations Perspective. *J. Tour—Stud. Res. Tour., Romania* **2012,** 90.

Asokastami. Tripura Tourism, n.d. http://www.tripuratourism.gov.in/asokastami (accessed Dec 30, 2020)

Barooah Pisharoty, S. Tourism in Northeast India: Industry Experts Urge Centre to Think of Revival Plan. *The Wire*. https://thewire.in/economy/tourism-northeast-india- experts-urge-central-govt-revival-plan

Bloom Consulting Journal. Bloom Consulting, n.d. https://www.bloom- consulting.com/journal/how-destination-brands-should-prepare-for-the-post-covid-19/

Butler, R. The Evolution of Tourism and Tourism Research. *Tour. Recreat. Res*. **2015,** *40*, 16–27. DOI: 10.1080/02508281.2015.1007632.

Charan Talukdar, B. COVID-19 & Tourism in Northeast Post 2020. Sentinel Assam, **2020,** Dec 30. https://www.sentinelassam.com/editorial/covid-19-tourism-in-northeast-post-2020-477561

Diwali. Tripura Tourism, n.d. http://www.tripuratourism.gov.in/diwali (accessed Dec 30, 2020).

Economic Times Brand Equity Team. Future Shock-25 Travel and Tourism Trends Post Covid-19. Brand Equity Economic Times, **2020,** May 30. https://brandequity.economictimes.indiatimes.com/news/business-of-brands/future-shock-25-travel-tourism-trends-post-covid-19/75463449

Garia Puja. Tripura Tourism, n.d. http://www.tripuratourism.gov.in/garia (accessed Dec 30, 2020).

Kapferer J. N. *The New Strategic Brand Management*, 4th ed.; Kogan Page: London and Philadelphia, 2008.

Kharchi. Tripura Tourism, n.d. http://www.tripuratourism.gov.in/kharchi (accessed Dec 30, 2020).

Kubickova, M. The Role of Government in Tourism: Linking Competitiveness, Freedom, and Developing Economies. *Czech J. Tour.* **2016,** 5. DOI: 10.1515/cjot-2016-0005.

Morgan, N., Pritchard, A.; Pride, R. *Destination Branding: Creating the Unique Destination Proposition,* 2nd ed.; Butterworth Heinemann: Oxford, 2004.

Morrison, A. M.; Anderson, D. J. Destination Branding. Paper presented at the Missouri Association of Convention & Visitors Bureaus Annual Meeting. Missouri, 2002.

Nirmahalfes. Tripura Tourism, n.d. http://www.tripuratourism.gov.in/nirmahalfes (accessed Dec 30, 2020)

Onsimo Cuamea, V.; Arely Bermudez, R. Factors for Destination Branding Based on Tourist's Perspective. *Int. J. of Adv. Res.* **2017,** *5* (Dec). 919–926] (ISSN 2320-5407). www.journalijar.com

Pike, S. Tourism Destination Branding Complexity. *J. Product Brand Manage.* **2005,** *14* (4), 258–259.

Pilakfes. *Tripura Tourism,* n.d. http://www.tripuratourism.gov.in/pilakfes (accessed Dec 30, 2020).

Pous. Tripura Tourism, n.d. http://www.tripuratourism.gov.in/pous (accessed Dec 30, 2020).

Stephens Balakrishnan, M. Strategic Branding of Destinations: A Framework. *Eur. J. Market.* **2009,** *43,* 611–629. DOI: 10.1108/03090560910946954.

Tripura State Portal. n.d. https://tripura.gov.in/. Retrieved December 30, **2020,** from https://tripura.gov.in/know-tripura

Tripura Tourism. Tripuratourism, n.d. http://www.tripuratourism.gov.in/ (accessed Dec 30, 2020)

Zikmund, W. *Exploring Marketing Research,* 8th ed.; Thompson South-Western: Ohio, 2003.

CHAPTER 16

Impact of Pandemic, Crises, and Challenges on Event Tourism

SANTUS KUMAR DEB[1] and SHOHEL MD. NAFI[2]

[1]*Department of Tourism and Hospitality Management, University of Dhaka, Dhaka, Bangladesh*

[2]*Department of Tourism and Hospitality Management, Noakhali, Science and Technology University, Noakhali, Bangladesh*

ABSTRACT

Research Problem: Events are considered not only as one of the significant parts of tourism, but also an inseparable part of human civilization was developed. However, this chapter will discuss the past pandemic and crises of event tourism. After that, it presents the impact of pandemic, crisis, and challenges of event tourism and learning for the future to overcome these crisis moments.

Research Significance: The tourism industry has experienced some economic and environmental crises and challenges like economic recession, terrorist attacks, and global pandemics. In 2020, the whole world was stuck in the COVID-19 pandemic, and the tourism industry has experienced an unprecedented loss. The $1.07 trillion event industry with 10.3 million direct jobs was one of the most affected sectors in the current pandemic. At that time, all types of events like sporting events, business events, cultural events, recreational events, and cancelations affected the overall event tourism industry. According to UNWTO, the overall tourism industry lost almost US $1.2 trillion in the first 8 months of the pandemic, which also affected event tourism. Consequently, any type of adverse situations also affected

Please note that few chapters were submitted during the peak of the pandemic. The long period of time to publish (due to supply chain and other issues) may have changed the perspectives presented in the chapter altogether.

Event Tourism and Sustainable Community Development: Advances, Effects, and Implications.
Ekta Dhariwal, Shruti Arora, Anukrati Sharma, Azizul Hassan (Eds.)
© 2024 Apple Academic Press, Inc. Co-published with CRC Press (Taylor & Francis)

community development because most of the events have emerged from the community people.

Method of the Study: This study is qualitative in nature, and data was collected from secondary sources like journal articles, relevant literature, and published materials.

Findings: This chapter discusses the past pandemic and crises of event tourism. Most of the crisis events impact on event tourism in a short-term basis while health-related crisis needs long time to recover. For short-term consequences, rescheduling is the best option to perform the event, and this measure will help to minimize the loss. This chapter presents some recovery suggestions to overcome the crisis events which will be helpful for event tourism.

16.1 INTRODUCTION

Event tourism is a significant part of tourism activities and acts as a travel motivator in many cases. Getz (2014) stated that "event tourism at the desti-nation level is the development and marketing of planned events as tourist attractions, catalysts, animators, image makers, and place marketers." From ancient times, some events are linked with the human civilization where some events are created with the demand time. So, events are very closely linked with human society and culture and sometimes reflect the intrinsic value of a civilization or a society. The formation of the event has been started from the ancient time. However, the concept of event tourism is relatively new than the development of the event. The concept of event tourism was first used in the late 20th century. In 1987, The New Zealand Tourist and Publicity Department first stated the term event tourism as "Event tourism is a significant and speedily increasing subdivision of global tourism...." (Getz, 2008). After that, the term event tourism is gaining popularity and uses as a concept of developing an organized event to attract tourists. Getz (2008) stated the importance of planned events in tourism which is already well documented and played a significant role to develop the competitiveness of a destination. The total value of the global event tourism industry is billion dollars which significantly impacts on the overall GDP.

In the 21st century, the global tourism industry has witnessed significant growth. The COVID-19 has bowed the world upside down. Every single activity of human civilization and economy has been halted by COVID-19. The global scenario has changed due to COVID, and people live and interact with each other differently, social norms have changed, and the travel restrictions have been imposed to control the people movement. For that reason, global travel and tourism have seen an unprecedented loss. In 2019, global tourism industry has contributed almost \$9.1 trillion dollars which is almost 10.9% of world GDP but suffered a loss of \$4.5 trillion dollars to reach \$4.7 trillion in 2020 (WTTC, 2021). A similar declining trend is also observed in all other indicators like employment creation, investment, and tourist arrival.

Getz and Page (2019) and Raj et al. (2017) stated that for many destinations, the event is the major earning source. Every year, thousands of tourists have traveled one country to another country to enjoy famous events. However, the outbreak of the COVID-19 has forced the governments and policy makers to restrict the travel movement. In this consequence, each country has imposed a complete lockdown for different timeframes, therefore banned travel and gathering for events. Moreover, event tourism, after gaining popularity, has experienced several crisis and challenges in the last three decades. However, it is inevitable that any crisis event that affects tourism will also impact event tourism. This chapter will discuss the impact of pandemic, crisis, and challenges of event tourism. After that, a recovery proposal and guidelines will also be presented in this chapter.

16.2 METHODOLOGY

The main aim of this study is to find out the impact of pandemic, crisis, and challenges of event tourism. Research article in the event tourism field is very scarce. For that reason, an qualitative research method was conducted to perform this study. Data were collected from secondary sources like journal articles, relevant literature, website data, and published materials. Boslaugh (2007) defined secondary data as the author not being involved in the data collection process and data collected by someone else. Secondary data may comprise data that have been previously collected and are under concern to be reused for new problems, for which the data collected were not initially anticipated (Vartanian, 2010).

To find the most desirable data, different keywords were used in search engines like "crisis in event tourism," "challenges of event tourism," "COVID-19 and event tourism," "pandemic and event tourism," and "events cancelled due to pandemic." Most of the crisis and tourism-related articles give a general overview of the crisis and their consequences in overall tourism and only a few articles stress the recovery process. Only a few studies have been published that examined the consequences of crisis events like COVID-19 on travel, tourism, and event tourism. But the crisis and event tourism is a very novel field of study and lack of organized information is the main limitation. This study attempted to find out the previous crisis and challenges of tourism and specifically event tourism and recovery process from these crisis events. However, COVID-19 is the most hazardous crisis moment for the tourism industry, and this study mainly emphasizes the current situation.

16.3 EVENT TOURISM

16.3.1 EVENT TOURISM

Getz and Page (2016) stated that events are the most significant factors for destination attractiveness and a key proposition for increasing global competitiveness. There is no universally recognized definition of the event (Oklobdžija, 2015). Events are the special short-term phenomena or activities and that each is distinctive appeal because of interactions among the people, arrangement, management, and design systems of the program (Getz, 2008). The term event means any specific cultural activity, religious ritual, performance, and exhibition, which are performed by a society or a community or an organization in a planned manner. Tourists are attracted by this type of event whether it is organized for profit or not. Getz and Page (2016) provided a typology of planned events from the event tourism perspectives and divided the events in four broad categories like business event, entertainment event, sports event, and festival and culture event. However, events can be categorized from local events to mega-events in terms of their size and attraction capability. Many events have very little or no impact on tourism and some events are mainly designed to attract tourists and earn huge profits. Oxford Economics (2018) stated that around 1.5 billion participants were involved in business events in 2017 and generated 2.53 trillion business output. Event tourism also generates huge employment opportunities for almost 26 million people (Gössling et al. 2020).

16.3.2 MAJOR CRISIS AND CHALLENGES OF EVENT TOURISM (TERRORIST ATTACKS, ECONOMIC CRISIS 2009, SARS, MERS)

The journey of modern tourism has started in the early 1950, and UNTWO estimates that only 25 million tourists traveled that year. Tourism has boasted practically continuous growth over time, regardless of intermittent shocks, representing the sector's strength and flexibility. International tourist arrivals have amplified from 25 million internationally in 1950 to 278 million in 1980, 687 million in 2000, and 1235 million in 2016. The average growth rate of tourist arrival is 3.3% from 2000 to 2010 and 5.1% between 2009 and 2019. This number has increased by almost 60% by 2019, and the number of tourist arrival stands at 1.5 billion in 2019 (UNTWO, 2020c). However, the achievement of the growth rate of international tourism was not a smooth path all the time. In this journey, the tourism industry has experienced many short-term and long-term crisis events confined to any geographical area to a global level. Ren (2020) stated that many crisis events have occurred in a specific area, and specific duration has a distinguishable time and space, and their effects may be long-lasting. The destruction of a similar event reaffirms the delicateness of the tourism industry (Jiang and Ritchie, 2017; Yeh, 2021).

But the impact of COVID-19 is unique and deadlier than any other previous crisis event. Due to COVID-19, the tourism industry came back to the position that it was 30 years ago. According to nature and impact, crisis can be classified into three broad categories, like political unrest or terrorist attack: short-term impact on people travel and event tourism, and effects are confined to the specific region; economic recession: negative impact on tourism sector but impacts on event tourism is very few; and health crisis or pandemic: worst impact on tourism and event tourism, and recovery depends on nature and spread of the pandemic.

International tourist arrival had seen an average growth of 6.6% between 1950 and 2005, and the global tourism industry sometimes observed downward as the average annual growth between 1990 and 2000 was 4.6% and between 2000 and 2005 was 3.3% (Hall, 2010). However, Hall (2010) provides complete information about the crisis events which are occurred between 1975 and 2010. Table 16.1 provides the previous crisis events from 1975 to the present day. Tourism as a major economic force has been disrupted by many social, economic, financial, political, disease, epidemic, and pandemic crisis events in that time.

236 Event Tourism and Sustainable Community Development

TABLE 16.1 Crisis Event Affecting International Tourist Arrivals.

Year	International tourist arrival (million)	Changes over the previous year (%)	Types of crisis
1974	205.7		Economic recession—W. Europe and N. America
			Oil or energy Crisis—Arab oil embargo
1975	222.3	8.1	
1976	227.4	2.3	
1977	246.1	8.2	
1978	260.1	5.7	
1979	272.1	4.6	Oil or energy crisis—energy crisis
			Political crisis—revolution in Iran; USSR invades Afghanistan
1980	278.1	2.0	Economic recession—USA
1981	278.6	0.2	Economic recession—W. Europe and N. America
1982	276.9	−0.6	Economic recession—W. Europe and N. America
1983	281.8	1.8	
1984	306.8	8.9	
1985	320.1	4.3	
1986	330.2	3.2	
1987	359.7	8.9	
1988	385.0	7.0	Political crisis—first intifada
1989	410.1	6.5	
1990	439.5	7.2	Economic recession—global
			Oil or energy crisis—oil shock
			Political crisis—First Gulf War
1991	442.5	0.7	Economic recession—global
1992	479.8	8.4	Economic recession—global
			Natural disaster—Hurricane Andrew
1993	495.7	3.3	Economic recession—global
1994	519.8	4.9	
1995	540.6	4.0	
1996	575.0	6.4	
1997	598.6	4.1	Economic recession—Asia
			Natural disaster—SE Asian haze
1998	616.7	3.0	Economic recession—global
1999	616.6	3.7	
2000	687.0	7.4	Political crisis—second intifada

Impact of Pandemic, Crises, and Challenges on Event Tourism

TABLE 16.1   *(Continued)*

Year	International tourist arrival (million)	Changes over the previous year (%)	Types of crisis
2001	686.7	00	Economic recession—global
			Political crisis—9/11 attacks
			Health crisis—UK foot and mouth
2002	707.0	2.9	Economic recession—global
			Health crisis—SARS
2003	694.6	−1.7	Political crisis—Second Gulf War
			Health crisis—SARS
2004	765.1	10.1	Natural disaster—Indonesian Tsunami
2005	806.8	5.5	Political crisis—Bali bombing
			Natural disaster—Hurricane Katrina
2006	842	4.5	Political crisis—Israeli invasion of Lebanon
			Natural disaster—US heat wave, SE Asian haze
2007	898	6.0	Natural disaster—European heat wave
2008	924	2.0	Economic recession—global
			Oil or energy crisis—oil high of $147
2009	880	−4.0	Economic recession—global
			Health crisis—swine flu
			Natural disaster—European and US cold wave
2010	940	6.6	Economic recession—global
			Oil or energy crisis—oil back above $80
2011	995	4.8	Political crisis—political turbulence in the Middle East
2012	1035	4.0	Political crisis—political turbulence in the Middle East
2013	1087	4.6	Health crisis—MERS outbreak
2014	1133	4.3	
2015	1189	4.5	
2016	1235	3.9	
2017	1329	7.0	
2018	1413	5.4	
2019	1465	3.8	
2020	398	−72.8	Health crisis—COVID-19 pandemic
2021		−83 (January–March)	Health crisis—COVID-19 pandemic

Sources: Hall (2010); UNWTO (2011, 2013, 2015, 2017, 2019, 2020b, 2021); Globetrender (2021).

Table 16.1 shows that major crisis events in tourism are related to economic recession, health issues, oil and energy crises, and political problems. However, before COVID-19, the economic recession was the worst event for tourism and the impact of these events was recovered in a short time period.

In the 21st century, major disturbing events in tourism are September 11 terrorist attacks in 2001, the economic recession, the SARS outbreak in 2003, the economic recession in 2008/2009/2010, swine flu in 2009, MERS outbreak in 2015, and COVID-19 pandemic in 2019. During these time periods, the world tourism industry observes negative growth in 2003, 2009, 2020, and 2021, and this trend is continuing at present. Figure 16.1 can help to visualize the impact of COVID-19 on tourist arrival and the overall tourism industry. At that time, the tourism industry is mostly disrupted by the health-related problem. Gössling et al. (2020) mentioned that the major reasons for increasing health crises or pandemics are mobility and rapid growth of the world population, urbanization trends of people, and technological advancement of the transportation network. However, the major challenge for event tourism is health issues. Mostly, events are postponed or canceled for health-related crisis for the short time period to long time period.

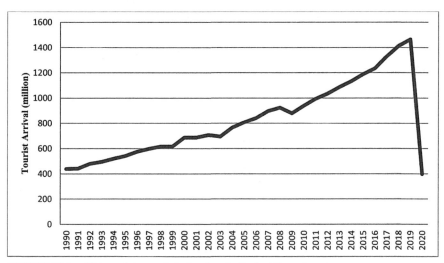

FIGURE 16.1 Major crisis events in tourism in the last three decades.

Source: Gössling et al. (2020); Hall (2010); UNWTO (2021)

In the COVID-19 situation, all types of people movement are completely restricted for several months, and to unlock, the situation countries are still maintaining social distancing. So, all types of events ranging from family events to national or international events are restricted. Business meetings and conferences are held on by using an online platform; family events are canceled or performed on a small scale; the majority of the national events are postponed or observed in a small scale; and some sports events are canceled or postponed or maintained strict rules to perform. COVID-19 has completely interrupted some rituals, such as the ritual of theaters (re-enactment of some events), rites of competition (games, sports, contests, etc.), and devalorization rites (ceremonials at the end of an event), because of the closure without any concessions of outdoor recreation venues, gathering and leisure venues (Getz, 2019; WHO, 2020; Seraphin, 2021).

Fingar (2021) stated that in 2019 the global value of the meeting, incentives, conferences, and exhibitions (MICE) industry was $1.1 trillion. Major sports leagues and events through Europe and North America and other countries have all finished their seasons with the opening of others including the 2020 Summer Olympic Games or the UEFA EURO 2020 postponed, and the combined economic impact is not yet calculated but it will be hundreds of billions of US dollars (Gössling et al., 2020). The event tourism is one of the most adversely affected subsectors of tourism by COVID-19.

16.4 IMPACT OF COVID-19 ON THE TOURISM INDUSTRY

Almost all the economic sectors in the world have observed the adverse impact of COVID-19. Travel and tourism industry is the most affected by this pandemic which is also proven by many studies. Before the pandemic, the annual growth rate of tourism sector was about 3.5% in 2019 (WTTC, 2020). In 2019, international tourist arrivals reached about 1.5 billion and experts expected that 2020 would be another successful year for tourism (Deb and Nafi, 2020). But COVID-19 has changed the overall scenario, and Table 16.2 presents the outlook of international tourists' arrivals from 2018 to 2020. At the same time period, WTTC also reported that travel and tourism industry contributes almost 10.3% of global GDP and the total value is $8.9 trillion. This industry enjoys a very sharp growth in the last few decades. Not only GDP growth, this industry contributes positively in all other economic and social parameters. However, travel and tourism play a significant role in employment creation which is almost 330 million employments where the women employment ratio is almost 50%.

TABLE 16.2 Outlook for International Tourist Arrival.

Region	Tourist arrivals (million)			Tourist arrivals change (%)			Average a year (%)
	2018	2019	2020	2018/17	2019/18	2020/19	2009–2019
World	1413	1466	398	5.6	3.8	−72.8	5.1
Europe	716.0	746.3	235.1	5.8	4.2	−68.5	4.6
Asia and Pacific	346.5	360.4	57.1	7.3	4.0	−84.1	7.1
American	216.0	219.3	69.7	2.4	1.5	−68.2	4.6
Africa	68.7	70.1	18.2	8.5	2.0	−74.0	4.4
Middle East	65.5	70.0	18.2	3.0	6.8	−74.0	2.7

Source: Deb and Nafi (2020); UNWTO (2021).

However, COVID-19 stopped the growth of the tourism industry at a drastic level. The GDP contribution of travel and tourism fell by 49.1% and stood at 5.5% in 2020 (WTTC, 2021). Figure 16.2 shows tourism contribution in GDP and employment in 2019 and 2020, and Figure 16.3 shows the regional performance of travel and tourism. The tourism industry has lost 41–59% of its share in 2020 than the previous year in different world's regions. The entire loss is quite predictable because the world saw almost 96% closing of all borders (UNWTO, 2020a).

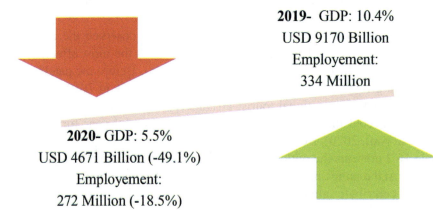

FIGURE 16.2 Tourism contribution in GDP and employment in 2019 and 2020.
Source: WTTC (2021).

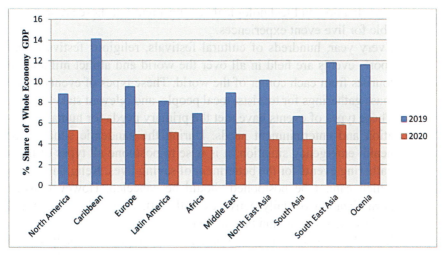

FIGURE 16.3 Travel and tourism regional performance.
Source: WTTC (2021).

Some countries impose a travel ban for international countries or selected countries. At that time, all kinds of domestic tourism and all forms of tourism activities are suspended for a long time. Event tourism, a form of tourism, is also significantly interference by COVID-19. All types of events in the entire world have been suspended for a long time that causes a billion dollar loss. In this situation, some sort of recovery plan is needed to restart tourism operation by maintaining the COVID-19 protocol.

16.5 RECOVERY PROPOSAL FOR THE EVENT TOURISM

- Most of the business meetings, incentives, conferences, seminars, and educational workshops are conducted in the online platform in all over the world. MICE tourism is one of the biggest segments of event tourism and a large number of tourism service providers are connected with this. Moreover, the major challenge is that some MICE tourism organizers think that this process is cost-effective for organizers and participants, and they are willing to continue it after the pandemic. Though the effectiveness of physical and virtual events needs to analyze in the future, virtual events are helpful for the pandemic situation but it will not be sustainable for a long time. Seraphin (2021) stated that virtual events are the blessing of globalization and technological advancement but these are not suitable for live event experiences.

- Every year, hundreds of cultural festivals, religious festivals, and sports events are held in all over the world and attract millions of tourists from each corner of the world. These types of events create mass gatherings for tourists, local people, and relevant stakeholders. These types of events have met the primary needs for human recreation and entertainment needs. During the pandemic situation or health emergency situation, it is wise to postpone all types of mass gathering events for the betterment of saving lives. Religious events which cannot be postponed should be canceled. However, when normalization of daily activities will start, event planners should review the scenario and take action.

- In COVID-19 situation, the normalization stage has already started after the starting of vaccination. Some countries, like the USA, the United Kingdom, Israel, and EU countries, demonstrated a positive result in effective COVID-19 vaccination as the infection rate has been dropped significantly. So, effective vaccination is the key for performing the events in a normal manner. However, it is a vexatious activity of vaccinating all the people in a short time period. In these circumstances, only vaccinated people should be allowed to participate in the events with all precautions prescribed by the regulatory authority.

- Many local, national, regional, international, and mega sports events are held around the year. Pandemic or any other crisis events have disrupted these, which lead to postponing or cancelation. Basically, the impact of natural disasters, political unrest, and economic recession on event tourism is temporary, and cancelation of events is very rare. However, the whole scenario in a health crisis or the current pandemic is different. In a pandemic situation, some measures should be taken to perform mega sports events, like matches should be arranged in various cities or venues to reduce the pressure, maintaining social distancing in the venue and use 50% or less capacity of the venue; diagnostic test report, such as negative report for COVID-19, should be applicable for the audience; only vaccinated audience can allow on the venue; less contract point for the players and other officials to avoid infection.

16.6 CONCLUSION

Event tourism is one of the biggest and fastest-growing segments in the tourism market in terms of size, activities, and economic contribution. The tourism industry and event industry have been disrupted by many crisis situations in the previous time. Most of the crisis events impact event tourism on a short-term basis, while health-related crisis needs a long time to recover. For short-term consequences, rescheduling is the best option to perform the event, and this measure will help to minimize the loss. COVID-19 is the most devastating crisis event in travel and tourism industry. From the beginning of COVID-19, all types of human movement and activities are being closed for several months, and after that, countries are gone through unlocking the situation. However, experts are assuming that it will take 2023 to normalize the situation. But the tourism industry will not return to its normal state until 2025. Some events are canceled and some events are rescheduled in this situation. But the nature of events is totally changed and observed by maintaining strict COVID protocol. This chapter presents some recovery suggestions to overcome the crisis events which will be helpful for event tourism.

KEYWORDS

- **event tourism**
- **travel and tourism**
- **crisis**
- **COVID-19**

REFERENCES

Boslaugh, S. *Secondary Data Sources for Public Health: A Practical Guide*; Cambridge University Press, 2007.

Deb, S. K.; Nafi, S. M. Impact of Covid-19 Pandemic on Tourism: Recovery Proposal for Future Tourism. *GeoJ. Tour. Geosites* 2020, *33* (4spl), 1486–1492. https://doi.org/10.30892/gtg.334spl06-597.

Fingar, C. Covid Continues to Wreak Havoc on the Events Industry- The Covid-19 Pandemic Has Decimated the Meetings, Incentives, Conferences and Exhibitions Space, with Online and Hybrid Events Enjoying Mixed Success Across Industries. Published Online, 2021.

https://investmentmonitor.ai/investment-monitor-events/covid-wreak-havoc-events-industry (accessed June 15, 2021).

Getz D. Festival and Event, Tourism. In *Encyclopedia of Tourism*; Jafari J., Xiao H., Eds.; Springer: Cham, 2014. https://doi.org/10.1007/978-3-319-01669-6_84-1.

Getz, D. *Event Studies: Theory, Research and Policy for Planned Events*; Routledge: London, 2019.

Getz, D. Progress in Tourism Management Event Tourism: Definition, Evolution, and Research. *Tour. Manage.* 2008, *29*, 403–428.

Getz, D.; Page, S. J. Progress and Prospects for Event Tourism Research. *Tour. Manage.* 2016, *52*, 593–631.

Globetrender. UNWTO Predicts Global Tourist Arrivals to be Down 85 Per Cent in 2021. Published Online, 2021. https://globetrender.com/2021/04/15/untwo-global-tourist-arrivals-predicted-2021/ (accessed June, 10, 2021).

Gössling, S.; Scott, D.; Hall, C. M. Pandemics, Tourism and Global Change: A Rapid Assessment of COVID-19. *J. Sustain. Tour.* 2021, *29* (1), 1–20. DOI: 10.1080/09669582.2020.1758708.

Hall, C. M. Crisis Events in Tourism: Subjects of Crisis in Tourism. *Curr. Iss. Tour.* 2010, *13* (5), 401–417. DOI: 10.1080/13683500.2010.491900.

Jiang, Y.; Ritchie, B. W. Disaster Collaboration in Tourism: Motives, Impediments and Success Factors. *J. Hospital. Tour. Manage.* 2017, *31*, 70–82. https://doi.org/10.1016/j.jhtm.2016.09.004.

Oklobdžija, S. The Role of Events in Tourism Development. *BizInfo J.* 2015, *6* (2), 83–97.

Oxford Economics. *Global Economic Significance of Business Events*; Published Online, 2018. https://insights.eventscouncil.org/Portals/0/OEEIC%20Global%20Meetings%20 Significance%20%28FINAL%29%202018-11-09-2018.pdf (accessed May 29, 2021).

Raj, R.; Walters, P.; Rashid, T. *Events Management. Principles & Practice*; Sage: London, 2017.

Seraphin, H. COVID-19: An Opportunity To Review Existing Grounded Theories in Event Studies. *J. Conv. Event Tour.* 2021, *22* (1), 3–35. DOI: 10.1080/15470148.2020.1776657.

UNWTO. Covid-19 Response: 96% Of Global Destinations Impose Travel Restrictions, UNWTO Reports. Published Online, 2020a. https://www.unwto.org/news/covid-19-response-travel-restrictions (accessed March 15, 2021).

UNWTO. International Tourism Growth Continues To Outpace The Global Economy, Published Online, 2020c. https://www.unwto.org/international-tourism-growth-continues-to-outpace-the-economy (accessed May 12, 2021).

UNWTO. UNWTO Tourism Highlights–2011. Published Online, 2011. https://www.e-unwto.org/doi/pdf/10.18111/9789284413935 (accessed May 29, 2021).

UNWTO. UNWTO Tourism Highlights–2013. Published Online, 2013. https://www.e-unwto.org/doi/pdf/10.18111/9789284415427 (accessed April 20, 2021).

UNWTO. UNWTO Tourism Highlights–2015. Published Online, 2015. https://www.e-unwto.org/doi/pdf/10.18111/9789284416899. (accessed March 29, 2021)

UNWTO. UNWTO Tourism Highlights–2017. Published Online, 2017.https://www.e-unwto.org/doi/pdf/10.18111/9789284419029 (accessed May 29, 2021).

UNWTO. International Tourism Highlights–2019. Published Online, 2019. https://www.e-unwto.org/doi/pdf/10.18111/9789284421152 (accessed May 29, 2021).

UNWTO. World Tourism Barometer–January 2020. Published Online, 2020b. https://webunwto.s3.eu-west-1.amazonaws.com/s3fs-public/2020-01/UNWTO_Barom20_01_ January_excerpt_0.pdf. (accessed March 22, 2021)

UNWTO. World Tourism Barometer–May 2021. Published Online: 2021. https://webunwto.s3.eu-west-1.amazonaws.com/s3fs-public/2021-06/UNWTO_Barom21_03_May_EXCERPT.pdf?HX6_a1qO47A3NC.WgFNaY6RtGjTkNNHM (accessed March 29, 2021).

Vartanian, T. P. *Secondary Data Analysis*; Oxford University Press, 2010.

WHO. COVID-19 Technical Guidance for Schools, Workplaces and Institutions. Published Online, 2020.https://www.who.int/emergencies/diseases/novel-coronavirus-2019/technical-guidance/guidance-for-schools-workplaces-institutions (accessed April 12, 2021).

WTTC. *Travel and Tourism—Global Economic Impact & Trends 2020*; UNWTO, 2020.

WTTC. *Travel & Tourism: Economic Impact 2021*. Published Online, 2021. https://wttc.org/Research/Economic-Impact (accessed April 29, 2021).

Yeh, S. Tourism Recovery Strategy against COVID-19 Pandemic. *Tour. Recreat. Res.* 2021, *46* (2), 188–194. DOI: 10.1080/02508281.2020.1805933.

CHAPTER 17

Opportunities and Challenges in Event Tourism Education

ABDULLAH USLU[1] and ERKAN GÜNEŞ[2]

[1]*Department of Tourism Management, Manavgat Faculty of Tourism, Akdeniz University, Manavgat-Antalya, Turkey*

[2]*Department of Travel-Tourism and Entertainment Services, Vocational School of Tourism and Hotel Management, Erzincan Binali Yıldırım University, Erzincan, Turkey*

ABSTRACT

Events are often viewed as tourist attractions. Therefore, small or large, all the destinations are in search for organizing local, national, or sometimes international events. In this sense, Turkey has an abundant potential for the event tourism thanks to its heritage and, natural and cultural resources. However, this potential is not well benefited since the organized events are mostly small in scale, local, or short in duration due to lack of appropriate planning and management. Events such as celebrations, festivals, fairs, and feasts are an indispensable part of cultural production and consumption. The event can also be defined as the systematic planning, development, and marketing of a number of activities as a touristic attraction and image-building for the natural and physical resources in the cities where it is organized (Getz, 1997). On the other hand, opportunities and challenges in event tourism education need to be well defined. Thus, students who want to work and make a career in event tourism can be guided easily. For instance, although more than 1600 events take place in Turkey per year, it is observed that there are not enough courses

---

Please note that few chapters were submitted during the peak of the pandemic. The long period of time to publish (due to supply chain and other issues) may have changed the perspectives presented in the chapter altogether.

Event Tourism and Sustainable Community Development: Advances, Effects, and Implications.
Ekta Dhariwal, Shruti Arora, Anukrati Sharma, Azizul Hassan (Eds.)
© 2024 Apple Academic Press, Inc. Co-published with CRC Press (Taylor & Francis)

in the curriculum of tourism departments students within the scope of event tourism. However, the effect of event tourism can be strong in ensuring local development and in the career development of students. With the training of conscious students, this will provide positive developments for sustainable tourism and the development of local community. Thus with this chapter is aimed to identify and exploit the opportunities in event tourism industry for the students in the future and career growth, event tourism strategy in the curriculum.

17.1 INTRODUCTION

Event management involves the functions of creating, planning, marketing, coordinating, supervising, and evaluating activities that require public gatherings for promotion, education, reunion, and celebration. However, event management also necessitates competencies in management, coordination, marketing, interpersonal skills, and the effective and efficient use of human resources (Hawkins and Goldblatt, 1995). In the context of tourism and event management education, many factors shape decision-making. At the macrolevel, these factors act to create a curriculum and pedagogy with almost universal similarities, while at the microlevel, they can determine priorities and values by producing a curriculum specific to each institution. On the other hand, the question "what makes the tourism curriculum in one institution different from others and what are the common elements in all curricula?" should be answered. Curriculum-shaping factors in event tourism education can be thought of as a mixture of influences forming curriculum, pedagogy, student experiences, and corporate governance. Although these factors are dynamic and interdependent, they will manifest differently in various institutional contexts (Dredge et al., 2013).

Event tourism education is a program that provides solid teamwork and critical thinking skills by exploring activities in both tourism and nontourism contexts such as sports, festivals, conventions, meetings, and other community events. The event tourism program offers students many benefits (University of Canberra, 2021).

In this section, the development process of event tourism education, what needs to be done in the field, general changes, and suggestions regarding event tourism education are presented. In this context, a broad literature review was conducted using secondary data sources, and a future-oriented evaluation was made with the current situation.

17.2 EVENT TOURISM

Tourism is a significant part of intercultural communication. While traveling, people get to know the culture and traditions of other people, learn about the features of contemporary life, and enrich their ideas about the world by communicating with each other (Kireeva, 2020). This vital feature of the sector also allows people from different cultures to come together in local and large-scale organizations and exchange cultures. The coming together of different cultures creates a meaningful economic input. This situation whets the appetite of all tourism destinations. Therefore, they want to host local festivals and events as well as national or international organizations.

Tourism destinations turn to strategies that focus on their own resources to stay competitive. The pressures of globalization and the problems caused by economic restructuring and the need to create new civic identities have led destinations to use "cultural" assets and resources to differentiate, renew the urban fabric and provide economic, social, and cultural welfare. Creating and promoting events such as festivals, shows, exhibitions, fairs, and championships has become a critical part of urban development strategy worldwide (Richards and Palmer, 2010: 2).

Event tourism is one of the fastest-expanding segments of the tourism sector. Whether large-scale events or local festivals, their economic impact, and sustainability aspects have only recently been scientifically measured (Hawkins and Goldblatt, 1995). On the other hand, events are a significant motivator of tourism, and they feature prominently in the development and marketing plans of most destinations. The roles and effects of planned events in tourism are well established and are of great importance to increase the destination's competitiveness. However, it is not long before event tourism has become established both in the tourism industry and research community (Getz, 2008).

Events are considered catalysts for positive social development through social cohesion, regional economic improvement, and tourist attractions (Armbrecht, 2021). Events play a key marketing role in promotion, both as animators of destination attractiveness and to attract visitor spending given the increasing global competitiveness (Getz and Page, 2016).

Event tourism has been adopted as a strategic approach in the destination management industry and recognized as a significant tourism product (Todd et al., 2017). Tourist events have a positive impact on a place or region by creating economic profits based on revenue from the sale of products and services of different activities associated with the event, as well as increasing tourist turnover, which improves the quality of restaurants and infrastructure (Hernández-Mogollón et al., 2014).

Tassiopoulos (2005) defines the term events as temporary and unique occurrences that have a specific duration, environment, and management and consist of human participation. Events are emerging as an integral and significant part of tourism development and marketing strategies. Event tourism can be used to describe this phenomenon and defined as "the systematic development, planning, marketing, and holding of events as tourist attractions" (Tassiopoulos, 2005: 4). The purposes of event tourism can be listed as follows:

- To create an image suitable for the destination,
- To expand the traditional tourism season,
- To spread the tourist demand in an area more evenly, and
- To attract foreign and domestic visitors.

On the other hand, events are classified as in Figure 17.1 in the literature (Masterman, 2009: 13):

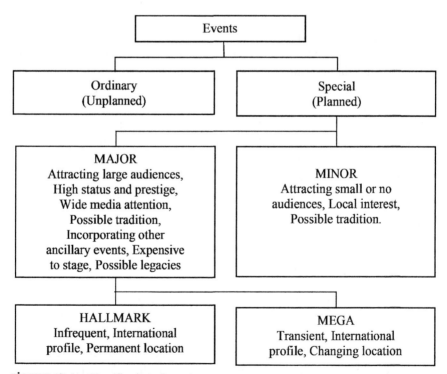

FIGURE 17.1 Classification of events.

Source: Masterman (2009: 13).

Opportunities and Challenges in Event Tourism Education

Planned events in tourism are formed for a purpose. These events, which were once the domain of individual or group initiatives, have largely become the domain of professionals and entrepreneurs. Getz and Page (2016: 594) gathered the main planned event categories and the typologies of the venues associated with each of them in four main groups in the event tourism context.

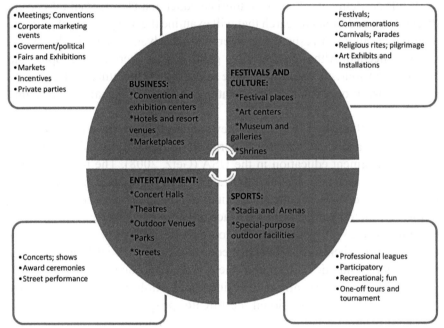

FIGURE 17.2 Event and venue typology from the event tourism perspective.
Source: Getz and Page (2016: 594).

Business events require convention and exhibition centers, including many small private parties and events held in restaurants, hotels, or resorts, while sporting events require specialized facilities, including athletic parks, arenas, and stadiums. Festivals and other cultural celebrations are less reliant on facilities and can be organized in parks, streets, theatres, concert halls, and any other public or private venue for these purposes. Entertainment events such as concerts are usually supplied by the private sector and take place in a variety of venues. (Getz and Page, 2016).

17.3 EVENT TOURISM EDUCATION

Various academic studies have been carried out in the literature on event tourism education. These studies are particularly relevant to students, educators (Barron and Knight, 2017; Lee et al., 2020), and curriculum development and certification programs (Hawkins and Goldblatt, 1995; Lee et al., 2009; Nelson and Silvers, 2009; Zeng and Yang, 2011).

While academic work in event tourism education is beneficial for current discussions, additional research that will examine the many facets of building a new curriculum in response to international advancements in the events sector is needed. Although there is a great deal of literature on topics and emphases in tourism education, there is not much literature that can fully address career opportunities in event management (Manaf and Ibrahim, 2008).

In the 1990s, there were very few undergraduate programs in event management and event tourism. George Washington University pioneered event management education in the USA (Getz, 2008). The mid-1990s are shown as the academic institutionalization of event management and, with it, the leap years of academic studies in the field of event tourism and event studies. Event tourism education and academic studies on event tourism took place roughly 25–30 years after the tourism, hospitality, and leisure industries took off. Therefore, university education for an event tourism career was similarly underdeveloped until these years (Getz and Page, 2016).

In the field of conventions, meetings, and exhibitions, there are many linkages between professional certificate program qualifications and available academic courses. Although event management necessitates a specific set of competencies and skills, no formal major or course leading to a specific degree in higher education could be identified until the 1990s (Hawkins and Goldblatt, 1995). These programs have faced mixed reviews, and there remains uncertainty about the career aspirations and goals of the graduates (Barron and Knight, 2017). In addition, although event management is conceptualized within the tourism discipline, it can be said that it is a developing field in the academic world globally (Manaf and Ibrahim, 2008).

In the last 20 years, the higher education curriculum in event management has started to grow exponentially. This situation showed itself, especially in hospitality and tourism programs. Examples of these universities and programs are University of Central Florida's Rosen College of Hospitality Management has introduced a Bachelor of Science with a major in Event

Management (2007); University of Nevada Las Vegas' William F. Harrah College of Hotel Administration has presented a Bachelor of Science in Hotel Administration with a major in Meetings and Events Management (2004) and Master of Hospitality—Executive Program in Event Management (2006); Indiana University—Purdue University Indianapolis has offered a Bachelor of Science in Tourism, Conventions, and Event Management; and the University of Houston's Conrad N. Hilton College of Hotel and Restaurant Management has introduced an Event Management and Hospitality Sales concentration (Nelson and Silvers, 2009). As professional job postings emerge, event management planning has been recognized more widely as a professional sector of the industry, including many educational institutions offering education and certification (Manaf and Ibrahim, 2008).

Meanwhile, international programs have taken the lead in curriculum development by giving diplomas in event management. For example, Cape Town University of Technology has offered a National Diploma in Event Management; University of Sydney has presented a Master of Management in Event Management; and Leeds Metropolitan University in England has offered Bachelor of Arts degree in Events Management, Master of Science in Events Management, Master of Arts in Responsible Events, Master of Science in International Events Management, and Master of Science in International Festivals Management. Increasing interest has led higher education institutions to develop both undergraduate and graduate programs in event management. Actually, hospitality and tourism programs respond to a demand from the sector and students for such programs. One of the indicators of the demand is the employment perspective of graduates from this field (Nelson and Silvers, 2009). Thus, an increasing number of students today show great interest in the event and meeting industry for their future careers (Lee et al., 2020). Efforts to improve event management curriculum and research activities should therefore be encouraged. These efforts should be carefully monitored and evaluated for measurable results before more comprehensive professional training programs are initiated. Event management appears to be a promising field that deserves attention by postsecondary institutions training tourism and hospitality staff (Hawkins and Goldblatt, 1995). Due to the wide variety of event types, job fields and job descriptions in the event industry also vary. Employer fields and job titles in event management are demonstrated in Table 17.1.

TABLE 17.1 Typical Employers and Typical Job Titles.

Typical employers	
Associations	Government Agencies
Attractions	Hotels & Casinos
Broadcasting Companies	Human Resources Departments
Catering Companies	Incentive Houses
Charitable Organizations	Marketing & Communications Firms
Municipal Special Events Departments	Political or Fraternal Organizations
Civic or Social Organizations	Professional Congress Organizers
Convention & Conference Centers	Resort Properties
Corporations	Retailers, Restaurants, & Museums
Country Clubs	Shopping Centers
Destination Management Companies	Sport Leagues, Teams, & Clubs
Event Venues	Tourism Bureaus
Festivals	Universities & Colleges
Typical job titles	
Account Executive	Event Coordinator
Catering Manager	Event Designer
Conference Coordinator	Event Director
Conference Planner	Event Manager
Conference Planning Manager	Event Organizer
Conference/Trade Show Manager	Event Planner
Conference Services Manager	Event Producer
Convention Services Coordinator	Executive Director
Convention Services Manager	Marketing Strategist
Director of Conference Services	Meeting Planner
Director of Development (Fund Raising)	Meetings Manager
Director of Education (Associations)	Operations Manager
Director of Events	Professional Congress Organizer
Director of Meetings	Special Event Director
Director of Sales	Wedding Planner

Source: Silvers and Nelson (2005) citing Nelson and Silvers (2009).

As Table 17.1 shows, the event management sector has a large number of job titles. However, this may pose some problems in career entry and advancement through job assignments (Nelson and Silvers, 2009).

In the context of event management education, several circumstances shape decision-making. At the macrolevel, these conditions work to produce a curriculum and pedagogy with almost universal similarities, while at the microlevel, priority values can be identified, magnified, and even changed by forming a curriculum specific to each institution. It is also necessary to look at what makes the tourism curriculum in an institution different from others and what are the common elements in all curricula. As in the whole tourism field, curriculum-shaping factors in event tourism education can be considered as a mixture of influences shaping curriculum, pedagogy, student experiences, and corporate governance. While these factors are dynamic and interdependent, they will also manifest differently in various institutional contexts (Dredge et al., 2013).

17.4 OPPORTUNITIES AND CHALLENGES IN EVENT TOURISM EDUCATION

With the rapid growth of the event and meeting industry, a growing number of students are interested in pursuing career opportunities in these fields. Responding to the increasing interest of students, hospitality and tourism management programs have reviewed and developed the event and meeting management curriculum to improve the quality of event and meeting education. Students seek to attend relevant event and meeting management courses and gain a wide range of work experience to build a competitive identity for their future profession. As a core academic discipline for event and meeting management, hospitality and tourism programs in higher education take on vital responsibilities by offering event and meeting management courses to better prepare students, meet industry needs, and develop students' competencies (Nelson and Silvers, 2009; Lee et al., 2020).

It is necessary to keep up with the fast-growing changes in the event tourism education field of the tourism industry. While service robots or advanced technologies are adopted in the tourism industry, on other hand, social media marketing becomes widespread. It can be necessary to direct students to consider designing interdisciplinary courses or multidisciplinary classroom projects for future business areas, with majors such as software or mechanical engineering, and to develop students' artificial intelligence knowledge. Virtual internships can be further developed in the future as a tool to broaden students' perspectives (Park and Jones, 2021; Seo and Kim, 2021).

The growing popularity of event management programs, as well as the resulting professionalization of the subject area in general, has encouraged institutions that provide event education, academic staff who teach on such programs, and researchers in the field to make for further research into this issue (Barron and Knight, 2017).

Even if event management education is now widely available in many countries, event tourism will inevitably create its own niche. This is due in part to an increase in the number of jobs specific to event tourism, as well as the value of merging tourism and closely linked topics like events. These new mergers' synergistic effects provide students with more options and opportunities and bring the practical management fields closer together (Getz and Page, 2016). There is also a requirement for the sector to contribute to this issue, and the availability of experience opportunities as well as the willingness of organizations to welcome, develop, and train students is critical for the sector's future success (Barron and Knight, 2017).

While colleges and universities consider curriculum development in event management as a focal point: efforts at the undergraduate and graduate level should address the following questions or issues (Hawkins and Goldblatt, 1995):

- Should event management be a separate degree program or a focus area?
- Can event management combine congress, festival, exhibition, and special event planning and management activities under a common curriculum?
- How does event management relate to general tourism and hospitality?
- At what levels should the event management curriculum be offered: technical, undergraduate, or graduate?

These questions can be answered from different perspectives. Today, event tourism education is on its way to becoming a major. Therefore, event tourism education should not be under any education area but should be a program that has its own place. Considering employment and career planning, the following suggestions can be offered to curriculum developers and educators for event tourism education:

- First of all, the event management curriculum should include a wide range of knowledge and skills and be planned comprehensively (Zeng and Yang, 2011). All areas of tourism education should demonstrate international business characteristics and provide tourism students with information technology skills along with business strategy skills, international business management, human resource management in multicultural work environments, and communication skills with multicultural customers (Wang and Ryan, 2007). A versatile, diverse, and therefore multicultural curriculum infrastructure should be prepared. The training programs should focus on communication skills as well as international management and organization.

- For the events industry, an emerging field for tourism graduates, educators face challenges when preparing students for their future careers. However, educators should play an active role in preparing their graduates both for the challenges of managing their careers and for gaining the skills and qualifications required by the industry (Robinson et al., 2008). In this context, managers or lower-level employees actively involved in event tourism can be invited to universities and brought together with students in various ways.

- For better collaboration in the event industry, education-related activities such as cross-industry internships, structured training programs for students, and communication and information sharing between industry, academics, and students through an online hub should be identified. Participation in these activities will create an opportunity for students to further develop their careers (Barron and Knight, 2017). In this way, students will have the occasion to get to know the industry and the managers in this field.

- In-depth researches have been conducted on event management curricula. The results demonstrate that event management students should have special knowledge about event planning, management, and marketing. In addition, students should also know event history and development trends, the motivation of relevant stakeholders, and their impact on the economy (Zeng and Yang, 2011).

- The establishment of university-based vocational education indicates that a field is moving towards professionalization. While events management programs exist at universities across the globe, it is necessary to assess their growth and determine if consistent terminology is used. As is apparent in event management job titles, the lack of clear and consistent terminology can be a barrier to further professionalization. Therefore, it should be evaluated whether inconsistent terminology is common among event management programs of universities (Nelson and Silvers, 2009). Developing a common terminology would be helpful for event tourism education. Also, researchers and academicians can improve an event tourism education glossary.

- University event management curriculum should be dynamic and up-to-date in line with the evolution of the industry. As a result, the research into industry perceptions regarding the event management curriculum should be undertaken on an ongoing basis. In addition, future event management curricula should be restructured to fight the challenges of this fast-growing industry. The curriculum should then be regularly evaluated and improved. This continuous development process will enable the graduates of event management programs to be better educated and qualified for their professional careers (Zeng and Yang, 2011). Therefore, curricula should be planned in accordance with development and change.
- University curriculum in almost all disciplines changes by adding or removing courses from the general flow of programs. The event management curriculum aimed at serving the industry and potential students should also reflect environmental and demographic changes in the industry. In addition, the linkage between key stakeholders' perceptions of the event management curriculum, the event industry, students, and the event academic community should be strengthened. Future event management curricula should be reconfigured to meet the challenges of the fast-growing events industry and to ensure that graduates of event management programs are better qualified for professional careers in the industry (Lee et al., 2009).
- In diploma programs that provide event tourism education, meeting and event management course contents should be associated with the tourism industry to ensure harmony and increase job opportunities. Practical training and event management should be included in the curriculum (Manaf and Ibrahim, 2008). Having experienced people in practical training will contribute to more qualified education.
- For students of tourism, events, and hospitality programs, internships encompass many values from "a stepping stone to full-time work, a vital source of income, and even a graduation requirement." Therefore, internships are vitally significant in event tourism education (Park and Jones, 2021: 176). Internship practice should be applied seriously, and employer opinions should be taken for this. Educators and supervisors should monitor internships. Internships should be expanded into other spheres of events as needed.
- Plans should be made for students to undertake virtual internships across the globe to learn how to manage international operations and interact with foreign customers (Seo and Kim, 2021).

- Job and career opportunities in event management (event coordinator, event designer, event director, event manager, event organizer, event planner, event producer, etc.) are diverse. This diversity should be taken into account for career development and conveyed to students accurately and clearly.
- The current COVID-19 pandemic is more of a reminder of societal importance as events are no longer staged. When life returns to normal, event organizers will face a new competitive market where they must do their best to regain their market share. Delivering quality experiences will be crucial to win back customers (Armbrecht, 2021). COVID-19 has brought critical changes to every corner of life and society. The higher education system in tourism, events, and hospitality should adjust to the changes produced by the current pandemic and be able to switch from traditional classroom environments to online classes when necessary. This transformation affects many aspects of the student learning environment, especially courses that include field experiences such as student internship programs (Park and Jones, 2021).

17.5   CONCLUSIONS

At every stage of event tourism education, students should be equipped with practical knowledge and skills. The tourism industry's dynamism necessitates a dynamic educational system. In other words, one of the fundamental conditions of being able to exist in an increasingly competitive environment is undoubtedly having a qualified workforce. This can only be achieved through effective and high-quality event tourism education and training, and employing tourism school graduates in this field. Due to all these reasons, this study emphasizes the significance of event tourism education in satisfying the demand for trained personnel in event tourism education. Thanks to this education, it will be understood that event tourism has a large number of fields and has attractive features for young people.

The number of academic studies in the field of event tourism education is quite limited. In this education, it is significant to produce a unique, macro-level, and microlevel curriculum. At the same time, curriculum development for event management education within tourism education is considered as a combination of pedagogy, student experience, and corporate governance concepts (Dredge et al., 2013). Although it has been delayed globally for event management, measurable evaluations should be made by encouraging research and development activities and curriculum development efforts, and the outcomes should be carefully examined.

Since event tourism education, which is essential for students to create a competitive identity, is unfortunately not sufficiently included in the education curricula, students tend to get certificates and gain various experiences by participating in the courses. However, if event tourism education is given adequately in higher education programs, students will not need to search for different things.

Like all sectors, the tourism sector is also transforming and changing quite rapidly, and the tourism sector has to keep up with this situation with all its stakeholders. Information communication technologies and social media channels are constantly developing, and online training, internships, and courses are organized in every field. These technological resources should also be used in a way that benefits students' personal growth.

Higher education institutions and students cannot be seen as the only ones responsible for event tourism education. At the same time, all public institutions, nongovernmental organizations, tourism, and travel industries with all their sub-branches related to event tourism should undertake their responsibilities. Just like the management of destinations, event tourism education will be successful with the active participation of all stakeholders.

Finally, tourism, like many other industries, has been severely damaged by the COVID-19 pandemic. With the new situation, all professionals and higher education institutions should take more critical and reformative decisions to re-establish market share. For example, many innovation tools such as online classes, online internships, and virtual reality should be seriously activated and used.

KEYWORDS

- **event tourism industry**
- **event tourism**
- **career growth**
- **education**
- **curriculum**
- **opportunities**

REFERENCES

Armbrecht, J. Event Quality, Perceived Value, Satisfaction and Behavioural Intentions in an Event Context. *Scand. J. Hospital. Tour.* **2021,** *21* (2), 169–191. DOI: 10.1080/15022250.2021.1877191

Barron, P.; Knight, J. Aspirations and Progression of Event Management Graduates: A Study of Career Development. *J. Hospital. Tour. Manage.* **2017,** 30, 29–38.

Dredge, D., Benckendorff, P., Day, M., Gross, M., Walo, M., Weeks, P.; Whitelaw, P. Drivers of Change in Tourism, Hospitality, and Event Management Education: An Australian Perspective. *J. Hospital. Tour. Educ.* **2013,** *25* (2), 89–102.

Getz, D. *Event Management and Event Tourism*; Cognizant: New York, 1997.

Getz, D. Event Tourism: Definition, Evolution, and Research. *Tour. Manage.* **2008,** *29,* 403–428.

Getz, D.; Page, S. J. Progress and Prospects for Event Tourism Research. *Tour. Manage.* **2016,** *52,* 593–631.

Hawkins, D.; Goldblatt, J. Event Management Implications for Tourism Education. *Tour. Recreat. Res.* **1995,** *20* (2), 42–45.

Hernández-Mogollón, J.; Folgado-Fernández, J.; Duarte, P. Event Tourism Analysis and State of the Art. *Eur. J. Tour. Hospital. Recreat.* **2014,** *5* (2), 83–102.

Kireeva, Y. A. The Current State of Event Tourism in Russia. *Turismo: Estudos Práticas* **2020,** *4,* 1–11.

Lee, K. M.; Lee, M. J.; Kim, H. J. A Comparison of Student and Industry Perceptions of the Event Management Curriculum in Korea. *J. Hospital. Leisure Sports Tour. Educ.* **2009,** *8* (2), 60–73.

Lee, S.; Shin, H. H.; Jeong, M. Are Students Ready for their Future Career in the Event and Meeting Industry? Lessons from a Comparative Study Between Students and Event and Meeting Professional. *J. Hospital. Tour. Educ.* **2020,** *32* (2), 77–87.

Manaf, N. A.; Ibrahim, S. The Knowledge and Exposure of Career Opportunities in MICE and Event Management for Tourism Students—A Study on Tourism Students at Sunway University College, a Local Private University. In *Proceedings of National Symposium on Tourism Research*; 2008; pp 116–123.

Masterman, G. *Strategic Sports Event Management*; Routledge: Abingdon, 2009.

Nelson, K. B.; Silvers, J. R. Event Management Curriculum Development and Positioning: A Path Toward Professionalization. *J. Hospital. Tour. Educ.* **2009,** *21* (2), 31–39.

Park, M.; Jones, T. Going Virtual: The Impact of COVID-19 on Internships in Tourism, Events, and Hospitality Education. *J. Hospital. Tour. Educ.* **2021,** *33* (3), 176–193.

Richards, G.; Palmer, R. Why Cities Need to Be Eventful. In *Eventful Cities: Cultural Management and Urban Revitalisation*; Butterworth-Heinemann: Oxford, 2010; pp 1–38.

Robinson, R.; Barron, P.; Solnet, D. Innovative Approaches to Event Management Education in Career Development: A Study of Student Experiences. *J. Hospital. Leisure Sport Tour. Educ.* **2008,** *7* (1), 4–17.

Seo, S.; Kim, H. J. (Jenny) How COVID-19 Influences Hospitality and Tourism Education: Challenges, Opportunities, and New Directions. *J. Hospital. Tour. Educ.* **2021,** *33* (3), 147–147.

Slaughter, L.; Reid, S.; Arcodia, C. Event Management Education in Finland. In *Advances in Convention, Exhibition & Event Research, Proceedings of Research and Academic Papers, Convention and Expo Summit*; Weber, K., Ed.; Hong Kong, 29–31 August, 2003.

Tassiopoulos, D. *Event Management: A Professional and Developmental Approach*, 2nd ed.; Juta Academic: South Africa, 2005.

Todd, L.; Leask, A.; Ensor, J. Understanding Primary Stakeholders' Multipleroles in Hallmark Event Tourism Management. *Tour. Manage.* **2017,** *59,* 494–509.

University of Canberra. Bachelor of Event and Tourism Management (MGB401.1), 2021. https://www.canberra.edu.au/course/MGB401/1/2021 (accessed July 10, 2021).

Wang, Z. H.; Ryan,C. Tourism Curriculum in the University Sector: Does It Meet Future Requirements? Evidence from Australia. *Tour. Recreat. Res.* **2007,** *32* (2), 29–40.

Zeng, X.; Yang, J. Industry Perceptions of the Event Management Curriculum in Shanghai. *J. Conv. Event Tour.* **2011,** *12* (3), 232–239.

CHAPTER 18

Enhancing Entrepreneurship in the Event Tourism Industry

ANURODH GODHA

Vardhman Mahaveer Open University, Kota, Rajasthan, India

ABSTRACT

Tourism has emerged as one of the most important economic factors for countries that contribute significantly to their GDP and encourage entrepreneurship. Events are a powerful tourism accelerator, and, as a result, they are heavily included in the growth and commercial strategies of many places. Globalization, immigration, transportation, tourism, and industry are all important factors when it comes to promoting tourism events. Tourism, of course, is a significant player in the age of globalization (by expanding new locations, new demand, and new markets), and it is also heavily influenced by it. Individuals are highly interested in and acquainted with many different sections of the country as a result of the travel and tourism industry's advantages. The event tourism business also offers immigrants a diverse range of entrepreneurial employment opportunities for locals and others, establishing social norms and financial activities in the process. Because of its versatility, low capital requirements, and social expectations, a considerable section of the population chooses to start a small tourism business between all types of tourism firms. The tourist sector has become a key feature in the growth and charisma of 'event management,' a fast-developing occupation for which tourists supply a potential market for organized events. As a result, event tourism is a key contributor to economic growth, with a major impact on entrepreneurship, employment, and household income. The purpose of this

---

Please note that few chapters were submitted during the peak of the pandemic. The long period of time to publish (due to supply chain and other issues) may have changed the perspectives presented in the chapter altogether.

Event Tourism and Sustainable Community Development: Advances, Effects, and Implications.
Ekta Dhariwal, Shruti Arora, Anukrati Sharma, Azizul Hassan (Eds.)
© 2024 Apple Academic Press, Inc. Co-published with CRC Press (Taylor & Francis)

study is to look into ways to improve entrepreneurship in the event tourism industry. This study discusses the variables that encourage the growth of entrepreneurship along with employment prospects in the event tourism business.

18.1 INTRODUCTION

Internationally and domestically, India is a fantastic tourist destination for both domestic and international visitors. In terms of our economy's overall growth and expansion, this potential may be seen. A multibillion-dollar industry, tourism in India is predicted to rise in profitability over the next few years. By virtue of its favorable linkages with other businesses, it is now exerting a direct impact on vital fields such as education, health care, and finance.

Public or private groups may organize an event at a specified site, which may involve a variety of activities. As a sort of touristic activity, events are a type of tourism offer that aims to attract visitors by highlighting the location's distinctive characteristics and preparing various tourism programmes related to nature and other tourist resources. Events can be categorized based on their content, location, scope, magnitude, and significance (Getz, 1997).

Hotels are controlled by conventions and conferences, which are only increasing in importance. With billions of dollars in revenue generated by events around the world, enterprises, hotel groups, and resorts are rethinking the way they operate. Events are the driving force behind tourism, and they play a major role in the progress and promotion of most destinations. Destination competitiveness is increasingly dependent on the role of planned events and their roles and impacts on tourism. "Event tourism" was coined only a few years ago by both the tourist and academic sectors, thus the industry's rapid growth can only be described as remarkable" (Getz, 2008). In today's world, events have become one of the most important tourist attractions, allowing visitors to learn more about the local people, culture, and history.

For example, the selling of items and services relevant to the event, increased visitor traffic, and the development of local entrepreneurship all contribute to the success of a place or region hosting a major tourist event.

An in-depth review of the literature on the genesis, classification, primary variables, and repercussions of events on the evolution of entrepreneurship is conducted in this article. As event tourism grows in relevance, we acknowledge that this endeavor can be twofold: First, it contributes to the growth of scientific knowledge in an area with significant potential for research development by identifying and discussing core concepts; on the other hand, it may be essential for professionals and future entrepreneurs because it provides a better understanding of the value of sustaining and holding events.

Hence, this article's three primary objectives are to (1) build a thorough viewpoint and importance of "events" within the tourism sector; (2) determine the economic function of event tour in promoting entrepreneurship; and (3) perform a comprehensive analysis of the financial role of event travel in supporting entrepreneurship

18.2 EVENT TOURISM AND INDUSTRY

Until recently, the hospitality business was dominated by the lodging and hotel industries, as well as transportation and entertainment, such as theme parks, amusement parks, sports grounds, and museums. In spite of the fact that people have always traveled for pleasure and comfort, there have also been those who have traveled for company or entertainment and these individuals have contributed to the growth of the places they have visited, whether to a summit, session, workshop, event, or other location. That brought everyone to those locations, resulting in the formation of the "event tourism" industry, which has since grown into a multibillion dollar industry (Etiosa, 2012).

Events, as previously noted, play a significant role in a location's growth and are a primary visitor incentive. They have been extensively studied in the literature for their role and impact on the tourism industry. Event tourism has only lately been recognized as a distinct field of study by both the tourism industry and academics. Events have been studied for a long time, but only as part of other disciplines, such as anthropology or geographic location. It was not until academics began publishing a huge number of essays and books on event studies, as well as creating journals and conferences dedicated to events, that event studies began to be taken more seriously. As a result of what they did, they were interested in that area. So "event management" as a rapidly increasing profession, with visitors providing revenue opportunities for organized events has taken off.

As the hotel sector in industrialized countries becomes more and more commonplace, many people fail to comprehend how it influences everyone's lives and how it is linked to the host town and the rest of the world (Cook et al., 2008). It has arisen from the recent development of events that a robust and effective event industry, including practitioners, suppliers, and

266   Event Tourism and Sustainable Community Development

professional bodies has emerged. There has been a considerable impact on the sector due to rapid globalization of markets and communication. A third issue affecting the sector is the increasing number of government laws and regulations, which has created a complicated and demanding environment in which the company must function. "As cited in Allen et al. (2011: 17)."

Special-interest markets have gained traction as a result of rising competition among host cities and tourist destinations in order to reap the benefits and meet economic, social, and environmental objectives. In the 1990s, event tourism organizations and companies sprang up all over the world to help promote and grow events. The number of tourist facilities and organizations, such as the Scotland Tourist Board, has also grown. It is important to note that different significant parties are currently working to improve events as vehicles for "economic development, nation-building, entrepreneurial development and location marketing" at the present time. A growing number of nongovernmental groups, such as businesses and corporations, are promoting their goods and services through the use of events. There has been a chain reaction of notable events because a topic or cause has grabbed the interest of local communities, social groups, and individuals (Allen et al., 2011).

18.3 FEATURES OR CHARACTERISTICS OF EVENT TOURISM

The key components of Event Tourism can be extrapolated from all associated information, based on the globally acknowledged concept of events. On the basis of this, a compiled overview of the most common elements of event tourism are as follows;

1. Generally "One in a Lifetime"—These are frequently "once in a lifetime" experiences for the performers (Wagen, 2009). Some only happen once or twice a year, if at all, and on predetermined dates (Getz, 1989).
2. Affordability—They can be fairly expensive to stage. Physical, environmental, and human resources in large quantities are required.
3. Short period—They often occur in a short period of time (Wagen, 2009). The duration is usually predetermined.
4. Open—"It must be open to the general public (Getz, 1989). It must be capable of attracting large groups of tourists" (Jago and Shaw, 1998).

5. Substantial and Precise Planning—They demand substantial and detailed planning (Wagen, 2009). It features a well-organized program of large activities that must be implemented in a scientific manner.

6. Development Objective—It must be able to develop locally (Jago and Shaw, 1998). "The purpose of a tourism event is to arouse travelers' interest in visiting a specific area, increase tourism and, as a result, economic development."

7. High-Risk—They pose a significant financial and bodily risk. There is typically a lot on the line for everyone involved, including the event management staff (Wagen, 2009).

8. Cross Communication—An event is organized in such a way that it can bring awareness among both citizens and tourists who attend the event.

9. Picture of the Location—An event can boost the picture of a location in the minds of tourists, followed by the image of the entire world. A social experience is provided by an event, as well as the distinction of being unique and special (Jago and Shaw, 1998).

10. One-of-a-kind attraction—"A tourist event must have highlights and attractions that are specific to the event's area. Apart from that, each event has its own unique appeal that acts as a major draw for tourists to come to the event's venue."

18.4 IMPORTANCE OF ENTREPRENEURSHIP IN EVENT TOURISM INDUSTRY

A wide range of academic disciplines has contributed to the study of entrepreneurship, which has been tackled using a variety of methods and theoretical frameworks (Cornelius et al., 2006). As an industry, event tourism has a significant advantage over other industries when it comes to finding entrepreneurial opportunities and the process of creating a consumable product for tourists. An event-centered strategy to building an essential component of the economy is more likely to bring together a wide range of stakeholders who have different motives for a coordinated approach to building a critical component of the economy.

Since it provides more jobs and stimulates competition, small business entrepreneurship is considered to be the most essential vehicle for starting new businesses in a country. Small businesses play a key role in the economy because they are the primary source of jobs. Innovation, entrepreneurship, and increased productivity are all at the forefront of government initiatives in many countries. Smaller enterprises have a specific significance in the supply chain. They are essential because they stimulate innovation and bring new products, services, and ideas to market.

The primary goal of event tourism is to boost tourism and the local economy in the area where the event takes place. Themes for corporate events are frequently chosen to reflect the company's objectives and ambitions. To encourage event tourism, factors such as the popularity of a certain form of tourism, accessible resources, and the area's unique traits all play a role.

18.5 STAKEHOLDERS ENTREPRENEURSHIP DEVELOPMENT IN EVENT TOURISM

1. Host Group—Anyone or any organization responsible for the conception, organization, and management of an event can serve as a host group. This could be a government agency, a nongovernmental organization, or a private company. National and state government authorities, as well as specialist event management groups, are usually involved in tourism events.

   National and local governments are interested in learning about the economic and social impact of tourism events, as well as how they relate to national and local development goals. They usually host events for "nonprofit" purposes, with the aim of promoting cultural, economic, environmental, and entrepreneurial growth.

2. Event Management Companies—They want to know how well the region's tourism is performing and what the ramifications of holding such events in the market will be, as well as the influence on business growth. The goal of these groups is usually to establish a brand image and to participate in promotional initiatives. These organizations create jobs for local residents, thereby encouraging entrepreneurship.

3. Host community—The term "host community" refers to the people who live at the venue, location, or venue where the event is being held. They may or may not attend the event, but they are interested in learning how tourism and related events will impact local livelihoods, culture, and the environment. Many members of that group

are helping to organize the event. Entrepreneurs concentrate on these activities in order to seize opportunities that develop as a result of regional events.

4. Participants—The targeted market or intended viewers for which the event is being arranged make up this group of stakeholders. These are the potential tourists and visitors in the case of a tourism event. They want to know what they are getting for their money.

5. Environment and Climate Change—One key element that is now affecting the staging of events is climate change, and as a result, there has been a growing global interest and dedication to sustainability and environmental protection (Etiosa, 2012). When it comes to event planning, environmental considerations arise at the same time. Environmental conservation organizations seek to investigate the effects of the upcoming event on the natural environment. This activity promotes new and aspiring entrepreneurs to adopt this exercise as their business plan and to support event organizers in terms of the environment.

6. Promoters— "People or firms who provide money, services, or other resources to events and event organizations in exchange for specified benefits are known as promoters. Many business owners and large businesses used to view sponsorship of an event as a public relations method to create community goodwill, but sponsorship is now viewed as a promotional element in the marketing mix, a way to improve brand awareness and drive sales." In addition, hosting facilitates the creation of strong commercial partnerships and the achievement of corporate goals and sales targets (Etiosa, 2012).

7. Coworkers—This refers to the human resource group that works for event management events, including the technological and logistical team, marketing and promotion team, consultants, event key managers, and even caterers and secretarial employees. As a result, it employs a variety of stakeholders. As a result, a number of event management companies encourage the growth of entrepreneurship.

8. Media and other Promotional Partners—Because they are obligated to disseminate and build the event's brand image, press, and advertising partners are essentially businesses in their own right. This means that choosing the right media source is more important than ever. Traditional media partners such as broadband digital television

and newspapers are being replaced by new-age technology providers who are utilizing the Internet. According to Allen, many events now include digital platforms on their websites that allow for feedback, comments, and suggestions, as well as the ability to trade events and even contribute to event planning and programming. Event communication can be more individualized and engaging using social media events such as "Facebook, Twitter, Youtube, Flickr, and LinkedIn." Allen et al. (2011).

9. Agents of Safety and Security—In the case of major events like the Olympics, the safety and security of the host people and the safety and well-being of visitors and tourists are of the utmost importance. Organizations tasked with the safety and security of the event site, as well as the venue itself, are interested in learning about the event's scope, size, anticipated attendance, and any other unique features. Moreover, they are concerned about the event's timing and duration in this scenario Entrepreneurs, on the other hand, see this as an opportunity to support event management businesses by providing security and surveillance services.

18.6 ROLE OF EVENTS IN PROMOTING ENTREPRENEURSHIP

The value or benefits of event tourism can be appreciated by looking at the function they play in tourism variety and the economy. Events play a significant role in the growth and reputation of any location. Hosting events has steadily become one of the methods for promoting the growth of tourism in the host destinations. This is due to the positive impact it has on a destination's community and economy. Crompton (1979) defines a person's picture of a location as the "total of beliefs, thoughts, and impressions that a person has of a location." Furthermore, according to Getz (2008), all organizations participating in hosting an event must have a primary goal of meeting the needs of visitors and promoting them through the most effective media in order to take full advantage of tourism in destination development. The following benefits of having an event at a place, as described by Hall (1992), are

- Improved infrastructure,
- Increased resident pride,
- Improved trade relations,

Enhancing Entrepreneurship in the Event Tourism Industry

- Increased external recognition,
- Increased experience in mass management, and
- Increased growth in the region of impact.

Tourism is boosted as a result of events. This is one of the main reasons why events play such a significant role in tourism. Role of events is given below:

- Stimulate area economic growth.
- Improve long-term imaging.
- Boost regional community pride.
- Historic or important events play a role in promoting a place since they are transmitted to millions of people. Thus, industry has followed in the media, entertainment, and tourism industries' footsteps in recent years.
- Cities and towns have added events such as expositions, arts expos, specialized markets, festivals, and fairs to their normal offers in order to attract more tourists and extend their stays (monuments, museums, mountains).

Events are becoming increasingly important in place marketing. Visitors from both domestic and other countries flock to them. By holding cultural events, a location can draw not only tourists but also investment. Job creation and occupation diversification are two benefits of event-related tourism. Using festivals and events, rural and small towns alike can now take advantage of the same advantages as big metropolis. Rural areas can benefit from tourism and the introduction of signature events. Because of the existing infrastructure, smaller events may be put on with minimal financial outlay.

In low or medium tourist seasons, events can help draw attention to and promote tourist sites and infrastructure, which is especially advantageous because it reduces seasonal unpredictability. Make the most and rationalize the use of certain spaces with these tools. In addition to sharing aesthetic and cultural heritage, the preservation of these locations may bring financial rewards.

The role of events and the destination image is becoming increasingly important for enterprises that have the potential to communicate the attributes, beliefs, and personality of the event and carefully advertise it. Organizing events, according to Dwyer and Forsyth (2009), can enhance the public image of a city or region, make it easier for businesses to network, and boost civic pride while also providing social and cultural benefits, educational opportunities, and conduits for the transmission of new technologies.

Host communities and the places they live in can both benefit from bringing in more short- and long-term tourists when they host events. According to Boo and Busser (2006), events have a significant impact on the perception of a place, and they suggest a study strategy based on empirical investigations to corroborate this link. According to Baloglu and Mangaloglu (2001), destinations compete primarily on the basis of their image among clients, which means that event communication and marketing are crucial events in the creation of any competitive strategy. Despite the fact that event-based tourism has a significant economic impact, it is becoming increasingly important in the context of destination branding (Simeon and Buonincontri, 2011). Destination managers can use events as part of their marketing strategy because they can be easily linked to a specific area (Baloglu and Mangaloglu, 2001). In the short and long term, branding can assist the place and group organizing the event improve its image while also increasing the number of attendees.

18.7 ECONOMIC IMPACTS OF EVENT TOURISM

The economic benefits of event tourism and tourism growth are the driving factor. Foreign tourist is easier to analyze than local tourism, yet depending on the scale and nature of the event, both groups often gain financially. Events can have a variety of effects on the host town, including the generation of revenue in foreign currencies and the development of new jobs (Etiosa, 2012). Host towns can use events to showcase their abilities, attract potential investors, and encourage new business opportunities. Economic advantages accrue to the local economy as a result of the events that host communities host annually. An additional benefit to the host community is the development of jobs as a result of visitors' spending during an event (Etiosa, 2012). It is therefore possible to declare the following advantages: Tourist visits and stay lengths will increase as well as jobs and tax revenue will rise as a result.

18.8 CHALLENGES FACED BY ENTREPRENEURS IN ORGANIZING EVENTS

Because event tourism is such a fiercely competitive market, any government interested in tapping into it will have to think far in advance. The success of an event depends greatly on human characteristics such as coworkers, attendees, and host cities when planning one. Both internal and external problems confront event planners. Decisions that are made in a methodical manner would take into account a country's distinct geography, economics, political, and social variables while deciding what events to pursue. Experts have identified five common issues that a country must overcome in order to successfully design and manage an event for international visitors. Organizing an event will get more difficult if you don't. In this section, we'll talk about the following issues:

The term "seasonality" refers to the occurrence of something at a specific period of year. Labor and capacity utilization are hampered in tourism destinations because of seasonality, according to Fletcher (2012). The issue of seasonality in event planning should be approached in a proactive manner by emphasizing activities that draw people off-peak times (Chalip, 2004).

Organizing an event requires a strategic match between the host site and the type of event to be held in terms of promotion and branding (Masterman, 2009). To have a successful event, it must be connected to the destination in some way, either whole or in part. For example, a roster of performers for an art concert should include local artists. In order for it to be effective, it must build a connection between its target audience and the intended goal. Linking an event with a location is insufficient, say Harrison-Hill and Chalip (2006). Effective negotiation and strategic planning are required by marketers when describing in marketing communications the characteristics and advantages they hope their event will bring to the destination brand.

18.9 GROWTH IN THE INDUSTRY

Local event organizers' skill, competence, and professionalism may make it difficult for an event management company to reach a global audience. According to Getz's (2013) work, these are all part of his facilitation function that includes crucial areas such as training and education.

18.10 FUNDING

One of the biggest challenges for event planners is raising money and finding sources of funding for their events Public or private support for an event can vary widely depending on its nature and expected return on investment. Government funding might take the form of grants, subsidies, or sponsorships.

18.11 PARTNERSHIP

One of the most significant aspects of partnership is the coordination and interaction between the many stakeholders. Event tourism should also be promoted to local governments and government entities. It is the responsibility of the many trades and professional organizations that represent tourism and events to identify and explain to their members the reciprocal advantages of event tourism. Involving and educating the local populace is also critical in order to make them aware of the benefits of event tourism. Event tourism has a few distinguishing traits, as the following list illustrates:

- In addition to the economic, social, and cultural benefits that it brings to a location, it is a temporary phenomenon.
- It can accommodate large crowds, eat up a lot of real estate, and cost a lot of money. Economic diversification and global integration are bolstered as a result of this.
- Community opposition, authenticity loss, reputational damage, exploitation, and opportunity costs are just a few of the drawbacks to mass tourism.

18.12 OPPORTUNITIES IN THE EVENT TOURISM SECTOR

The term "entrepreneur" is widely used in business and economics, both colloquially and technically. Even while entrepreneurship has many different names, it is impossible to pin down one concept that encompasses all of them. According to Davidson (2003), entrepreneurs are typically regarded as agents of change who offer new and innovative ideas to companies in order for them to grow and prosper. They are innovative because they start from scratch and develop a concept from the ground up. From the point of view of events management, one or more individuals are said to be "event entrepreneurs" when they design and implement their own events. If the event is to be a success, the event entrepreneur must identify a market gap and create an event that meets the demands of the intended audience.

Most people do not consider event tourism to be a legitimate vocation in and of itself. Location marketing and administrative institutions, such as national tourism offices, are commonly seen as having this purpose or specialization. Event development agencies (as opposed to policy, arts, and culture agencies that also deal with scheduled events) fully embrace event tourism, and there is a rising number of associated professional pathways

Enhancing Entrepreneurship in the Event Tourism Industry 275

or technical responsibilities, as depicted in Figure 3. Many of these activities have been studied and practiced extensively, as the following literature review shows.

TABLE 18.1 Event Tourism Career Paths and Their Areas of Expertise.

Events tourism career paths	Tasks; areas of expertise
Event enabler/ manager	• Involvement with conference and exposition centers, as well as other venues, as a liaison for the purpose of helping events in the destination fulfil their tourism potential
	• liaison with sports and other organizations that put on sporting and other activities
Event producer	• organize and produce events for the sake of tourism
	• management of stakeholders (with numerous event partners)
Planner	• Create a plan for reaching your destination
	• Event planning and product development should be integrated.
Strategist and research analyzer	• Promote event tourism by working with policymakers
	• Conduct an investigation (e.g., feasibility studies, demand forecasting, impact assessments, and performance evaluations)
Event auction	• Be a part of the action by bidding on events
	• Establish connections that will lead to the establishment of successful events for the area
Event support	• Assist events by providing fundamental as well as specialized services (e.g., travel and logistics; accommodation and venue booking; supplier contacts)

Source: Original (created by author).

For tour operators and tour guides, there is a wide range of options to choose from because the hotel sector has grown steadily over the previous few decades. Because a tour guide's modes of transportation are often highlighted, making choices can be difficult. Most typical tours offered by tour operators include comprehensive trips, charters, whisked deluxe trips, fishing/sports tours, historical/art tours, four-wheel drives, journey, day and group tours as well as wine tastings and cookery classes. It was a 2015 Tourism Booster. With this type of company, you don't need a large amount of money to get started, and you can expect to see great results. In addition to helping you organize the entire event, a company that specializes in event planning can assist you in securing venue space and providing guidance on specific themes. Creative problem solving and a willingness to try new things are essential to success in this sector. (Wilson, 2009).

18.13 EXPECTED CONTRIBUTIONS OF THE RESEARCH

An in-depth review of the existing literature, as well as a qualitative method approach, are used in this study. Academics and practitioners alike will benefit greatly from the study's findings. Event tourist motivation and visitor management, and entrepreneur motivation, are two areas where the study contributes. As a second benefit, the insights can be used as strategic tools to inform future organizational initiatives. The research offered in this well-written essay has the potential to contribute in the expansion of event tourism as a viable business model.

18.14 CONCLUSIONS

According to the current article, the growth of event tourism entrepreneurship has become increasingly relevant for entrepreneurs who recognize the importance of organizing events to a location's brand and positioning. A deeper knowledge of the role that events play in fostering entrepreneurship and giving environmentally friendly tourist experiences will be gained through the examination of these factors.

While providing a wide range of entrepreneurial employment options for locals and others, the event tourism industry also helps migrants build social norms and financial activities. Because of its adaptability, low startup costs, and cultural expectations, a tiny hotel business attracts a sizable section of the general population. Visitors provide a potential market for organized events, and the tourism industry has become an important factor in the growth and appeal of "event management," a rapidly increasing profession. As a result, event tourism has a significant impact on both enterprise and population income.

It was determined in this study that tourism offerings and demand might be enhanced through events, and that these events may also contribute to entrepreneurship growth. Special events, especially those that are well-planned and well-marketed, can be a powerful tool for drawing a diverse range of people. For this reason, events must be assessed not just in terms of their monetary value but also in terms of their contribution to the development of a positive entrepreneurial mindset.

18.15 FUTURE SCOPE

Future research should examine the role of event tourism in promoting entrepreneurialism, with a specific focus on the impact of event tourism on startup growth. Using the findings of these studies can help young entrepreneurs in their growth by supporting them with marketing and investment plans that are designed to compete with other regions of the same demographics.

KEYWORDS

- **entrepreneurship**
- **event tourism industry**
- **employment**
- **stakeholders**
- **career**
- **challenges**

REFERENCES

Baloglu, S.; Mangaloglu, M. Tourism Destination Images of Turkey, Egypt, Greece, and Italy as Perceived by US-Based Tour Operators and Travel Agents. *Tour. Manage.* **2001,** *22* (1), 1–9.

Boo, S.; Busser, J. A. The Hierarchical Influence of Visitor Characteristics on Tourism Destination Images. *J. Travel Tour. Market.* **2006,** *19* (4), 55–67.

Bowdin, G.; O'Toole, W.; Allen, J.; Harris, R.; McDonnell, I. *Events Management;* Routledge, 2006.

Chalip, L.; McGuirty, J. Bundling Sport Events with the Host Destination. *J. Sport Tour.* **2004,** *9* (3), 267–282.

Chaulagain, M. K.; Maskey, A. Sport Tourism: Development and Promotions of Finnish Cricket, 2013.

Connor, K. M.; Davidson, J.R. Development of a New Resilience Scale: The Connor-Davidson Resilience Scale (CD-RISC). *Depress. Anx.* **2003,** *18* (2), 76–82.

Cornelius, B.; Landström, H.; Persson, O. Entrepreneurial Studies: The Dynamic Research Front of a Developing Social Science. *Entrepreneurship Theory Pract.* **2006,** *30* (3), 375–398.

Crompton, J. L. Motivations for pleasure vacation. *Ann. Tour. Res.* **1979,** *6* (4), 408–424.

Dwyer, L.; Forsyth, P. Public Sector Support for Special Events. *East. Econ. J.* **2009,** *35* (4), 481–499.

Etiosa, O. The Impact of Event Tourism on Host Communities. Central Ostrobothnia Universitiy of Applied Sciences, Pietarsaari, 2012. https://www.theseus.fi/bitstream/handle/10024/43714/omoregie_etiosa.pdf?sequenc e=1

Fletcher, Q. E.; Speakman, J. R.; Boutin, S.; McAdam, A. G.; Woods, S. B.; Humphries, M. M. Seasonal Stage Differences Overwhelm Environmental and Individual Factors as Determinants of Energy Expenditure in Free-Ranging Red Squirrels. *Funct. Ecol.* **2012,** *26* (3), 677–687.

Getz, D. Special Events: Defining the Product. *Tour. Manage.* **1989,** *10* (2), 125–137.

Getz, D. *Festivals, Special Events, and Tourism*; Van Nostrand Rheinhold: New York, NY, 1991.

Getz, D. *Event Management and Event Tourism*; Cognizant Communication: New York, NY, 1997.

Getz, D. Trends and Issues in Sport Event Tourism. *Tour. Recreat. Res.* **1997,** *22* (2), 61–62.

Getz, D. *Event Management and Event Tourism*, 2nd ed.; Cognizant: New York, 2005.

Getz, D. Event Tourism: Definition, Evolution, and Research. *Tour. Manage.* **2008,** *29* (3), 403–428.

Getz, D. The Nature and Scope of Festival Studies. *Int. J. Event Manage. Res.* **2010,** *5* (1), 1–47.

Harrison-Hill, T.; Chalip, L. Business Studies: Concepts and Paradigms Marketing Sport Tourism: Creating Synergy between Sport and Destination, 2006.

Hernández-Mogollón, J. M.; Folgado-Fernández, J. A.; Duarte, P. A. O. Event Tourism Analysis and State of the Art. *Eur. J. Tour. Hospital. Recreat.* **2014,** *5* (2), 83–102.

Jago, L. K.; Shaw, R. N. Special Events: A Conceptual and Definitional Framework. *Fest. Manage. Event Tour.* **1998,** *5* (1–2), 21–32.

Piva, L.; Cerutti, S.; Prats, L.; Raj, R. Enhancing Brand Image Through Events and Cultural Festivals: The Perspective of the Stresa Festival's Visitors. *J. Tour. Cult. Territor. Dev.* **2017,** *8* (15), 99–116.

Simeon, M. I.; Buonincontri, P. Cultural Event as a Territorial Marketing Tool: The Case of the Ravello Festival on the Italian Amalfi Coast. *J. Hospital. Market. Manage.* **2011,** *20* (3–4), 385–406.

Trueman, M.; Cook, D.; Cornelius, N. Creative Dimensions for Branding and Regeneration: Overcoming Negative Perceptions of a City. *Place Brand. Public Diplom.* **2008,** *4* (1), 29–44.

Van der Wagen, L. *Human Resource Management for Events*; Routledge, 2009.

Wilson, J. Social Networking: The Business Case. *Eng. Technol.* **2009,** *4* (10), 54–56.

CHAPTER 19

Rural Event Tourism: Developing Sustainable Rural Event Tourism for the Development of the Community

ANILA THOMAS

Department of Tourism and Travel Management, Jyoti Nivas College Autonomous, Bangalore, Karnataka, India

ABSTRACT

Community involvement in rural event tourism offers a deeper sense of social values. Local/regional festivals and fairs are a source of income for communities and are vital for the development and preservation of ethnicity by promoting the aesthetic value of the local community. This chapter reflects on the theoretical understanding of rural event tourism and rural events and festivals as a driving force for sustainable development. The main objective of this study is to establish a creative and practical, socially responsible method for economic development by supporting rural/regional/local event tourism initiatives. The paper also aims to recognize and appreciate the role of the society in strengthening and enhancing the authentic cultural values of rural areas.

The study uses qualitative research methods using an exploratory approach to synthesize the conceptual foundations of rural activities, with a view to recognize the ethical and credible cultural practices through different theoretical or literary perceptions. The paper utilizes conceptual methods of study in order to establish a theoretical structure, based primarily on the observation and interpretation of findings, previous simulations, and related works. The results of the study provide an insight into possibilities

---

Please note that few chapters were submitted during the peak of the pandemic. The long period of time to publish (due to supply chain and other issues) may have changed the perspectives presented in the chapter altogether.

Event Tourism and Sustainable Community Development: Advances, Effects, and Implications.
Ekta Dhariwal, Shruti Arora, Anukrati Sharma, Azizul Hassan (Eds.)
© 2024 Apple Academic Press, Inc. Co-published with CRC Press (Taylor & Francis)

of conserving various rural activities and suggests interventions to construct an ecosystem that is fully sustainable. The results also indicate that rural stakeholders carry out a variety of activities and event managers will initiate measures that encourage satisfaction and sustainable development.

19.1 INTRODUCTION

The importance of community involvement in tourism has been widely recognized as critical to its long-term viability. It is emphasized from the considerations of profitability, innovation, and business development. Community ownership, sustainable rural surveillance, limited outflows and reverse supply, efficient in resolving disputes, enhances in the local community's sociocultural habitats, and upgraded sustainability are all advantages of this type of tourism. The income generated by tourism in the communities is circulated in terms of expectations; either equally divided among all residents or spent wisely. Several rural tourism projects are intended to enhance in regional development. In its face of escalating agrarian upheavals in emerging regions, the hardest task persists supplying inclusiveness to enormous sectors of the society who have been repeatedly denied of essential services such as health and skills training. Rural tourism cannot be a yet another service for achieving objectives like equality and emancipation. Moreover, if someone is aiming for people-centered tourism, this attribute is both important and useful. The development of Rural Tourism destinations not only transforms an area's physical landscape but also greatly impacts the community's social relationships (Hwang et al., 2012). If tourism growth goes beyond the capabilities of a community, a society's social status endures enormous changes and upheavals. It is imperative to analyze the community-based influence of the tourism development and to clearly show to what extent communities seem to be ready to coordinate with tourism support collaborators. Because the comprehensive development of tourism reflects on meaningful deliberations between tourists and hosts, it is local residents who will help tourism over time. In order to recognize the sustainable growth of tourism, both community behaviors and attitudes are critical. In social sustainability, identifying effects of tourism activities and influencing communal circumstances are extremely important. Community participation promises to improve the efficiency of a society to demand the effectiveness of sustainable tourism initiatives and to safeguard itself against harmful effects (Hwang et al., 2012). It is accountable in relation to the environment, the various benefits to the society, and the restoration and progression of cultural aspects, art and craft, and ethnicities that can often stagnate in rural locations.

Getting involved in a traditional village life is the focus of rural tourism. It is found that nearly 70% of the Indian population still lives in rural areas of the country and relies on agriculture for a living. Rural tourism provides people in rural areas with an additional source of income in the nonagricultural sector and undoubtedly increases our export earnings. Rural tourism will accelerate the development process and provide an opportunity for village residents to connect with others around the world (EQUATIONS, 2008). The merchandise of rural artisans will find a favorable environment. As per the "Evaluation cum Impact Study of Rural Tourism Projects" by ACNielsen ORG-MARG Pvt. Ltd. (2012), the majority of Indians live in villages, and for the rest of the world to understand the true spirit of India, it is necessary to look into the sociocultural life in rural areas. Understanding the role of rural tourism for the ultimate growth of the industry, the Government of India initiated the procedures of rural tourism development, brand management, and promotion. During this process, the government subsidized a lot of initiatives targeted at enhancing the country's rural tourism industry. The Government of India's Ministry of Tourism initiated a number of strategies to encourage rural tourism in order to create opportunities for the rural communities to strengthen their living conditions through initiatives. The quantity of sports and cultural events seeking to encourage vacationers from all over the world has increased several times around in the last couple of decades (Jamieson, 2014). To increase its customer base and elongate their accommodation, urban centers have introduced new events such as art shows, craft fairs, themed marketplaces, festivals, and fairs to their traditional offerings.

19.2 RESOURCE SUSTAINABILITY OF RURAL REGIONS IN INDIA

Events allow us to find recognition and focus on promoting the tourist destinations and infrastructural facilities of rural areas. They enable the optimization and rationalization behind the use of particular areas and their resources. The sustainability of these assets may yield economic advantages as well as the dispersal of architectural and cultural legacy. Locations may stimulate not only visitors but also investment opportunities through cultural events. The tourism industry that endorses events creates jobs and diversifies the economy. Event-based tourism, according to Kotler et al. (2006), is an essential element of development initiatives. Living in rural or remote societies mostly use festivals and events to significantly expand and generate relatively similar financial advantages as larger cities. Tourism and the institutionalization of connector events can assist in addressing the problems that rural areas face. Since the facilities seem to be in central location, different events necessitate very less funding to progress.

Each village seems to have something locally inspired, and it is what we want to enhance and strive to do even if, at the end of each day, our goal was to identify specific rural areas that were connected to existing circuits and destinations. The motive has always been to stimulate tourists toward these localities and succeed in making them a part of the destination, so that even though tourists move to different locations, they must also go over there, representing a significant compounding impact in terms of quality of life and work opportunities. As such, in several rural areas, people educate natives to be facilitators, whereas in other places, clients are using the existing strategic position to offer each other advanced-level investment returns since services are available there and can acquire. Consequently, there seems to be a number of ethnic encounters in some of these rural communities, and there was still a lot of interaction easily accessible. The idea of socially responsible tourism on a community basis offers significant benefits in terms of community resource utilization (Nicolaides, 2020). It also promotes a more efficient management of rural resources.

Rural tourism initiatives are fundamentally a societal interference in rural areas, and it is quite inclined that certain confrontations will arise. While societies actively participate in tourism, it must also be recognized that perhaps the extend where a particular location partakes can and will differ considerably on a series of influencing variables, both intrinsic and external (Huang and Stewart, 1996). Tourism cannot and may not be the alternative to the agrarian conflict, and its adoption should not be viewed as an alternative for yet more balanced and safe livelihood options. This is especially important given that tourism is a consumption-based strategy that helps to replace production-based livelihood opportunities in rural areas (Fun et al., 2014).

In effect to extreme weather conditions, diminishing agricultural activities, and productions and trade relations, rural communities in India have encountered substantial economic, lifestyle, and societal changes. Mostly as a result, local communities are dealing with mental and behavioral challenges. Events in rural communities offer additional valuable recreational prospects for the community to come together through a frame of reference (Irshad, 2011). However, event planning and administration place emphasis on the participation of various agencies with equally strong ideologies.

19.3 RURAL EVENT TOURISM: ATTRIBUTES AND PRACTICES

Events become such an essential component of tourism product development and are a part of the culture. Events are indeed an essential part for local and global communities by acting as an intermediary in the emergence, revitalization, and rebuilding of places, paving the way for new progression and awakening (Pernecky, 2015). When considering several other service providers such as the hospitality business, event management functions are absolutely remarkable. Events come under the purview of service sector and experience-based enterprises that cause responsiveness and working toward the distinct expectations of divergent companies, clients, and persons. Events not only consider local people's outlook on life, but also demonstrate social values and practices, expectations and aspirations, and linkage with the environment (Pernecky and Luck, 2013). Events embedded with our sociocultural framework are interdependent with many facets of society and cover the sociocultural, monetary, contemporary, and spiritual dimensions.

Economically viable areas of digital recognition have expanded mostly in practise of difficulties such as inaccessibility, emotional instability, expertise, and access to resources. Tourism itself is tested to identify of that as well, with events and festivals playing a major role. Amidst the idea that the number of festival and event-related published research focuses on either their strategic thinking requirements or their business viability, the terminology of "triple bottom line" technique has recently converted into festivals/events research.

Special events nowadays are enormously popular in rural areas mostly as mechanism of reviving regional economy. Festivals and community events contribute in destination attractiveness as image makers, animators of transient attractions, and catalysts for several other innovations. The term "event" is sometimes used to identify a variety of operations, most of which have very unique attributes. Getz (2008) stated in his work "Event tourism: Definition, evolution, and research," that events are momentary occasions, either intentional or accidental, and also that they usually have a constant range, which will be classically determined or broadly testified for scheduled events. Events can also be identified and sometimes even described in various ways based on their size, shape, and functionality. Special events, hallmark events, mega events, carnivals, trade shows and exhibitions, explorations and displays, social events and other corporate and academic events, major sporting events, and theatre events are some different forms.

Communities are affected by events in both direct and indirect ways. They offer opportunities for social interaction, skills enhancement, getting involved, and the recognition of interpersonal, ethnic, monetary, and environmental development. Community events have the power to stimulate residents and visitors on a regional, national, and international scale (Backman et al., 1995). Events aid in creating interest and promoting tourist destinations and infrastructural facilities. They allow you to maximize and rationalize the use of specific spaces. The sustainability of these areas may lead to significant financial gains as well as the dissemination of historical and literary legacies. Festivals can have a wide variety of benefits for local community, especially when they attract people outside the area. It is indeed recognized that the higher the involvement of community residents and service providers in the delivery of services, food, beverages, and entertainment venues, the higher the opportunity for the growth of the local area (Mair and Duffy, 2015). Local retailers, craftsmen, artisans, restaurant workers, hoteliers, and innkeepers may earn a substantial portion of their total revenue during an event.

Local events are indeed commercializing enterprises and spurring economic growth of the country. Government agencies provide an array of goods and services to effectively boost community events in rural areas. Community events can contribute significantly to regional development with strategic management, well-defined objectives, regional-level collaborations, and financial support (Moscardo, 2007). Rural communities, on the other hand, frequently organize tourism events in order to boost their regional economy. Such an estimation is insufficient to achieve sustainable rural macroeconomic stability. Events help the area's tourism activities, but they are insufficient to revitalize the nation's economy. Apart from the financial benefit of tourism growth, carnivals and special events extend the location's tourist season, build a sense of cultural identity, and make a significant contribution to long-term development. Shift in weather patterns (e.g., increased droughts and heavy rains) have necessitated industry expansion in regions completely dependent on regional economies like agriculture or particularly focused tourism sector. Events and festivals are already used successfully in many of these areas to attract people to areas that have conventionally seemed to have a seasonal tourist appeal (Backman et al., 1995).

The potential benefits of sustainable implications in organizing local festivals and events (Pirnar and Celebi, 2020) are as follows:

- Sustainable festivals and events are often regional in nature, offering chances for local investors to showcase innovative strategic operations and maximizing their local economic gains.
- Sustainable-based festivals and event operations focus on improving standard of living and well-being of local community.

Rural Event Tourism

- Such events have productive, resilient, and distributive effects for the generations to come and revitalize ethnicities of local traditions and beliefs.
- Sustainable festivals and events emphasize the importance of social responsibilities and duties and critical issues such as changes in climate and its adverse effect, environmental problems of global concern, sustainable frameworks such as waste management practices, the utilization of renewable sources such as solar energy, etc.
- These events facilitate effective social community behavior of customers and enhance cohesiveness and collective ethical stimulation and capacity building.
- Sustainable festivals and events also enhance regional economy by producing skilled jobs, increasing the implications of revenue multipliers and generating significant working environment.
- The interaction, insights, and the appreciation between the people involved in organizing the festivals and events and host communities are supported by efficient and sustainable use of the resources.

Rural events allow for the publicity of the indigenous culture and all it has to show, that might motivate those around relocate to the area for wellness reasons and to establish additional establishments. Trying to attract inhabitants is critical for rural communities that have experienced internal migration as a result of deliberate difficulties and water scarcity. Studies have identified that village events necessitate the involvement of well-established and highly regarded residents from the community in planning and coordinating, leveraging their established networks and perceptions of the brand to resolve the said resentment (Capriello and Rotherham, 2011). Besides that, adaptation strategies must try to persuade and identify opportunities in order to maintain their contentment and, as a result, participation in the event.

Event competition has resulted in a significant overdependence on project governance in event organization. To maintain community participation, event managers must address the requirements of target audience while also answering to desired outcomes. The involvement of qualified and able stakeholders in event processes and operations is really required to support rural communities (Reid, 2011). Substantially, if event stakeholder involvement declines, rural events will descend into chaos, decreasing the number of social and recreational possibilities for inhabitants who are already suffering from insecurity, declining agricultural produces, and famine. Rural event working groups are purely voluntary and are comprised of inhabitants and/or community groups mostly from surrounding neighborhoods. Additionally, the number and efficiency of people who are prepared to coordinate social events and activities in rural communities are relatively small. The implications of rural events highlighted the pattern of the initial framework of associates, recognizing the importance of common standard in depiction and competence. To accomplish strategic goals, rural events companies rely on the skill sets, expertise, and productive capacity of members of society from the community. The community, local organizations, regional office, commercial enterprise, manufacturing sector, corporate partners, investors, benefactors, volunteer groups, and associated groups are some of the broad segments of rural event stakeholders (Pernecky, 2015).

19.4 METHODOLOGY

A thematic content analysis approach (Cho and Lee, 2014) has been used to identify patterns of information obtained related to explore the effects and implications of events and festivals for community development by encouraging sustainable event tourism initiatives. The accurate coding of words and themes entailed a number of risks, particularly when dealing with aggressive societal and environmental issues. The content analysis methodology greatly helped in identifying and classifying the gathered data sources on three different levels, namely based on themes, location, and event typology. At the first level, the sources were divided into three main themes:

- Economic—regarding financial benefits to local, regional, and national economies as a result of organizing events and festivals;
- Social and cultural—repercussions include rapid expansion and revitalization of ethnic diversity, as well as social heritage.
- Environmental—factors relating to the substantial ecological impact of events and festivals on rural areas.

During the second level of analysis, the sources were documented with regard to the location of the events and festivals. Rural, urban, and suburban were the categories used to define them in the literary sources that described them.

The third level of analysis was linked to the event's typology:

- Cultural: events focusing on the ethics or lifestyle of a rural community or the heritage or cultural exchange of a rural area
- Rural sports and games: community events or practices that expose people to a broader range of rural sporting activities (Jamieson, 2014).

- Diverse art forms: The events showcased a variety of artistic talents, including martial arts and folk arts.
- Events/melas with a specific theme, such as culinary skills, handicrafts, pottery-making, and so on, are of particular interest.

Several significant findings emerged from the content analysis. Even though number of literary sources trying to cover the effects of rural events is relatively small, it still accounts for a sizable proportion of all sources pertaining to festivals and events observed during preparatory reviews. Overall, 39% of the source coverage of the effects of events and festivals is purely related to economic implications, 28% with comprehensive socio-cultural pertinence, and 19% with local community welfare. Environmental effects account for 14% of source coverage.

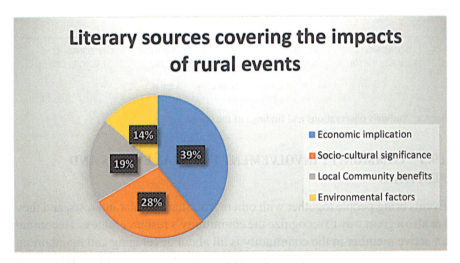

Source: Author's observations and findings of the study

Comprehensively, studies are indeed focused on economic consequences of events, which may reflect broader social understandings of the possible effects of events and festivals. Furthermore, it is evident from the content analysis that there are a few previous studies with definite explanations to sociocultural importance. The study also reveals that there are very few studies on the influence of events on the regional concept of sustainability.

According to an evidence on the impact documented by event location typology, 81% of the reviews, which mostly focused at social implications, have been talking about festivals in either urban or suburban areas. In addition, half of the articles, that stressed the importance of environmental impacts, were about events and festivals hosted in rural areas. Local community was clearly a key element of media interest, with 60% of articles describing festivals in rural areas. The graph below depicts these findings:

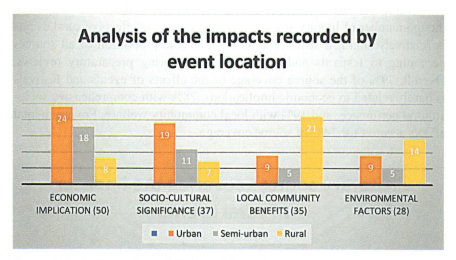

Source: Author's observations and findings of the study

19.5 COMMUNITY INVOLVEMENT IN RURAL EVENTS AND FESTIVALS

Events bring people together with others who share similar interests, and they are also a great way to recognize the community's resourcefulness. Becoming an active member in the community is all about developing and maintaining relationships. There seems to be little research into why some communities really are involved in event planning and make a significant contribution to the special event. This study explores how events engage local residents and recognizes methods for appreciating and broadening community involvement. The magnitude of community participation however depends on the interests of the involved parties and their inclusiveness. It is because the local people may not have a clearly defined, standardized interest. The aspirations change over time between communities and in the social groups, depending on various societal expectations, responsibilities, and value systems (Panyik et al., 2011). Although not all interested parties ought to be and must never be involved uniformly in the decision-making procedures, it is important to identify and understand all preferences.

Rural Event Tourism

The available resources assisted toward the development of a conceptual framework showcasing the appropriate community participation in rural events (Reid, 2003). The framework illustrates the inter-relationships between communities, as well as active involvement in the development of events and the implications of that collaboration.

19.6 MODEL FRAMEWORK FOR COMMUNITY INVOLVEMENT IN RURAL EVENTS

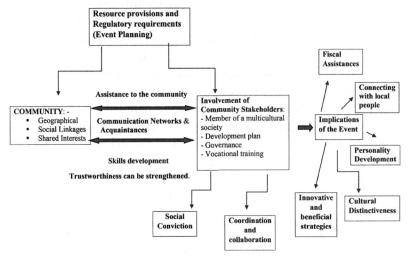

FIGURE 19.1 A conceptual framework of the importance of ethical community participation in rural events (Source: Thematic Analysis of the collected Sources and observations)

A community's cultural norms will have a significant impact on the society as well as its practices and events. Through common ties, people are able to recognize and express affiliation in the community. The links and patterns of collaborations within communities serve to enhance the community by magnifying the sociocultural credibility and trust of participants and transferring knowledge among members (Ayazlar and Ayazlar, 2015).

Furthermore, community cohesion, solidarity, appreciation, and collaboration are probable outcomes of incorporating and developing these social relationships. Community participation in event planning makes use of these strong ties to evaluate specific event stakeholders and to focus on ensuring that multicultural community groups are represented and could communicate their thoughts, beliefs, and strategic goals in event planning (Ayazlar and Ayazlar, 2015). These affiliations and encounters are reinforced further by incorporating the community's indigenous knowledge. Furthermore, those in the community stakeholder group are building leadership skills, understanding through experience, and knowledge transfer. All of these features are intended to increase social trust, reciprocity, respect, and cooperation.

Participative leadership appears to be another ideologically charged term, and it can be interpreted as encouraging and facilitating societies to have a greater connection to and control over what happens in their regular lifestyle. This simply means that a motivated community may have complete control and power over existing resources, fully accountable and reflective local leadership, and fragmented and liberalized facilities, all within equitable surroundings (Ertuna and Kirbas, 2012). This is especially important for rural communities looking to mitigate the negative consequences of recent events and strengthen resources for future growth.

It further supplies the rural community with various motivational attributes. Financial benefits can be achieved from attracting tourists to the community to attend these events, as well as from the money that they spend within the community that might not otherwise actually happen. The event gives the community an awareness of celebrations and special occasions, as well as a chance to build relationships. This is significant for strengthening community social networks and the well-being of associates in rural areas who have had to take into consideration trials and tribulations. Events could indeed help to foster a commitment to social ethnicity both internally and externally. Locally, through some kind of shared vision and admiration in the event, and regionally, by people recognizing the area's location and the reality of an event. Furthermore, the use and progression of these systems and linkages in developing and planning the event make a significant contribution to the management of resources inventory of social value within the community as well as the development of attributing even further to these returns.

19.7 IMPACTS OF COMMUNITY EVENTS AND FESTIVALS ON RURAL PLACES

Communities organize special events and festivals to encourage participation, skill development, volunteerism, and social, cultural, economic, and environmental growth (Allen et al., 2020). Community events and festivals can attract tourists and visitors at the regional, national, and global levels. It is impossible to overestimate the significance of community events in our lives. It helps with capacity expansion and plan development. Providing sustainable events seems to be a more comprehensive process to event governance that can stand to gain both event stakeholders and communities affected by the event (Holmes et al., 2015). There are both progressive and idealistic

Rural Event Tourism

intentions for the continuous development of events. Events must recognize three dimensions in order to be sustainable: environmental, economic, and social concerns. Subsequently, event organizers were primarily associated with the economic impacts of events, but the environmental and social impacts have emerged in great significance (Wise, 2020). In recent times, governments and industry groups issued guidance to assist event organizers in creating more sustainable events.

Events provide chances for host communities to demonstrate their knowledge and experience and host prospective buyers and to promote commercial opportunities. Events also affect the host community financially by optimizing operational efficiency because it reflects the advantages for local companies and the community as a whole (Omoregie, 2012). The following table summarizes the various impacts of events on host communities highlighting both benefits and detriments.

TABLE 19.1 Impacts of Events: Benefits and Detriments.

	Benefits	Detriments
Sociocultural Effects of Events	• Collective opinions—values and culture • Revitalization of ethnicities • Establishing community dominance • Validation of community groups • Greater community contribution • Acquaint with new and challenging ideas • Expansion of cultural perspective	• Community alienation • Manipulation of community • Negative community image • Bad behavior • Substance abuse • Social dislocation • Loss of amenity
Economic Effects of Events	• Destination promotion and increased tourists visits • Extended length of stay • Job creation • Increased tax revenue • Business opportunities	• Community resistance to tourism • Loss of authenticity • Damage to reputation • Exploitation • Opportunity costs
Environmental Effects of Events	• Showcasing the environment • Provision of models for best practice • Increased environmental awareness • Infrastructural legacy • Improved transport and communications • Transformation and restoration of countryside resources	• Environmental degradation • Pollution • Destruction of heritage resources • Noise disturbance • Traffic congestion

Source: ÇOBAN (2016), pp. 465–467.

A number of factors influence the proportion and sharing of benefits, including the desirability of the tourism asset, the type of operation, the nature and extent of community involvement, and whether earnings are retained as private income or regulated partially or entirely into development initiatives or other productivity mechanisms.

Well-managed festivals and events provide a variety of potential benefits to communities in addition to being enjoyable. By definition, festivals attract tourists, which boosts the economy. When visitors return home, they talk about their experiences, so festivals provide free promotional strategies for local businesses. Festivals and events were not only an instrument for tourism growth, destination expansion during different seasons, image building, and regional economic development, but have also evolved over time along with cultural practices (Okech, 2011).

Organizing festivals and events in local communities is a prominent tourism marketing technique. They attract tourists, create jobs in the tourism industry, and spread economic benefits throughout the destination (O'Sullivan and Jackson, 2002). Festivals and local events that provide leisure activities and pleasant visitor experiences also have an impact on the quality of life of the local residents (Allen et al., 2020). Destination marketers and community leaders may be unable to use festivals and local events as a strategic approach to improve people's quality of life because of some kind of unfamiliarity about them.

These are few reasons why more social activities should be organized in every rural region:

- Festivals and fairs help to define a community's identity. Many rural areas hold social events to keep old customs alive or to introduce new ones. Often, communities can highlight what makes them unique, which helps citizens feel proud of their community (Alves et al., 2010). Citizens take better care of their village as a result of their increased sense of belonging, which helps to reduce criminal activity and property destruction.
- Events are beneficial to both tourism and local businesses. Festivals can help local businesses like shops and restaurants grow. Larger events may even attract visitors from outside the area, who will spend more money in the community. As a consequence of rising income, more tax money is necessary to enhance the community across all inhabitants.
- Social gatherings are simply interactive and rewarding. Public activities provide something for all citizens to look forward to,

regardless of age, color, or occupation. Festivals provide residents with the benefits of collaborating to create the event, the excitement of participating in it, and the opportunity to reflect on it afterward.

Culture that reflects a society's practices; its authentic beliefs, social views, and rituals are transferred down from generation to generation, whereas a society is a community or a large gathering of mutually reinforcing traditions, institutions, activities, and interests (Alves et al., 2010). In this context, the potential consequences or effects of events or tourism on a society's culture are critical issues for the host community, event organizers, and other stakeholders in the planning system as a whole (Reid, 2007). This is because events frequently bring visitors or "external stakeholders" into a host community or "society," with the potential for transforming the cultural identity.

Since celebrations and event tourism have the potential to have a sociocultural impact on a host community by reinforcing regional values or traditions, they also have the potential to introduce social and cultural costs. Every event held in a community has immediate social and cultural ramifications for the participants, as well as, in some cases, the relatively large host communities. Sophisticated encounters, such as sporting events or concerts, can have a significant impact (Jamieson, 2014). Events have the power to boost community pride, introduce new and challenging ideas, and revitalize the local village's traditions.

Another benefit that an event can have on a host city is the opportunity to generate additional revenue streams. Local councils utilize events to showcase their expertise, host potential investors, and promote innovative products and services. Economically, events have an impact on a host community by optimizing business strategies to enable local businesses and, through them, the community at large. Another way an event can impact the host community is through employment generation, as tourist spending during events can result in more job openings for the host community. There might be more significant adverse effects than realistic actions on a host community, especially when there has not been adequate research, evaluation, or mitigation put in place. Crowd movement and management, traffic congestion, connectivity and parking, and, most importantly, waste disposal are all significant attributes. Any destination or host community that wishes to offer services to visitors must first build the infrastructure required to sustain these facilities.

Events have a broad spectrum of applications for rural host communities. They have the potential to attract organization's external investment and financial resources to local areas, potentially resulting in economic benefits. This is especially important for rural communities suffering from drought, lower yields and profitability, and outmigration. Participation in events may also help to empower a community to begin the process of revitalizing their rural region through community-driven development (Fong and Lo, 2015). Rural towns must foster their own growth in order to survive and thrive, particularly in light of declining assistance from different stakeholders.

Events could perhaps serve as the basis for community outreach, cognitive ability, and economic expansion, which can have significant implications for future community-driven development (Alves et al., 2010). However, the majority of event research has focused on the economic concerns of events. Only in recent times has there been such a transition in the nature of this research area, with plenty of emphasis placed on the social implications of events. While event tourism can also be used by local community as a catalyst for sustainable development and positioning of destinations, it may have adverse consequences if not carefully planned and structured for the social environment (Omoregie, 2012). One reasonable observation would be that events primarily influence the host communities by establishing a brand equity and ensuring greater sense of responsibility.

19.8 STRATEGIC APPROACH AND INFERENCES ON RURAL EVENTS' FUTURE DEVELOPMENT

The current study was focused to validate those events as effective means for small regions because they can contribute to a wide range of benefits. This study highlighted the importance of assessing the impact of rural events and, as a result, the importance of developing suitable techniques for gathering the data order to generate such dimensions on a continuous basis. This assessment could provide information about the festival's return on investment as well as its impact on the local community. The resulting impact can be quantified to help justify the government's investment. The following strategies and plans may be adopted to provide the intended impacts by analyzing the possible and desired positive outcomes that could result from the events:

- The ecological damage on rural areas is being significantly reduced: Social effects are growing concern that have an impact on the community and should be considered when formulating and implementing the event. Road conditions, overcrowding, and a lack of infrastructure to community facilities available can all have a detrimental societal influence, leads to a feeling of social marginalization and isolation.

- Optimizing the welfare programs requires a degree of community support and inclusion in the strategic planning, which can be accomplished through community events, reviews, participant observations, and other means.
- Limiting the negative effects on rural society: Every event has some sort of environmental impact, which will inevitably increase in proportion to the magnitude of the event. Pollution from automobile emissions, noise, chemicals, sewage, and other negative environmental effects are all common.
- Seeking to make use of all the rural tourism's financial benefits: Events should always aim to benefit the host community and the surrounding region. Tourists who spend money in the area frequently generate economic benefits. To capitalize on this advantage, however, tourists must be encouraged to stay in the area and patronize local services and businesses. As a result, events may be used to target consumers outside of peak tourist seasons, encouraging the use of untapped tourism facilities when demand is lower.
- Productivity gains may be spontaneous, such as those likely to get from the event's staging, or informally, such as creating a convenient background for event attendees can increase the probability of repeat visits and suitable digital and traditional evaluations. Using local producers whenever possible will invariably yield a high profit for the local population than bringing in dealers from outside the region.
- It's indeed important to incorporate a wide range of people in order to obtain a better understanding of their aspirations and inclinations, as well as to facilitate ideas and feedbacks for suitable and feasible alternatives. The best way to accomplish this is through an interactive and resilient framework that addresses a diverse variety of community representatives as partners in the process and support in the tracking out of community values in terms of what appeals most and what transactions are relevant (Ezeuduji, 2015).
- The transport infrastructure to the rural tourist destination should be available to ensure the average rural tourism enthusiast to reach the desired location.
- Tourist accommodation should be provided or developed in such a way that tourists should not have to travel far to connect with the rural tourism venture.

296 Event Tourism and Sustainable Community Development

- Water supply, sewage facilities, power generation, food outlets, and so forth should be included in the proposal so that travelers to rural tourism destinations do not have to drive to a nearby town for these amenities.
- To allow the whole event to be a success, tradesmen require support and assistance for marketing their products, obtaining raw materials, and gaining exposure.
- Discovering if the venture has been economically and socially important to the local people, and whether there will be any socio-economic discrepancies in the proposal.
- Evaluate the inclusion and commitment of the state government, local governments, and nongovernmental organizations in terms of operational involvement, governance, and financial involvement (NGOs).

19.9 CONCLUSIONS

Destination events and festivals, fortunately, are not the only way for a community to strengthen its economic system. The revenue of local events can be accurately measured by looking at consumption habits, demographic characteristics of participants, and market dynamics. As a matter of fact, it is indeed completely obvious that events have the potential to greatly affect societies. Because of the slowdown in rural areas, it is appropriate for them to use as well as expand their own potentials in order to manage the declining trend. By leveraging existing inventories in rural areas, the community is effectively capable of doing things, activate and manage the resources, communicate, and solve problems. As a result, these communities may be able to mobilize expansion and investigate opportunities to alter some of the deterioration and challenges they have faced. Involvement in events is a vital resource for empowering communities to take dominance of their circumstances and lay the groundwork for future growth. However, guaranteeing that everyone, who is involved, is beyond the capacities of even the smallest communities. As a result, the whole observation indicated that even community event stakeholders enhance the likelihood of success for involvement in community events (Reid, 2011).

Event planning experts are in greater competition as the event industry grows and diversifies. Trade groups are becoming enormously important in providing support and guidance to these professionals. As a result, more research is required to determine the active participation of rural communities in event planning, which will assist individuals in developing and utilizing their skills, knowledge, and experience, as well as their resource potential (Simmons, 1994).

The community volunteers have key roles during event planning phases, and this will cut down the cost incurred on professional assistance. This is because the event takes place in their own location, and it is much more effective since people know what exists in the community to benefit and help in organizing events. The participation of local people serves as an advantage as a result of possible implications. Event tourism could perhaps advance only if the stakeholders are sufficiently aware, and the industry benefits from their diverse thoughts and perspectives. Being one of the major influencers, any such indifference reduces the efficiency and resilience of event tourism when members of society are underestimated. It seems that every stakeholder has a right to showcase their apprehensions and a potential to redefine with collaborative work and sensitization (Ololo et al., 2018). These tactics are necessary to guarantee the sustainable growth of event tourism.

Event tourism may lead to economic variability and revenue growth by creating jobs, improving essential services, and growing financial account-ability among urban and rural people. Community-based Tourism develop-ment and participation of local community in various regional events and festivals can help people to become aware of their talents, seek alternative employment and business opportunities, and focus on improving their overall quality of life (Okazaki, 2008). Community events may attract local, national, and international tourists and visitors. Events help to draw attention to and promote attractions and infrastructural facilities. They enable you to make the most of and validate the use of specific areas. The restoration of event venues may lead to significant financial profits including the trans-mission of innovative and societal records. Based on the latest systematic reviews, the greater the region's economic effectiveness, the more efficient local people and vendors are in rendering assistance, food, beverages, and amenities. Local dealers, artists, crafters, entrepreneurs, hotel chains, and shopkeepers may earn a large portion of their yearly revenue during the event (Mottiar et al., 2018). Organizers should build relationships with as many local businesses as possible. Community events should be considered an investment in the village's long-term efficacy by organizers, who should weigh all of the benefits.

Community events and celebrations can contribute significantly to regional development. It is because they are strategically organized; have

298   Event Tourism and Sustainable Community Development

well-defined goals; are collaborative at the local level and are financially supported. Rural areas frequently organize tourism events to uplift their local economies. But, this amount of money is not enough to achieve sustainable rural economic progress. Events help the region's tourism businesses, but they are insufficient to revive the entire economy. Events and festivals help to put an area on the map and differentiate its attractions from those of other comparable areas. Events can also provide a higher return, such as increased community pride and an enhancing brand image.

KEYWORDS

- **rural event tourism**
- **rural events and practices**
- **sustainability**
- **community development**

REFERENCES

ACNielsen ORG-MARG Pvt. Ltd. *Evaluation Cum Impact Study of Rural Tourism Projects*; Ministry of Tourism, Government of India: New Delhi, 2012.

Allen, J.; O'Toole, W.; Harris, R.; McDonnell, I. *Festival and Special Event Management Interactive Wiley E-Text*; John Wiley & Sons, 2020.

Alves, H. M. B.; Cerro, A. M. C.; Martins, A. V. F. Impacts of Small Tourism Events on Rural Places. *J. Place Manage. Dev.* **2010**.

Ayazlar, G.;Ayazlar, R. A. Rural Tourism: A Conceptual Approach. *Tour. Environ. Sustain.* **2015,** 167–184.

Backman, K. F.; Backman, S. J.; Uysal, M.; Sunshine, K. M. Event Tourism: An Examination of Motivations and Activities. *Fest. Manage. Event Tour.* **1995,** *3* (1), 15–24.

Capriello, A.; Rotherham, I. D. Building a Preliminary Model of Event Management for Rural Communities. *J. Hospital. Market. Manage.* **2011,** *20* (3–4), 246–264.

Cho, J. Y.; Lee, E. H. Reducing Confusion About Grounded Theory and Qualitative Content Analysis: Similarities and Differences. *Qual. Rep.* **2014,** *19* (32).

ÇOBAN, Ö. Event Tourism. *Global Iss. Trends Tour.* **2016,** 465–467.

EQUATIONS. Community-Based Rural Tourism in Developing Countries. Some Insights & Lessons from the Endogenous Tourism Project in India. *Making a Difference. Dossier on Community Engagement on Nature Based Tourism in India*; **2008,** 62–68.

Ertuna, B.; Kirbas, G. Local Community Involvement in Rural Tourism Development: The Case of Kastamonu, Turkey. *PASOS Revista de Turismo y Patrimonio Cultural* **2012,** *10* (2), 17–24.

Ezeuduji, I. O. Strategic Event-Based Rural Tourism Development for Sub-Saharan Africa. *Curr. Iss. Tour.* **2015**, *18* (3), 212–228.

Fong, S. F.; Lo, M. C. Community Involvement and Sustainable Rural Tourism Development: Perspectives from the Local Communities. *Eur. J. Tour. Res.* **2015**, *11*, 125–146.

Fun, F. S.; Chiun, L. M.; Songan, P.; Nair, V. The Impact of Local Communities' Involvement and Relationship Quality on Sustainable Rural Tourism in Rural Area, Sarawak. The Moderating Impact of Self-efficacy. *Procedia-Soc. Behav. Sci.* **2014**, *144*, 60–65.

Getz, D. Event Tourism: Definition, Evolution, and Research. *Tour. Manage.* **2008**, *29* (3), 403–428.

Holmes, K.; Hughes, M.; Mair, J.; Carlsen, J. *Events and Sustainability*; Routledge: New York, 2015; pp 1–206.

Huang, Y. H.; Stewart, W. P. Rural Tourism Development: Shifting Basis of Community Solidarity. *J. Travel Res.* **1996**, *34* (4), 26–31.

Hwang, D.; Stewart, W. P.; Ko, D. W. Community Behavior and Sustainable Rural Tourism Development. *J. Travel Res.* **2012**, *51* (3), 328–341.

Irshad, H. Impacts of Community Events and Festivals on Rural Places. *Government of Alberta, Agriculture and Rural Development Division*, 2011.

Jamieson, N. Sport Tourism Events as Community Builders—How Social Capital Helps the "Locals" Cope. *J. Conv. Event Tour.* **2014**, *15* (1), 57–68.

Mair, J.; Duffy, M. Community Events and Social Justice in Urban Growth Areas. *J. Policy Res. Tour. Leisure Events* **2015**, *7* (3), 282–298.

Moscardo, G. Analyzing the Role of Festivals and Events in Regional Development. *Event Manage.* **2007**, *11* (1–2), 23–32.

Mottiar, Z.; Boluk, K.; Kline, C. The Roles of Social Entrepreneurs in Rural Destination Development. *Ann. Tour. Res.* **2018**, *68*, 77–88.

Nicolaides, A. Sustainable Ethical Tourism (SET) and Rural Community Involvement. *Afr. J. Hospital. Tour. Leisure* **2020**, *9* (1), 1–16.

O'Sullivan, D.; Jackson, M. J. Festival Tourism: A Contributor to Sustainable Local Economic Development? *J. Sustain. Tour.* **2002**, *10* (4), 325–342.

Okazaki, E. A Community-Based Tourism Model: Its Conception and Use. *J. Sustain. Tour.* **2008**, *16* (5), 511–529.

Okech, R. N. Promoting Sustainable Festival Events Tourism: A Case Study of Lamu Kenya. *Worldwide Hospitality and Tourism Themes*, 2011.

Ololo, N. G.; Unit, H.; Dieke, P. U. C.; Eze-Uzomaka, P. I. Collaboration and Sensitisation as Strategies for Community Involvement in Nigeria's Event Tourism Development: The Abia State Example. *Collaboration & Co-Creation Opportunities in Tourism* 2018; p 135.

Omoregie, E. The Impacts of Event Tourism on Host Communities: Case: The City of Pietarsaari, 2012; pp 29–34

Panyik, E.; Costa, C.; Rátz, T. Implementing Integrated Rural Tourism: An Event-Based Approach. *Tour. Manage.* **2011**, *32* (6), 1352–1363.

Pernecky, T. Sustainable Leadership in Event Management. *Event Manage.* **2015**, *19* (1), 109–121.

Pernecky, T.; Luck, M. Events in the Age of Sustainability. *Events, Society and Sustainability: Critical and Contemporary Approaches*; 2013; pp 1–12.

Pirnar, İ.; Celebi, D. Sustainable Festival and Event Tourism Management. *Fest. Event Tour. Impacts*; 2020; pp 53–66.

Reid, S. Community Participation in Rural Events: The Potential to Develop and Utilize Social Capital. In *Advances in Convention, Exhibition and Event Research*; Hong Kong Polytechnic University Hong Kong. 2003; pp 42–51.

Reid, S. Identifying Social Consequences of Rural Events. *Event Manage.* **2007,** *11* (1–2), 89–98.

Reid, S. Event Stakeholder Management: Developing Sustainable Rural Event Practices. *Int. J. Event Fest. Manage* **2011.**

Simmons, D. G. Community Participation in Tourism Planning. *Tour. Manage.* **1994,** *15* (2), 98–108.

Wise, N. Urban and Rural Event Tourism and Sustainability: Exploring Economic, Social and Environmental Impacts. *Sustainability* **2020,** *12* (14), 5712, 1–5.

Index

A

Amenities, 22–23
Ashokastami festival, 215–216
Attractions, 22
Australian heritage commission (AHC), 163

B

Biological factors, 171–172
Branding, 219–223
Bunong tradition, 179–180

C

Case studies, 213
    Ashokastami festival, 215–216
    branding, 219–223
    Diwali festival, 218
    events, 214–219
    festivals, 214–219
    Garia puja, 214–215
    Kharchi festival, 217
    Neermahal tourism, 217–218
    Pilak archaeological, 216
    postpandemic tourism, 223–227
    Pous Sankranti fair, 219
    pristine natural beauties, 214
    rich culture, 213–214
    Tirthamukh mela, 219
    tradition, 213–214
    Unakoti festival, 215–216
    unique fairs, 214–219
Catamaran
    growth and development, 65
        literature review, 67–68
        marketing strategies, 71–72
        sustainable development, challenges, 72
        tourism industry, 68–69
        types, 69–70
Citrawarna, 19
    amenities, 22–23

attractions, 22
Cronbach's Alpha analysis
    results of, 24
cultural festival, 20
    attribute, 21
    factor, 21
entertainment, 23
findings
    coefficients of model, 26–27
    correlation analysis, 25–26
    descriptive statistic, 27–28
    general questions, 24–25
    regression analysis, 26
    reliability analysis, 24
    respondents background profile, 24
frequency, 25
mean, 27–28
methodology, 23–24
millennial pull factors, 21–22
model, 27
programs, 22
questionnaires, 24
R square, 26
respondents profile, 25
significant, 26
Collective responsibility model (CRM), 124
Community development
    attributes, 283–286
    community involvement, 288–289
    impacts, 290–294
    methodology, 286–288
    model framework, 289–290
    practices, 283–286
    resource sustainability, 281–282
    strategic approach, 294–296
Community events
    stakeholders, involvement, 113
        assigned responsibilities, 123
        collective responsibility model (CRM), 124
        community-based events, 120

major challenges, 118–119
organizing community events, 121
process, 119–120
public private partnerships, 117–118, 121
shared responsibilities, 123
social capital, 121–122
social networks, 122
Content marketing, 134
Cornish wrestling, 148
Crises and challenges
impact
COVID-19 on tourism industry, 239–241
economic crisis 2009, 235–239
MERS, 235–239
methodology, 233–234
recovery proposal, 241–242
SARS, 235–239
terrorist attacks, 235–239
tourists, 234
Cronbach's Alpha analysis
results of, 24
Crowd movement, 293
Cultural festival, 20
attribute, 21
factor, 21

D

Data analysis method, 56–57
Data collection, 56–57
primary, 166–167
secondary, 167
Destination management organizations (DMO), 78
Digital marketing tools
consideration, 136–137
content marketing, 134
e-mail marketing, 135
e-wom, 134
information and communications technologies (ICTs), 133
pay per click (PPC), 135
search engine marketing (SEM), 135
search engine optimization (SEO), 135
social media, 133
tools to promote events, 132–136
tourism destinations

importance for, 130–132
web portal, 134
Disabled youths
event organization issues and challenges
finding, 206–207
methodology, 205–206
people with disabilities (PWD), 202
problem, 203–204
studies, 205
Malaysian government, 204
Diwali festival, 218

E

Edirne city
destination, 149–151
tourism, 151–152
province's destination, 148–149
Elephant marriage, 174
ceremonies in
aim, 159–160
alternative, 181–182
analysis, 167
Australian heritage commission (AHC), 163
background, 159
Bunong tradition, 179–180
captive, 164
characteristic, 182
conceptualization, 160–161
data collection technique, 166
ethics, 168
event feasibility criteria, 180–181
feasibility, 162–163
framework, 165–166
indigenous culture, 163
key stakeholders, 162
Lao people's democratic republic (PDR), 164–165
objectives, 159–160
operationalization, 160–161
organization for economic cooperation and development (OECD), 163
problem, 159
product, 161–162
research design, 166
research questions, 160
sample selection, 167
scope and limitation, 168

Index 303

Thailand, 165
validation, 168
E-mail marketing, 135
Entrepreneurship
event tourism industry
challenges, 272–273
characteristics, 266–267
contributions, 276
economic impacts, 272
funding, 273
growth, 273
importance, 267–268
industries, 265–266
opportunities, 274–276
partnership, 274
role, 270–272
stakeholders, 268–270
climate change, 269
community, 268–269
coworkers, 269
host group, 268
management companies, 268
media, 269–270
participants, 269
promoters, 269
safety and security, agents, 270
Event tourism
challenges, 252–255, 272–273
career, 255–259
tourism, 249–251
characteristics, 266–267
contributions, 276
crises and challenges, impact
COVID-19 on tourism industry,
239–241
economic crisis 2009, 235–239
MERS, 235–239
methodology, 233–234
recovery proposal, 241–242
SARS, 235–239
terrorist attacks, 235–239
tourists, 234
economic impacts, 272
education, 252–255
career, 255–259
tourism, 249–251
funding, 273
growth, 273

importance, 267–268
industries, 265–266
opportunities, 252–255, 274–276
career, 255–259
tourism, 249–251
pandemic, impact
COVID-19, 239–241
economic crisis 2009, 235–239
MERS, 235–239
methodology, 233–234
recovery proposal, 241–242
SARS, 235–239
terrorist attacks, 235–239
tourists, 234
partnership, 274
role, 270–272
E-wom, 134

F

Findings
celebration
Pu Tang village, 176
Pu Trom village, 175–176
challenges, 178–179
opportunities, 178–179
results
perception of proposed even, 169–170
profile, 168–169
recommendation, 170–171
tourist interest, 169
visit, pattern of, 168–169
semi-structure, 171
biological factors, 171–172
capacity, 176–177
celebration, 175–176
elephant marriage ceremony, 174
indigenous Bunong, 172
non-breeding taboo, 173–174
process, 175
stakeholder interest, 177
status, 171–172

G

Garia puja, 214–215
Glima, 148
Government Official (GO), 57
Greco–Roman wrestling, 147

I

Information and communications
   technologies (ICTs), 133

K

Kharchi festival, 217
Kirkpinar oil wrestling festival
   destination tourism, effects, 144–145
   Edirne province's destination, 148–149
      city, 149–151
      tourism, 151–152
   hallmark event, 143
   local event, 143
   regional event, 143
   sports events, 145–148
   types, 142–144

L

Lalon academy official (LAO), 57
Lao people's democratic republic (PDR),
   164–165

M

Malaysian government, 204
Mall–Yuddha and Koshti Pahlavani
   wrestling styles, 148
MICE (Meetings Incentives Conferences
   Exhibitions), 79
Millennial pull factors, 21–22
Mondulkiri
   data collection technique
      primary, 166–167
      secondary, 167
   elephant marriage ceremonies in
      aim, 159–160
      alternative, 181–182
      analysis, 167
      Australian heritage commission
         (AHC), 163
      background, 159
      Bunong tradition, 179–180
      captive, 164
      characteristic, 182
      conceptualization, 160–161
      data collection technique, 166
      ethics, 168
      event feasibility criteria, 180–181

   feasibility, 162–163
   framework, 165–166
   indigenous culture, 163
   key stakeholders, 162
   Lao people's democratic republic
      (PDR), 164–165
   objectives, 159–160
   operationalization, 160–161
   organization for economic cooperation
      and development (OECD), 163
   problem, 159
   product, 161–162
   research design, 166
   research questions, 160
   sample selection, 167
   scope and limitation, 168
   Thailand, 165
   validation, 168

N

Neermahal tourism, 217–218
   and water festival, 217–218
Non-breeding taboo, 173–174

O

Oil wrestling festival
   destination tourism, effects, 144–145
   Edirne province's destination, 148–149
      city, 149–151
      tourism, 151–152
   hallmark event, 143
   local event, 143
   regional event, 143
   sports events, 145–148
   types, 142–144
Organization for economic cooperation and
   development (OECD), 163
Ottoman empire, 148

P

Pay per click (PPC), 135
Pehlwani wrestling style, 148
People with disabilities (PWD), 202
Pilak archaeological, 216
   and tourism festival, 216
Pontoon catamaran boat, 70
Postpandemic tourism, 223–227

Index 305

Pous Sankranti Fair or Tirthamukh Mela, 218, 219
Pu Tang villages, 176
  data collection technique
    primary, 166–167
    secondary, 167
  elephant marriage ceremonies in
    aim, 159–160
    alternative, 181–182
    analysis, 167
    Australian heritage commission (AHC), 163
    background, 159
    Bunong tradition, 179–180
    captive, 164
    characteristic, 182
    conceptualization, 160–161
    data collection technique, 166
    ethics, 168
    event feasibility criteria, 180–181
    feasibility, 162–163
    framework, 165–166
    indigenous culture, 163
    key stakeholders, 162
    Lao people's democratic republic (PDR), 164–165
    objectives, 159–160
    operationalization, 160–161
    organization for economic cooperation and development (OECD), 163
    problem, 159
    product, 161–162
    research design, 166
    research questions, 160
    sample selection, 167
    scope and limitation, 168
    Thailand, 165
    validation, 168
Pu Trom villages, 175–176
  data collection technique
    primary, 166–167
    secondary, 167
  elephant marriage ceremonies in
    aim, 159–160
    alternative, 181–182
    analysis, 167
    Australian heritage commission (AHC), 163

background, 159
Bunong tradition, 179–180
captive, 164
characteristic, 182
conceptualization, 160–161
data collection technique, 166
ethics, 168
event feasibility criteria, 180–181
feasibility, 162–163
framework, 165–166
indigenous culture, 163
key stakeholders, 162
Lao people's democratic republic (PDR), 164–165
objectives, 159–160
operationalization, 160–161
organization for economic cooperation and development (OECD), 163
problem, 159
product, 161–162
research design, 166
research questions, 160
sample selection, 167
scope and limitation, 168
Thailand, 165
validation, 168
Public private partnerships, 117–118, 121

R

R square, 26
Rajasthan tourism
  women's roles and empowerment
    Covid-19, 109–110
    ecotourism culture, promotion, 105–106
    enterprises, culture tourism, 106–107
    medico tourism, contribution, 107–108
    religious tourism, radiant beauty, 108–109
Rural event tourism, 51
  attributes, 283–286
  communities, 283–284
  community involvement, 288–289
  discussions, 57–60
  Government Official (GO), 57
  impacts, 290–294
  India
    resource sustainability, 281–282

Lalon academy official (LAO), 57
literature review, 53–54
  social impacts, 55
  sociocultural development, 55
  sustainability, 54
  sustainable rural economic
    development, 54–55
local community (LC), 57
local events, 284
methodology, 286–288
model framework, 289–290
practices, 283–286
research method, 55–56
  context, 56
  data analysis method, 56–57
  data collection, 56–57
  sampling, 56–57
respondents, 57
strategic approach, 294–296
tour operator (TO), 57

S

Schwingen, 147
Search engine marketing (SEM), 135
Search engine optimization (SEO), 135
Security guards, roles
spectacle and worker, 87
  Argentina, 97–99
  events, 91–94
  expectancies, 94–97
  limitations, 94–97
  mega-events, organization, 90–91
  terrorism, 91–94
  tourism, 91–94
terror, 87
  Argentina, 97–99
  events, 91–94
  expectancies, 94–97
  limitations, 94–97
  mega-events, organization, 90–91
  terrorism, 91–94
  tourism, 91–94
Sri Lanka
literature
  implementing, 190–191
  need, 191
  sustainable event management,
    189–190

methodology, 191–192
SLAPCEO, 191
Sri Lanka Association of Professional
  Conference, Exhibition, and Event
  Organizers (SLAPCEO), 191
Stakeholders, 268–270
climate change, 269
community, 268–269
coworkers, 269
host group, 268
involvement, 113
  assigned responsibilities, 123
  collective responsibility model (CRM),
    124
  community-based events, 120
  major challenges, 118–119
  organizing community events, 121
  process, 119–120
  public private partnerships, 117–118,
    121
  shared responsibilities, 123
  social capital, 121–122
  social networks, 122
management companies, 268
media, 269–270
participants, 269
promoters, 269
safety and security, agents, 270
Sumo wrestling, 148
Sustainable event management
literature
  implementing, 190–191
  need, 191
  sustainable event management,
    189–190
methodology, 191–192
Sri Lanka Association of Professional
  Conference, Exhibition, and Event
  Organizers (SLAPCEO), 191
Sustainable Event Planning Guide Denver
  Convention Host Committee Greening
  Initiative, 190

T

Tirthamukh Mela, 219
Tour operator (TO), 57
Tourism destinations
importance for, 130–132

Index

Tourism in economic and social
development, 75
community development, 80
economic benefits, 80–81
social benefits, 81–82
destination management organizations
(DMO), 78
direct business associated, 79–80
inclusive development, 82–83
indirect business associated, 79–80
MICE (Meetings Incentives Conferences
Exhibitions), 79
synergetic relationship, 77–79
T-DIGD, 82
Tourism-driven inclusive growth diagnostic
(T-DIGD), 82
Tracing journey of event tourism, 1
coevolution
synergy, 9–11
diachrony, 5–8
synergic merger, 11–12
trends, 3–5
Tripura as destination brand
case studies
Ashokastami festival, 215–216
background, 213
branding, 219–223
Diwali festival, 218
events, 214–219
festivals, 214–219
Garia puja, 214–215
Kharchi festival, 217

Neermahal tourism, 217–218
Pilak archaeological, 216
postpandemic tourism, 223–227
Pous Sankranti fair, 219
pristine natural beauties, 214
rich culture, 213–214
Tirthamukh Mela, 219
tradition, 213–214
Unakoti festival, 215–216
unique fairs, 214–219

U

Unakoti festival or Ashokastami festival,
215–216
Unique fairs, 214–219
United Nations Sustainable Development
Goals, 188

W

Water-plane area (small) catamaran boat
with twin hulls (SWATH)
cruise catamarans, 70
sailing catamarans, 70
Web portal, 134
Women's roles and empowerment
Covid-19, 109–110
ecotourism culture, promotion, 105–106
enterprises, culture tourism, 106–107
medico tourism, contribution, 107–108
religious tourism, radiant beauty, 108–109

9781774912416